The House the Rockefellers Built

The House the Rockefellers Built

A TALE OF MONEY, TASTE, AND POWER
IN TWENTIETH-CENTURY AMERICA

Robert F. Dalzell Jr. and
Lee Baldwin Dalzell

A JOHN MACRAE BOOK

HENRY HOLT AND COMPANY   NEW YORK

Henry Holt and Company, LLC
Publishers since 1866
175 Fifth Avenue
New York, New York 10010
www.henryholt.com

Henry Holt® and 𝕳® are registered trademarks of
Henry Holt and Company, LLC.

Library of Congress Cataloging-in-Publication Data
Dalzell, Robert F.
The house the Rockefellers built : a tale of money, taste, and power in
twentieth-century America / Robert F. Dalzell, Jr. and Lee Baldwin Dalzell.
    p.   cm.
Includes bibliographical references and index.
ISBN-13: 978-0-8050-7544-1
ISBN-10: 0-8050-7544-5
1. Rockefeller family. 2. Rockefeller family—Homes and haunts—New York
(State)—Pocantico Hills. 3. John D. Rockefeller House (Pocantico Hills, N.Y.)
4. Mansions—New York (State)—Pocantico Hills. 5. Pocantico Hills (N.Y.)—
Buildings, structures, etc. I. Dalzell, Lee Baldwin. II. Title.
CT274.R59D35 2007
974.7'100922—dc22   2007001171

Henry Holt books are available for special promotions and
premiums. For details contact: Director, Special Markets.

First Edition 2007

Designed by Kelly S. Too

Printed in the United States of America
1   3   5   7   9   10   8   6   4   2

With heartfelt gratitude
to all those Williams students
who have taught us both so much
over the years

There were places much grander and richer, but there was no such complete work of art, nothing that would appeal so to those who were really informed.

HENRY JAMES, *The Spoils of Poynton*

F. Scott Fitzgerald: The rich are different from you and me.

Ernest Hemingway: Yes, they have more money.

An exchange widely believed to have taken place
between the two men, though no evidence
exists to prove it ever actually occurred

CONTENTS

There is nothing more public, and at the same time more intimate, than a house. Whatever its setting, it stands, a palpable object in the landscape, often built to be seen, seldom easy to miss. Yet inside it events occur and feelings ebb and flow that only its occupants can truly know. Indeed, one of its primary functions is to shield such privacies from public notice. Silently woven into its fabric, as well, are all the thoughts, hopes, fears, and dreams that went into building it. In time most of them recede from view, though occasionally enough survives to permit informed speculations about matters like style and period. But such speculations miss much that determined the origins and history of the place. Who built it, and why? How did those who lived there use the house? How did they feel about it? And what beyond its walls gave shape and meaning to their lives?

To study houses, in short, is to study people, which is our goal in this book. The people at the center of it belonged to a single family—the Rockefellers—notable in American history for several reasons, but above all for being tremendously rich. The house is Kykuit,* which was lived in by the leading members of three generations of the Rockefeller family. Two of them were responsible for building it, and the third, after making sweeping changes, left it in his will to an organization he hoped would open it to the public. It is a complex story, full of surprising twists and turns. It is also a story that reveals the Rockefellers—behind the carefully constructed facade of their public presence—as far from united, in fact often sharply at odds with one another about how to use the vast fortune that had come to them, all of which left an indelible stamp on Kykuit, as the chapters to come will show.

---

*Kykuit, a Dutch word meaning "lookout," rhymes with high-cut.

In writing about Kykuit and the Rockefellers, we are in some measure crossing familiar ground, for a number of years ago we published a similar book about George Washington and Mount Vernon. He too was rich, and Mount Vernon mattered mightily to him. During every year of his adult life, work of some sort was being done on it. Twice he rebuilt it almost completely, both times doubling it in size. In the same way, Kykuit was never far from the Rockefellers' thoughts. They doted on it, agonized over it, and decade after decade spent several kings' ransoms embellishing and maintaining it. Indeed, neither house was ever simply a place to live. Both were indivisibly linked to how their owners saw themselves and how they hoped to be seen by others. Yet in one of those marvelous coincidences that historians love, in the end both houses were relinquished by the same proud individuals who owned them—given up to futures they could only dimly see, indeed ultimately given back to the public.

Both houses, too, are emblematic in significant ways of the eras that produced them. Mount Vernon was by no means typical of American houses during the Revolutionary period, but it does provide a revealing picture of the values and aspirations of the Virginia gentry that played so large a role in opposing Great Britain and establishing the new American republic. Similarly, Kykuit speaks in unmistakable terms of the enormous wealth produced by the nation's industrial expansion during the late nineteenth century and of the dilemmas that wealth posed in a society committed to faith in equalitarian democracy. By the same token, the decision to let go of the two houses may well have reflected a sense of how, at least in America, surrendering wealth became a moral requirement for all those desiring fame more than fortune.

Inevitably, working on Washington and the Rockefellers also posed for us the question of how we felt about them as people. All of them went at life with a will, meeting its challenges with rare, sometimes ruthless, boldness and determination. All of them faced difficult moral choices. Of those confronting Washington, slavery was the most wrenching; those with which the Rockefellers had to deal were both more numerous and less clear-cut. As our research on Mount Vernon progressed, our estimate of Washington's intelligence and character rose steadily. Though not without faults, he truly seemed to be, as Thomas Jefferson said of him, a "great and good man." The Rockefellers struck us as more complicated. "Great" one or two of them were; "good" most of them conscientiously tried to be. Yet among them it was a woman—and not by birth a member of the family—who most impressed us. Abby Aldrich Rockefeller, John D. Rockefeller Jr.'s wife, was an extraordinary human being.

But more important than our personal feelings, obviously, is the historical evidence, including the prodigious amount of material on Kykuit and the Rockefellers available at the Rockefeller Archive Center and detailed on its Web site. In interpreting that material we owe much to the work of other authors who have written both about the family and about American country house architecture during the Gilded Age. Over the years the Rockefellers have provoked an endless torrent of debate, ranging from unrelenting criticism to earnest defense by those who believe the magnitude of the family's philanthropic contributions—unparalleled until the recent efforts of Bill and Melinda Gates and Warren Buffet—effectively erased the stain created by the source of their wealth. Among the early critics, Ida Tarbell, in a series of articles published initially in *McClure's Magazine*, led the way, followed by historians like Matthew Josephson, in his *The Robber Barons*, and writers David Horowitz and Peter Collier, in their highly popular book, *The Rockefellers: An American Dynasty.* The defenders, in turn, include one of the leading American historians of the middle years of the twentieth century, Allan Nevins, who produced both a one- and a two-volume biography of John D. Rockefeller. Equally sympathetic are Raymond Fosdick's biography of John D. Rockefeller Jr. and John E. Harr and Peter J. Johnson's two fine volumes focusing on John D. Rockefeller 3rd and to a lesser extent on the other members of "the brothers" generation, *The Rockefeller Century* and *The Rockefeller Conscience.*

Together this second group of studies, each carefully researched and thoughtfully written, constitutes an impressive achievement, yet one to which there are also certain limits. As Ron Chernow, in his superb *Titan*—unquestionably the best biography of John D. Rockefeller to appear thus far—says of Nevins's work, "Rockefeller vanishes for pages at a time amid a swirl of charges and counter charges." To which he might have added that even when Rockefeller does move to the center of the stage, it is almost exclusively as a businessman and philanthropist that we encounter him; the man himself eludes us. That defect Chernow's biography definitely avoids, as do several other books on members of the family, including Bernice Kert's *Abby Aldrich Rockefeller*, Clarice Stasz's *The Rockefeller Women*, and Cary Reich's *The Life of Nelson A. Rockefeller*. In all of these one finds compelling portraits of complex individuals who emerge as much more than simply the sum total of assets accumulated and dispersed across time. It is our hope that we have accomplished something similar, using Kykuit as our principal text.

As for the literature on American country houses of the Gilded Age, it too runs the gamut, stretching from E. L. Godkins's bitingly critical article, "The Expenditure of Rich Men," published in *Scribner's Magazine* in 1896, to the recent spate of handsome books documenting the careers of many of the major country house architects of the period, including Peter Pennoyer and Anne Walker's *The Architecture of Delano & Aldrich*, a study of the firm that served as Kykuit's principal architects. Quietly celebratory, works like Pennoyer and Walker's are both informative and lovely to look at. What they tend not to do is connect their subjects in any very systematic way to the larger culture in which a small number of people, suddenly flush with money, set out to use architecture to help define places for themselves in an environment rife with controversy about the meaning and significance of that wealth. More useful in broadening the picture in this regard are studies like Richard Guy Wilson's *The American Renaissance* and his *The Colonial Revival House*, Clive Aslet's *The America Country House*, and Mark Alan Hewitt's *The Architect and the American Country House*. Also indispensable to understanding the cultural context out of which houses like Kykuit rose are the strikingly perceptive observations of Herbert Croly, a leading architectural critic of the time. Our views have been much influenced by his.

In writing the book we relied as well on newspapers, on interviews with people involved in the events we were describing, and finally—as all historians must when confronted with gaps in the evidence—on our own educated guesses. If at times the ice beneath us seems to stretch too thin, any book can do no more than hope to persuade its readers. Whether it succeeds is a question they alone can answer.

R.F.D. Jr and L.B.D.
Sweden, Maine, August 2006

The House the Rockefellers Built

Sic Transit . . . December 1991

It had always felt like the most private of places. Now after more than eighty years that was about to change, and though arguably the entire family was losing a part of its heritage, it was the youngest among them, the children of "the cousins," who seemed to feel most deeply the need to mark the break. So it was that on a December night in 1991 the fifth generation of the Rockefeller family—counting from John D. Rockefeller Sr. and his wife, Laura Celestia ("Cettie") Spelman Rockefeller, for whom the house had been built—gathered in the dining room of Kykuit for a farewell dinner. "It was an extraordinary evening where everyone reminisced about their childhood experiences on the estate," remarked one person afterward. Someone else recalled walking through the house and gardens, "just thinking how sad it was that it was changing. It was the end. It wasn't going to be a family house anymore. It was going to be a public place."

In the past, the dinner served that night would have been prepared by the house's own staff of servants, but since only a skeleton crew remained indoors the food was brought in by hired caterers. Still, with the china and crystal gleaming softly in candlelight as the four courses of the meal were passed to person after person, everything must have seemed much as it always had, except that this was indeed the last family dinner in the house. Two weeks later Kykuit was turned over to the National Trust for Historic Preservation to be readied for a long-heralded program of public tours of "the Rockefeller Family Home."

In May 1994, the month the tours began, the *New York Times* ran no fewer than three articles on Kykuit. By the time the third appeared, reservations were booked for the remainder of the year, and the newspaper was describing the attention focused on the opening of the house as "more or less akin to that surrounding the start of public tours of Buckingham

Palace." As for the place itself, the *Times* architectural critic, Paul Gold-berger, was guarded in his assessment, but overall his verdict was favorable. "Oddly restrained, almost hesitant, and rather tight in its proportions" was one comment, yet that was tempered later in the same article by another observation: "The house's mix of idiosyncrasy and restraint stands in wel-come contrast to the self-important hauteur of the average pile of stone in Newport . . . There is nothing vulgar here, and that alone separates Kykuit from almost every other great house produced in the golden age of Ameri-can wealth," a judgment with which the public seemed to agree. "You know it really was a very livable mansion," remarked one woman, who had come from two hours away in Connecticut to see Kykuit.

As the guides on the tours explained, it was Nelson Rockefeller, the longtime governor of New York and the last member of the family to live in the house, who had paved the way for opening it to the public by stipulat-ing in his will that his share of the estate, along with much of his large col-lection of modern art, should go to the National Trust. Left undescribed on the tour, however, were the complex and often strained negotiations neces-sary to give reality to Nelson's plans for Kykuit, negotiations that stretched on for fourteen years. Nevertheless, in the end his wishes were honored, and the house, together with its contents and eighty-six acres of land, passed out of the Rockefellers' hands and into those of the National Trust.

During most of the interim between Nelson's death and the transfer, no one lived in "the Big House," but the family continued to hold events there, including weddings, birthday parties, christenings, and gatherings of rep-resentatives of at least half a dozen different Rockefeller charities. Several fifth-generation members even organized a seminar on the family's his-tory, including the life and career of its patriarch, John D. Rockefeller Sr. himself. In addition, there was that final dinner, planned by the same gen-eration, and purposely timed to precede the annual family Christmas luncheon scheduled for the next day. Over the years the number of people attending the Christmas luncheon had grown so large that it had to be held next door in the estate's coach barn. But after the meal, those present de-cided to go up to the house and hold "a simple ceremony to say good-bye to the place" they had known all their lives. Not all of them had been fond of Kykuit, and at least a few had decidedly negative feelings about it. Still, standing in a circle they shared their memories, lighting candles as they spoke, "until there was a ring of light commemorating all that had been and all that was being let go."

Let go? Yes. An ending? Unquestionably. But not quite, perhaps, the change from private to public that some people saw, at least in any simple sense. For Kykuit's privacy had always been more a matter of illusion than reality; given the individuals who built the house and lived there, it could not have been otherwise. The Rockefellers, particularly in the first three generations, were too rich and too prominently involved in too many different areas of American life to enjoy the luxury of privacy as most people know it. For much of his life John D. Rockefeller Sr. managed to ignore that fact, but his son and namesake discovered it soon enough, as did his children. Yet at Kykuit it had still seemed possible to will away the ever-present spotlight of public attention. That was the charm of the place. The great granite-clad house perched high on its hilltop overlooking the Hudson River, the handsome high-ceilinged rooms filled with works of art, the acres of beautifully tended gardens adorned with arresting sculptures—what else was it all for if not to serve as a private refuge, a source of pleasure for its owners and those lucky enough to be invited to see it?

What else indeed, yet neither John D. Rockefeller nor his son thought of it that way. In their eyes life was not about pleasure; it was about work and accumulation and the careful disposition of what had been accumulated. That was the lesson father taught son, as he himself had learned it from his mother, the redoubtable Eliza Davison Rockefeller. Moreover, as the family moved into the twentieth century the emphasis would increasingly shift from "getting" to "giving," as John D. Sr. liked to put it, from constantly piling up money to using it on an ever-grander scale to do good in the larger world. The building of Kykuit both coincided with that shift and was intimately connected to it.

Writing about Thomas Jefferson's Monticello, the architectural historian Dell Upton describes it as both "a hermitage"—a private retreat—and a "republican" place, designed to teach those who encountered it the principles of civic virtue. Upton also sees this dual identity as characteristic of more than a few American elite houses, and certainly, given the history of its building, Kykuit meets the test. But as with so much else about the Rockefellers, the scale of things tended to change the usual formulas. Thomas Jefferson died deeply in debt, in no small part because of what he spent building and rebuilding Monticello. The day John D. Rockefeller moved into Kykuit he was widely assumed to be the richest man in the world, and the bulk of his wealth would remain either in family hands or in the hands of institutions controlled by the family.

Yet for all its durability, the Rockefellers' wealth could not be made infinitely elastic. With each succeeding generation the great fortune was divided into smaller and smaller pieces. By the time Kykuit was turned over to the National Trust, no one in the fourth and fifth generations of the family could have afforded to live there, even if they had wanted to. In this way, too, the passing of the house from family ownership marked a change, and no doubt a poignant one for many people present at those farewell events.

To be sure, reactions varied. One person at that final dinner described stripping off his clothes later in the evening and striding naked into his great-great-grandfather's "incredible shower with the millions of nickel-plated spigots, shower heads, and liver sprays." A bit of good-natured fun, undoubtedly, but showers of that sort had once been badges of the kind of near-limitless wealth no single Rockefeller any longer possessed, just as being a Rockefeller had once meant—and now no longer would—claiming Kykuit as your "family seat."

Still, the house itself survives and remains a fascinating artifact, rich in historical significance, which it is the purpose of this book to unravel. On one level, it is a story of money, power, and taste—that elusive entity, which at Kykuit was meant to both fuse the other two and lift them to a higher plane. On the subject of taste, too, the *New York Times* was definitely right: Kykuit *is* different from other houses built by the American rich. The taste that shaped it was not the taste of a particular group or class. It was, quintessentially, the Rockefellers' taste. And what gave it its distinctive character was the underlying conviction that things, the tangible props of daily life, ought to mean something beyond the ordinary ends they served. If taste is the pursuit of excellence, excellence at Kykuit invariably came to a matter of moral judgment. It was not enough for things to be useful, or fashionable, or even beautiful; they also had to be *good*.

The Rockefellers were hardly alone in imputing moral qualities to physical objects. Every human culture has had its sacred totems. But their creation generally depends on long-standing, deeply rooted structures of collective consensus. In the Rockefellers' case it all happened so quickly, fueled by energies coming from so many different directions at once, that consensus constantly eluded the family. Indeed, what most surprised us while we were working on the book was how often and how sharply they disagreed with one another in their anxious search for the proper material forms in which to clothe their moral aspirations. And from the beginning a major source of those disagreements was Kykuit itself. John D. Rockefeller Sr. had wanted to build a simple family home; his son had much loftier ambitions for the place. The same son, John D. Rockefeller Jr., disliked modern art, yet his wife, Abby, became one of the founders of the Museum of Modern Art, and the chastely banal nudes he chose for the gardens at Kykuit would eventually have to share the space with works by Picasso, Lachaise, Maillol, and Henry Moore put there by *their* son, Nelson Rockefeller. Husbands and wives, sons and brothers, they all had their own opinions.

Still, they pressed on with their quest, for on a deeper level what was at stake was one of the most perplexing issues in American life: the proper place of great wealth in a democracy. The twenty years before, Kykuit's building had witnessed, in the United States, an altogether unprecedented accumulation of riches in private hands. Should that circumstance be celebrated as a triumphant affirmation of the benefits of a social order unfettered by fixed position and privilege? Or was it fundamentally inimical to the health and well-being of such a society? "Plutocrats," "robber barons," "malefactors of great wealth"—the less flattering labels widely applied to the possessors of the new wealth made clear just how uncomfortable many Americans were with the phenomenon. And no family was more thoroughly condemned for its wealth and the methods that had produced it than the Rockefellers. How could a fortune the size of theirs, earned as it had been, possibly be compatible with the nation's traditional democratic ideals? That was the question that confronted the family.

John D. Rockefeller Sr.'s answer was to live frugally and give an ever-increasing portion of his fortune away. But there were those who argued that in so doing he ignored the higher cultural values that it was also the duty of the rich to promote, for great democratic societies do not, cannot, live by bread alone. Nor was this just the view of his critics; it was also what his own son came to feel. If evidence was needed to prove that wealth and democracy were in fact compatible, "Junior," as he was called, believed Kykuit ought to serve that end by being modest and unpretentious—no opulent palace, certainly—yet still beautiful, its architecture and contents displaying the highest, most noble values. Since the values were universal, the connection to democracy would be obvious. Obvious too, or so the family hoped, would be the fact this was the home not of greedy, self-seeking individuals but of decent, civic-minded people, determined to do good with the riches that God and the American system of capitalistic enterprise had showered upon them. And if all that seemed like a heavy burden for any house to bear, through most of the twentieth century the Rockefellers never doubted for a moment that it was possible, however strenuously they disagreed about the details.

Great Good Fortune

1

Heir Apparent, 1902

The fire began at night. One of the maids smelled smoke near the wall separating the parlor and the dining room. A hurried search revealed that flames, darting upward, could be seen through the slot for the sliding door between the two rooms. The cause seemed to be faulty wiring, and in apparent confirmation of that theory the electric lights failed almost at once, plunging the house into darkness.

By the time someone chopped through the plaster for a better view of the blaze, it was already too late to stop it. The problem was more the shortage of water than the fire itself, which actually burned rather slowly at first. There was even time to move many items—including a piano and a large bookcase—to safety out on the lawn. In the flickering amber light, family members, servants, and estate workers pitched in together, hurrying in and out with furniture, rugs, and hastily made-up bundles of whatever came to hand. But all the while the fire continued to burn, spreading inexorably through room after room in the twenty-five-year-old wooden structure, gaining momentum as it went, leaping from floors to walls to ceilings.

Meanwhile, hundreds of people had gathered from every direction and stood for hours on the lawn, watching as the flames spent themselves. After all, it was not every day you had a chance to see the home of the world's richest man burn to the ground, though as it happened—elusive as always—he was away that evening.

In the great scheme of things, 1902 was not a good year for John Davison Rockefeller and his family. There were some happy moments: two grandchildren were born. But then came the night of September 17, when fire destroyed the house at Pocantico Hills, in Westchester County, New York, and barely two months after that the first installment of Ida Tarbell's devastating exposé of Standard Oil appeared in *McClure's Magazine.* At the time the two events—the Pocantico fire and Tarbell's assault on the enterprise that had brought the Rockefellers both great riches and tremendous public notoriety—might have seemed unrelated. And so they were. But in the aftermath, each, like pebbles dropped in a pond, sent ripples circling outward, and eventually the circles intersected.

A prime example of the thundering industrial expansion that had swept the United States into the twentieth century, Standard Oil and Rockefeller, its creator, were a reporter's dream of a story, and Tarbell went at it with a passion. Reared in the oil regions of Pennsylvania where Standard had battled for control with particular ferocity, she saw her father go down to defeat in that war, and her account of Standard's rise was indelibly marked by the experience. It was also a first-rate piece of journalism, exhaustively researched and deftly written. Within nine years the storm of angry protest it fueled would lead to the breakup of Standard Oil by the U.S. government.

During those years, the Pocantico Hills house was replaced with a new one, far grander than its predecessor, though the process that led to its building was anything but smooth or easy. By that time the nation's industrial barons had been dotting the landscape with hugely expensive new country houses for more than a decade, but erecting yet another millionaire's "palace" was most definitely not what John D. Rockfeller had in mind. On the other hand, deciding what to build instead provoked, from the outset, sharp disagreement within the family. Indeed, in the beginning it was unclear whether anything at all would be built.

Certainly money was not the problem. In 1902 Rockefeller's annual *income* had reached $58 million. Still, he prided himself on living as simply as possible. Forest Hill, the family's country home outside of Cleveland, the city where he began his business career, was a failed tourist hotel he had invested in initially with other local businessmen. When he transferred the center of Standard Oil's operations to New York City, he lived with his family in hotels for almost ten years before finally buying, in 1884, a house on West Fifty-fourth Street that was notably less imposing than his brother William's place, around the corner on Fifth Avenue.

Rockefeller's dislike of spending money was not lost on Tarbell. Along with the secret deals, the rebates, the kickbacks, the brutal treatment of its rivals that marked Standard's relentless drive to dominate the oil industry, she duly noted—in a two-part treatment of Rockefeller's character that followed her series on the company—what she called his "cult of the unpretentious." Far from finding it attractive, she considered it petty and mean-spirited, as well as inimical to any appreciation of higher cultural values. "Here was parsimony made a virtue," she declared. Rockefeller's houses struck her as especially telling in this regard. "Unpretending even to the point of being conspicuous," they showed him to be a person who took "no pleasure in noble architecture" and appreciated "nothing of the beauty of fine lines and decorations." Forest Hill she dismissed as "a monument of cheap ugliness."

Fifteen years after the fact, Rockefeller's fabled composure could still crack when, in private, he spoke of some of Tarbell's charges, for example, her claim that he had acquired his monopoly of Cleveland's oil refineries by threatening to force his competitors out of business. Her scathing treatment of his father, William Avery Rockefeller, a traveling patent medicine salesman who had led a thoroughly irregular life and in fact bigamously married a woman other than Rockefeller's mother, he also found deeply offensive. But toward Tarbell's assault on his stinginess and taste in architecture he adopted a more philosophical attitude, or at any rate there is no record of his ever complaining about it.

Publicly, meanwhile, Rockefeller said nothing at all about any of Tarbell's charges, though his apparent calm was not shared by John D. Rockefeller Jr., his only son and namesake (the Rockefellers' other surviving children were daughters—Bessie, Alta, and Edith), who seemed determined to do something. Admittedly, much of Tarbell's case focused on the rise of Standard Oil, about which Junior knew little, but her attack on Rockefeller as an individual was another matter. There the battle could be joined confidently, and by the end of 1902 a dutiful son had already begun considering how that might be done. Moreover, one strategy he gravitated toward with growing conviction was persuading his father to build that new house in Pocantico Hills, something "Senior" appeared to have little if any desire to do.

The young man thus occupied was also to find, in 1902, the salary he received for working in the family office at 26 Broadway raised to $10,000. He had started there in 1897, three months after graduating from Brown

University, at $6,000 a year with no clear-cut duties. In a preview of things to come, some of his earliest assignments involved supervising renovations to the family homes. But at the same time he began to familiarize himself with his father's business commitments, which included far more than simply Standard Oil. He also took an early interest in the family's burgeoning philanthropic activities, and in both cases his tutor was his father's brilliant, tirelessly energetic factotum at 26 Broadway, the former Baptist clergyman Frederick T. Gates.

Junior's early forays into business were not auspicious. In 1899 he lost more than $1 million speculating with money that he did not in fact have in the stock of the United States Leather Company. But then two years later he more than redeemed himself in a series of highly important negotiations with J. P. Morgan over the sale of the Mesabi iron ore mines, which Senior had developed and which Morgan hoped to make part of U.S. Steel. At their initial interview the crusty banker had kept Junior and Gates waiting and then gruffly demanded to know what price they were asking, to which Junior coolly replied, "Mr. Morgan, I think there has been some mistake. I did not come here to sell. I understood that you wished to buy." Senior's reaction on hearing this story was to exclaim to his wife, Laura—or "Cettie," as she was called—"Great Caesar, but John is a trump!" to which she herself added, "Are we not proud, as parents, of our boy!" As it turned out, the Mesabi properties sold for $88.5 million, which Gates calculated represented a clear profit of $55 million on Rockefeller's investment.

As yet another way of being of service, Junior occasionally spoke in public on various topics, including religion, although his efforts sometimes backfired, as happened in February of 1902 in a talk he gave to the Brown University YMCA. Picking "Christianity in Business" as his subject, he endeavored to show that sound business principles and Christian faith were not in the least incompatible. Unfortunately, in making his point he chose to draw an analogy between the benefits of consolidation as opposed to competition in business and the process of developing superior roses by pruning away unwanted, lesser buds. Labeled the "American Beauty Rose Speech" by the press, his remarks provoked a blast of derisive criticism and seven years later could still prompt an irate clergyman to remark, "A rose by any other name will smell as sweet, but the odor of that rose to me smacks strongly of crude petroleum."

The press also had a field day with Junior's earnest determination to teach a men's Bible study class at the Fifth Avenue Baptist Church. With painstaking care he prepared for each session, only to find himself both heckled on the spot by enterprising reporters and made the butt of endless jibes in newspaper stories on the subject. Quipped the *Pittsburgh Press:* "With his hereditary grip on a nation's pocketbooks, his talks on spiritual matters are a tax on piety." Still, he doggedly persisted in leading the class for eight years, remarking, "This work has meant so much to me . . . that I feel, from a selfish point of view, that I cannot afford to give it up without good cause." When he finally let the Bible class go, he did so only because his philanthropic energies had become increasingly caught up in other, more ambitious projects.

In that regard one of the signal events of 1902 was the creation of the General Education Board. Building on the deep commitment of Cettie Rockefeller's parents to the cause of abolition, she and Senior had contributed heavily over the years to institutions like Spelman Seminary in Atlanta. In the same spirit, in 1901, Junior had joined a train trip planned by Robert C. Ogden, a wealthy department store executive, for the purpose of interesting northern philanthropists in southern black colleges. The General Education Board grew out of that trip on the so-called Millionaires' Special. Organized at a meeting at Junior's house lasting until after midnight on February 27, 1902, it was funded in large part by his pledge of $1 million to support the board's work. The money came from his father, and over the years, Senior continued to pour funds into the effort, making it one of a small number of premier Rockefeller philanthropies.

As significant as the donations themselves was the way the General Education Board's finances were structured. The year before its establishment, a similar body, the Rockefeller Institute for Medical Research, had been created to further basic research in the field of medicine. In that case too Rockefeller's initial gift was followed by others, eventually totaling tens of millions of dollars. For the most part the gifts consisted of shares of Standard Oil stock, which were kept by the institute as a permanent endowment, with only the income used for the purposes designated. Today organizations that function this way are known as philanthropic foundations, and there are literally thousands of them in the United States; at the time the form was relatively novel, and more than anyone else it was the Rockefellers who gave it its modern shape.

In doing so they were responding to a situation that was itself unprecedented. Unlike most of his contemporaries among the very rich, John D. Rockefeller Sr. was a committed philanthropist all his life. In 1855, the year he began his business career in Cleveland as a clerk at the firm of Hewitt and Tuttle, earning three dollars a week, he had tithed. In 1889 he founded the University of Chicago with a gift of $600,000. Three years later his charitable giving reached $1.35 million. Yet all the while, the value of his holdings continued to spiral upward. By 1901 it totaled $200 million, not to mention the millions in income that flowed into his coffers every year. How was "charity's share" of all that to be spent? It was a question to which there was no ready answer. Such riches had never existed before, at least not in the United States.

In his autobiography Rockefeller would promote philanthropic foundations as an ideal means of keeping money profitably invested in business, since the assets donated did not have to be sold. He would further claim that sound businesses were themselves the very "best type of philanthropy" by virtue of their ability to employ people and create wealth. But it was Gates who stripped the issue to its core when he wrote in a letter to Senior in 1905: "Two courses are open to you. One is that you and your children while living should make final disposition of the great fortune in the form of permanent corporate philanthropies for the good of mankind . . . or at the close of a few lives now in being it must simply pass into the unknown, like some other great fortunes, with unmeasured and perhaps sinister possibilities." Here was the system of philanthropic foundations laid out for Rockefeller's approval with all its key features in place: the commitment to doing good; the determination to control how it was done; the determination as well to hang on to the power that went with great wealth; the blending of family responsibility and corporate power; and the promise of permanence that would make of it all a lasting monument to the Rockefellers' generosity. The letter ended with a detailed plan calling for the creation of no fewer than six foundations, each in a different field.

While the problem Gates was addressing would continue to preoccupy the Rockefellers for decades, his letter had about it an air of urgency that plainly bore the stamp of the time in which it was written. Five months earlier in Washington, D.C., the House of Representatives had passed a unanimous resolution urging an immediate antitrust investigation of Standard Oil. This was Gates's view of how the Rockefellers should respond. And Junior, every bit as concerned, wrote his father, "Mr. Gates's letter to you seems to me a powerful and unanswerable argument," adding, "I very much hope it may seem wise to carry out this plan." For his part, Senior responded with notable promptness. Within two weeks he arranged to give

$10 million to the General Education Board, the beginning of a veritable flood of gifts to that and other family foundations, which in time would swell to over $446 million.

Bowled over by his father's generosity, Junior hurried to thank him for the $10 million, writing, "I believe this is a great thing, far greater than any of us can conceive today." The fact that the first of the new gifts went to the GEB must have been especially gratifying to Junior, too. In effect it amounted to a tacit endorsement of the path he had already tentatively embarked upon and would continue to follow with growing self-confidence and energy in the years ahead, as he progressively limited his involvement in business and turned instead to managing the ever-expanding philanthropic universe his father's millions had called into being.

In 1902, however, all that lay in the future. Junior had no idea what would become of his life, or even any very clear sense of what he wanted to do. He continued to take on whatever seemed to require his attention at 26 Broadway. The year before, when his sister Alta married, he had not only supervised the purchase of a house for the newlyweds but planned its decoration and furnishing down to the last pair of lace curtains. He also worried constantly about whether he did enough to help his father. On hearing that his salary had been raised that year, he wrote, "My breath was completely taken away by what you told me regarding my salary . . . I cannot feel that any services which I can offer are worth to you such a sum as $10,000 a year."

Grounded in genuine affection on both sides, the relationship between Junior and his father was complex. As a young parent, Rockefeller had often taken afternoons off from work to be with his children. But at every turn their upbringing had been strictly molded to conform to the moral standards he and Cettie drew from their unwavering Baptist faith. Not only had that precluded all "sinful" amusements like card playing, dancing, and the consumption of alcoholic beverages; it also demanded constant acts of service to others. "My mother and father raised but one question," Junior would say in later life, "Is it right, is it duty?" Living with such pressures was not always easy. During the winter of his thirteenth year, Junior had shown sufficient signs of stress to convince his parents to send him from New York to their summer home in Cleveland, "dear old Forest Hill," for a season of strenuous outdoor activity, and four years later, as he was about to finish school before going off to college at Brown, the experiment was repeated.

On that occasion a grateful son had humbly thanked his father for "the trouble and expense you have incurred in order that I might stay here this winter," to which Senior replied in terms he would use again and again over the years: "Be assured the appreciation you show is ample payment for all we have ever tried to do for you, and I have not words to express our gratitude for what you show us in your daily life, and for the hope you give us for the future time when our turn comes for us to lean more on you."

After the rigors of his early upbringing, college proved to be something of a liberating experience for Junior. Choosing to ignore his parents' disapproval of dancing, he regularly attended dances and even hosted one himself, which his mother could not bring herself to attend. He also made a number of lasting friendships and enjoyed his first taste of power as junior class president and, later, manager of the football team and organizer of his class's senior supper. And without a strikingly distinguished academic record, he still did well enough to be elected to Phi Beta Kappa. At the end of it all his mother proudly wrote, "How very thankful we are for your college record and with what just pride does it fill our hearts." To which he happily replied—proving that he had not wandered too far from the nest—"I have been in many homes during the last four years . . . but nowhere have I seen such kind and loving parents, such sweet harmony and love and so healthful a general atmosphere as by our own fireside."

Yet for all its charms, Junior could still imagine ways of improving life by the Rockefeller fireside. In the same letter to his mother, he noted that "some phases of home life" he had seen elsewhere "might well be introduced into our own." Exactly what those "phases" were, he neglected to say. Certainly it is difficult to picture his parents taking up the social graces he encountered at the parties given for Providence debutantes, or Junior wanting them to. A more likely explanation is that he was referring, however obliquely, to a specific individual, and if so surely the person he had in mind was Abby Greene Aldrich, the woman who eventually became his wife.

The "eventually" here is no mere figure of speech, for though the two met in 1894 during Junior's sophomore year at Brown, more than seven years were to pass before they finally married. They were introduced at his first dancing party. Probably because he was too shy to ask, they did not dance together, but he remembered afterward being treated by her as if he had "all the *savoir-faire* in the world," and from that evening he marked the time he "began thoroughly to enjoy the social aspects of college life." It was to be the first of literally dozens of other "firsts" he would owe to Abby during their life together. The daughter of Nelson Aldrich, the all-powerful Republican leader of the U.S. Senate, she had far more experience of the world than Junior, and her sophistication was matched by a warm and outgoing manner as well as considerable self-confidence. She was a young woman who knew her own mind and spoke it freely. That never changed.

She also seemed eager to make a place for Junior among her many beaux, and plainly he was taken with her. But even though they were constantly together in the weeks before his graduation from Brown, he left immediately afterward for a bicycle trip in Europe having made no declaration to Abby, and for the next three years they saw each other only intermittently. In 1900, no doubt hoping to bring matters to a head, Senator Aldrich invited him on a cruise to Cuba aboard President McKinley's yacht. Abby was also a member of the party, yet at the end of the trip the two seemed no closer than before to the engagement that many people, including the press, assumed was imminent.

The chief problem was Junior himself. "Marriage either makes or breaks a life," he confided to his biographer long afterward. "I felt I couldn't afford to make a mistake." But if fear of making a mistake was one reason for hesitating, Junior was also going through a time of intense self-doubt on other grounds. While Abby and the world at large were waiting for some sign of his romantic intentions, he was struggling to find his niche at 26 Broadway, with mixed results and little direction from his father. His losses in the stock market were particularly painful, and lacking the funds to cover them he had no choice but to go to Senior, hat in hand. Patiently, Rockefeller listened to his explanation, questioning him closely about the details. "Never shall I forget my shame and humiliation," Junior commented later. But when he had finished, his father said simply, "All right, John, don't worry. I will see you through."

Overwhelmed with gratitude, Junior poured out his soul in a letter to his father several days afterward: "Because of your forbearance and gentleness you have caused me to feel the more deeply the lesson which this has taught. I would rather have had my right hand cut off than to have caused you this anxiety." But despite his father's kindness and the lesson the incident taught Junior, the chief difficulty he faced at 26 Broadway remained unchanged: he had no definite duties, no real job. Anxious not to impose his will or demand too much, Senior left him free to do whatever he wished. Doubtless he believed he was doing his son a favor. Yet Junior felt otherwise and would long remember his acute discomfort in the situation. "Why, the girls in the office here have an advantage I never had. They can prove to themselves their commercial worth . . . I never had that kind of reassuring experience."

To help deal with his anxieties, he split firewood and ran for miles every day. On the social front he found little to amuse him. "I lived in a sort of vacuum . . . There was no social life of any kind at first." He spent his evenings at home with his parents and sister, Alta, and even the occasional party he attended provided nothing more than "a fairly nice time." What he badly needed was a success of some sort, which finally came in the negotiations with Morgan over the Mesabi mines, and as much as anything else, that probably moved him to do something about his relationship with Abby. The agreement with Morgan was complete by the middle of May 1901; two months later Junior proposed, and she accepted.

Even then, there had been obstacles to overcome. The couple had agreed earlier not to see each other for six months in order to test their feelings, but then at the last minute Junior seemed to develop fresh qualms. In the end his mother gave him the push he needed, saying simply, after a long conversation with her son on the subject, "Of course you love Miss Aldrich. Why don't you go at once and tell her so," which he did. There followed a whirlwind of preparations, for with the issue finally settled the couple wanted to be married as soon as possible. The ceremony took place on October 9 at the Aldrich summer home in Rhode Island. A lavish affair with vintage wines and champagne served in a huge tent festooned with exotic greenery, it was definitely more in the Aldrich than the Rockefeller mode. At the last minute, the groom's mother found herself too ill to attend, but if she objected to anything it was to the "worldliness" of the event, not to the bride. When her son wrote joyously after eight months of marriage, "each day is happier than the last," and remarked that she had never told him what she thought of Abby, she hurried to reassure him: "She seems a wife made to order for you—and this I fully believe. So sweetheart, you have made no mistake, nor are you any longer in doubt as to your Mother's opinion."

Cettie Rockefeller may have spoken more wisely than she knew. Abby *was* the ideal wife for Junior, though not all of her virtues were those his parents prized. Physically passionate herself, she brought out a corresponding passion in him, which they both delighted in. She also had little use for some of the more rigid patterns of behavior stressed in Junior's upbringing. When he suggested that she keep a weekly record of her expenses, as he had done at his father's request since he was a boy, her response was a resounding, "I won't."

She had definite ideas, too, about what Junior ought to do with his life. Within a few years she would be writing ("instead of speaking of it because I am afraid it may cause you some pain") to urge him to give up his Bible study class. She did so in part because of the nervous strain it caused, but also because she felt the time and energy involved could be, as she put it, "better employed on philanthropic work along broader lines." Her hope was that he would not lessen his chance to do what she called "really big things." And in such larger ventures, she herself was fully prepared to participate. The night in 1902 when the General Education Board was conceived, she was there, at the meeting, in the family library with Junior—"the only woman present," as he proudly wrote his father the next day, and as she often would be on similar occasions in the future.

As satisfying as working with organizations like the GEB could be, however, there was a part of Abby's nature—and, she may have suspected, of Junior's as well—that such activities left unfulfilled. Self-made man though he was, her father, the great senator, had a keen interest in art and architecture. He collected paintings and delighted in planning the decoration of his various houses, particularly Indian Oaks, the seventy-room country house he built overlooking Narragansett Bay. Abby shared his interests. She valued beautiful things and elegant surroundings, and if high philanthropy of the sort the Rockefellers favored failed to nourish those impulses, the Rockefeller houses offered even less in the way of sustenance.

Senior actually preferred buying places that were already furnished, presumably to save the trouble and expense of having to do the job himself. He wanted things well maintained, with kitchens and bathrooms in good working order. He also enjoyed planting trees, a hobby that he described at length in his autobiography, though principally as a lesson in how leisure time activities could be usefully organized as business ventures. The only major changes he made in the properties he acquired tended to be the addition of elaborate carriage barns for the horses and buggies he delighted in driving at high speeds whenever he had the chance.

A fair example of what the senior Rockefellers considered adequate housing was the four-story brownstone they had purchased on West Fifty-fourth Street, in New York City. For the land, house, and furnishings they traded various pieces of Manhattan real estate valued at roughly $600,000.

The property's previous occupant was Arabella Worsham, the mistress and later wife of railroad magnate Collis Huntington. On Huntington's death, she had inherited half his fortune, with the other half going to his nephew, Henry, who subsequently courted and married her. In short, the Rockefellers' new house had been a love nest, and behind its rather dour exterior it looked the part. In the basement there was a Turkish bath and on the ground floor a Moorish salon furnished with richly cushioned ottomans, its walls and ceiling draped to look like a tent. On the floor above, Arabella's bedroom, with its Turkish corner, vividly painted ceiling, and black ebonized woodwork done in the Anglo-Japanese style (now installed in the Museum of the City of New York) became the Rockefellers' own, as did the adjacent dressing room, crafted in rare woods with mother-of-pearl inlay and a running frieze of gilded cupids.

The contrast between these flights of decorative fancy and Senior and Cettie's stern moral views could hardly have been sharper, but on moving into the house they did little more than replace several worn carpets. Though if they were oblivious to it all, Abby would not have been. It was ridiculous to think of her in-laws living amid such gauchely voluptuous trappings. On top of that, by the time she saw the house, its decoration and furnishings were hopelessly out-of-date. Arabella Huntington had not been alone in her passion for the exotic; in the years after the Civil War many of New York's wealthier citizens filled their rooms with finery echoing styles from faraway places like Morocco and Japan. Yet the taste for such things had definitely passed. Moreover the Rockefellers' other houses, Forest Hill in Cleveland and the place in Pocantico Hills, if less opulent, were equally old-fashioned, but there seemed little likelihood any of this would change soon—until, that is, the September night in 1902 when the Pocantico house burned down.

Though Junior and Abby were in New York City at the time, they took the train out to Westchester early the next morning. It was his sister Alta, and her husband, Parmalee Prentice, who had been staying in the house that evening. In the confusion someone had saved Junior's violin from the blaze, but many of Abby's clothes, as well as everything she had bought on a recent trip to Scotland and all of the couple's letters to each other, were gone. They could be thankful, however, that no one had been injured, and for the moment there was a great deal of work to do. With the senior Rockefellers in Cleveland, it fell to Junior and Abby to supervise the moving and storage of the things that had been carried out to the lawn the night of the fire. They also took charge of readying the Kent House, a modest frame dwelling farther down the hill, to receive Junior's parents when they returned. It was a complicated task, which they managed to complete in only a week.

There was, however, another issue raised by the fire that took much longer to settle. From the time he began acquiring property in Pocantico Hills, Senior had talked of building a house on the highest point of land overlooking the Hudson River, and he had actually begun to develop the site. The house that burned—known, like the Kent House, by the name of its previous owners as the Parsons-Wentworth House—had stood a short distance away, on lower ground. Logically, its loss seemed to point the way toward an accelerated building program on the heights above, but Senior had earlier called a halt to the work because of mounting costs. What would he do now? It was a question that from the first caught Junior and Abby's attention. They fervently hoped he would build a new house, and they were even prepared to give him a significant push in that direction.

On October 24, 1902, Junior wrote Chester H. Aldrich, saying he would like to see him "on a little business matter" at his "earliest convenience." A distant relative of Abby's, Aldrich was an architect and partner in the newly organized firm of Delano & Aldrich. He had been trained at the École des Beaux-Arts in Paris, and he and his partner, William A. Delano, had earlier worked for Carrère and Hastings, the firm that directed the renovation of William Rockefeller's house overlooking the Hudson River. Only a few miles from Pocantico Hills, Rockwood Hall, as the place was renamed, had cost Senior's brother $100,000, but by the time he finished he had spent more than $3 million making it one of the most lavish houses on the river, an immense baronial pile, peppered with turrets and towers, boasting more than two hundred rooms.

The "little piece of business" Junior wished to see Aldrich about was discussing arrangements for drawing up plans for a new house to be built at Pocantico Hills for his father. Five days later, he asked specifically what a preliminary ground-floor plan and a set of elevations would cost, and Aldrich apparently went ahead with the drawings. What neither of them reckoned with was Senior's opinion on the subject.

Almost certainly, Junior had spoken to Aldrich without first telling his father, but at some point after his meeting with the architect such a conversation did occur, and much to Junior's chagrin he discovered that, at least for the present, Senior had no intention of building a new house. On the contrary, having come back from Cleveland early in October, he was already up to his elbows in plans to renovate the Kent House, which Junior had seen as nothing more than a temporary residence for his parents. Furthermore, he seemed intent on making it a virtual copy of Forest Hill, "his ideal for a summer house," as Junior wrote his mother archly, and that was the only building project that interested him. Hastily, Junior wrote Aldrich saying that his father's plans were "so indefinite" and "the question of whether he will build at all so undecided, that for the present I think it best to lay this matter on the table."

Yet laying the matter on the table, in Junior's mind, meant exactly that. He was not prepared to give up the idea of a new house, and he would continue to promote the project, whenever possible, in conversations with his father. At issue, too, was a fundamental disagreement between father and son, one that would reverberate throughout Kykuit's building.

Senior's position was the simpler of the two. He genuinely believed in the virtues of plain living. In his mind it was a matter of moral principle. If the Kent House, an unpretentious dwelling already available for occupancy, could be made comfortable, it seemed wrong not to use it. What he knew of Chester Aldrich and his association with Carrère and Hastings probably also suggested to him that the kind of house Junior and Abby wanted built was considerably more ambitious than anything he himself would be happy with. Added to all this was another factor. With Ida Tarbell's attack on Standard Oil taking hold of the nation's imagination more tenaciously every month, it hardly seemed wise for the Rockefellers to be embarking on elaborate and expensive changes in their personal living arrangements. In fact it was the worst imaginable time for such a thing. Far better to concentrate on philanthropy, which had the benefit of sound, moral principle to recommend it.

Agreeing completely with his father about the value of philanthropy, Junior would still have rejected the case against building a new house. Above all, he and Abby—for they were to be equal partners in the venture—would have challenged the notion that a house of the sort they wanted to see Senior build was immoral simply because it promised to cost a lot of money. If all money could buy was tasteless opulence, then yes, expensive houses were immoral, but money could buy far more than opulence. It could buy beauty; and who could dispute that beauty had moral value? In the face of Tarbell's charges, indeed, here was a way for Senior to prove that he was not in fact a doomed soul, driven by nothing more than greed and love of power. The man who appreciated beauty could never be such an individual.

Nor, at bottom, was there any conflict between beauty and the kind of wholesome simplicity that the Rockefellers had always seen as essential to their domestic happiness. As Junior would explain later, his instructions to the architects and designers who worked on Kykuit constantly aimed at "a residence so outwardly simple that friends . . . coming from no matter how humble an environment, would be impressed by the homeliness and simplicity of the house; while those who appreciated fine design and were familiar with beautiful furnishings would say, 'How exquisite!' "

Both father and son, then, were planning their separate building projects with an audience in mind. Junior, however, was more explicit about that fact and also about the nature of the audience he hoped to reach. It was to be as broadly inclusive as possible, to combine both ends of the spectrum of American society and presumably everyone in between. Could a single house appeal to such a diverse collection of individuals? And not only appeal to them, but persuade them that the people who lived there, in spite of their enormous wealth, were after all decent, caring, moral human beings? And what of the idea, which father and son surely must have shared, that houses were meant first and foremost to be family places, private refuges from the larger world?

No doubt in 1902 these questions were only just beginning to take shape in Junior's mind. But at least he was determined to keep the issue of a new house open. And as time passed and Tarbell's salvos rumbled on, making all of the Rockefellers increasingly anxious, he would become more and more adamant on the subject. At a minimum, building a new house was something he could do for his parents, and who was to say that it might not, in the end, like the tens of thousands of shares of Standard Oil stock pledged to further medical research and improve the quality of southern education, help redeem his beloved father in the eyes of his fellow Americans? When the issue was put that way, the fact that Rockefeller himself seemed quite uninterested in building a new house was irrelevant. He *needed* a new house, and one way or another he had to be persuaded to build one.

2

Titan, Husband, Father

Lean, yet upright and sinewy, the boy slipped stealthily through the half-light of dawn, ax in hand. His movements were easy, assured. He had grown strong doing chores, but this was no chore. Far from it. As he approached his objective, he would have looked around quickly to make sure no one was watching. Then, ax raised, the swift, arcing blows began, one after another, each precisely aimed, yet not too hard lest the noise wake those sleeping inside. Soon enough the deed was done, leaving the remains to be cut up and carried off, which took a bit more time. Yet all that would have been carefully planned. The great thing was to finish before anyone noticed what was happening, so that finally there would come that magic moment when they walked in and saw what he had done—and the wonderful difference it made!

The tree had stood outside the dining room window of the house where they were living at that point, blocking what he was sure was a fine view. Driven by his father's erratic ways, they moved often during those years, though each time there was an effort, in which everyone joined, to find attractive quarters, to keep up appearances. But when he proposed cutting down the tree, several members of the family objected. Later, while he and his mother were alone together, however, she suggested that if the tree were removed some morning before the family sat down to breakfast, the resulting view might well settle the argument in his favor.

And that was exactly what happened, as he reported afterward with more than a little glee.

A modest triumph, certainly, but one that remained fresh in John D. Rockefeller's memory fifty years after the fact. Improvement through subtraction, turning less into more; in time he would make it a potent formula for business success. And here too it seemed to work exactly as he hoped it would, just as, given his mother's advice, cutting down the tree had not been a completely reckless act. Nor was there any need to save himself from paternal disapproval by ostentatiously refusing to lie to his father about what he had done—the tactic that other boy used in the story Parson Weems invented for his biography of George Washington. If William Rockefeller was angry at his son, there is no record of it.

As for his mother's role in the drama, she was described as having "sympathized" with the boy. Perhaps she agreed with him about the tree. But this was the same woman who regularly appeared in family legend as a stern teacher of moral lessons. More likely her point was that if you were truly convinced of the rightness of your opinions, you should go ahead and act on them, regardless of what other people thought, a principle her son would follow all his life.

In his autobiography, *Random Reminiscences of Men and Events*, Rockefeller put the tale of the tree at the end of the first chapter, much of which described the friendships he had made in the oil business over the years and how important they were to his success. The chapter also contained a discussion of his passionate interest in moving trees and laying out roads, activities he believed he was at least as good at as any professional landscape architect. So in effect the story brought together the separate strands of his disarmingly casual ramblings. Here, at least by his own account, was the man of vision, who nonetheless enjoyed simple earthly pleasures and preferred to act as most people always have: with friends to support him, in this case his beloved mother.

The truth was, of course, that John D. Rockefeller was not at all like other people. With friends and family members his manner was kind and gracious. He was a thoughtful employer, who both delegated responsibility freely and paid close attention to the opinions of his associates. Yet always there remained that other side to his nature, solitary, secretive, plotting his course by signs he alone could see, and utterly determined to have his own way. This was the man whom, half a century later, his son hoped to persuade to build a house he neither wanted nor thought he needed. If Junior knew the story of the destruction of the unwanted tree, and surely he must have, did it give him pause? Perhaps, but it might just as easily have emboldened him, heredity being what it is.

As for the boy the senior Rockefeller had been, he had set out that morning convinced he could clear the way to a better view, and events proved him right. No doubt, too, eliminating the tree let more light into the house, an added benefit that must have appealed to him. Or certainly it would have been ironic if it had not, for it was to light—brilliantly commoditized, affordable light—that he would one day owe his fortune. Inexpensive artificial light would also be his greatest gift to his fellow human beings, though few of them seemed inclined to thank him for it. Candles and whale oil had been for the rich. It was cheap kerosene that banished the night for millions of people of modest means around the globe, and though Rockefeller did not invent the process that distilled this useful product from the dark slimy petroleum that fairly bubbled out of the ground in parts of western Pennsylvania, he did figure out how to produce and market it more efficiently than anyone else on earth, an achievement that earned him not only vast riches but the undying hatred of his competitors. Those, that is, who failed to heed his often repeated call to join him in his dizzying assent.

Afterward his enemies would claim that the entire saga, from start to finish, was the result of a single, enormous plot, hatched in Rockefeller's devilishly fertile brain. They were wrong. He could see far, but not that far. Indeed, it had all begun quite simply. In the early 1860s kerosene was the hot product of the moment; the profits were there for the taking. As a commission merchant in Cleveland, Rockefeller started selling kerosene, and if selling it made good sense, refining it promised even higher returns, so he went into the refining business like scores of other people at the time. That was in 1863. In 1865 he bought out two of his partners and grossed $1.2 million. Two years later, oil prices crashed in what would become a recurring pattern in the industry.

His response, then and later, to the mad gyrations in both crude oil and kerosene prices was to cut costs and steadily expand operations. He made his own barrels and sulfuric acid, a key ingredient in the refining process; he built warehouses and fleets of lighters and tankers. He also began negotiating highly favorable shipping rates with the railroads—rates not available to most of his competitors in the refining business. In 1870 Standard

Oil of Ohio was founded. The following year oil prices crashed again, and the year after that Rockefeller, in a stunning coup relying on Standard's privileged position with the railroads, forced most of the other oil refiners in Cleveland to either sell out to him or abandon the business. From there, using similar tactics, he swept on to cherrypick major competitors in Pittsburgh, Philadelphia, Long Island, Baltimore, and West Virginia. By 1875 the Standard "alliance," with a capital of $3.5 million, controlled more than half of the refining capacity in the United States. That was also the year the Rockefeller family began spending winters in New York City, at the Windsor Hotel on Fifth Avenue.

Behind all of this activity lay a great deal of hard work and careful planning, plus a constant struggle to find the capital needed for so rapid an expansion, and above all Rockefeller's implacable determination to bend the world to his will. Yet in later years he invariably claimed that the results surprised him. "None of us ever dreamed of the magnitude of what proved to be the later expansion," he wrote in his autobiography. "We did our day's work as we met it, looking forward to what we could see in the distance and keeping well up to our opportunities." This was one way of explaining what happened, certainly, but it left out a great deal, including any very clear sense of what drove Rockefeller during those years. Nor did he ever answer that question in so many words.

If pressed, he probably would have said that his primary goal was hanging on to the money he had already invested in the oil industry. In his autobiography that was how he explained his other great business success of the period, the "many millions" of dollars he earned developing the Mesabi iron ore mines. There too he had put money into something that initially he knew little about, and there too—this time in the panic and depression of the 1890s—values had suddenly plummeted. Not to have acted at that point would have doomed the enterprise to ruin, which to Rockefeller was unacceptable. As he said, he abhorred the thought of any venture in which he was involved becoming bankrupt, "for receiverships are very costly in many ways and often involve heavy sacrifices of genuine value." To avoid that fate, the mines needed a strategy for development; they also needed fresh capital, a great deal of it. Sent to evaluate the situation, Frederick Gates devised the strategy, and Rockefeller provided the capital. He set out to buy, at bargain prices, sole control of the mining properties. Next, rail lines were extended from the mines to Lake Superior, and finally an entire fleet of ships was built to carry the ore to ports around the Great Lakes.

To a more cautious soul, all of this might have seemed like throwing good money after bad, especially in the midst of a major economic downturn, but Rockefeller knew better. In good times, businesses grew or they slipped backward; in hard times, they grew or they went under. More often than not, too, hard times actually created opportunities, as frightened investors hurried to unload their holdings in falling markets. So in business one did not simply ride out the storms; saving the ship invariably meant forging ahead with all engines running at full bore.

Yet for Rockefeller to explain Standard Oil's dazzling success, and his own role in bringing it about, by pointing to something as uncomplicated as a determination not to lose money would have amounted to a highly selective interpretation of what happened. Above all, it drastically oversimplified the forces at work in the oil industry during those years. For under the Standard's ever-lengthening shadow, a distinct climate developed: one in which good times and bad for others in the industry came and went less in response to broad market conditions than to the company's own activities. Bigness brought it steadily growing economies of scale. More important still, however, was the increasingly preferential treatment Standard demanded from the railroads, as rebates and kickbacks proliferated, giving it a tremendous advantage over its competitors. And for all of Rockefeller's claims to the contrary, he systematically used that advantage—with devastating effect—to Standard's benefit.

The most memorable example remained "the Cleveland Massacre" of 1872. Oil prices were severely depressed at the time, but adding mightily to Standard's leverage were rumors of a vast combine it had secretly entered into with all three of the major railroads serving Cleveland, providing it with absolute control over freight rates into and out of the city. The so-called South Improvement Company never went into operation, but the panic it produced, ruthlessly manipulated by Rockefeller, served him well. In a matter of months twenty-two out of twenty-six Cleveland refiners, faced with the prospect of having to pay disastrously high transportation costs, succumbed to Standard's offer to buy them out. Even though few of them had been overtly threatened, most were convinced they would be ruined if they refused to sell, and Standard's representatives made clear to the holdouts that was precisely what would happen. Selling, too, meant selling at Rockefeller's prices, which many felt, with good reason, grossly undervalued their companies. But for the beleaguered sellers there was at least a consolation prize of sorts, for Standard invariably offered to pay them in either cash or Standard Oil stock, a choice that gave those astute enough to take the stock excellent reason to congratulate themselves in future years. The sense of injustice may have lingered, but few assets were to appreciate more dramatically over the next half century than stock in Standard Oil.

Meanwhile, with the great victory in Cleveland won, the fundamental nature of the game changed. As Rockefeller charged relentlessly onward, extending his strategies to the oil fields and incorporating pipelines in his arsenal, while forcing competitor after competitor to join his alliance or go out of business, his vision grew ever larger until at last it came to embrace the entire industry, dominated, as he imagined it, by a single great enterprise under the Standard Oil banner. The chief virtue of such an arrangement, he would eventually claim, was the order it promised to bring to the oil business, an order that would replace the prevailing chaos in the industry and end forever the terrors and wastefulness of unbridled competition. At the time, however, he said as little as possible about any of this, for it was revolutionary in substance as well as in theory, flying as it did in the face of some of the most cherished beliefs of his fellow countrymen, who persisted in placing a high value on competition in the economic realm, a view Rockefeller would one day pay dearly for challenging.

In 1881 Standard Oil formally became a "trust," and the same year the first full-fledged journalistic attack on Rockefeller's creation appeared, written by Henry Demarest Lloyd for the *Atlantic Monthly*.

The agreement establishing the trust was one of a series of attempts to gather the sprawling collection of firms Standard had assembled under a single, national corporate umbrella. It was necessitated by the fact that technically only states could create corporations, yet Standard operated in many different states. Under the terms of the agreement, designated trustees of Standard Oil of Ohio would issue "certificates of interest" to stockholders in the individual companies that made up the larger enterprise, pledging to manage the whole in their behalf.

Lloyd's "Story of a Great Monopoly" was as sloppily done as Standard's trust agreement was tight and efficient. Still, he made of the company's rise a marvelously entertaining story, thanks to a gift for vivid prose. "The greatest, wisest, and meanest monopoly known to history" was how he characterized Rockefeller's creation at one point, and on the subject of the company's political machinations he quipped, "The Standard has done everything with the Pennsylvania legislature except refine it." As Lloyd spun out his tale, Standard owed its success to its corruptly unprincipled dealings with its competitors and the railroads, and as a result of his article both the company and the issue of rebates began receiving national attention.

However, it was the states, not the national government, that took the first steps to collar Standard's power. Two years before Lloyd's article, a New York investigation had exposed the details of the special treatment the company was receiving from the railroads. In 1882 the Pennsylvania legislature undertook to tax Standard's entire property, in as well as out of the state. Then in 1886, testifying before a New York Senate committee, Rockefeller was forced to reveal the terms of the trust agreement, and as a result in 1890 the attorney general of Ohio brought suit against the company for monopolistic practices, which led to an Ohio State Supreme Court order invalidating the existing arrangement.

Throughout this chain of events, Standard's executives and the lawyers they hired worked tirelessly, and often with notable success, to protect the company, but the strain on Rockefeller personally was enormous. Endlessly pilloried in the press and in the rhetoric of politicians, he became the great villain of the piece. The notoriety brought with it a different kind of pressure as well: for whatever it suggested about the morality of Rockefeller's actions, it at least made clear that he was a very rich man, and the calls on his generosity rose as rapidly as the fervor with which he was condemned by his critics. If anything, the pleas for money were even more difficult to cope with because he had always been generous with his wealth and meant to remain so. Yet sorting through the mass of appeals and deciding which were legitimate and which were worthy of favor was, by the 1890s—as he would write himself—threatening to consume all his energy.

In time, with Frederick Gates and Junior to help him, Rockefeller would organize his philanthropy as efficiently as he had his business activities, establishing appropriate routines, delegating responsibility, and framing a comprehensive plan to guide his giving. But for now he needed to worry less about both giving and getting, and one way he found to ease his cares during those years was travel. In 1884 the family crossed the continent to San Francisco. Returning to the West two years later, they experienced the wonders of Yellowstone, and the year after that they traveled to Europe for the first time, taking the entire summer to do it.

Yet as pleasant as these excursions may have been, none of them seemed to leave a deep impression on Rockefeller. Certainly he gave no signs of wanting to join the growing troop of wealthy Americans who routinely traveled abroad every year. Nor did exposure to the art and architecture of the Old World appear to have much impact on either his tastes or his character. Indeed, one of his most memorable experiences on that first European tour seems to have been the discovery that he was being cheated by the guide he had hired to accompany the family and handle the details of the trip. Promptly dismissing the culprit, he took over the job himself, including paying the bills, which to him meant checking and rechecking every last charge to be sure it was correct. In Rome a lengthy discussion developed within the family about whether, in a given week, they had eaten one chicken or two, as their hotel bill indicated. Cettie finally established that two was the correct number. "Such care in small things might seem penurious to some people," Junior commented later, "yet to him it was the working out of a life principle."

Teaching his children to be careful "in small things" was important to Rockefeller, and perhaps doubly so while they were traveling abroad, far from their American roots, and if this made him seem like a Philistine, he would not have minded in the least. He was who he was, and he saw no reason to improve upon the model in his own case, or in the next generation. Before long he passed the role of chief bill-checker during their trips on to Junior, whose duties in that regard would grow steadily over the years.

So while travel had its uses, its value to Rockefeller as a diversion was limited. He preferred things he could do at home like bicycling, which he took up with great enthusiasm during the 1890s. Ultimately, however, his chief passion would be golf. Though he did not play his first game until 1899 when he was almost sixty years old, from then on golf became the center of his life. Courses were laid out at both Forest Hill and Pocantico Hills, and to extend the season of play he bought two other houses, one in New Jersey and another in Florida, each of which had its own golf course. Like clockwork, he played every morning. When it rained his caddy held a large umbrella over his head so he could continue, and on at least one occasion at Pocantico he had the course cleared of several inches of snow rather than forgo his daily game.

As golfers always have, Rockefeller worked ceaselessly to improve his swing, even to the extent of having himself photographed so he could correct its flaws. In this and other ways he brought to golf the same meticulous attention to detail that he had to business, which was probably no accident, for by the time he took up the game he had in fact officially left the world of business behind. He had been talking of retirement for years, but the reverberating impact of the depression of the 1890s kept him in harness until 1897. From then on, however, Standard Oil was run by the individuals he had groomed for command, with John D. Archbold, his combative handpicked successor, at their head. Rockefeller went no more to the company's offices at 26 Broadway, though he did have both a direct telegraph line and the telephone if he wished to communicate with his former associates.

But mostly he was content to stay at home and enjoy the pleasures golf offered that business never had. Playing with friends gave full vent to his charm, as he laughed and joked his way around the course. On the golf course, too, he was in total control; nothing intruded on his pleasure except the occasional player foolish enough to ask for a favor of some sort, and such people were never invited back. The physical setting was also a vital part of the experience, for golf placed Rockefeller in precisely the kind of landscape that most appealed to him. Well-laid-out golf courses were "natural" in the sense that they avoided the artificialities of imposed symmetry and order, but the "nature" visible in all those gently rising hills and drifts of trees shimmering in the sunlight remained one purposely managed by human will to create the finest vistas, to lead the eye ever onward to new delights. Here indeed was that green and inviting world that had filled the imagination of the young boy with the ax, all those years ago. And now at last he was free to enjoy that world, which for the moment was all he needed, or wanted, to know.

Unfortunately for his sake, it was not all his fellow countrymen wanted to know. Together, the writings of Henry Demarest Lloyd and the revelations before legislative committees had created a hunger for information about Rockefeller that would not die. And with it had grown a sense that serious injustices had been committed, injustices that cried out for correction. But in a stunning display of unconcern, Rockefeller said nothing at all in his own defense. And whether it was the endless golfing or simply his retirement from business, in many ways his health seemed better at the end of the century than it had been several years earlier, when he suffered from severe bouts of fatigue, digestive problems, and depression. Then in 1901 he suddenly lost all the hair over his entire body. The cause of alopecia, as the condition is known, is unclear, though it is sometimes thought to be stress-related. In Rockefeller's case it produced a jarring change, aging him decades in appearance in a few months, which was only partially remedied when he began wearing wigs.

Still, life continued to afford its pleasures. In addition to golf, there was the improvement of his Pocantico Hills estate to occupy his mind. With the family headquartered in New York, it made sense to find some place outside the city where they could spend time, especially after Rockefeller retired. Accordingly, in 1893 he had begun buying property not far from his brother William's home, overlooking the Hudson River, above Tarrytown. To keep prices from escalating, the purchases were made as quietly as possible under "dummy" names. In August of that year contracts were signed for four parcels, totaling just over sixty acres, at an average price of $2,515.52 per acre—the core of an estate that in time would grow to more than three thousand acres.

The land itself was magnificent. Rising steadily upward from the valley, it overspread the heights above, offering glorious views of the river to the west and beyond it the Palisades. Delighted with his new domain, Rockefeller was soon tramping over every acre of it, often with Junior by his side. There was already an observation tower on the property, and from it he spied out the most picturesque sites for the roads and paths that would make the place truly his own. To help him, he hired the landscape firm founded by Frederick Law Olmsted, the creator of New York's Central Park. Later the man the firm sent him, Warren H. Manning—who went on to have a brilliant career as a landscape designer working in the "naturalistic" style—continued the project alone. A large stone coach barn was also built, and there was talk of building a new house, though as the costs began to mount, Rockefeller backed off, calling a halt to the work.

For the present he and Cettie were comfortably settled in the Parsons-Wentworth House on one of the original parcels he had purchased. Junior and Alta, the two of their children who were based in New York, often joined them at Pocantico Hills, as they married and began families of their own. Junior especially seemed to like the place, and in recognition of the fact, in the spring of 1902 Senior gave his son and daughter-in-law the use of a rambling Dutch-style house on the property, which soon became known as Abeyton Lodge. Then came the fire that destroyed the Parsons-Wentworth House, followed by the dispute within the family over whether to replace it with a new house, a dispute in which Junior proved surprisingly adamant. In spite of his father's opposition to the project, he pursued it without letup over the next four years, working quietly with Delano & Aldrich, the architectural firm he and Abby had chosen, and stating the case repeatedly to Senior.

Under ordinary circumstances, Rockefeller would undoubtedly have agreed to anything his son seemed to want so much, despite his disagreement with Junior in the matter. But in this case other tensions within the family circle had to be taken into account. Those tensions, too, would continue to shape the project in crucial ways even after Senior capitulated and reluctantly decided to go ahead and build.

It was the end of October 1902 when Junior first met with Chester Aldrich on the subject of a new house, and less than two weeks later when he wrote Aldrich that Senior was not in fact interested in the project. In the meantime Aldrich had drawn some sketches to indicate what might be done. Unfortunately they no longer exist, nor do any of the other early drawings of Kykuit, but evidently Junior liked what he saw, for in May of 1903 he gave Delano & Aldrich the job of designing a pergola for Abeyton Lodge. He also assured Aldrich that he would let him know when and if his father "comes to the point of having an architect draw plans" for a new house.

As further proof of their enthusiasm for Aldrich's sketches, Junior and Abby showed them to her father, who was suitably impressed, and they took them along when they visited the senior Rockefellers at Forest Hill later in the summer, though in that case they might have saved themselves the trouble. Senior was willing to have a look, but his reaction was decidedly cool. "They were all much pleased with the plans," Junior wrote Aldrich somewhat disingenuously before going on to note that Senior had "made no criticisms or suggestions" and did not seem inclined to consider the question further "at this point."

But Junior's "at this point" at least suggested that Senior might change his mind, so Aldrich, undaunted, went ahead with various revisions he had discussed earlier with Abby and Junior. After all, this was not a commission one wanted to lose! Nor was Rockefeller himself quite ready to let the subject of a new house drop. In December Junior wrote Aldrich that his father "talks from time to time of building and enjoys studying over his mental picture of a house." He even had in mind "a definite plan for the first floor of the house including the size as well as the location of the rooms." But this was for a "much smaller house" than the one Junior and

Abby had imagined. If the project was to go forward, Junior continued, it would have to be taken up from his father's standpoint "and his ideas first laid out on paper . . . as to size and interior arrangement."

No further word on the subject materialized for several months. During that time Junior and Abby's attention was much taken up with the birth of their first child, a daughter, which occurred at the end of 1903. In April of the following year Cettie suffered the strokelike attack that left her paralyzed for months. But then two months after that a letter from Junior, written at his father's request, clearly indicated that Senior had not ruled out the idea of building a new house. The letter went to Lamont Bowers, an uncle of Frederick Gates's, who had served as manager of Rockefeller's fleet of ore ships on the Great Lakes and was currently supervising construction of the Rockefeller Building in Cleveland, a large office complex. The purpose of the letter was to ask if Bowers would be willing to play a similar role in connection with "a house at Pocantico Hills" that Senior was "contemplating building." Junior further indicated that the house would cost at least $100,000 "including furnishing and decorations, although this is a wild guess." Senior also had an architect in mind. While Junior did not mention his name, he described him as having worked "pleasantly and satisfactorily" on the renovation of Senior's house at Lakewood, New Jersey, which had originally been built as the clubhouse of a golf club that had since failed.

So the idea of a new house was indeed not dead, but Junior's reaction to the information he sent Bowers must have been decidedly mixed. If the fact that Senior was still thinking of building a new house was encouraging, his choice of architects did not at all please his son. The individual in question was Dunham Wheeler. Apparently, when Senior mentioned the project to Wheeler he went ahead and drew up a ground-floor plan and later an elevation. In a letter to his cousin, Percy Rockefeller, Junior remarked that he had tried to persuade his father to use "various architects of standing in the city," implying that Wheeler had no particular standing in New York as an architect, which was true. After seeing Wheeler's drawing of the house, he was even less enthusiastic, complaining to Abby that it seemed "crude and mongrel and suggests the Lake Mohawk Hotel"—in other words, a great barn of a place surrounded by an endless piazza, with none of the elegant flourishes that someone like Aldrich routinely provided.

Also upsetting to Junior must have been his father's decision to put Lamont Bowers in charge of building the new house. If Bowers accepted, what would be left for Junior and Abby to do? What effect, too, would it have on the house itself? Before coming to work for Rockefeller, Bowers had been involved in a string of small ventures in upstate New York, including a real estate agency and a wholesale grocery. Admittedly he had done well with the ore fleet in spite of his modest background, but what did that say about his knowledge of the finer points of architecture? Precious little that would have satisfied Junior and Abby.

How much of all this Senior sensed is unclear. As perceptive as he was, he probably understood a fair amount of it, but by refusing to say more than he did he preserved his freedom to act as he wished. Plainly Junior and Abby wanted him to build. But if he did decide to go ahead with a new house, it was unlikely to be the kind of place they wanted it to be, and size was only part of the problem. Of far greater importance was how the house would work, what its function and purpose would be.

In the years when he was still making only occasional trips to New York, Senior had written Cettie, "The world is full of Sham, Flattery, and Deception, and *home* is a haven of rest and freedom." As unremarkable a sentiment as this may have been for a Victorian husband to utter, what remains striking is how completely it shaped the domestic life that Senior and Cettie constructed for themselves and their children. Their houses truly were places apart from the turmoil and temptation of the sinful world outside. Always and quintessentially they were family homes. The activities that went on in and around them—daily religious devotions, the singing of hymns, swimming and skating, bicycling, and simple parlor games—were all family-centered, participated in by parents and children alike. By the same token, home was a private world, with little if any public side. As Junior said later, speaking of his parents' activities in Cleveland, "They had no civic or social relations with anything or anyone in the city." The people who came to call were Baptist ministers and other worthy individuals interested in good works. They were there for earnest conversation and plain fare, not entertainment.

To design a house to accommodate this kind of life was not difficult. There did not have to be a great many rooms; nor did they have to be very large or arranged in any particular way. Comfort and convenience were more important than anything else. The house that Junior and Abby envisioned, on the other hand, had to satisfy a more complex agenda. It too was to be a setting for family life, but in addition it was meant to be an object of beauty, and above all beauty cast in the time-honored forms of classical architecture. Presumably Aldrich understood this, and the plans he did for

Junior had the requisite features: large rooms, symmetrically arranged around a central axis; the ground floor, especially, a series of imposing spaces, leading formally from one to another; the whole composition grand, ordered, hierarchical.

At the best of times it is hard to imagine Senior, given his passion for plain living, wanting to build such a place, and in 1904, with the furor produced by Tarbell's series at its height, the arguments against doing so were stronger than ever. There was as well another, equally important if less obvious reason for not building the kind of house Junior and Abby wanted, and that was what it would mean to Cettie Rockefeller.

When they were younger, Cettie had shared fully in her husband's triumphs and worries. Intelligent, strong willed, and high-minded, she both sustained and guided him in his rise; their marriage had been a true partnership. But that time had passed. The business had become so vast that she no longer seemed to understand it. Or perhaps she understood only too well what it had become and the moral costs it exacted. In any case Senior had slipped beyond her into a world she hung back from entering and could only half glimpse. He continued to write fondly whenever they were apart, yet his letters contained little news of any importance. Two things that Cettie had not lost, however, were her rock-solid religious faith and her abiding commitment to their shared ideal of family life. Both were enshrined in their homes in Cleveland, and the ten years they spent living in hotels in New York City before buying a house there may well have reflected a reluctance on her part to attenuate those ties any further. But the step could not be postponed forever. Eventually they moved into the house on West Fifty-fourth Street, and if Cettie was disappointed, at least she still had Forest Hill to hang on to.

In her mind Forest Hill would always remain the family's true home. Every year she and Senior spent much of the summer and early autumn there, and certainly no one was proposing to replace their cherished Cleveland retreat with a new house in Pocantico Hills. But how could she be sure that in time gradually, ineluctably, that would not happen? So much in her life had already changed in ways she could never have predicted or controlled. Also, her health was deteriorating, and her children were marrying and leaving home, most recently John, her favorite, the one to whom she had always felt closest. And even though he had chosen an excellent wife, their backgrounds were different, and John himself had changed: those dancing parties at college, and now sly jokes about how Forest Hill was his father's "ideal for a summer house," an ideal Junior apparently did not share. Finally, rumbling on every side, was the mounting barrage of accusations leveled at Senior, accusations that she desperately wanted and needed to believe were untrue.

As a loving husband Rockefeller could afford to ignore none of this in weighing the question of a new house. If one were to be built, it had to be something Cettie could be comfortable with. In no way could it be seen as a replacement for Forest Hill, yet it was equally important that it have the same qualities: that it be first and foremost a family home.

However, it was also true that Cettie's feelings were not all that mattered. For as the months passed, it became increasingly clear that despite everything that might have seemed good in Junior's life—his fine wife, his new baby, his growing involvement in projects like the General Education Board—his emotional stability was crumbling. The symptoms were familiar; he had suffered from them before, as had Senior: insomnia, severe headaches, perpetual fatigue. But this was more serious than those other times. Years afterward Junior would confide to a friend of his son David's (as he had to none of his own children up to then) that he had actually suffered a nervous breakdown, though "nervous exhaustion" was as much as anyone spoke of at the time.

There was no single cause of his condition. Anxiety at having to share with the new baby the affections of Abby, on whom he would always be deeply dependent, may even have played a role. But on top of that, his mother's failing health plus all the unresolved doubts about his future pressed down upon him. And finally, complicating everything, there was Tarbell's series on Standard Oil, which appeared in book form at the end of 1904, to be followed eight months later by the publication in *McClure's Magazine* of her two-part dissection of Rockefeller's character and personality. Every ounce of Junior's instincts would have cried out that Tarbell had to be wrong, but in fact it was not that simple. As much as he wanted to believe his father innocent of her charges, he had come to know through personal contacts with John Archbold, Senior's successor at Standard, about the bribes the company paid to political figures, and had actually been asked himself, and agreed, to lobby his father-in-law, Senator Aldrich, on Standard's behalf. If Archbold was as unscrupulous as he appeared to be, and as ready to involve Junior in his schemes, what did that say about Senior, the man who had trained him? Then, too, there was his father's refusal to answer publicly the charges against him. Was it because he was unwilling or in fact unable to do so?

Ultimately Junior had to resolve all such doubts in Senior's favor, and without ever mentioning them to his father. He could not have carried on otherwise. But the resulting strain was something he alone could fathom. Not even to Abby was he likely to have expressed his deepest anxieties. It was bad enough that by bringing her into the family circle he had subjected her to the Rockefellers' collective destiny, which at the moment seemed singularly bleak.

So Junior suffered alone, but everyone was terribly kind, including Senior. He had come to rely on his son in countless ways. None of his three sons-in-law were up to taking Junior's place in that regard, and among his daughters, two—Bessie, married to Columbia professor Charles Strong, and Edith, the wife of International Harvester heir Harold McCormick— were themselves already showing signs of the chronic ill health and emotional instability that would mark the rest of their lives. The future of the family, in short, lay in Junior's hands; everything depended on his recovery. And if building a new house at Pocantico promised to help in that regard, the price was hardly too high to pay. At the very least it would express confidence in his son's judgment and give him something to fill his days with, something tangible and down to earth. By a curious coincidence, as a young man Senior had taken on the task of overseeing the construction of a house for his parents in Cleveland, and by all accounts he handled the job well.

It remained essential, however, that any house built at Pocantico be the kind of place Senior, and ultimately Cettie, could be comfortable with. Hence his determination to control the planning process as well as the actual work of construction. For the first of those tasks he would use Dunham Wheeler, and for the second Lamont Bowers. Both men were already beholden to him and would follow his wishes to the letter. Evidently Junior's role would be to relay his father's instructions to them and serve as paymaster for the project. Senior was also careful to stipulate that he wanted, as he wrote Junior, "no responsibility on Mother and little or none upon myself."

Such was the plan Senior outlined in midsummer 1904. But while some features of it remained constant—the ban on involving Cettie, for example—others began to change almost at once. When Senior suggested that Bowers might wish to choose an architect other than Wheeler, Junior pressed his father to make the final choice himself. The answer that came back was precisely what he must have hoped it would be: Senior liked Wheeler's "interior plan of the house," but he would not object if "some other architect" were called in to provide, as he put it, "a sketch or picture" of the exterior, "without changing the interior plans, though it might be that the interior plans could be improved." He was not, as he said, "wedded to Mr. Wheeler if we can do better with another architect," to which Junior hurried to reply, "I think you are wise in suggesting that someone else be called upon to look over the ground plans which you and Mr. Wheeler have worked out for the house with a view to making any suggestions which may occur."

Armed with his father's approval and determined to move as quickly as possible, Junior wrote Aldrich the next day telling him how matters stood and asking if he would be willing to go over the plans Wheeler had done for Senior and "make any suggestions which occur to you and also work out an elevation." Aldrich was about to leave on a trip to Europe, so he passed the assignment along to his partner, William Delano. "I have seen Chester Aldrich. He sails tomorrow, his partner will make sketches for me," Junior informed Abby, adding what must have been particularly heartening news: "They do not seem to feel hopeless." Abby was delighted. "I am sorry that Chester Aldrich is going abroad but very glad and thankful that they are willing to undertake making plans."

From that point the design process moved quickly ahead with regular meetings between Junior and Delano. If absent in person, however, Senior remained very much part of the process. On August 23, 1904, just as Delano was beginning work on the project, Junior forwarded the contents of two telegrams to him. The first, from Junior to his father, read, "Would you object to enlarging first floor of Pocantico house somewhat and making the third story less extensive? Think effect would be better." More than likely the suggestion had come from Delano, and the answer ought to have given both him and Junior pause. "Think utility and convenience of the first importance and that the third floor as I planned it the most desirable in the house," declared Senior, adding, "I would not have the first story so large as it is but could not see the way to make it smaller." In short, Senior was holding fast to his vision of the house. The rooms on the third floor were to be bedrooms for children and grandchildren; they were what mattered most. The spaces on the first floor were less important; there was no need to make them any larger. This was still to be emphatically, at least in Senior's mind, a family house.

Perhaps reluctant to sound quite so uncompromising, Senior did add that he was "agreeable" to seeing the plan Junior described, "assuming the expense of the same is reasonable." Taking their cue from that assurance—though it might have been wiser not to—Junior and Delano went ahead with what was plainly a full-scale revision of Senior's plans. "Mr. Delano spent several hours here yesterday . . . and this afternoon showed me a rough sketch of the first floor," Junior wrote Abby. "He has run a hall across the hall by putting the dining room and the library adjacent. I think it is a real improvement. Already things look better and he is full of hope." And two days later: "I stopped in to see Mr. Delano on my way down this morning. He has several new ideas regarding the arrangement of both the first and second floors which are admirable, also about the elevation. I think you will like his work and am quite hopeful Father will."

All too soon that hope was to be dashed, however. At the beginning of September 1904 Junior went, as he had the year before, to visit his parents with a set of architectural plans under his arm, only to have them, again, rejected. "My father's mind was not on building," he wrote Delano. "He did not feel inclined to look at the plans until the last day and then only casually. He made no expression whatever regarding the ground plans." Junior added that he doubted anything further would be done until his father came east again in October.

As it turned out, much more time than that was to pass before the matter arose again, for by now Junior's precarious emotional state was becoming a subject of grave concern to the family. Nor did his anxiety over the house-planning project help in that regard. In the latest round of planning, he and Delano had dutifully started with Senior's design, but talk of enlarging the ground floor and adding a hall to intersect the one shown in Wheeler's drawing suggested that they were transforming the house into something quite unlike Senior's vision of it—something larger, more formal, less dedicated to the domestic ideal that mattered so much to Cettie Rockefeller. Senior had detected the change readily enough on seeing the plans and, without saying so explicitly, made clear that he considered them unacceptable.

Did all this bespeak a still more basic conflict between father and son? Quite possibly it did. Junior cannot have liked continually disagreeing with his father about the house, yet whatever larger issues may have been at stake, apparently he could not, or would not, face them. By December of 1904 his condition had become sufficiently troubling that it seemed best for him to embark on an extended trip abroad. Living quietly with Abby and the new baby in the south of France, he followed a rigorous program of diet and exercise. With the coming of spring he appeared well enough to travel a bit alone with Abby, after which the family returned to America, though throughout the summer Junior's secretary continued to answer most of his incoming mail, explaining that he remained too ill to do so himself.

Being home did have its brighter side, however. Over the winter it seemed his father had changed his mind and was now committed to building a new house. Though he never announced his decision in so many words, in January of 1905 he asked the housekeeper at Pocantico to send him all the various plans and sketches done thus far. As he poured over them, the differences between his version of the place and Delano & Aldrich's would have been obvious enough. But surely with a few modest changes his ideas could be made acceptable to Junior and Abby. After all, these were just lines on paper; there was every reason to hope it would all work out—that he could find a way to be both a good husband and a good father.

And hope was something Rockefeller must have felt a particular need for that winter. February 1905 brought the unanimous vote in the House of Representatives in Washington, D.C., on the resolution calling for an antitrust investigation of Standard Oil, and the month before that had seen the inauguration of Theodore Roosevelt, now elected president in his own right, and no friend to Standard Oil. Indeed, TR privately confided to his attorney general that he considered Standard's directors "the biggest criminals in the country," a view that would be reflected eventually in the federal antitrust suit brought against the company.

For all its apparent inevitability, however, the government's suit was not a foregone conclusion in 1905. The calculus of business consolidation was a subject Rockefeller grasped more thoroughly than anyone of his generation; politics he understood less well. Roosevelt did not want to break up Standard Oil. If the company's executives had been more cooperative in dealing with the government, the results would almost certainly have been less draconian. A decent show of obedience and contrition, a due regard for the power of the government and the president, in short a compromise, would have been enough. Unfortunately, compromising with the government was something Rockefeller never seriously considered.

In that sense the question of the new house was different, for there an earnest concern for his family's future had mandated a compromise. Yet in that case another calculus was at work as well, one Senior knew even less about than the conventions of political compromise: the calculus of taste. In his mind the issues were personal. He knew what he liked, and he hoped to build a house that would please both his wife and his son; their opinions and his own were all that mattered. But in reality the design of the house had significance beyond the Rockefellers' wishes, and taste lay at the heart of it, taste and the symbolic power of taste.

For the fact was that in the minds of not a few thoughtful observers the ways in which many of America's newly rich industrial barons were choosing to house themselves raised fundamental questions about the health of American society, questions that endowed things like classical cornices and artfully laid out garden terraces with a higher order of meaning. Moreover, the issues at stake were not at all unlike the ones that divided Senior and his son in the case of the Pocantico project. So whether he liked it or not, Rockefeller was also involved in creating not just a home but a text that would find a place in an ongoing debate in American culture about the proper place of wealth in a democracy, and the role of taste in defining that place.

Building

3

Kykuit Rising I

Was the architect standing there, watching as the extraordinary performance unfolded in yet another demonstration of the client's boundless determination to have his way? For the great man had indeed made his plan, and now the time had come to carry it out.

Once again it was about light, this time bright streaks of it, piercing through strategically cut holes in the large wooden box he had ordered built and set up on a turntable at the top of the hill. Waiting impatiently until everything was ready, he took his seat inside the box, before a small stand holding a model of the building, and as the box turned he carefully noted how the light fell on the model from angle after angle.

His goal was to arrange things exactly as they were at his New Jersey house. But there, since he had bought the place already built, it happened without his willing it; here he had to make certain himself that there were no mistakes, that nothing was left to chance. The crucial point was to position the house so that the sun would follow him throughout each day, greeting him in the morning in his office and glowing sublimely in the west above that glorious sweep of river, out his dining room windows, as he ate his evening meal. When his calculations were complete he gave instructions making clear how he wanted it done: precisely where the great hole should be dug and the house raised up out of it.

So much for the notion that architects designed houses.

Rockefeller, hidden from view in a machine of his own creation, single-mindedly managing the world around him; it could have been a metaphor for his entire life up to then. His architects had their own opinions on the point at issue, starting with a dislike of positioning houses on the tops of hills, because without a substantial amount of flat land on which to build, a feature Kykuit's site lacked, it could be difficult to integrate the house gracefully into the surrounding landscape. For all their romantic picturesqueness, hilltop aeries were seldom elegant, at least as Delano & Aldrich would have defined the term.

But in this case the site was a given, just as the character and personality of John D. Rockefeller were. As he saw it, you hired architects to give you what you wanted, to worry about the nuts and bolts of the job, to produce plans that builders could build from. The idea that their primary function was to exercise independent artistic creativity would have struck him as dangerous in the extreme. If architects were allowed to design whatever they liked, where would it all end, and more important, who would be in charge?

Again, Delano & Aldrich took a different view of the matter. In later years the partners regularly provided their country-house clients with a self-published handbook titled *For You to Decide*. Though ostensibly their intention was to describe the various choices that needed to be made during the design process, they also wished to establish, in a polite way, the primacy of their authority in matters aesthetic, once the client's basic preferences had been made known. This was how the architect-client relationship was supposed to work, at any rate from the firm's perspective. At stake, too, was considerably more than the usual floor plans and exterior elevations. Designs for interiors and, on the outside, for drives, terraces, walkways, and gardens were all declared to be "essential parts of the architect's work." Only if that was so would the result become a coherent, integrated whole, a sensible enough goal, certainly. But reality can trump even the most sensible of goals, which for Delano & Aldrich would become the story of Kykuit's building. In the nine years the firm worked on the house, six of them as the principal architects for the project, the process violated every one of the precepts laid down in *For You to Decide*. "Bitter" is how a recent book on the firm's work characterizes the experience, "fraught with client interference and . . . so many designers," according to the authors, "that [it] became a thoroughly compromised commission."

Excessive client interference, a surfeit of designers, a thoroughly compromised commission—all true. Yet under the circumstances it could hardly have been otherwise. That Kykuit was built at all was a wonder; that it could have been simply or easily built was never in the cards.

At the beginning of 1905, however, all of that lay in the future, including Senior's labors in his box at the top of the hill. For the moment the great thing was that he had finally made up his mind to go ahead and build, a fact signaled by his request to have all the various plans for the new house sent to him in New York. Conveniently his decision came at a time when he had the field to himself. Dunham Wheeler's services had been dispensed with, Delano & Aldrich had been paid for the work Junior had asked them to do, and Junior, with Abby, was in Europe recovering from his nervous collapse. By the time they returned, the plans for the house were virtually complete, done by Delano & Aldrich, the firm Junior had chosen, but working this time at Senior's request and under his sole direction.

Presumably the basis of the plans was that "mental picture of a house" he had been carrying in his head for the past year or more. Dunham Wheeler's design had captured its essence, though like Junior and Abby he envisioned a much larger house than Senior wanted, just as Delano & Aldrich once had. But now all such issues would be settled by Senior; that was *his* view of how the design process ought to work. It was up to his architects, therefore, to manage as best they could, and however little they may have liked it, that was precisely what they hoped to do. For if John D. Rockefeller represented a rising class of vastly rich industrialists, William Delano and Chester Aldrich belonged to a growing coterie of professionally trained, gentlemen architects who had staked their careers on pleasing the rich.

Born to socially prominent families and educated at Yale and Columbia respectively, before enrolling in the École des Beaux-Arts in Paris, Delano and Aldrich would come to move effortlessly through the social and professional milieu that provided the commissions that made their firm, during the first third of the twentieth century, one of the premier designers of American country houses of the grander sort. In achieving that distinction they followed a path pioneered by Richard Morris Hunt, the first American architect to study at the École. After Hunt's death in 1895, McKim, Mead & White became the leading firm in country-house design, and trained in its offices, in turn, were John Carrère and Thomas Hastings, in whose firm Delano and Aldrich began their careers.

Like Delano and Aldrich, all of these men came from privileged backgrounds, and all of them spent time traveling and studying abroad. The lives they led outside their handsomely appointed offices also followed similar patterns. They lived in the same neighborhoods (Delano and Aldrich two blocks apart in the Murray Hill section of Manhattan) and summered in the same places. At dinner parties and exclusive private clubs in the city they mingled with the moneyed individuals who already were, or would eventually become, their clients. Between them, Delano and Aldrich belonged to no fewer than six New York clubs: the Century Association, the Coffee House, the Digressionists, the Knickerbocker, India House, and the Brook. And if all those memberships made for a hefty outlay in annual dues, in addition to providing contacts with wealthy clients, the clubs could and did become clients themselves. Thus the Knickerbocker, the Colony Club, the Brook, and, most prestigious of all, the Union Club of New York would each build clubhouses designed by Delano & Aldrich. The firm also executed dozens of commissions for elite schools and colleges, as well as for various charitable organizations supported by the rich, including the Greenwich Settlement House, the Kips Bay Boys Club, and the New York chapter of the American Red Cross.

Such was the world in which the gentlemen architects built their careers. Helix-like, it operated as a series of interlocking circles bound by a complex network of personal and institutional ties that firms like Delano & Aldrich manipulated with singular skill and energy. Ultimately, however, what drove the system forward was something more palpable than skill and energy, and more basic, even, than good breeding and good manners. What drove it forward was money, unprecedented amounts of it, suddenly pouring into private hands.

Of all of this, the Rockefeller family with its ever-burgeoning wealth was a prime example, though different only in degree were the other fortunes that financed the building of the clubs, the charitable headquarters, the college and school buildings, and the houses designed by the gentlemen architects. As a body of work another characteristic those buildings shared— foursquare, symmetrical, sheathed in brick and limestone richly decorated with appropriate classical detail—was an unmistakable monumental quality. But monuments to what exactly?

In point of time, the country house as monument first appeared in America in what would simultaneously become its apogee: George Washington Vanderbilt's colossal Biltmore, designed by Richard Morris Hunt for a vast estate in Asheville, North Carolina. Begun in 1889 but not finally finished until 1895, Biltmore is still regularly described as the largest private house ever built in America. With its 255 rooms stretching for almost four hundred feet across the landscape, in style it followed the French Renaissance mode Hunt had used earlier for the Fifth Avenue mansion of George Vanderbilt's brother, William, and his wife, the redoubtable Alva. Topped by tall, steep roofs densely packed with towers, chimneys, and dormer windows, both buildings had a certain liveliness about them, but essentially the impression they created was one of grandeur, eye-grabbing, mind-stopping grandeur.

Both houses also turned out to be notably significant in social as well as architectural terms. It was Caroline Astor's fear of being excluded from the housewarming ball Alva Vanderbilt gave at her new "palace" that finally persuaded her to admit the Vanderbilts to the inner circle of New York society. And though no one undertook to match Biltmore's heroic size, in the decade after its completion the number, scale, and opulence of American country houses all rose sharply. As important as the house itself was its setting on tens of thousands of acres of land, amid correspondingly lavish outbuildings and gardens. Biltmore as a totality, as a kind of all-sufficing world of its own—that was what set it apart for both the public and George Vanderbilt's fellow millionaires. Here, as a contemporary observer remarked, was "the ancestral seat of one line of Vanderbilts"; not just another big house in the country but a true aristocratic domain of the sort that dotted the European countryside.

To see places like Biltmore as ancestral country homes, havens of aristocratic position and privilege—as family seats in short—was a powerful vision. Yet the reality was never that simple. From time immemorial European country houses had functioned not only as badges of social standing but also as productive economic units, literally supporting the ruling classes. More important still, such places were bastions of political power, by law and custom linking local interests to politics on the national level. At Biltmore George Vanderbilt constructed an English-style village for his estate workers and on the advice of his landscape architect, Frederick Law Olmsted, began reforesting his land as both a moneymaking scheme and a public-spirited venture aimed at developing new systems of land use for the impoverished hill country of North Carolina. But the rules he imposed on his tenants were highly unpopular, and arsonists set fires that destroyed thousands of acres of his timber. Even in social terms, life at Biltmore seemed at best a pale reflection of life in its European counterparts. Edith Wharton and Henry James came to stay at one point, but the guest books would record few large house parties. Such visitors as there were generally belonged to a small circle of friends and family members.

So it would be at most American country houses. In economic terms they were sites of consumption, not production, and their political functions were nonexistent. Instead, people busied themselves with socializing and sports of one kind or another, to facilitate which "colonies" of elaborate country houses grew up in the Berkshires and Bar Harbor, and nearer at hand on Long Island, joining already established locations like Newport and the Hudson River valley. Yet the more people clustered in such places, the more suburban, the less truly aristocratic, life in them tended to seem.

Still, the vision of aristocracy persisted, and it was left to the gentlemen architects to create the settings that would give it the substance it needed. More often than not they worked with the children or grandchildren of the men who had made the great fortunes—as Hunt did with the Vanderbilts and Delano & Aldrich did initially with Junior and Abby—and it was those children who came to embrace most enthusiastically the foursquare, the symmetrical, and the monumental in country houses.

The results also turned out to be of great interest to the public, as the growing number of publications treating country houses indicated. Among the most popular were *American Homes and Gardens, Country Life in America, House and Garden, House Beautiful,* and *Town and Country*—all established about this time, and all handsomely illustrated as well as carefully calculated to appeal both to people fortunate enough to own country houses and to those who only dreamed of doing so. In a more serious vein, journals like *Architectural Record* and *Architectural Forum* each published annually an entire issue on country houses, and after 1900 the number of books on the subject also multiplied steadily.

For the most part this literature was unabashedly enthusiastic, not only about the new country houses but also about what they seemed to stand for: a true "American Renaissance"—a coming of age of the nation's taste, even, by extension, of American civilization itself. The buildings were acclaimed, their owners lionized, and their architects regularly, if somewhat illogically, praised for the skill with which they employed traditional European styles in designing houses for modern use in New World settings. Not all commentators shared such feelings, however, and some intrepid souls went so far as to deplore both the houses and the attitudes they represented.

A favorite topic of the critics was what they saw as the blatant contradiction between American democratic values and vast houses designed to copy European palaces in what appeared to be a mindless trumpeting of aristocratic pretensions. In addition there was the matter of simple fairness. Wrote E. L. Godkin in an article in *Scribner's Magazine,* "To erect palatial abodes is to flaunt, in the faces of the poor and the unsuccessful and greedy, the most conspicuous possible evidence that the owner not only has enormous amounts of money, but does not know what to do with it."

Aptly enough Godkin's article was titled "The Expenditure of Rich Men," but the true master of that subject was Thorstein Veblen, whose *Theory of the Leisure Class* appeared in 1899. Less about houses per se than the mores that led the rich to spend in ever more lavish orgies of "conspicuous consumption," Veblen's analysis was utterly devastating. Far from being the bearers of progress much of the world considered them, such people were, as he portrayed them, not only supremely wasteful but driven by dark, atavistic impulses harkening back to the most brutal forms of primitive society. The fact that Veblen was a faculty member of the University of Chicago, which owed its existence to John D. Rockefeller's millions, made his ideas seem all the more intriguing, though ironically Rockefeller detested ostentation almost as passionately as he did.

Gentler than Veblen, while still sharing some of his opinions, was another commentator, Herbert Croly, who did concern himself specifically with the houses of the rich. A member of the editorial staff of *Architectural Record,* Croly later went on to found the *New Republic* and become active in Progressive politics. As an architectural critic he published dozens of articles and two books on domestic architecture, *Stately Homes in America: From Colonial Times to the Present Day* (1903) and *Houses for Town or Country* (1907). At times his remarks could be quite biting, as when he declared, "Americans do everything with their wealth except 'forget it.' The result is that there is too much of everything: too much gilt, too much furniture, too much upholstery, too much space, too many styles, too much ceiling." Yet Croly also believed there was a reasonable chance all this would change. "In regard to the houses of the present day, it looks as if many of the most expensive 'palaces' will fail to be interesting at the end of thirty or forty years. I certainly hope that such will be the case because these houses . . . are places in which a man not stupefied by his own opulence could not possibly live."

Croly's optimism about the country-house movement grew from what he saw as an emerging trend toward smaller, more "suitable" houses. Designed by younger architects—who continued to favor, as Croly himself did, styles that bore the stamp of historical authority, but in simpler, less palatial versions—such places seemed to indicate that country-house architecture in America might finally become what he most deeply believed it could be: simultaneously an affirmation of the nation's traditional democratic values and a civilizing force of the highest order.

Croly's *Stately Homes in America* was published the same year Junior and Abby began working on plans for Kykuit with Delano & Aldrich, and given their views they may well have read the book. But again, it was Senior, not Junior and Abby, who sat down with Chester Aldrich to plan the new house in the winter of 1905, and he almost certainly knew nothing of Croly's ideas. Nor was he the least bit smitten with visions of aristocracy, or even, as Croly described the typical industrial tycoon, interested in building houses simply as "one of the spoils of his financial conquests" to advertise his prowess at making money. All of which must have made him seem like an odd bird to his elegantly trained architects.

At the same time, however, it would have been a great mistake to imagine that Rockefeller had no interest in architecture or lacked ideas about how houses ought to be designed. Quite the reverse was true. Along with his personal requirements for the new house—that it be above all a place dedicated to the kind of family life that mattered so much to Cettie Rockefeller—he had definite opinions about architecture, opinions that fell well within the broad sweep of American architectural taste as it had evolved during his lifetime.

On more than one occasion Junior noted that his father "had no conception of art or beauty" except for the beauty he found in nature. When it came to houses, he further described Senior as loving to "change things" yet added that the changes he made to the houses he owned, usually for the sake of convenience, had more the character of "excrescences" than anything else. But in truth both notions—the primacy of natural beauty and the importance in domestic architecture of functionally organized, free-flowing spaces—had long enjoyed solid support in architectural practice and theory, however little they figured in the teachings of École des Beaux-Arts.

Interestingly enough, hints of some of Senior's ideas on these subjects found their way into an article titled "John D. Rockefeller's Pocantico Estate," which appeared in the November 1905 issue of the *Country Calendar*, one of the many popular magazines dealing with country houses and country life. Though no author's name was given, the article had every appearance of having been written by someone in close touch with the family, perhaps even with Senior himself, which if true would have been extraordinary, given his notorious aversion to publicity. In any case, the author chose to present Rockefeller and his estate in a highly appealing light, emphasizing the beauty of the property's more than two thousand acres and the fact that it remained open to everyone as "a great public park." The only two activities Rockefeller was described as pursuing there were golf and road building. Houses were barely mentioned. "Anything is good enough for me" was Rockefeller's declared view on the subject, to which the article added that he had lived in one house already on the property when he bought it, then moved to another after that house burned down, and more recently had been giving thought to building a new house of his own devising; "but when it will be begun and when finished, no one pretends to say."

Plainly the author's intention was to convince readers that in no sense was the place being described (and much was made of the fact that it had as yet no name) a typical millionaire's estate. Even less did it resemble a great aristocratic establishment, a point the author made explicit in noting of Rockefeller, "He seeks not to play the country gentleman with his neighbors and tenants, and never assumes the lord-of-the-manor air." Instead, all he seemed to want was a peaceful spot with beautiful views where he could enjoy, for a while each year, a few simple pleasures. "Here, if anywhere," the article concluded, "could the millionaire safely get away from his wealth."

Living modestly in a house of no great pretension in a setting of striking natural beauty was in fact the essence of Rockefeller's notion of what country life ought to be. While neither his son nor his architects seemed to share that vision, fifty years earlier a young American nurseryman named Andrew Jackson Downing had developed something quite similar to it in a number of highly popular books, including *A Treatise on the Theory and Practice of Landscape Gardening, Adapted to North America* (1841) and *The Architecture of Country Houses* (1850). No writer on such subjects was more influential through the middle years of the nineteenth century than Downing; if Rockefeller read anyone on landscape design and country houses, it was almost certainly him. (An inventory of Junior's library done in 1959 lists early editions of both *The Architecture of Country Houses* and *A Treatise on the Theory and Practice of Landscape Gardening.* More than likely, given their publication dates, they had originally been Senior's.)

"In our republic there are neither the castles of feudal barons nor the palaces of princes" was how Downing began his chapter "What a Country House or Villa Should Be" in the *Architecture of Country Houses.* His point was that wealthy Americans preferred modest "villas" to more elaborate country establishments, a fact he considered an unalloyed blessing. Except for being larger and more "refined" than the cottages pictured earlier in the book, his villas were not noticeably different from them in other ways. Fully as important as their character and style was the setting cottages and villas shared as "rural dwellings." "For," Downing proclaimed, "it is in such houses that we should look for the happiest social and moral development of our people."

Two other characteristics that villas possessed according to Downing were truthfulness and individuality, which together defined their essential Americanness. The property of particular individuals, they were most definitely not the "country seats" of a class of hereditary aristocrats. For while it might be tempting to try to create on this side of the Atlantic places like those in Europe, where, as Downing described them, "age after age the descendants of one family have lived and loved, and suffered, and died," such a thing could never be, he declared, "more than a delusion" in America. There the only true country house would forever be "the home of the individual man—the home of that family of equal rights, which continually separates and continually reforms itself in the new world."

Downing was killed in a steamboat accident in 1852 at the age of thirty-six, but his ideas proved remarkably durable. By the end of the Civil War, *The Architecture of Country Houses* had gone through nine printings, and for the next forty years the great majority of country houses built by wealthy Americans fell comfortably within the parameters he had prescribed for his villas. Over time the styles he favored—Gothic, Tuscan, and Tudor—gave way to houses done in the Queen Anne, stick, and shingle styles. Yet wood remained the preferred building material for such houses, and they tended to be open rather than formal in plan, with rooms casually massed, now pushing forward, now receding, as function required. Everywhere, too, there were porches and jaunty, steeply pitched roofs of varying shapes, all making for a lively, engagingly picturesque appearance. Most often, as well, the landscape followed suit, with everything made to seem as "natural," as irregular, informal, and picturesque, as possible.

It was precisely this sort of place that Rockefeller most admired. Forest Hill fit the pattern perfectly, and until 1895 some of the leading architects of the day routinely designed such houses. No less a luminary than Richard Morris Hunt did, and to the end of his life he hoped to be as well remembered for them as for the vast palaces he created later for clients like the Vanderbilts. McKim, Mead & White, in its early years, designed extensively in the shingle style, doing some of its finest work in examples like the Samuel Tilton House, the Isaac Bell House, the Skinner House, and Ochre Point, all built in Newport during the 1880s. Of those and other houses like them, the architectural historian Vincent Scully writes:

> The dark shingles welcome the changing light from the surrounding foliage, and the porches create shadowed pavilions like the sheltered spaces under great trees. Architectural sensitivity to void, to volume, and to structure, merges here with a sense of nature . . . This is not architecture conceived in an academic fashion, two dimensionally upon a sheet of drawing paper, but architecture felt in the densities and properties of materials, in the reality of the three-dimensional space. Appropriate to their place and climate and expressive theory, these houses represented in their time a living architecture of originality and . . . considerable power.

Over the next decade, however, the work of McKim, Mead & White, like that of so many of the gentlemen architects, would veer sharply away from such houses toward a very different aesthetic. Pulled back into rigid, geometric forms, axially laid out inside and lavishly embellished outside with historically accurate detail, the firm's later country houses embraced unequivocally the monumental, the symmetrical, and the academic. Two notable examples, both built overlooking the Hudson River not far from Kykuit, were the Ogden Mills and Frederick William Vanderbilt houses (1895–97 and 1895–99, respectively). Modeled on the White House in Washington, D.C., the front facade of the Mills House featured a large classical portico with columns rising two stories to a projecting pediment. Grander still, the Vanderbilt House boasted no fewer than four columned porticos, one on each side of the building. The author of a recent book on McKim, Mead & White's work describes the house's architecture as "imperial, with no concession to images of rural domestication."

But whatever McKim, Mead & White had come to see as appropriate for its clients, "images of rural domestication" remained John D. Rockefeller's touchstone in country-house architecture. Only in such surroundings, as the article in the *Country Calendar* had declared, could "the millionaire safely get away from his wealth." Nor was there ever much chance that Delano & Aldrich would change Rockefeller's feelings in that regard, however impressive their training and connections. The most to be hoped for was some sort of compromise, and even that eluded the firm. Still, after what Chester Aldrich later described as "many interviews with Mr. Rockefeller," plans for the new house did find their way onto paper in the winter of 1905.

Starting, as the firm was obliged to do, with Senior's "mental picture" of the ground floor, the long axis of the building was laid out in an east-west direction, perpendicular to the Hudson River. The principal entrance was placed on the narrow end to the east, while to the west the structure was widened a bit to take advantage of the view and the afternoon light. The result thus became a T-shaped building, and within that basic form, beginning at the entrance, there would be a hall, flanked by an office and a drawing room, leading to a larger central space, which was to become a music room, featuring a very large, built-in player organ. Beyond that, in the widened, western portion of the building, would be three additional rooms: a library, an "alcove" or "tea room," and the dining room. The main stairway was tucked in a separate space, off to the side of the music room.

From that basic configuration, the house expanded both downward and upward. Below, and projecting beyond the ground floor on all four sides, were two basement levels primarily devoted to service functions, including the kitchen and a "golf room," with lockers and a shower for the convenience of those joining Rockefeller in his favorite pastime. Above the ground floor would be three stories of bedrooms and related spaces, with Senior and Cettie's quarters on the second floor, other family bedrooms on the third, and servants' rooms on the fourth.

Stacking three full stories on top of Senior's ground-floor plan produced a building awkwardly tall relative to its width, though almost as much of its bulk lay below the level of the first floor as above it. The house also looked larger or smaller depending on the point from which one viewed it, both because of the T shape and the way the land fell away to the west. Inside, however, there would not be the least shred of ambiguity. At every turn, the palatial and the opulent had been avoided. The rooms were of generous dimensions without being unduly large. There was a certain amount of symmetry in their layout, but comfortable bay windows poked out here and there, and no rigid axial lines thrust their way through the structure. The most telling element of the plan in this respect, however, was the entrance hall, the space in which visitors would first encounter the interior of the house. In the typical great house of the period this often became the most imposing room of all, a towering monument in its own right, rising two or even three stories, replete with the obligatory grand staircase, tier upon tier of classical columns, and marble, gilt, and mirrors glittering everywhere. Yet here there would be nothing more than a rather narrow passage, one story in height, with no stairway in sight at all.

To have made more of the entrance hall would have been to emphasize the public functions of the house. Instead, the heart and soul of Kykuit would lie enshrined in the music room, that most intimate and private of spaces, where the family gathered to play and listen to music and sing hymns and pray together. One senses that Rockefeller first imagined Kykuit by starting there, at the center, and only after that moved outward to the rest of the house.

Yet, as carefully conceived as all this was, it still left a great deal unresolved. What of the outside of the house? What would its walls be made of? How would its doors and windows be arranged? What shape would its roof have? Here, if anywhere, was Delano & Aldrich's chance to leave its imprint on the house, and to a certain extent that did happen. The windows, if not symmetrically placed on all four sides of the building, were at least positioned that way on the east and west facades, and elsewhere they marched along with considerable regularity as to size and shape. There were even a few classical touches, arched windows on the ground floor, for example. By and large, however, Senior's wishes prevailed outside the house just as they had inside.

One feature that made this instantly apparent was the cordon of porches that lined all four sides of the building. Each was no more than a single story high, and with their roofs supported by simple wooden pillars, none would have been confused for a moment with the classical porticoes that had become so fashionable in country-house architecture. They were porches, just that and nothing more, and they gave to the house a decidedly *un*grand look. Expansive and informal, such porches abounded at all of Rockefeller's other country houses, and Downing had incorporated them in almost every one of his designs. Describing his "Lake or River Villa for a Picturesque Site," for example, he noted that, in contrast to the sense of "power" suggested by the bulk of the house and the height of its roof, the "veranda" that ran around three sides of the drawing room lent an air of "domesticity" with its "peculiarly homelike look." At Kykuit, Rockefeller doubtless hoped the effect would be the same, and the porches did stretch the building out visually, making it seem less imposingly tall and narrow.

Two other important elements that the house would share with Downing's "Lake or River Villa for a Picturesque Site" were the design of its roof and the building material used for its exterior walls. Of all the features of Kykuit, the roof was to be the most distinctive, and it mirrored exactly the design Downing used for his Lake or River Villa. In shape it was high, rising through two full stories, and steeply pitched, with a strong, outward-flaring curve at the bottom. One critic likens it to a huge slab of pastry dough, awkwardly draped over the building; another refers to a "billowing tablecloth of roof " pinned to the walls below by the house's tall chimneys. As Downing saw it, however, the sharply sloping line of such a roof, in a picturesque setting, would compliment perfectly the hills and valleys of the surrounding landscape, just as the "delicious curve" at the bottom would repeat "the grand hollow or mountain curve formed by the sides of almost all great hills rising from the water's edge." Roofs of this sort were occasionally used on grander American houses built in the French style, the most notable example being Biltmore. But rather than mentioning their French antecedents, Downing chose to point out instead that they were often found on buildings along the Rhine in Germany, adding that they would, he was sure, serve equally well "on our picturesque river banks." The tower atop Forest Hill also had such a roof.

For the exterior walls of the house, Rockefeller's initial preference was probably wood, since his other country places were built of wood, but in the end he chose or was persuaded to use stone. Yet what kind of stone would it be? The smooth, dressed limestone of places like the Mills and Vanderbilt houses at Hyde Park hardly seemed appropriate, but Downing had another solution to recommend for his Lake or River Villa, one that better expressed its "character and picturesqueness": "Common quarry stone, that may be found in any hilly country, will best answer for the walls of such a residence as this; and the effect will be better, if only roughly dressed by the mason's hammer, and even laid in random courses, than if cut with the chisel, and laid in smooth ashlar." Which is exactly how it was done at Kykuit. The walls were built of rough-cut stone quarried from the same hill on which the house would rise, and laid in random courses.

Was Rockefeller consciously borrowing from Downing while working with Delano & Aldrich on the plans for Kykuit? Much about the house makes it tempting to think so, as does the fact that he appears to have owned a copy of *The Architecture of Country Houses*. But it was not his style to reveal the source of his ideas, so the question remains unanswered. It may have been, too, that Delano and Aldrich suggested using Downing. They can hardly have admired his work, and none of the other houses they designed over the years bore even a passing resemblance to it, but considering who their client was and recognizing his preferences, the partners must have thought it prudent to give him what he wanted. If so, Downing was an obvious place to turn. Yet either way Rockefeller would have succeeded in controlling the design process, making of Kykuit, as planned, what he seemed determined to have it be: *his* house, the quintessential expression of his taste, his convictions.

But thus far that house existed only on paper.

As frustrating as Delano and Aldrich must have found their dealings with Rockefeller, their feelings would have paled in comparison with Junior's. He had no more interest than his father in building a great glittering pile like the Vanderbilt houses, but he had imagined something tastefully elegant, a place that bespoke the great historical traditions of Western architecture. Instead, on his return from Europe in the spring of 1905 he found plans for a house fifty years out-of-date and utterly lacking in grace or beauty. Indeed it could almost have been the old Parsons-Wentworth House raised from the ashes. Picturesque and homelike it surely was, but he and Abby had dreamed of something altogether different.

At least the house was going to be built, however, so all was not lost. It also promised to take a fair amount of time, which meant there might well be opportunities to make changes later. Meanwhile, a dutiful son would play the role his father had envisioned for him: serving as bill-checker and paymaster for the project, under the direction of Lamont Bowers, though as it turned out Bowers was less involved than originally planned. Much of his time was still committed to various Rockefeller projects in Cleveland,

and his wife's health was failing, making it necessary eventually for the family to resettle in the West. Increasingly, therefore, the important decisions would fall to Junior.

Yet in the beginning what he was most conscious of was how slowly everything seemed to move. Not until the early months of 1906 did work on the house finally commence in earnest, and even then, with the approach roads being laid out, Senior still seemed reluctant to go ahead with the project. In two separate letters, one written in March 1906 and the other early in April, after carefully assuring his father that he had no personal stake at all in the matter, Junior pointed out that if construction was to begin that year the decision had to be made promptly, so the foundations could be closed in before winter. In March he suggested—hoping against hope for a positive response no doubt—that if Senior was uncertain about the plans for the house, they could "revise them or plan from the beginning again." But Senior neither took this suggestion nor seemed ready to start. So in April Junior, repeating that his sole concern was recommending what would be "the most comfortable and agreeable thing" for his parents, again argued they should build and begin at once.

Actually he need not have worried. Before the first week of April was out, Senior was making arrangements to visit the site to supervise (in the memorable way he did) the precise placement of the house. By May 9 Junior was able to write Bowers, "We are now digging the cellar for the house." Within another two days the stone coming out of the cellar hole had been analyzed and judged to be satisfactory for building purposes. At that point more than three and a half years had passed since the Parsons-Wentworth House burned down. Now at long last, and despite whatever doubts and uncertainties lingered, the new house, high on its hill overlooking the Hudson, was under way.

The estate's own workers dug the excavation for the foundation (for which each of them received a two-hundred-dollar bonus), but for the actual building of the house Bowers recommended hiring a large construction firm. Plans were made to get competitive bids, but in the end the job went to Thompson-Starrett Company, the firm he had favored from the beginning. The total cost of the house stipulated in the contract was $223,105, a figure at least within range of the $100,000 to $200,000 Junior had talked about two years earlier. On the other hand, it was above the high end of that range and included nothing for furnishing or landscaping.

That Senior was already nervous about costs became clear in a protracted debate early the following year over what provision to make for getting the family's laundry done. Junior favored building a separate structure of stone, matching the main house and including quarters for the laundry staff. When the estimate came in at better than $70,000, Senior vetoed the idea, declaring, "I do not feel we are justified in investing such a large sum of money for a laundry . . . I confess I am scared, and think we better call a halt." Junior was determined to build his "laundry house," however, and eventually got permission to do so, but for less money, using cheaper materials.

Arguably, with a very large stone carriage barn already on the property and a brand-new "palm house," to winter-over exotic plants, being built at the same time as the main house, the proliferation of outbuildings on the property—even before talk of a separate laundry house—was giving it an air not unlike that of some of the more elaborate country estates of the period. Though ostensibly the disagreement over the laundry house focused on money, it was probably also about how much farther down that particular road the Rockefellers ought to go. Predictably, Senior chose to buck the trend while Junior seemed ready, even eager, to follow it.

But for the most part Junior's time was taken up with more mundane issues during the months when the foundations of the house were being laid. Literally scores of decisions had to be made, some minor, some not. Where would the heating plant go, in the basement of the house or in the coach barn? Should iron, copper, or brass pipe be used for the plumbing system? Could the "flower closet" next to the music room be sacrificed to provide space for the organ pipes? Where else might the flower closet go? What brand of telephones should they order for the house? What sort of cooking range should they plan on using? And on, and on, and on. At the same time, Thompson-Starrett's agreements with its subcontractors had to be painstakingly checked, not to mention its bills. And then there were the contracts that Junior and Bowers entered into independently for items like the built-in vacuum cleaner system, the elevator, and the dumbwaiter. Each of them was a part of the larger whole, and each carried a cost.

The entire process was also complicated by the fact that technologies of all kinds were available to Kykuit's planners that twenty or even ten years earlier were undreamed of. Naturally the Rockefellers wanted the best of everything, but they were often using items sufficiently new and novel that no one had much experience with them. Nor did the complications end there, because the house was also meant to operate in traditional ways, with a large staff of servants ready to do whatever was necessary to ensure the comfort and well-being of the family and its guests. That meant separate servants' quarters, service passageways, flights of back stairs, and call systems were all essential parts of the house and had to be carefully considered along with everything else.

Happily for his sake Junior sometimes had a chance to break free of such issues and accomplish something useful on his own initiative. In the autumn of 1906, when the building schedule threatened to become hopelessly snarled for lack of structural steel, he managed to expedite matters by personally contacting the president of U.S. Steel not once but twice and asking him to speed up shipment of the orders. At such moments being a Rockefeller had its advantages. But then in spite of Junior's instructions to Thompson-Starrett to omit the usual inspection of the steel since the company's executives had already provided assurances on that point, Thompson-Starrett went ahead with the inspection anyway. Worse still, the firm charged the Rockefellers for it. Testily, Junior refused to pay.

By the end of 1906 he was also complaining about delays in construction. Some of them were not Thompson-Starrett's fault, he recognized; the excavation for the foundation had taken longer than he and Bowers had estimated it would, for example. But part of the blame, he believed, ought to be put down to poor scheduling and lax management by the company. He would pay for seven weeks of delays, but not for the two additional weeks for which Thompson-Starrett billed him. He also objected to having the charges for the delays that the Rockefellers were obliged to pay calculated on the basis of seven-day weeks when the normal workweek was six days.

Worrying about small amounts of money and making sure that he was not being cheated were habits Junior had acquired at an early age, and he truly believed they mattered. Sooner or later small sums added up to bigger ones. Presumably, too, this sort of vigilance was what his father expected of him, and as a rule he seemed to get genuine pleasure out of it. Still, in this particular case any satisfaction it afforded—compared to the high hopes he had once had for the new house—would have been limited at best. If Senior imagined this was the therapy his anxious son needed, he was wrong.

But as he waded through the hip-deep morass of contracts and bills that confronted him every day, Junior was also, it turned out, giving increasing thought to more interesting matters, for he had in fact decided to change in significant ways, if he could, his father's plans for the house. In that respect the laundry was a test case of sorts, and there he got at least part of what he wanted. Making comparable changes in the main house would be a much tougher nut to crack, yet he was prepared to try, and several factors strengthened his hand. As had been true from the start, he and Abby would be fighting the battle together. ("I am crazy to hear about the house," she had written as construction was about to begin.) Also, for two months during the latter half of 1906 Senior and Cettie were in Europe visiting their daughter, Bessie Strong, who had fallen ill with a mysterious malady never fully diagnosed. Tragically, she died soon after her parents' return to America. And to further distract Senior's attention, the day the news arrived also brought word that the federal government had begun antitrust proceedings against Standard Oil.

As distressing as Junior himself must have found these developments, they did give him the opportunity to master the details of Kykuit's construction without his father constantly looking over his shoulder. As a result, he would always grasp the innumerable complexities of the project better than anyone else, and as Senior could have told him based on his experience in the business, such knowledge amounted to real power. Junior also came to understand, as Senior had, that Delano & Aldrich's drawings were simply collections of lines on paper; they could be and were changed constantly. To a lesser extent the same was true of the actual fabric of the building, even as it rose higher with each passing month. Walls could be moved; windows could be shifted around; decorative details could be added. All it took was an order to the builders and, of course, added expense.

For anyone wishing to change Senior's design of the house, however, the most striking thing about the project was how much had not yet been decided at all. By the beginning of 1907 the basic shape of the building was established, its outer walls were fixed in place, and the floors stretching between them soon would be. To Thompson-Starrett's credit, after a slow start, the work was moving ahead rapidly. Yet it was work on what remained an empty shell in the middle of a barren construction site, which in turn left very substantial opportunities to embellish, to perfect, to alter the final result.

In particular, no detailed plans had been made for either the interior finish of the house or whatever landscaping would be done around it. Rockefeller had not asked Delano & Aldrich for such plans, and the firm had not provided them. So the field lay open in at least two directions. And it was precisely on those fronts—behind the palimpsest of daily contract and bill-checking—that Junior and Abby were about to start turning the house Senior had planned with such care into something that, as yet, they themselves probably only half glimpsed, and which he surely had never even begun to imagine.

4

"For the Sake of Harmony"

How to answer the letter? He had hoped to avoid written forms of confrontation by going to see the architect a few weeks earlier and presenting the new arrangements to him in person. However, the grievances before him were firmly outlined and given added weight by the formality of the signature at the end: the name of the firm, not the partner they had always dealt with.

Worse still, the facts in the letter were not at all inaccurate. In hiring someone else to do the interiors, he was giving that person authority over what the architects saw as "expressions" of their own plan. It was equally true, as they so bluntly reminded him, that he was simply a go-between in this case. "We feel sure," they wrote, "that you will get the best results by entrusting the interior as you have the exterior, to those who have conceived and worked out the plan in detail with your father." And in the same patronizing tone they went on to point out that his actions were wholly at odds with prevailing professional practice: "While we recognize that you may not be conversant with the necessary standards of professional ethics," those ethics were violated by employing a designer for the interiors who was not merely a decorator but also, himself, a practicing architect.

Here indeed was where the partners' letter came closest to the mark. Yet he had no intention of entrusting the interiors to them; to give in now would mean sacrificing all he hoped to accomplish. They would simply have to swallow their troublesome objections and work with the person he had chosen.

Junior had decided to hire a different architect for the interiors of the new house at least six months before Delano & Aldrich's angry letter to him. In this, as in so much else, Abby was his inspiration and collaborator. While visiting his parents at Forest Hill in the summer of 1906, he had chosen a relaxed moment after dinner to have a "nice quiet talk" with Senior about the house, and it all went just as he hoped it would. As he wrote Abby afterward, "I spoke of the furniture question and he liked the idea of getting handsome old pieces . . . I think he will be pleased to have us do what we think desireable [sic] in the matter. He could not have been nicer about it."

The "handsome old pieces" Junior and Abby had in mind were the type of eighteenth-century American and English "antiques" Abby had watched her own father collect: furniture suited to the federal, classical-style houses in Providence where she grew up. But therein lay a dilemma: the furniture they had in mind would not have harmonized with Delano & Aldrich's informally organized interior spaces or with the firm's apparent determination to cover the walls with dark paneling broken into endlessly repeated small rectangles. Clearly someone else would have to be brought in to work on the project. But who could they get to do it?

Earlier that summer, with an eye to answering that question, Junior and Abby had embarked on a tour of New England to look at interiors and had admired several examples of the work of Ogden Codman, whose name would already have been well known to them through the highly influential book, *The Decoration of Houses,* he had coauthored with Edith Wharton a decade before. (Two copies of the original edition were listed in Junior and Abby's library when it was cataloged later.) Of Codman's contribution to the success of the book, Wharton would write, "[He] had been at great pains to cite suitable instances in support of his principles . . . we found that people were only too eager to follow any guidance that would not only free them from the suffocating upholsterer, but tell them how to replace him."

There were two approaches, the book began, that could be used in decorating: "by a superficial application of ornament totally independent of structure," or, preferably, "by means of those architectural features which are part of the organism of every house, inside as well as out." Crucial to the architectural approach was a scrupulous attention to proper proportions everywhere inside a house, including doors, windows, and fireplaces. Even the walls of a room had to be architecturally correct; likening them to the structure of a classical Greek order, the book suggested that baseboards and dados should be thought of as the base of a column, the cornice abutting the ceiling as the column's capital, and the walls in between as its shaft, articulated by decorative plasterwork or paneling.

Equally critical was a strict adherence to symmetry. The instinct for symmetry, the book argued, was "more strongly developed in those races which have reached the highest artistic civilization." Also, the most important rooms should be the most elaborately finished, but escalation toward them should be gradual, with all the rooms in harmony and no sharp breaks in the progression. What followed these opening dictums was a compelling rationale for banishing every trace of Victorian clutter in favor of a purer, more suitable style endowed with the unpretentiousness that Junior and Abby were seeking. It was a taste reflecting Abby's New England background. "There is no question in my mind but that I am very much a New Englander," she wrote later to one of her sons, "and I won't get over it." For Junior these were also historically sanctioned architectural rules, reassuring emblems of culture and civilization.

The problem was what to do about the architects already on board. Ironically Delano and Aldrich had the training to do the same kind of thing Codman did, yet they worked for Senior and were committed to following his wishes. Codman would be working for Junior and Abby. But bold solutions required bold action: in Junior's initial discussion with Chester Aldrich after hiring Codman, he arrived already armed with some of Codman's suggested revisions, confronting Aldrich, in effect, with a fait accompli. Of course, he pointed out, Delano & Aldrich could submit competing designs of its own, but Junior's assurances on that point only added insult to injury. The partners were already the architects for the project; why should they have to "compete" with someone else? So they had written that indignant letter to Junior, and now he had to respond.

His first move was to invite Aldrich to the site for a discussion. Next he prepared a memorandum outlining point by point his interpretation of their exchange. The pronoun he used throughout was not *I* but *we*, meaning the family, meaning Abby, meaning Senior, however the firm chose to interpret it. In defending his decision to add Codman to the architectural team, he recollected that from the outset he had "frequently" brought up the idea of having a decorator from outside of the firm. He had "suggested" the change now because he and Abby had no "practical demonstrations" of Mr. Aldrich's work of that kind (though examples must have been available in New York for them to see). Regarding Pocantico, too, he spelled out several examples of blunders he felt the architects had made, for instance, placing the boiler room in the subbasement under Senior's office, "a fatal error" costing a full three-week delay. Those mistakes had resulted from Aldrich's carelessness.

But that sidestepped the issue. "We had thought of Mr. Codman solely and wholly as a decorator and never for a moment as an architect," Junior claimed. Yet Delano and Aldrich had every right to be angry. Working from his offices in Boston, Newport, and New York, Codman did much more than simply decorate interiors. He had been a practicing architect for over a decade. Besides, as he and Wharton had written in their book, informed interior decoration *was* architecture.

Gifted, dedicated, and lavishly provided with all the confidence of a self-proclaimed tastemaker, Codman traced his descent to several long-established Boston families and was always quite conscious of, indeed obsessed with, his ancestral background. Exposed during his youth to the region's eighteenth-century architecture, including the Grange, the Codman family homestead in Lincoln, Massachusetts, he had also lived in Europe while his family recouped their financial resources, and along the way he developed a passionate interest in historic buildings, especially their interiors. "Do write me a long letter about furniture. There is hardly anything I take so much interest in. Houses and furniture and genealogy are my three hobbies," he wrote his mother after coming back to America in 1884 to finish his education at MIT. He was twenty-one.

Though it was one of the few schools in the United States that offered formal training in architecture, Codman disdained MIT's instruction (he later had his name removed from the student roster) and stayed there only a year. Under the tutelage of John Hubbard Sturgis, an uncle who was an architect, he then embarked on a program of making scale drawings of historic structures, which both suited his interest in eighteenth-century design and his sense of independence. By his own account, studying the buildings so closely proved to be a far more successful apprenticeship than the several "dreary" years he spent working for architectural firms in Lowell and Boston. But despite his unconventional training, his social credentials gave him ready access to the moneyed clients who would launch his career once he started distributing his calling cards in Boston and Newport.

Particularly crucial would be his friendship with Edith Wharton, who became one of his first clients in Newport. Early on they discovered a mutual appreciation of Italian and French art and culture, as well as a shared aversion to the stifling, overbuilt, and overstuffed mansions being put up by the nouveau riche in New York and places like Newport. "I wish the Vanderbilts did not retard culture so very thoroughly," wrote Wharton. "They are entrenched in a sort of *thermopylae* of bad taste, from which apparently no force on earth can dislodge them."

Yet surprisingly enough it was at Cornelius Vanderbilt's hugely opulent "Breakers" in Newport, that Codman won his first major commission. While every inch of the house's downstairs rooms, done by J. Allard et Fils, a fashionable French firm, glittered with marble, gold, and richly painted decoration, Codman's designs for the bedrooms and bathrooms upstairs— finely detailed with classical moldings, pilasters, and cornices—were a studied contrast in their lightness and simplicity. The rooms were also a fitting precursor to his further collaboration with "Pus," a pet name for Wharton. (She called him "Coddy," and they referred to the two of them together as "Puscod.") Nurturing and expanding upon their distaste for the "vulgarity of current decoration," by 1897 they were ready to publish their instantly successful *The Decoration of Houses*. From there Codman went on to serve numerous clients, and by the time Junior hired him his career was fully established.

One can only wonder at Junior's first impressions of Codman himself, so sharp was the contrast between them. Where Junior was intensely private and self-deprecating, Codman was aggressively social and confident. He was also a self-styled dandy. "You would scarcely recognize me I am so smart," he once wrote to a friend, describing his monocle, his boutonniere, top hat, and his "very smart gloves . . . everything from the swellest London people." In the same spirit he curled his mustache, "the ends set nearly into my eyes." A great snob, he freely labeled the rich newcomers encroaching on the social scene "common" and "vulgar" yet cultivated their company and their trade. In New York his circle included the Hewitt sisters and J. P. Morgan's daughter, Anne, whom he toyed with the idea of marrying, but as he wrote, "she considers me too frivolous and too fond of pretty things." Although not above making disparaging remarks about dinners at Elsie de Wolfe's, also one of his clients, who later became a leading interior decorator herself, he still attended her evening salons, which drew writers like Wharton and Henry James. His marriage in 1904 to another of his wealthy clients, Leila Griswold Webb, a Westchester County neighbor of the Rockefellers, secured his place in a social circle that included the Vanderbilts (related to Leila by marriage), the William Rockefellers, and the V. Everit Macys, close friends of Junior and Abby's.

By the time Junior told Delano & Aldrich that Codman had been hired, he had had almost three weeks to review the firm's plans, and his revisions already went well beyond minor adjustments. Challenging the very character of the house, they called for giving symmetry and proportion to the downstairs rooms by changing window and door openings in the library, alcove, dining room, office, and drawing room. There was also to be a coffered, barrel-vaulted ceiling, complemented by a marble floor, in the entrance hall, heralding the classical nature of the rest of the house's interior. The only room on the first floor that had yet to succumb to Codman's remedial help was the music room.

Plan after plan appeared over Codman's signature during the winter and spring months of 1907: interior elevations with renderings of Georgian entablatures, classically inspired ogee moldings, architraves over doorways, and paneling graced with Grecian urns, acanthus leaves, and swags. After Codman sketched the designs, his drawings made their way to Abby and Junior before being returned for any revisions. Junior then took the results to the aggrieved Aldrich, who was instructed to go over them carefully with Codman, since it soon became clear that sometimes "certain points [were] insufficiently shown in his drawings."

Each of the ground-floor rooms was to be done in a particular style. Paneled in oak (stained in the same shade Codman used for his own library), the office would be in the earliest style of all: late seventeenth-century William and Mary. The rest of the rooms, painted cream with decorative plasterwork, would be done in later styles: eighteenth-century Chippendale for the dining room and library, and lighter, neoclassical Robert Adam for the drawing room. In each room, too, the furniture would harmonize with the style Codman had chosen, as would the mantelpieces, all of which were to be done in marble. Upstairs, the rooms were to be furnished in either Hepplewhite or Sheraton style, continuing the Georgian theme of the house, so the same studied effect would prevail everywhere.

But all this still left the most important room of all—the music room at the house's center—to be decided upon, and what Codman proposed as a cynosure there was a great "hole" in the middle of the ceiling. Piercing through to the second floor, it was to be a classical *oculus*, as such openings were called, based on a seventeenth-century design by Inigo Jones for Ashburnham House in London. The space above it, originally meant to be a large hall with a fireplace, was reconceived as a gallery, with a balustrade around the oculus. Further signaling the centrality of the music room below, Codman planned to have eight symmetrically placed pairs of arched, mirrored doors, spaced around its perimeter.

The main feature of the music room, however, would be a very large pipe organ. In selecting it, Junior had sought the advice of Harry Shelley, the organist at the Fifth Avenue Baptist Church, and Senior himself had taken a hand, insisting that whatever they chose be "as extensive and as comprehensive as we could hope to have in the given space." Dressed with Codman's decorative casings, the Aeolian instrument eventually decided on came with "self-playing attachments" (Junior later calculated that the self-player was used nine times more than manual playing) and an additional keyboard that could be played from the third floor. Whatever Senior thought of Codman's "hole" in the ceiling, Junior would be armed with a ready argument in its defense: through the open oculus the organ music so important to his father, including the sonorous notes of Baptist hymns, would rise heavenward to the highest reaches of the house.

Along with some of Codman's other changes, plans to cut through the ceiling for the oculus prompted yet another letter from Aldrich. Not only would the work involved cause delays in construction; it would also be costly, necessitating the removal of steel beams already in place on both the second and third floors, and it would require new drawings as well, for which Delano & Aldrich asked to be compensated. Two weeks later Junior's response, though cloaked in civility, was unequivocal: he was sorry they had even asked. The changes to "certain parts" of the house had, he wrote, "been suggested to some extent by [Codman], but to quite as great, if not a greater, extent by Mrs. Rockefeller and me." In a phrase that could have been taken straight from *The Decoration of Houses*, so close was it to Codman's tenets, Junior added, "They are all changes in the interest of symmetry and convenience." And since "the whole expense involved can in no event be great," the partners should meet the cost of the drawings themselves, in the "broad, liberal spirit" with which all parties were expected to operate. All parties, that is, but the Rockefellers. For whether it was Junior's inbred parsimony or simply a matter of insensitivity, he was in fact treating Delano and Aldrich anything but liberally.

Nor were they about to let the matter drop. Three months later they wrote again, this time pointing out that Codman was in fact changing completely the planned ambience of the house: "Many of these changes seem to be necessary more on account of . . . a certain fixed idea of symmetry." If symmetry had been "disregarded" in the firm's own plans, it was because of "the direction of the original ideas of the house." Yes, Junior replied, the changes were due to a "broadened conception"—a departure from "my father's and Mr. Aldrich's ideas in their earlier interviews." But so confident was he about the new designs that, as he wrote, "I do not hesitate to assume the entire responsibility for the changes and my father's eventual satisfaction therewith." In other words, when it came to matters of architectural design, Senior was no longer in charge. Junior would decide.

On other fronts, too, Junior's responsibilities were growing. With Lamont Bowers gone from his supervisory position, every aspect of the project now came under Junior's command, and the complexities of it all were made even more cumbersome by his propensity to obsess over details. Long accustomed at his parents' New York City house to exercises like holding wallpaper samples up against walls, studying them in different lights, and then carefully reporting to his mother on the results, at Kykuit, in his eagerness to achieve the best possible outcome, he constantly made changes in the midst of construction that upset previous decisions. More than once he substituted high-cost materials for cheaper ones. On his instructions the hardwood floors in the hallways leading to the south porch were ripped up and replaced with marble. At another point, he ordered thirty-two doors remade to be a full two inches thick, which meant that the special French hardware Codman had ordered for them had to be altered as well.

Though Codman cared as much about the details as Junior, he could be careless about sending his designs in time to be used during construction, and since he provided no on-site supervision, Junior was often left to pick up the pieces. The situation was further aggravated by the fact that the year Codman undertook the commission for the Rockefellers turned out to be the busiest and most profitable one of his career, and in the words of his biographer, "success had done nothing to soften his tongue"—or to increase his patience. He cared neither "to be doubted nor crossed." Having chosen him to do Kykuit's interiors, however, Junior had no choice but to work with him on those terms.

Meanwhile, in the spring of 1907 he and Abby had begun shopping for furnishings for the new house. A few years earlier she had taken him to "old furniture" shops while they were in New Orleans. Now they began looking for antiques in earnest, a venture they both enjoyed. In March they went to a dealer in Baltimore and liked a number of pieces. When Codman visited the city later, Junior asked if he would tell them what he thought of their choices. In April, at Koopman & Company on Beacon Street in Boston, they selected more pieces, and they continued to look for others in both Boston and New York.

Always mindful of the high charges that would be encouraged by the Rockefeller name, Junior went to great lengths to bargain for lower prices, arguing that the country was facing hard times or pointing out that he had plenty of other sources to go to. He could also use the need to have Codman's approval to his advantage, and as a rule he stipulated that he be allowed to make returns without penalty. It is unclear how often Codman rejected Junior and Abby's choices, but not all of them passed muster. Among the things returned after he saw them were some engravings, a small dressing table for Senior's bedroom, as well as two "Directoire jardinières," about which Junior wrote to Abby, "He thinks these very beautiful but feels strongly that they will not harmonize with the style of the new house."

Apart from looking for furniture during the spring of 1907, Junior and Abby concentrated on reviewing Codman's plans. Timing was becoming an urgent consideration. In April a flurry of decisions had to be made about various items: elevations for the music room; designs for the vestibule door, to be made of glass with ornamental bronze and ironwork; a final plan for the entrance hall; the placement and design of hardware and electric light fixtures; and what Junior referred to as "the completion of the mantle question." With the mantelpieces for the first and second floors all being custom-made abroad, the designs for their overmantles and surrounds could not be completed until the selections were made. Meanwhile, after marrying into wealth, Codman had taken up the habit of spending the summer months in Europe—in part for his own pleasure, in part to shop for his clients, including the Rockefellers—yet everything had to be worked around his schedule.

If Junior was uneasy about Codman's disappearance from the scene, he had good reason to be. A crucial issue still outstanding was the choice of a firm to execute his designs. Junior sought bids from several companies, but

Codman was accustomed to working with W. C. Baumgarten & Company, and in the end, after several meetings plus a tour of the construction site and a delay in getting detailed enough specifications for the firms' bid from Codman's office, the contract was finally signed in August. Baumgarten would do the plastering and woodwork for the house's interiors; the firm would also supply carpets, wallpapers, fabrics, and both new and old furniture, which could be refurbished and upholstered at Codman's direction.

By then the construction was far enough along that coordination among the various parties involved had become vital. All the plumbing, as well as the wiring for the twenty-seven house "telephone stations"—fifteen of them connecting with public lines—and for electric boxes and switches, base plugs, and fixtures had to be installed at the same time Thompson-Starrett's crew built the terra-cotta tile interior walls of the house. The builders also needed detailed plans from Baumgarten so that they would know where to place the wooden furring strips to hold Codman's paneling. Only when this was done could the Baumgarten people plaster the walls, allow the time for the plaster to dry, and finally fashion Codman's decorative finishes.

None of this ran smoothly, and Junior contributed to what ultimately amounted to a five-week delay by making, throughout the fall, small changes in placing electrical plugs and switches. In September the builders still did not have detailed plans for the overmantles, apparently because the mantles themselves were taking so long to order. More serious still, in October someone noticed that the staircase off the music room had been constructed so that the stairs protruded into Codman's symmetrically designed music room, causing one pair of doors to be shorter than the others. Blame was tossed from one party to the other, but in the end the staircase had to be ripped out and replaced with a new one.

Yet for all the tribulations, construction proceeded. Early in February of 1908, Codman designed interiors for the rooms above the second floor. He also reviewed the furniture in storage and made up room plans accordingly. Abby and Junior had continued looking for old furniture, but having found out that several pieces they purchased, including a set of twenty Chippendale-style dining room chairs, were later copies, they also started ordering reproductions, something Codman had recommended all along. And while Codman was continuing with his designs for the upper stories of the house and for Senior's "golf room" in the subbasement, he was working with Abby and Junior to choose furniture, carpeting, wallpapers, and chintzes for the second and third floors—choose and sometimes re-choose, as happened when Junior decided that the furniture for Cettie's bedroom was "rather more girlish than possessing the dignity . . . appropriate to [his] mother."

Carpets for the main floor also became a major problem. Codman recommended Savonnerrie designs woven to order by the French house of Hamot for most of the rooms. Samples had been sent back and forth across the Atlantic, yet the final ones still needed approval before the weavers could begin work. When Codman arrived in Paris in May, he stopped by Hamot's offices, but the weavers had not finished the samples he needed to see. Thereupon he left Paris, not to return until midsummer. Faced with repeated inquiries from Junior, Hamot finally sent the samples directly to Baumgarten's, and Junior and Abby asked for changes. When Codman saw their choices, he was less than pleased. "The changes will take all the style from the designs," he wrote, though in the end he seems to have acquiesced. In the meantime the delays meant the carpets could not possibly be completed until well past the time Senior and Cettie were due to move into the house.

On the other hand, by the end of July Junior was able to report from Pocantico to Abby, who was spending the summer in Bar Harbor, that the third and fourth floors were nearing completion, including wallpapering and carpets, and that (in what he described as debilitating heat) he was personally putting the servants' furniture in place according to plan. One day Codman unexpectedly appeared at the house, explaining that he had only come back from Europe for the week, as Junior bemusedly noted to Abby, "because 'the other client' wouldn't wait! He was agreeable . . . and stayed but a few minutes." Yet Codman did stop in the city to look at an Adam-style bed Junior had found for his mother's bedroom, and Junior's response was gracious: "I particularly appreciate your taking the time . . . when here for so short a time and so fully occupied."

During the last week in August, when all was done but a few of the downstairs rooms, Junior had the servants from the Kent House—where his parents had been living when they were in Pocantico—move to the new house and began staying there himself, eating with the housekeeper in her dining room. In September Abby joined him, spending several nights a week in the new house, sampling the bedrooms and taking a few meals there each time. In a general way Junior also kept his mother informed of their progress. Once when she mentioned bringing some of the framed

family photographs she had in the city house to Pocantico, he tactfully suggested that she "see the house and possible locations" before deciding to
bring them. Perhaps he feared the old family pictures would clutter the new
house's delicately balanced room plans. (Even picture frames, according to
Codman, had to be architecturally harmonious.)

Meanwhile he wrote Codman, who was still abroad: "Mrs. Rockefeller
and I feel your absence most seriously . . . Mr. Baumgarten is also abroad . . .
so we are quite helpless. We are hoping that it is your plan to return to New
York in the very near future." With Senior and Cettie due to move in October 1, the engravings sent to France to be framed and the custom-designed
lampshades had yet to appear. A week before his parents were expected to
arrive Junior wrote again. Had Codman found andirons and fire tongs,
shovels and pokers for the fireplaces on the first floor? The curtains for Senior's office had not been shipped, nor had the material that was supposed
to cover the settees in the alcove room. What could Codman do to expedite
matters?

At that point Codman claimed to be looking in France for the things
that would give the house "that homelike touch," including hooks for pictures (Junior wanted the gold bowknots Codman himself used in his city
house), china, silverware, mantle ornaments, vases, and dressing table ac-
coutrements. Junior and Abby had expressed an interest in seeing a large
silver service he was purchasing for another client—"based on some of the
most beautiful models . . . made during the eighteenth century." Would
they like one like it? he asked. Yes, Junior replied, although he and Abby had
not thought of getting so "complete or elaborate" a service. They might
also be interested, Codman prompted, in seeing the French china that he
found less costly there, "while the designs are so much more interesting and
beautiful and the field of choice so much larger." Desk sets and clocks for
most of the rooms were needed too, Junior reminded him. And what about
an umbrella stand? he wondered just two days before his parents' arrival.

Codman's shopping for "pretty things a bit out of the common" continued
into the late fall. At a shop in Paris he described picking up a number of
objects for his other clients. "Every time we have done this, Mrs. Codman
has said 'Why do you not ask Mr. Rockefeller to let you get some of these
lovely things?'" Still, the French-made fireplace tools took him another
year to find and order, and as if to soothe Junior, Codman wrote, "My ex-

perience has been that it takes a great deal of time and pains to get really good things." In the end, he added, "one soon forgets all the petty annoyances." Yet characteristically, as he received Junior's repeated entreaties over the summer and fall of 1908, he could not resist summing up his client to someone else as "all perspiration and prayer."

Such a remark was disparaging, certainly, but Codman was well aware of the opportunity the Kykuit project brought him and was careful to tell Junior, "As a rule my clients . . . have only allowed me to go part way," while Junior and Abby had, as he said, "been good enough" to allow him to complete a "carefully thought out scheme of decoration . . . in which all the furniture and objects of art harmonize." His shopping, he recognized, took time, though he reminded Junior and Abby of the very high standard they had set together: that the items purchased to complete the house be "as handsome as possible, yet quiet and in good taste." And if working with Codman had its fretful moments, Junior's letters to him (unlike those to Delano & Aldrich) were unfailingly polite and patient, even to the point of ending with his and Abby's hopes that the Codmans were enjoying their time abroad.

Meanwhile the costs continued to rise. The estimate for the house's construction as originally planned was $250,000; the final cost, including Codman's flourishes, more than doubled that figure. Significantly, however, though all other charges for the house were routinely vetted by Senior, Junior alone took responsibility for Codman's work. This was his project and Abby's; by no stretch of the imagination could the new house's quietly elegant interiors have been seen as an expression of Senior's taste. Yet a rather different story would be told when *House Beautiful* featured Kykuit in its pages the following June.

"Mr. and Mrs. John D. Rockefeller, Jr.," the article declared, "were so well acquainted with the wishes of Mr. and Mrs. Rockefeller that, with the assistance of Messrs Delano and Aldrich and that of Mr. Ogden Codman, they were able to finish it in the absence of the owners." The major point made by the article, however, was that if readers envisioned the house as "the palace of a Croesus," they would be disappointed. On the contrary, its principal qualities were "comfort" and "refinement and reserve." The decoration of the Adam-style drawing room, for instance, was "entirely removed from the elaborate and overdone schemes often found in the homes of American millionaires." The harmoniousness of the interiors was also much praised: "A series of rooms has been produced remarkable for unity, for what might be called a unified variety." Nothing was there to upset the balance.

The fact that the article had been published at all was equally noteworthy, for it represented a sharp break with the Rockefellers' usual preference for guarding their privacy. Obviously Junior thought there was an important point to be made—doubtless exactly the point the article did make about the house's careful blend of restraint and quiet good taste. Such were the results of Codman's knowledge of eighteenth-century styles and his strict adherence to them. Perhaps William Welles Bosworth, who planned the gardens at Kykuit, put it best decades later when he wrote of Codman's approach to design, "The word 'grammatical' suited his character as well as his architecture . . . His motto was 'Order, for the sake of harmony and in the hope of beauty.'"

Which was indeed what Codman brought to Kykuit, as Junior had imagined he would. But to what end? Why had it mattered so much to have him there; why put up with the quarrels with Delano & Aldrich, the steadily rising costs, the maddening delays—especially over something that was so palpably not what his father had intended or wanted? Here perhaps interiors of a different sort came into play. For despite Junior's conflict with Senior over the house, they both continued to believe that the family's actions—all of them—had somehow to fulfill a higher purpose. And in Codman's work there was at least the germ of an idea about how all the time and money spent on the new house might eventually bear fruit in that regard.

While he was a student at Brown in 1896, Junior's carefully penned class notes had assigned credit for the flourishing arts in another age to the Medicis, who "gave to the renaissance its life and its fecundity" by commissioning artists who were "the direct and legitimate successors of the Greeks and Romans." Though he later claimed he remembered nothing of his art history classes at Brown, as a Rockefeller in the twentieth century Junior was in fact patronizing a modern version of design rooted in precisely the same classical past that had captured the Medicis' imagination. Could that effort have an impact beyond, even, rescuing his family's reputation by building a better, more tasteful kind of house for his father? Codman was no Michelangelo, but the house was, after all, a Rockefeller house, and in *The Decoration of Houses* he and Wharton had declared that "changes in manners and customs usually originate with the wealthy or aristocratic minority, and are thence transmitted to the other classes," adding, "When the rich man demands good architecture, his neighbors will get it too." So possibly in true democratic fashion others might profit from the lessons Junior had learned from Codman, or at any rate he could hope that might be the case.

Yet there was also a formality to the relationship between the two men, a distance that seemed to define it finally as what it was for Codman: a fine professional opportunity. His chief concern was getting the job done to his own satisfaction and producing an acceptable result for his clients. If Junior hoped for more—including the emotional gratification of sharing a fuller bond with the designer of Kykuit's interiors and exploring with him the possibility of elevating taste more broadly—one senses that Codman, often engaged with his other work and absent for months on end each year, had little interest in such an effort.

Just outside Kykuit's walls, however, another designer was at work, one with whom Junior would eventually share a very different kind of relationship.

5

"The Fruits of the Spirit"

From the moment he saw it he knew he had to begin with that extraordinary view. To experience it was to understand why the house was sited as it was. For all the awkward cragginess of the spot, it commanded everything for miles around. Even if the property did have boundaries somewhere off in the distance, they were hidden; nothing halted the heart-stopping sweep of it all. It was as if the entire world belonged to his client. But considering who the client was, that was not surprising.

Meeting the son that day had been a piece of good fortune. Still, he had to proceed cautiously—to learn as much as he could first. So he had taken care to befriend a carpenter on the place, who had shown him the client's old lookout tower, which would be essential for his task. Yet he remained an interloper there.

He had also seen the architect's drawings of the house, with its old-fashioned porches and its even more awkward roof. Deplorable! But it was a given, something to be worked around, to be settled properly on the land and embellished with all the magic his art could conjure. It would not be cheap—no indeed! Which left the client himself as the central problem: people said he did not part with a dollar easily. Yet it looked as if the son might become an ally. With luck, and his help, it could all be made to work. How could it not, given that amazing view?

Apart from Junior and his father, no one would contribute more to making Kykuit what it became than its landscape architect, William Welles Bosworth. He did not appear on the scene immediately, however. By the spring of 1907 Junior had already tackled two projects outside the house, with varying degrees of success. Senior had rejected the initial plans for a stone, Palladian-style laundry house, which according to Lamont Bowers, who reviewed them, had "the look of being put up for a century or two." But the second project—renovations for the coach barn—had gone more smoothly, perhaps because Senior saw the practicality of adding spaces for automobiles. Motoring was becoming a popular amusement for those enjoying country weekends (*Country Life in America* was to feature an issue on the sport the following November), and the twenty or so miles of roads Senior had enthusiastically engineered could be used to great advantage for that purpose. Yet now it was time to embark on what was likely to prove a far more controversial course of action: designing the grounds around the house.

Although Senior had explicitly given Junior and Abby control over "the furniture question" inside the house, he had yet to delegate its landscaping to anyone. The golf course circling the hill was already in place, and from the outset planning the roads and the lookouts afforded by the natural beauty of the estate had been a favorite pastime of his. Earlier, too, he had hired Warren H. Manning from Frederick Law Olmsted's office to plan both the grading around the house site and the approach roads to it, though as he made clear in his *Random Reminiscences,* he saw the results largely as an opportunity to compete: "After this great landscape architect had laid out his plans and had driven his line of stakes, I asked if I might see what I could do with the job . . . It was a proud moment when this real authority accepted my suggestions."

For his part, Junior shared his father's deep appreciation of natural beauty, and together they had spent hours exploring the estate's terrain and vegetation. But now the challenge was landscaping the grounds immediately adjacent to the house. No doubt had he been asked, Senior would have said that the landscape was already there, and it should be trifled with as little as possible. Yet Junior disagreed. In his opinion something else was needed, some way of both enriching and enhancing the natural landscape by adding more formalized elements to it. Though at first he was not sure how this was to be done, clearly his ideas placed him in direct opposition to Senior. And like their conflicting tastes in architecture, their disparate approaches to landscaping Kykuit would mirror trends that had divided professionals in the field for some time.

The natural style—lakes, ponds, clumps of trees and shrubbery, rolling hills, all contrived to look as though God, not man, had arranged them— early on found its leading American advocate in Frederick Law Olmsted, the renowned designer of Central Park. Pointedly expressing his disdain for formality in landscape design, Olmsted had written to William Platt, who was about to set out on a trip abroad to explore Italian gardens, "I am afraid that I do not think much of the fine and costly gardening of Italy . . . I urge you again to hunt for beauty in commonplace and pleasant conditions."

Yet for those Americans inclined to disagree with Olmsted, a key source would be a book by William Platt's own brother, Charles, entitled *Italian Gardens.* Published in 1894, it brought its author dozens of commissions for country houses as well as gardens, just as Ogden Codman's success had begun with *The Decoration of Houses.* And for both gardens and country houses Platt favored formal layouts. Writing in 1904, he observed that in the country his clients did not wish to "return to a state of nature," but rather would continue to "read, dine, entertain, dress, and have leisure much as in town." In Cornish, New Hampshire, where he summered with a coterie of artists and writers, he created a series of garden "rooms" steeped in classicism, with carefully framed views of the surrounding New England hills, a felicitous blend of the formal and informal that established a new American prototype in country living. Meanwhile, Edith Wharton— lamenting that "the American landscape has no foreground and the American mind no background"—had joined the campaign with a series of articles richly illustrated by Maxfield Parrish that were later published in book form as *Italian Villas and Their Gardens.*

Gardens like the one Platt designed for the architectural critic Herbert Croly in Cornish were also featured in the monthly magazine *Country Life in America,* where subscribers (among them Abby Rockefeller) could not but notice the typical features of formal country-house landscape design: forecourts around main entrances, terraces with overhanging pergolas, leveled garden spaces enclosed by either stone or hedged walls, and straight axes cutting through the landscape, punctuated at end points by teahouses, temples, or green exedras with classical statuary, giving way to vistas of the natural landscape in the distance. Moreover, just as Codman and Wharton had advocated an architectural approach to interior design, Croly, in

Houses for Town and Country (1907), advised his American readers that failing to consult with an architect in laying out the grounds of an estate meant "sinning against their own opportunities just as flagrantly as if they erected a vulgar and tawdry house." Junior had spent most of his conscious life avoiding sin; here was one of another sort that he and Abby were not about to commit. But of course architects could make mistakes too.

It was no surprise, then, that scrutinizing the long, gracelessly crude retaining wall Delano & Aldrich had designed to separate Kykuit's future lawns and garden beds from the more natural landscape of the hillside, Junior quickly concluded that the firm was not up to the job—that he would have to find someone else, and soon.

Casting about for other designers, he asked Charles W. Leavitt Jr., the surveyor then working with Senior on the new house's approach roads, to draw up a general plan. Leavitt had the wit to suggest terracing, particularly on the steep slope to the west of the house, but his ideas were trumped by the fortuitous appearance of another contender, first encountered while Junior and Abby were meeting with the artists Albert and Adele Herter, in their apartment in New York, one afternoon in May of 1907.

They did not know the Herters well, but they would in time. The following summer Adele Herter painted Abby's portrait (the only one the family felt captured her true spirit) in Easthampton, where both were summering, and through the three weeks of sittings the two became fast friends. "I hope that you and I too and my husband may all grow to have the friendship which has come to Abby and me," Adele wrote Junior after the portrait was finished. "It is based on such real things—and will increase, we feel sure, with the greater experience of our lives." Presumably the Rockefellers' initial visit to the Herters' in May was to see Adele's work and arrange for Abby's portrait. But something in the conversation prompted Adele to knock on the door of her neighbor, Welles Bosworth, an architect with a special interest in landscape design, asking if he would join them at tea.

Bosworth was a talented, European-trained architect without Codman's attitude or need to condescend to his rich clients. His lineage extended back to the *Mayflower*, and, like Delano and Aldrich, he was a member of several important clubs in the city, so he knew well the value of social connections. His ambition, however, was softened by a manner that was at once charming, tactful, and refined. He was also sophisticated and knowledgeable about the arts, as well as a good conversationalist. He and Junior might have found a number of topics to touch on that afternoon. They were close to the same age. Born and raised in Marietta, Ohio, a region known for its oil wells and the new wealth they brought around the time Senior was buying out his competitors in Cleveland, Bosworth, like Junior, had the Buckeye State in his blood.

Would he, in answering Junior's casually phrased inquiries, have mentioned the buildings he had designed for Hampton Normal and Agricultural Institute, a black college in the South that Junior and Abby had visited several years earlier and that had benefited in a major way from Rockefeller largesse? Or did he talk instead about his travels in Europe with William Roach Ware, who was for many years the editor of *American Architect*? Or perhaps he caught Junior's attention by describing his more recent experience in urban design: working on the Cleveland Plan, a project directed at managing the city's burgeoning growth. He had also designed a number of summer cottages on Long Island and was planning a garden for a friend and neighbor of Junior's, V. Everit Macy, at his estate at Briar Cliff Manor.

As a rule Junior moved cautiously in life, but that very afternoon he mentioned that his father needed a landscape job done at Pocantico and asked if he could see some of Bosworth's current work. Bosworth obliged by taking him to his apartment and showing him working drawings for a new campus plan for Vassar College. Though Junior left without any sign of commitment, apparently he was impressed with what he saw. The next morning he was in Bosworth's offices, and the following day the two were at the Tarrytown site, discussing how to address its problems and the great opportunities afforded by the magnificent view.

Junior showed him the plans for Leavitt's approach road, deliberately designed both to provide an easier grade and to capture the view while crossing the lawns in front of the house, then reversing direction to arrive at the front entrance. All of this was wrong, Bosworth explained, no doubt with a fair measure of diplomacy. One of the dictates of both French and English landscape planning was that you never passed your destination only to come back to it.

As important, too, was how to best capture the house's chief asset: its wondrous view. According to Bosworth, it was not to be thrown away at first blush, but saved, something that could be managed by planting large numbers of evergreens to obscure the view along the approach to the house. Then, only after entering and passing through the house, toward its west end, would the onlooker discover the vista in its full glory. All of this he probably demonstrated with a quick sketch. Junior would always wonder why architects seldom carried pencils with them, as he always did, while consulting on-site, but Bosworth was an exception. His hastily drawn sketches on the backs of whatever paper he happened to have with him were confident, robust, and captivating.

More compelling than Bosworth's knack for sketching, however, was his training and experience. He had graduated from the architectural program at MIT in 1889 and then worked at various times in the offices of Shepley, Rutan and Coolidge, one of Boston's leading architectural firms, as well as those of Frederick Law Olmsted and Carrère and Hastings in New York. In the early 1890s he moved to London to study painting under Sir Lawrence Alma-Tadema, an artist best known for his learned and scrupulously detailed paintings of ancient Greek and Roman subjects, who was probably responsible for the skill Bosworth demonstrated later in drawings published in the journal *Pencil Points*.

But Bosworth's greatest asset was his training at the École des Beaux-Arts, where he studied landscape design under Gaston Redon. "It was seven years after leaving the Institute, when I came to live in New York, before I realized that the methods of the École . . . were necessary to fit one for those great opportunities," he later remarked. Yet even before then, his training had led him to eschew the informal landscape style, in which designs were arrived at by a process he described derisively as "stick a few pins at random on the paper to represent trees, then crumple up a piece of twine and drop it over them for paths." The École's approach, in contrast, was systematic to its core: strict in its adherence to symmetry and proportion and zealous in its attention to all the varied parts of a well-conceived plan. The design for a house should extend into the landscape surrounding it; the design of each component had to be integral to the whole. Bosworth's own words of advice to students at the Columbia Department of Architecture were that they needed to know "how to make each part perfect . . . each link strong in order that the chain may be strong . . . that the whole may be perfect."

In the spring of 1907 the challenge for Bosworth was how to apply those principles to Pocantico. That Senior had to be dealt with somehow was clear at the outset. The design also had to be thought of in terms of its relation to the house he and Delano & Aldrich had designed, as well as to his partiality for a landscape that was seemingly uncontrived. Doubtless on Junior's advice he took care to win the confidence of Mr. William Turner, a carpenter working on the place who Senior himself often consulted before embarking on projects. And again it was Turner who suggested Bosworth use Senior's observation tower.

As he later wrote in an article on Kykuit's gardens published in the *American Architect*, the tower was vital to him, for the sense it gave him of what the "natural disposition" of the gardens ought to be. From it he could also gauge perspectives at different levels, so the garden could be enjoyed from every floor of the house, "as all gardens should be." The major challenge, though, was how to marry the house, perched as it was on its "inverted oyster shell, flat only at the top, and hardly flat there," to the grounds below, something that could be satisfactorily achieved only by terracing in the Italian style. And almost as much of a dilemma was where to place the main axis, to which the terraces and gardens would be linked, and then a second axis crossing it. As complex as it all was, however, within a month Bosworth had arrived at a basic scheme, which, it seems, Junior promptly accepted. "As compared with the plans . . . by Mr. Aldrich and Mr. Leavitt," he wrote to his father, "his is not to be mentioned in the same day."

Essentially what Bosworth's scheme did was to conceive of the grounds around the house as a single, large composition, with individual parts that were integral to it. This was landscape gardening in the grand European tradition. It went far beyond what most people (including the Rockefellers) thought of as "gardens," which were basically flowerbeds, filled with colorful plants blooming in profusion, preferably through the long season from April to October. Flowers and flowerbeds there would be at Kykuit, but trees, shrubs, stretches of lawn, walks, paths, terraces, and statuary would all be part of the gardens too, indeed the most important part of them, for such things would provide the structure blending the house, the site, and the view into a harmonious whole.

For Junior, Bosworth's ideas were enticing from the start. Especially appealing was his theory of what a "true" garden should be. A true garden, he later explained in his article on Kykuit, was not designed to overwhelm at first glance. To "have the right quality" it also needed to "feel as though its owners really live in it," to offer opportunities for walking and moving about, for sitting in the sun or the shade, for discovering "obscure" and "sequestered" spaces that were "tempting . . . to explore." It had to appeal to all the senses. It needed different colors, shapes, and the sounds of birds and water, and also elements of antiquity. Like a magician, Bosworth with his words and charcoal pencil brought it all to life.

But the basic plan, organized around its two axes, remained the key to everything. Because of the sharper grades to the north and west, the main axis ran not through the house but beside it, to the south. Centered on an "inner" garden shimmering with displays of flowers, particularly in the spring and fall when Senior and Cettie would be there, it was to be punctuated at its ends by a teahouse to the east and an arbor with a central pavilion to the west, which in turn would be the entryway to a series of terraces spreading down the hill and providing some of the variety—gardens, pools, and vantage points—Bosworth considered so important. The perpendicular axis, running north–south in line with the bay windows in the library and dining room, was to be terminated by a Greek temple to the south, and to the north by pergolas, looking out onto a semicircular rose garden, in which that most beguiling of all flowers would bloom in dozens of varieties, filling the eye with color and the air with fragrance.

Within this scheme the west porch would be reserved for the view; no distracting gardens or terraces would compete there. Instead, a broader platform was to be achieved by extending the level of the west porch to the south. Immediately below this platform would be a formal orange-tree terrace, and then, below that, formality would give way to a more rustic world of pools and grottos, including a swimming pool rimmed with flat irregular boulders. None of these wonders, however, were to be casually or even easily experienced. As the view toward the west was to be saved until one proceeded through the house, the bay windows in the library and dining room looked directly out on Bosworth's north–south axis, but the way to get there was through French doors on adjoining walls. Even the stairways leading up and down the terraces were to be angled for sideways approaches. To see the gardens one also had to move fully through each one to get to the next, giving the whole added depth and mystery.

Nor did the entrance side of the house escape Bosworth's plan. Instead of being open and informal, it was now to be an enclosed space, setting the house apart from the surrounding countryside. Roads that ran across the lawns in front were to be obliterated. Replacing them would be a new road, swinging well out of sight of the house before approaching it through wrought iron and bronze gates leading to a rectangular forecourt surrounded by masonry walls, pierced by occasional "windows" of open grillwork. On the north side of the house, more garden areas were planned for the housekeeper's entrance, as well as for the walk from Senior's golf room in the subbasement to the links.

With respect to the practical side of all this, Bosworth's charges to the Rockefellers would cover his office time and a sum agreed upon with Junior (three payments of five hundred dollars each) "for the art in the work." Thompson-Starrett was to build the stone walls buttressing each level of the terracing, and as much of the labor and materials as feasible would be furnished from the estate. Bosworth added other stipulations, too. He was to design all garden structures. There had to be "a trained foreman" to supervise the work not falling under Thompson-Starrett's direction. On another point—perceiving correctly Junior's intense interest in everything going on—he was tactful but forthright: "You remember a little story I told you about an effort of the Pan American officials to coerce my best judgment . . . Should any question arise between us, where in my opinion, an artistic error would be committed . . . you will not insist on going contrary to my judgment." To soften his conditions, he took care to say to Junior several times, "My chief interest in the work is in the artistic result."

In July two of Bosworth's perspectives showing the gardens from various levels were ready to show Junior. "They are enchanting," he wrote Abby. "I shall have prints of them to show you later."

As irresistible as they were, the terraces and gardens pictured in Bosworth's "perspectives" (which unfortunately have not survived) entailed an extraordinary amount of earth-moving and stone wall construction. Large boulders for the walls were quarried on the estate, but to give a feeling of rustic antiquity to appropriate parts of the gardens dozens of individual rocks, found half buried in the woods and covered with moss, were carefully dug up and relocated. As many as forty men at a time worked on the walls. Teams were also sent to scout the surrounding acres for full-grown trees to transplant.

Characteristically, Junior kept a close eye on the work and made a few modifications of his own after consulting with Bosworth—for example, changing the materials for the garden steps—but basically the two worked in concert. It is difficult to tell exactly what was done when, in part because Bosworth's design work (unlike Codman's) flowed so smoothly. There was also a steady stream of "additions." Seventeen pieces of statuary were bought from the Stanford White estate, and Junior and Bosworth explored Baumgarten's storerooms looking for more. When a neighboring estate came on the market, its old boxwood was acquired for the borders of the forecourt, and when suitably mature ivy plants were found in England, they were imported and attached to the forecourt's walls, all to give a sense of age. Clipped trees, some in the shapes of animals, were imported from Holland for the inner garden. Six orange trees said to be over two hundred years old and not even, according to Bosworth, to be rivaled by those at Versailles, were shipped in from a château in France.

Embellishments of all kind proliferated as well. If rocks were too smooth for rustic places in the gardens, they could be grooved to provide more dramatic character. If stalactites were needed for the wall niche framing the fountain on the orange-tree terrace, they could be imported from Italy. If an outcropping of ledge interfered with the Italian terracing, it could be enhanced artificially as a picturesque feature. If one wanted to sit on the terrace by the pools, summer pavilions could be designed for each end. If the gardens were to be enjoyed in the evenings, lanterns could be hung from pergola beams and iron gates, and lights imbedded in all the fountains and waterways. If ideas for fountain statuary were needed, Bosworth knew Renaissance examples that could be copied. If sculptors had to be recruited to fashion classical figures in stone or plaster, Bosworth could introduce Junior to the best available artists. And if Senior wanted a flagpole put up somewhere, a place could be found overlooking the tennis courts, below the set of terraces angled to one side.

Also, for Bosworth water was an essential ingredient of any garden, and at Kykuit water—springing upward in fountains, meandering through man-made brooks and pools, dripping from the mouths of statues—was to be carried to every level, experienced in every part of the gardens. In true École fashion, too, each water detail had to be thought out in terms of how and from where it was to be seen—and heard—how it played into the whole.

All of which promised—in preparation for Senior and Cettie's move into the house in September of 1908—a busy year ahead. By the end of the fall of 1907, however, most of the terracing on the west side of the house and some of the pools and fountains that graced those terraces were in place. The new pergola for the west porch, which Bosworth had designed, was presumably finished as well. Frederick Smythe of Wadley & Smythe, who had been commissioned to search for plants abroad, was compiling a list for Junior, which would exceed the original estimate of $10,000 by nearly half.

Excavation for a hidden grotto room underneath the classical temple planned for the terminus of the north–south axis was another project undertaken that fall and winter. Grottos, signifying the mystery of the primeval and set off from the formality of the gardens closer to the house or villa, were standard features of Italian gardens. This one was to be an especially flamboyant creation. It would be approached from inside the house by means of a long, basement-level passageway (with tiles laid out smoothly enough for roller skating and bicycling, and also a bowling alley) and from the outside by a narrow stone stairway winding down from the temple above. Dressed on the exterior in massive, crudely shaped rust-colored granite, on the inside around its perimeter it would feature sandstone columns capped with ancient-looking, godlike carved heads. In the center, under the Guastavino tile ceiling would stand a giant jar, which Bosworth would later describe as a copy of "the great Borghese vase . . . with lights hidden in the top . . . [making] the effect mysterious." Man-made "lava" stone around the doors and windows would add to the effect, and later, green stalactite ceiling lights made by Tiffany would contribute their eerie glow, as would the mirrored doors reflecting the "dreamy and delightful" tangle of greenery outside. Water, too, was incorporated into the scheme, trickling from a bronze head of Pan in a dark cave of coral and stalactite stone on one wall.

Another major new structure was a "tree storage house" or "orangerie," copied from one at Versailles to winter over all the bay trees, oleanders, myrtles, jasmine, and citrus trees being acquired for summer display. With its boiler pit underneath the floor, its white interior walls and skylights, its tall, arched windows, made so that they could be swung open at the bottom, and its wide doors at each end through which the huge tubs of trees could be moved, it was both practical and monumental. The fact that the boxes containing the plants were copies of the *caisses* used at Versailles added an extra touch of elegance.

Nor were the wonders of the gardens to end there. While the orangerie was going up and Bosworth's terraces were cascading down the hillsides, two Japanese artisan-gardeners trained at the Imperial Palace in Tokyo, a Mr. Takahashi and a Mr. Uyeda, arrived to create a Japanese brook winding through the irregular terrain on the lower slopes to the south and west. Whether deliberate or not, the brook would prove to be an entering wedge for a much larger project: adding an entire Japanese garden to the mix. For Americans of taste—many of whom were already seasoned collectors of Japanese prints (Abby and Junior had bought some from the American Art

Gallery in March of 1907)—Japanese gardens, always with ponds and earth mounds suggestive of seas and mountains, were a growing attraction. *Country Life in America* featured examples of all sizes, down to one of only thirty-six square feet, which cost just twenty-five dollars. In another instance a "teahouse" from which to view the finished product, a must in Japanese gardens, was described as having practical qualities as well, by virtue of functioning on its backside as a henhouse. The Rockefellers scarcely needed to resort to such practicalities, but acquiring a Japanese garden to add an element both exotic and ancient to the landscape had its appeal.

The Japanese artisans had been working on the brook for two and a half months when Junior decided it was time to approach Senior about constructing a pond that could be the central feature of a larger Japanese garden. As usual, he prepared his arguments carefully: the ground there was already a swampy depression; the pond would be small and would not "materially increase the difficulty" of the golf course; costs would be low, and any dirt that was excavated could be used as fill elsewhere. Did he mention the idea of a larger Japanese garden with a teahouse by the pond? Probably not yet.

Meanwhile Junior's updates to Abby remained enthusiastic during the summer of 1908. In June she had left to follow her obstetrician to Bar Harbor, where her third child, Nelson, would be born shortly before Senior and Laura were scheduled to take up residence in the new house. Although both the large stone teahouse and the temple remained unfinished, the inner garden was leveled and sodded while she was away, and the marble walk from the living room out along the terrace to the south was laid. In high spirits Junior wrote humorously too of a "séance" he had discussing with Bosworth his "really exquisite" design for the great arbor sheltering the marble walk.

Usually shy and reserved, Junior obviously enjoyed not only Bosworth's ideas and designs but also his company. "Mr. Bosworth came up after lunch," he wrote Abby late in June. "We were at the house till half past five and then . . . drove through the nursery, to the new quarry, and to Raven Rock. Mr. B. was infatuated with the latter. We were late to dinner but the drive was delightful." When Bosworth had business with another client in Bar Harbor, Junior urged him to stay with Abby. "It might be a diversion for you," he wrote her. But Abby's delight in Bosworth's company seems not to have matched Junior's. Later, during one of Junior's absences, Bosworth would join her for lunch along with a sculptor he had commissioned to work at Kykuit. "I think they are both foolish," she declared to Junior. "They think women like flattery and they don't."

With so much planting and finishing still to be done near the house by the time Senior and Laura were due to move in, Junior reluctantly had them postpone their arrival until the beginning of October. At that, his scheduling proved hopelessly optimistic. Even over a year later, in June 1910, when he presented Bosworth's foreman with a gold watch, signaling his work was "practically completed," much remained to be done. That same summer Abby arranged to invite the residents of Pocantico village to view the grounds one evening. About three hundred came. With everything lit, "it was quite like fairyland," Junior wrote elatedly to his mother. The following January Bosworth's article, sharing his masterpiece with the readership of *American Architect*, appeared. Still, the gardens would not finally be finished until 1915.

What Bosworth's article did not say, of course, was that it had all cost a great deal of money, a fact that had never escaped Senior's notice. Later, sitting on the Pompeian chaise lounge in the stone teahouse, looking out over the inner garden in the afternoon, he may have seemed to his family to take pleasure in the results, just as he did in demonstrating to guests that all the lights outside could be turned on with a flick of the switch, or in quipping, "Those little brooks run mighty high," referring tongue-in-cheek to how expensive they were. Through much of the time the gardens were being worked on, however, his mood was anything but jocular.

For months, as he watched the endless digging and building, the constant moving of huge boulders and towering trees, there had been little to show for the burgeoning costs. The scale of it all, too—the diameter of the semicircular rose garden, for example, which was greater than the length of the house itself—turned out to be far beyond anything he had imagined. In the beginning, seeing hills leveled and turned into fill for terrace after terrace, he had sought out his carpenter friend Mr. Turner, asking if he thought Bosworth was "crazy," only to be told that Bosworth seemed "pretty straightforward." Yet all the while the costs continued to escalate. When they reached five times the original estimate, Junior's rejoinder to his father's anxious questioning was "I am not in the least afraid but that you will regard the finished result as well worth its cost. I am increasingly enthusiastic about it as the work goes on." He also offered to pay half the expense himself. And when Senior proposed halting the work altogether, Junior responded that it would be cheaper and more convenient to continue what was already under way.

In April of 1908 Senior had come out to review Bosworth's suggestion that one of the golf greens be modified to accommodate the gardens. After observing the multitude of workers and foremen on the site, and noting the high commissions the family was paying, he wondered whether they should have used their own people to do the work. He also noticed that a path already laid with stone was being moved. "It seems to me," he wrote Junior, "that Mr. Bosworth has done a good deal of cutting and trying . . . Do you still like him as well as ever? His manner is pleasant; his method is luxurious."

But Junior remained unwavering in his faith. "I like Mr. Bosworth increasingly," he answered, adding, "I believe him to be a man of more real genius than any with whom we have been associated in this work." Urging his father to be patient, he declared, "A year from now when the gardens are all completed . . . and you have an opportunity to enjoy them, if you do not agree that Mr. Bosworth has done a truly wonderful thing and that all of the work and expense is more than justified in view of your own enjoyment [here he had changed the word *judgment* in a prior draft to *enjoyment*] . . . I shall be more disappointed than I can tell."

Confronted with Junior's enthusiasm, Senior had tried to soften his objections by saying they were "simply reflections." But his "reflections" were unceasing. The notion that they should construct a Japanese garden (when Junior finally broached it) provoked a fresh burst of skepticism: "My thought was that we ought not to allow these men to run us into an indefinite expenditure for a thing that may not be invaluable." A year later the issue was still alive. Seizing on particulars as if to grab at the whole, Senior wrote, "I can hardly understand how the little Japanese house, which I supposed was to be a very superficial affair, would reach $10,000." The culprit, he supposed, was not Junior ("I am very appreciative of what you have done") but Bosworth. "I do not charge that he has deliberately planned, with unfair intent, to cause the expenditure of the large sum of money which we have been compelled to pay." Yet, he added, "I should pity the man of moderate means who fell into his hands. It seems to me he has done a vast amount of experimentation, at our cost . . . He does not command my confidence to the extent he does yours."

The following January, when he learned that the costs for the gardens now exceeded the original estimate by *"twenty-five times"* (Senior's emphasis), he observed sarcastically of Bosworth, "It was conceded by his architectural friends whom I met here on one occasion that he had had a very rare opportunity to proceed." But between the lines his anger was obvious. In Bosworth's hands, the family had been exploited; the gardens were unnecessarily expensive; worse, what Bosworth's "costly art" had produced was far too grand for their needs. However, unlike the fur coat and hat that Junior had once given him as a Christmas present, and which he had promptly returned as far too luxurious to wear, there was no going back in the case of the gardens. As both father and son knew, the game had been played. Yet it was, after all, Senior's house. How had he been outmaneuvered so thoroughly?

When the issue of building a house had first come up six years before, Junior had begun by presenting his father with a series of plans, all of which had been decisively rejected. Then in his and Abby's absence, Senior had taken matters into his own hands, leaving Junior to work as best he could around the plan his father and the architects had produced, all of which Bosworth seemed to understand perfectly. It was a delicate situation calling not only for tact and diplomacy at every turn but also a healthy dose of ingenuity. Whose idea was it, then, *not* to have a grand plan for the gardens, committed to paper, at the outset of the project? For that appears to have been the strategy adopted. Senior's continual complaints about Bosworth's "cutting and trying" and his "experimentation" strongly suggest that he was never given a fully developed plan to review. Were not the high costs, as he wrote, due to "[Bosworth's] not having definite ideas at the outset," plus "the many changes made in his program" as time went on?

Certainly, with his Beaux-Arts training, Bosworth had to have had a clear, overall idea of how the gardens would evolve, beginning with the two main axes to which they were oriented. To Abby, Junior had written of the "perspectives" that he was anxious to show her, and several times he mentioned a plan. Yet had he actually seen that plan, or had it simply been described to him? Was he plotting openly with Bosworth, or did the plan (as seems more likely) simply fail to appear? There were separate designs—eventually hundreds of them—for everything from temples and teahouses to lampposts and flowerpots. There are also, in Bosworth's article appearing in the *American Architect* in 1911, sketches of the cross sections of each of the two main axes, showing the garden structures punctuating them. But in no sense did any of those constitute a comprehensive plan.

So month by month, year by year, the gardens grew, quite possibly with no one but Bosworth knowing for sure what would come next, and through all that time the costs rose steadily higher, confounding at every turn Senior's attempts to control them. It may have been advantageous, too, that the gardens were *not* finished for so long a time. Unlike interior rooms, which were complete when they were plastered or paneled and furnished, the work outdoors had no clear-cut conclusion. From Junior's standpoint it would also have mattered that he had Abby's unqualified support. Loving gardens herself, she could see how much the landscaping project meant to him, and though not a spendthrift, she believed wealth was an advantage to be enjoyed. As his wise and steady confidante, she could help him achieve his goal of formalizing the grounds in ways that set him inescapably in opposition to the father he worshipped.

But now, for added support, Junior had Bosworth, someone he related to quite differently than he had to the august yet often difficult Ogden Codman, and with whom he would share a steadily deepening relationship. In 1911 he chose Bosworth to design his and Abby's nine-story town house at 10 West Fifty-fourth Street, the formal, neoclassical architecture of which perfectly suited Junior's tastes and disposition. Whether it was introducing him to talented artists, taking him to look for statuary at Duveen's, or seeking with him just the right color for the walls to set off his Chinese porcelain collection, Bosworth also continually broadened Junior's aesthetic world. Significantly, it was through Bosworth that he met George Grey Barnard, a neoclassical sculptor and avid collector of medieval art, who in turn led him to the Unicorn Tapestries, and whose fragments of French monasteries he would eventually purchase and make the basis for the Metropolitan Museum of Art's collection at the Cloisters. "Long ago," Junior wrote Bosworth in 1913, "we ceased to regard you as a business acquaintance and placed you among our personal friends." For his part Bosworth, who was more openly emotional than Junior, went even further: "My work with you and Mrs. Rockefeller has never seemed like work to me . . . every hour spent with you [is] one of benefit to heart and brain, as well as pleasure. To have you think of me as 'friend' is a happiness indeed, a very sacred one." He kept a framed photograph of Junior in his bedroom, and he signed his letters, "Devotedly yours."

As Senior remarked, Bosworth benefited greatly from Junior's generosity, and not only from his work for the family but from the commissions he later received, chief among them supervising, as "Secretaire Générale du Comité pour la Restauration des Monuments de Versailles-Fountainebleau et la Cathèdrale de Reims," the restoration projects that Junior financed in France after the Great War. Junior was also sensitive to the Bosworths' financial situation—which worsened in the 1950s after some unfortunate investments—and stepped in to cover the expenses for a kidney stone operation for Bosworth that led to complications necessitating extensive nursing care. He paid as well for alterations to the Bosworths' house so that part of it could be rented.

The association went well beyond commissions and financial support, too. On occasion the Bosworths lunched with the Rockefellers at Pocantico or hosted them along with the Herters at dinner in what Junior described once to his mother as his "artistic apartments." Even after Bosworth moved to France in 1922 to carry out the restoration work, the two stayed in touch. Bosworth sent Junior cravats at Christmas. When the Bosworths were expecting their first baby, Junior hunted for the latest edition of Dr. Luther Emmett Holt's *The Care and Feeding of Children* (which he and Abby had used) to send the new parents. Whenever the Rockefellers or their children were in France, they visited the Bosworths, often going on excursions to Bosworth and Junior's restoration sites. But Bosworth found himself saddened by the loss of the closer contact he had had with Junior before leaving the States to live abroad. "I miss you very much," he wrote. "The lack of having you more in my life is about the only thing I yearn for over here." If Bosworth had business in New York, he invited Junior for lunch at the India Club, or the family for dinner at the Plaza, and in turn, the Rockefellers shared their box at Carnegie Hall with him. When Bosworth built his own grand house, Marietta Villa, outside of Paris, Junior and Abby sent a piano as a housewarming present, and their daughter Babs Milton and her family were his first dinner guests. Once Junior paid for a spring visit to Williamsburg so the Bosworths could see the restorations there, and when France fell during the Second World War and the German army commandeered Marietta Villa, Junior helped the Bosworths get to a temporary refuge at Glen Cove on Long Island.

The two even shared a dislike of modern art. In 1929 a visit by Lucy Aldrich, Abby's sister, prompted a tongue-in-cheek reference by Bosworth to the subject when he wrote Junior: "I am trying to entertain her as best I can. She wants to see this modern art and I am showing it to her with the hope that she may not give you the impression that I am overenthusiastic about it. I hope I appreciate what is good in it as in all the phases of Art, but so far at least the result has not touched our home."

Yet essentially the relationship between Bosworth and Junior was based on a mutual love of art, not a critical study of it. And if Bosworth's superior knowledge and understanding fed that love in Junior, he had in him an eager and appreciative student, though it was Bosworth's idea that *both* were students. It was more than flattery when he wrote Junior, "Every hour spent with you [is] one of benefit to heart and brain." Each would say later, at different times, but in exactly the same words, that all of what they had worked so hard to accomplish was done "in the hope of beauty," and toward the end of Junior's life Bosworth mused: "Our country is still too immature for any general appreciation of the value of idealism to human life. When the majority have leisure enough to learn about the benefits of the 'unnecessary,' the fruits of the spirit will ripen on family trees; a lesson you have done so well to teach, at Williamsburg, and the Cloisters, the Agora; and out West; in fact, I'd say, by the beautiful picture your whole life makes."

Such was Bosworth's epitaph for his friend and benefactor. For Junior, on the other hand, working with Bosworth to shape the gardens at Kykuit had meant crossing yet another frontier, moving beyond the bounds his parents had set for him, beyond, even, the terrain he had crossed with Codman. Learning to appreciate "the benefits of the unnecessary" in the gardens, he came to see the world anew, and more, to feel that he had actually participated in the creative process. That was Bosworth's greatest gift to him, and it would change his life forever, pointing the way, as Bosworth said, for him to make broader use of what he had learned in projects like Williamsburg and the Cloisters—each of them dedicated to rescuing and preserving the art of the past in the cause of educating the public, teaching the citizens of a modern democracy all that they owed to those who had gone before them and what they had created; teaching, too, future generations of Rockefellers the value of such things. Thus would "the fruits of the spirit" ripen, as Bosworth had said, "on family trees."

But there were still other lessons Kykuit's building had to teach Junior, and some a good deal less sunny and bright than those he had learned form Bosworth, yet in their own way just as important.

6

Kykuit Rising II

*The newspapers had a field day with it—headlines about a "Laborer . . .
Shot" in his own vegetable garden, in broad daylight. The bullets had hit
him in the stomach, piercing his liver. Later, when the authorities investi-
gated, they found footprints in the garden, along with the gun, shoved in a
cornstalk nearby.*

*But much remained murky about the incident. What caused it? Was it
a quarrel over a job, a woman, or was there something darker, more ominous at the heart of it? Two men had already been murdered and more
robbed, at least twelve so far that summer. There were letters too. Letters
demanding money, threatening to kill people who did not pay up. Or people who talked. Letters with drawings of skulls, of coffins, and most
dreaded of all, a handprint with a dagger. La Mano Nera. The Black
Hand. No doubt the victims thought there would not be this terror any
longer, not in America, but its tentacles had reached even here.*

*The man who had been shot had come to the country nine years earlier.
His team dumped and spread dirt in front of the big house, the place they
said was being built for the richest man in the world. Who could tell, however, whether he cared anything about the crews? There were guards everywhere, yet the women wanted their men to stay home, to be safe. Most
continued to show up, but many went armed with guns and knives. Going
to the police was too dangerous. If they talked to others, it was only to their
own kind. Now there were rumors that they might decide not to go back to
work at all.*

Although no one thought he would, Giuseppe Russo—one of the Italian laborers working on the Rockefeller estate—survived the shooting. His story to the police was that he had shot himself by mistake. The coroner had doubts, but hoping to calm things down, the sheriff asked him to list the case as an accident. Meanwhile Russo told his priest that he was shot by an "enemy."

That Kykuit's building should have been marked by the sort of violence that nearly cost Giuseppe Russo his life was certainly no part of anyone's plans for the place. Indeed, given Junior's hopes for it and Senior's bucolic vision of country life, the entire episode had an almost surreal quality. But Russo was an employee of the Rockefellers, and the shooting did occur in an Italian settlement not far from Kykuit. His experience was also less surprising than it might have been at other times, coming as it did in 1912, in the midst of a summer rife with turbulence, including other violent acts and threats from the Black Hand.

Quite possibly, too, none of it would have happened if things had gone better four years earlier, when the senior Rockefellers finally took up residence in their new house. For incredibly enough, in spite of everything— all the money, all the time, all the care—that had gone into building the house, it was not a success. Far from it.

Always reluctant to leave Forest Hill, Cettie had arrived at Pocantico in the fall of 1908 prepared to enjoy the place Junior and Abby had worked so hard to create, and the first words about it in her diary were admiring and hopeful: "It is beautiful and convenient within and without." Yet all too soon she began noticing problems. She would have planned for more closet space. The bedrooms on the upper two floors, awkwardly shoehorned in under the high, sloping roof, were too small to be suitable for servants, let alone guests. Then there was the noise. The clamor of the dumbwaiter, making its way up from the kitchen in the basement, could be heard at the dining room table; rumblings from the elevator disturbed anyone in the adjoining bedrooms; and the sound of Cettie's toilet flushing was "plainly" audible in the library and alcove room below. Equally irritating to Senior was the racket made by deliveries in the service court below his bedroom windows, particularly—once the heating season began—the sound of the coal car. He also found the noise from the furnace in the sub-basement annoying, and winter revealed still other, even more serious problems. The heating system was unbalanced, leaving some rooms uncomfortably chilly. During a rainstorm in December water from the chimneys ran out onto the floors of both the dining room and the library, though luckily the butler saved the Savonnerie rugs from damage. Worse still, the chimneys sometimes belched clouds of smoke into the rooms.

How on earth could so much be wrong with a brand-new house? Even more to the point, who was to blame for the whole fiasco? Quick to absolve Junior from any responsibility, Senior faulted the architects and the contractors. Yet what of his own part in it? More than anyone else, he had shaped the basic design of the house, which plainly accounted for several of the most serious problems, including the cramped upper-story rooms and the malfunctioning chimneys.

But happily for his sake, Senior had never been one to dwell on past mistakes, least of all his own. What counted was putting matters to rights as quickly as possible. For Junior, dealing with the disappointment at the way things had turned out was harder; still, he began looking for solutions at once, attacking problems piecemeal, which seemed sensible enough. He soon discovered, however, that almost everything was more complicated than either he or Senior had imagined. In reality there were few quick fixes to be had. On the contrary, before they were finished father and son would find themselves presiding over an outcome that even in retrospect seems astonishing: the all but total rebuilding of the new house. And among the many unexpected consequences of that effort would be the shooting of Giuseppe Russo.

Junior did manage to find some simple solutions. Contained within their shafts, the elevator and dumbwaiter could be made quieter through electrical modifications. More perplexing was how to soundproof water pipes buried deep in Thompson-Starrett's terra-cotta tile walls. "What can now be done to remedy this defect," Junior wrote Aldrich, "and what could we have done in the installation of the plumbing system to have prevented it?" From there the difficulties multiplied steadily.

Because of Senior's fondness for wood fires, the fireplaces had always been considered a central feature of the house. There were eight chimneys in all, each capped below the ridgeline of the roof. Sensing the problem as early as 1908 (according to country wisdom, chimneys had to rise above the roof to draw well), Senior had put the case in the strongest possible terms to Junior: "Let us spare no expense to make them right." Dutifully, during the construction, Junior had consulted the John Whitley firm, specialists in chimney construction, and several times he tested the fireplaces himself. Yet what everyone had failed to take fully into account beforehand was Kykuit's position high on a windy hilltop.

Should the chimneys be raised, then? Or could they be covered in some way? Perhaps movable extensions could be tried. Much of 1909 was taken up with such discussions, and in the end Junior authorized Delano & Aldrich to design, with Whitley's advice, temporary extensions for some of the chimneys as an experiment. At first they seemed to work, yet the following spring there was smoke in the house from both the extended and unextended chimneys. Junior suggested raising them even higher, but would such tall chimneys stand up in the wind? Finally in June 1910, having struggled with the problem for almost two years and taking aim at Delano & Aldrich's "ignorance or negligence," Senior proposed an even more radical solution. "So desirous am I to have the chimneys right . . . I would be willing to run the walls of the house up higher, so that the main chimney could extend to the top of the roof . . . I suppose this is not to be thought about, although I think it would be well to call it up with the architects."

Raise the walls! If Junior was surprised, he must have been intrigued as well. Could it be that all the problems with the house might turn out to be a blessing in disguise? Not only would running up the walls solve the chimney problem and address Cettie's objections to the cramped "roof rooms," but it would also modify the slope of the roof and thus go far toward blunting the awkwardness of the house's old-fashioned profile. The day after receiving his father's suggestion, Junior scheduled a conference with Delano & Aldrich.

The question put to the architects was whether a new roof could be placed on a third floor raised to full height. The house would be the same style, but (mercifully!) the roof's slope would be shallower. Delano & Aldrich agreed to draw up new plans along those lines, and from abroad, Codman consented to return to the job, though he minced no words in his reply to his office manager, which clearly was intended for his eyes alone: "I am glad to hear that Mr. Rockefeller is going to try to improve those horrid little attic rooms; I feel sure he cannot hurt the looks of the exterior of the house; for it is so ugly already . . . what a pity he did not have the house built by a real architect."

More ideas about the changes emerged over the summer. Could the east wall of the house above the main entrance be extended out over the porte cochere, thereby enlarging the upper-story front rooms? Junior also asked the architects about doing away with the roof's slope altogether and using a flat roof instead. That idea, however, Delano & Aldrich summarily rejected as both impractical and aesthetically out of keeping with the rest of the house: "It would . . . introduce an alien form into the general landscape of the slopes." A flat roof—appropriate for a house of a "more artificial and formal character"—would also mean "the whole building would have to be transformed from the type of country house of a domestic type . . . to the palace or villa of Italy." For example, the porches with their wooden pillars would have to be supplanted by a "more monumental" design in stone or marble. So for now the modified sloping roof prevailed.

As the new plans were made and revised, Junior told Delano & Aldrich to send them to Codman and Bosworth, as well as to his father, for approval. Yet autumn came with no final decision from Senior. In October Junior told him he had to make up his mind soon, if work was to begin in the spring. In November Edith Rockefeller McCormick proposed that her father hire her architect, Charles Platt, as a consultant, an idea Junior readily supported and Senior rejected. Still, the suggestion may have spurred him into action, for shortly before Thanksgiving Delano & Aldrich were instructed to proceed with the plans they had, leaving the winter for minor modifications. Under that heading, Senior suggested enlarging the hall and increasing the closet space on the second floor, and as the snow flew, he proposed adding a second elevator for freight and extending and enclosing the west porch. Junior replied that with the pads and movable wood-slat floor the existing elevator already had, handling freight was not a problem. He also told Bosworth's assistant to disregard Senior's ideas for the west porch.

Then, toward the end of February, with Delano & Aldrich's plans finally ready to be sent out for bids, Codman broke through the problematic schemes agreed on thus far with an extraordinary suggestion. Sketching on tissues overlaying the plans, he showed Junior a design for extending the house forward all across the entrance facade and raising the fourth story by replacing the still-sloping top of the house with a low, hipped roof. Junior heartily approved. But what about the forecourt? Might it not be too short for so high a house? Codman thought it would, and Bosworth, rushing to Codman's the same day, agreed. If the new plan was adopted, the forecourt would have to be redone, as would some of the gardens. For the moment that seemed out of the question.

Yet the thought persisted, and Junior spent the next two weeks conferring with Codman and Aldrich, as well as Bosworth, who was delighted to be working on a design more in harmony with his gardens. By March Junior was ready to lay out the case for Senior. Cettie's room would be enlarged, and she would gain a boudoir, or dressing room, with a large additional closet. The servants on the fourth floor would have full headroom, and supporting the extension of the upper stories at the ground-floor level would be stone piers topped with archways, forming a loggia connecting the walls of the forecourt in a "flat and unbroken" line, which would "improve rather than hamper" the gardens and forecourt. Junior's enthusiasm for the entire plan—"unquestionably the best thing"—was palpable, though he chose not to mention yet the need to enlarge the forecourt. Senior too liked it. "[The plan] strikes me favorably," he replied. Always thinking about light, he suggested adding a skylight at the top of the house, as well as a balustrade around the roof so it could be used as an observatory.

Junior had already begun to work on costs with Aldrich. When finished, the new plans went to five contractors for bids, including Thompson-Starrett, with Charles T. Wills Company eventually chosen to do the work. (There had been too many problems with Thompson-Starrett before.) At the same time M. A. Munn, an engineer from Cleveland, was hired to oversee the rebuilding, and Fred Briggs, shortly to become the acting superintendent of the estate, was given responsibility for managing any laborers not provided by Wills. Baumgarten's crews would execute Codman's new interiors on the upper floors, and William Turner, Senior's trusted carpenter, would stay in the house during the construction to prevent damage to the existing structure.

In April 1911 all the books, prints, and bric-a-brac in the house were packed up and taken to Manhattan Storage. Silver was stored at a local bank, and some of the lighter furniture, curtains, rugs, slipcovers, and cushions went to Baumgarten's. By the end of the month, except for furniture piled up and covered in a few of the larger rooms, the house was emptied of the contents so long and carefully assembled and ready for the rebuilding to begin.

Even as the work commenced, however, more "pretty things" from Codman's French suppliers continued to arrive. Outside in the gardens, too, the pace never slowed. By now the borders of the sunken lawns of the inner garden next to the house were ornamented with topiaries, clipped in the shapes of animals and birds, and lined with boxwood "enlivened" by drifts of candytuft and yellow pansies. At the inner garden's east end, the interior of one of Bosworth's main garden structures—the stone teahouse inspired by the sixteenth-century Loggia of the Muses at the Villa Lante— was also receiving its finishing touches: on the ceiling, painted panels of Venus in a shell-shaped chariot drawn by dolphins, plus miscellaneous cherubs, swans, cranes, sparrows, and doves; and on the walls, neoclassical scenes of musicians, maidens, and fawns, dancing in low, carved relief.

At the same time, the furniture for the teahouse, constructed by Baumgartner to Bosworth's design ("the most artistic furniture ever executed in our shop," Baumgartner wrote later, explaining the cost overruns), was being made. Consisting of leather-covered, silver-finished, inlaid Pompeian-style chairs, stools, and a couch bed, plus a circular marble table, it all passed Senior's review unchallenged. The tipping point came with estimates for the brown tapestry curtains being woven by Herter Looms. Looking rather plain to an untutored eye, they were slated to cost $2,500, which seemed utterly outrageous to Senior. Could the order be postponed and reconsidered? he asked repeatedly. But evidently Cettie was enjoying the teahouse, providing Junior with a useful argument: why deny her anything that might add to her pleasure? It would also be easier, he claimed, to proceed with the curtains while the "data" were still "fresh" in everyone's minds. The order would, of course, be canceled if Senior wished, but, Junior continued, "I have given so much time and thought . . . have made so many visits to the factory . . . arranged for so many experiments, all with a view to getting the thing just right," that he was sure the final result would be to his parents' liking.

Though in time Senior grudgingly gave in on the issue of the teahouse curtains, questions of taste and aesthetics never engaged him to the extent that technological matters did. There he considered his expertise matchless and expected others to accept his ideas without dissent, setting him further at odds with Junior as the house was being rebuilt.

One of his major complaints remained the heating system—the rumbling of the coal cart as it passed through the service court and the uneven distribution of heat in the house, which enlarging the upper stories would only worsen. Why not solve both problems by connecting the house to a utility system in the coach barn, as had been done at the Parsons-Wentworth House and Abeyton Lodge? Junior, burdened with a multitude of other matters, waited almost a month before answering. In his reply he reminded his father that putting the heating system in the coach barn had been proposed as early as 1906, but Senior had vetoed it. To make the change now would mean tearing up gardens already completed. Junior also had Munn looking into ways of reducing the noise of the coal cart, so for the time being nothing more was done, though Senior continued to explore the matter.

Another, notably more radical scheme of his—this one for addressing the general clamor and dust of the service court—was not so easily sidetracked. The idea, he wrote Junior, came from Mary Hargreaves, the housekeeper, who suggested routing deliveries through an "aqueduct" or tunnel leading to an underground service court at the level of the subbasement. Senior was intrigued. Looking across at the house from Abeyton Lodge two days later, Abby noticed him "busy surveying something." Never one to waste time, he was happily planning the new project while waiting for Junior's reply. It was just the kind of challenge he loved.

Yet Junior liked this idea no better than Senior's others. "It would be costly; it would require additional help; it would be inconvenient; and," he went on, through the cloudburst of semicolons, "it seems to me entirely impossible." Senior answered that it was both "feasible and easier than [he] had expected." So he continued to study the scheme with Turner and Munn, while Junior continued to voice his objections to it. What about his father's golfing companions? How would they get to his golf room? Another problem was Senior's decision to hire D. E. Howatt, Forest Hill's former superintendent, as a consultant. Howatt, Junior reminded his father—to no avail—was noted for his bad temper and for mixing his personal business with the estate's.

Confronted with his father's persistence, Junior asked Delano & Aldrich to confer with Munn about where and how a tunnel could be attached to the house and requested that Bosworth be consulted "at each step" of the planning, though he still hoped, as he told his father, that Senior would give up his "subway" idea. Senior's response was to write Munn at the end of June, "Mr. John does not sympathize with my enthusiasm about the scheme but we will pursue it exhaustively," and not waiting for Junior to contact Bosworth, he wrote his old adversary himself, suggesting that it would be an opportunity "to do one of the finest pieces of work" they had done. He was sure, he added, that Bosworth and "Mr. John" would come to see things his way.

While Junior was in Seal Harbor, Senior—urging him to stay longer and get plenty of rest—also consulted Howatt about adding a baggage compartment to the underside of the existing elevator car in addition to planning for the tunnel. As for bringing in Delano & Aldrich, he wrote Howatt that he saw no need for an architect, except for Bosworth "so that Mr. John will have no necessity of complaining. He is very favorable to Mr. Bosworth." Yet Junior continued to point out problems: "These I have mentioned to father," he wrote Bosworth, "but he has apparently not given them consideration." When it came to the service tunnel, however, he left the directing to Senior, returning Delano & Aldrich's plans for the tunnel entrance because, as he wrote, it was "father's project." Senior had indeed carried the day: the tunnel would be built.

Nor was this the only time the division of authority between father and son led to confusion. Another instance—and one that might well have had serious consequences—involved the plan to attach a baggage carrier to the bottom of the elevator car in lieu of building the added freight elevator Senior had proposed earlier. In order to accommodate the carrier at the subbasement level, which Senior and his golfing companions used, a pit would have to be carved out of the bedrock under the house. Both Turner and Howatt had advised against any blasting there, so Senior's solution was to have the elevator go only to the basement level. He and his golfing companions could use either the baggage compartment or the stairs perfectly well. Yet Junior felt his father would regret that decision, and in the end a pit—to be dug by hand—was decided on. But one day arriving at the house, Junior discovered to his horror that an estate worker, John Reilly, was using dynamite in the subbasement to blast out the pit. What would all that jarring do to Kykuit's foundations, not to mention its waterproofing, plaster, and ceilings? Furious, he ordered Reilly and his men out of the house and put Munn in charge of the digging, which, whatever the extra cost, did produce the result Senior wanted.

During the summer and fall of 1911 plans were also being made for the altered entrance facade and roof. If the house were to be reconceived as an "Italian palace or villa," Junior wanted Bosworth, not Delano & Aldrich, to design its newly formalized exteriors. Sensitive to the firm's prior difficulties with Codman, he offered the partners the option of bowing out altogether or having Bosworth as a consultant "in order that the house and the gardens might make a harmonious whole." They chose to stay with the project, and Bosworth set to work, taking Junior as a first step around the city to see various house exteriors. The fall was taken up with finalizing designs—subject to Abby's review—for lining the new loggia with lime-stone, for changing its floor to Tennessee marble, and for a new iron and glass marquise, or canopy, above the front door, to replace Delano & Aldrich's old-fashioned porte cochere.

Meanwhile, the heavy structural portion of the rebuilding was moving forward, though its progress was marred by what turned out to be a major accident. Inspecting the work after returning from Seal Harbor that fall, Junior suddenly noticed that some steel beams being hoisted to the roof had broken free of the ropes around them and were about to crash to the ground. Turning, he shouted to the Italian stonemasons working below, warning them to jump clear, as he himself was doing, but apparently they did not hear him, for in the next instant he watched with horror as the beams fell on them. Frantically he and others worked to rescue the trapped men, his hands and clothes, as the *New York Times* reported later, "bathed in blood." Of the five workers injured, one eventually died. Having done what he could to administer first aid, Junior arranged for the men to be treated in a makeshift infirmary set up in the coach barn, providing both doctors and trained nurses after he learned that all the local hospitals were full. Abby too rushed to the scene of the accident to help. Unfortunately, as harrowing as the incident was, it would not be the last tragedy to occur at Kykuit during those years.

With most of the major design issues raised by the rebuilding settled by the autumn of 1911, one still remained unresolved: the size of the forecourt in front of the heightened house. Just how long should it be, and with auto-mobiles now a major factor, what was the best way to lay out the drive? Se-nior, favoring the picturesque as always, opposed "a thoroughfare" running straight up to the house. Bosworth, however, felt strongly that a central axis to the main entrance was essential. But perhaps because of his other com-mitments (at that point he was designing Abby and Junior's New York City house), he was slow to provide a solution that satisfied everyone. Just be-fore Christmas, Senior telephoned him, asking for a revised plan. "I had not given this matter much thought," he answered, but a few days later he wrote, "The 'best thing' would involve a more radical measure than any we have so far considered." To have the entrance gates "an ideal distance from the front door," the forecourt would have to be longer than anyone had imagined, requiring, if it was to be level, "heavy" infilling where the land

sloped sharply away from the house to the east, plus a twenty-foot-high retaining wall to hold the fill in place. A longer, "very simple" forecourt was all
right with Senior, but not the driveway as Bosworth designed it. Finally, by
April 1912, enough of the plan was agreed on to begin preparing the site.

Meanwhile, Junior hoped that his parents could move back into the
house the following summer, but time was getting short. Also, after re-
drawing the plans for the forecourt and consulting with "[his] friend Platt,"
Bosworth recommended adding even more to its length, bringing it to a
full two hundred feet, though how to construct so large a forecourt was no
simple matter to resolve. Where would they find that much fill, and how
would it be transported to the site? Senior proposed using steam to power
a network of cables and buckets, but most of the fill was likely to come
from sources too distant for such a system. Instead, the method settled on
was to dig up the dirt and cart it to the site, in untold hundreds of loads,
shoveled into horse-drawn wagons—a truly massive undertaking, calling
for an immense amount of labor, which would have to be found somewhere. As it happened, however, the area already had a sizable supply of
labor, thanks to New York City's ever-increasing demand for water.

By 1911 the system that brought water to the city from the Croton River
in Westchester County—begun more than half a century earlier—was
nearing the end of a major overhaul. A much larger aqueduct had been
built, as well as a "final" dam at Croton Falls, not far from Kykuit. At the
same time, work was under way on an entirely new system, using water
from the Catskills. Described by an engineer from the city's Department of
Water Supply as "probably second only to the Panama Canal," it called for
eight large gathering reservoirs and an aqueduct stretching for almost a
hundred miles, parts of it tunneled deep beneath hills and mountains as
well as under the Hudson River. Huge aerators, "of far greater volume
[than] . . . the fountains of Versailles," would keep the water pure along the
way. To build all this, as many as fifteen thousand workers, earning an average of two dollars for a ten-hour day, would furnish the muscle for work
that was often as dangerous as it was hard, and a large number of those
workers would be Italian.

Altogether between 1890 and 1920 more than a quarter of Italy's population emigrated, bringing tens of thousands of newcomers to America.
Most who came were unskilled laborers, from the poorest areas of southern Italy and Sicily. Typically, they were recruited in Italy by the agents of
padrones, who acted as a bridge between employers and workers once they

The two John D. Rockefellers, Junior and Senior, in New York, early twentieth century (Courtesy of the Rockefeller Archive Center)

Junior and Abby Aldrich Rockefeller soon after their marriage (Courtesy of the Rockefeller Archive Center)

Forest Hill, John D. Rockefeller's Residence, Cleveland Sixth City

Postcard of Forest Hill, the Rockefeller family's summer home in Cleveland (Courtesy of the Rockefeller Archive Center)

Chester Aldrich, Kykuit's original architect (Courtesy of the Century Association Archives Foundation)

Kykuit under construction in 1907 (Courtesy of the Rockefeller Archive Center)

Senior's office at Kykuit, as designed and furnished by Ogden Codman (Courtesy of the Rockefeller Archive Center)

The music room, with its organ, mirrored doors, and Codman's oculus in the center of the ceiling (Courtesy of the Rockefeller Archive Center)

The exterior of Kykuit as completed in 1908 (Courtesy of the Rockefeller Archive Center)

Excavation work for landscape architect Welles Bosworth's terraces and pools, stretching downward from the hilltop on which Kykuit sat (Courtesy of the Rockefeller Archive Center)

The completed terraces, crowned by the long arbor at the west end of the inner garden, with the rock-rimmed swimming pools below (Courtesy of the Rockefeller Archive Center)

The stone teahouse at the east end of the inner garden (Courtesy of the Rockefeller Archive Center)

The interior of the stone teahouse, with its Pompeian furniture and the curtains, the cost of which so annoyed Senior (Courtesy of the Rockefeller Archive Center)

The teahouse and pool in the Japanese garden (Courtesy of the Rockefeller Archive Center)

Kykuit's new entrance façade, with its pediment, elaborate limestone panels, and loggia, designed by Bosworth (Courtesy of the Rockefeller Archive Center)

William Dunson, who oversaw the teams working on the forecourt, often with gun in hand, during the troubled summer of 1912 (Courtesy of the Rockefeller Archive Center)

Junior and Bosworth watching the construction of the Oceanus fountain (Courtesy of the Rockefeller Archive Center)

The view from the front of the house looking out across the lengthened forecourt to the Oceanus fountain (Courtesy of the Rockefeller Archive Center)

The Aphrodite standing in the gardens of Kykuit before she was placed in her circular temple (Courtesy of the Rockefeller Archive Center)

An illustration accompanying a *Harper's Weekly* article on the Ludlow Massacre, depicting Senior watching from afar (*Harper's Weekly Magazine*, May 23, 1914)

Mackenzie King and Junior about to enter the mines in Colorado during the summer of 1915 (Courtesy of the Rockefeller Archive Center)

arrived. Since often no other quarters were available, workers on the water projects and their families lived in labor camps that kept them contained and the neighboring areas "safe." Schools to teach the children during the day and the adults at night were provided, and in addition the Department of Water Supply hired mounted policemen to keep order.

One of the largest camps for the Catskill project was located just a few miles up the road from Pocantico Hills, in the town of Kensico, the site of a key component of the new system: the dam for a huge reservoir that would ultimately flood the town itself and act as a holding tank for the other reservoirs upstream. During the summer of 1912, while Bosworth was doing his drawings for the enlarged forecourt at Kykuit, the Catskill Aqueduct, running to the new reservoir, was almost complete, and construction was scheduled to begin soon on the dam, but between the two projects there would doubtless be workers happy to accept the Rockefellers' wages. With them, however, was likely to come yet another feature of Italian immigrant life: the much-feared Black Hand.

Originating "back home," where mafiosi traditionally offered security against oppressive government officials (and taxes), Black Handers were in fact gangs of extortionists. As Stanislas Pattenza, an Italian immigrant on trial for kidnapping, told his lawyer, "I knew [the Black Hand] before I could even talk . . . Children are brought up to dread it. I was. The Black Hand is everywhere." Yet for the most part the Black Hand in America remained a many-headed, loosely organized phenomenon. To the victims went threatening letters demanding money, usually written in Italian, which most law enforcers could not read. Threats of violence were translated into action with dynamite sticks, easily smuggled out of excavation sites, or with guns, which were even more readily available. Such methods were also used by amateur imitators, sometimes by gangs numbering only a few. Still, they terrorized the Italian immigrants they preyed upon, who were disinclined to trust the police.

By 1905 Black Hand–type crimes were becoming a major concern to law enforcement agencies. The following year, arresting officers found an account book listing extortion payments for labor camps in outlying areas of New York State. In 1909 the *Independent,* a journal of commentary on public affairs, described the phenomenon occurring "especially out on the line of the new aqueduct," and the same year a secret squad was organized by the New York City police to investigate the Black Hand's operations—a squad, according to speculations in the press, financed by a group of private citizens including both Carnegie and Rockefeller. Even before the summer of 1912, too, workers at Kensico went armed to protect themselves from the Black Hand agents, who regularly laid claim to a cut of their pay.

Nor had Kykuit been spared troubles involving its Italian workers. Several years earlier one of the Rockefellers' employees, John Cadenza, had been shot and stabbed by two other Italians at the gates of the estate. According to a *New York Times* account, the killing was caused either by a quarrel over a woman or because Cadenza had refused to "pay up" to a Black Hand "secret society." Senior was staying at the Kent House at the time and was "so horrified," the paper reported, that he wanted the assailants "heavily punished." After several Italian societies in New York and Westchester County retained a lawyer for the trial, however, the men were saved from the electric chair and sent to nearby Sing Sing Prison instead.

In 1910 Rockefeller's secretary had referred, in a letter to him, to the "Italian troubles" among his employees. The following winter, an Italian bank manager in New York City was beaten to death, ostensibly for revealing a plot to blackmail Senior. This happened shortly before Tony Ditto, a "well-to-do" Italian, who lived less than half a mile from Kensico and was rumored in the press to have had trouble with Black Hand operators, was shot in the head close to the Rockefeller estate. Apparently he had gone there expecting trouble; his bull terrier and a fully loaded pistol were found beside his body. A few months later, during the summer of 1911, one of the Italians who had worked on the estate for a short time was jailed for extortion, after having shot someone for turning state's evidence. Separately these incidents may not have been so alarming, but together they were ominous.

How much of this entered Junior's consciousness as he began to organize the extension of the forecourt is hard to tell. As usual, a dozen different matters clamored for his attention, and as trivial as many of them were, they had to be dealt with one way or another. How could it possibly have happened, for example, that a waste pipe from a third-floor bathroom had been run below the ceiling in Cettie's sitting room, and what, if anything, could be done about it? Of all the projects indoors and out, however, enlarging the forecourt remained the most important and ambitious.

Ultimately work on the forecourt increased by as many as two hundred men an estate crew already close to that size. Hiring the added recruits—a significant percentage of whom turned out to be Italian—fell to Briggs.

The going rate in the area, as he told Junior, was two dollars for a ten-hour day, which was enough higher than the $1.75 rate normally paid estate workers to cause friction among the different groups. Loading eight to ten wagons efficiently from widely scattered sites and keeping them moving also meant that the project's success would depend heavily on the foremen directing the work. A key figure in that regard would be William Dunson, an intrepid black southerner, who worked for the estate and was placed in charge of the teams digging and loading the fill. To avoid trouble, he and the other regular estate hands were told not to fraternize with the temporary workers. But inevitably there were delays in the work, leaving the men standing idle, free to gossip and quarrel with one another.

By July of 1912 the situation was alarming enough for Briggs to write Senior. Among other things, one of the carpenters had decided to return to Italy with his brother after receiving threatening letters. Senior's advice was to act cautiously but also to "do what you think best for protection." Rather than have the estate's own people ferret out the "bad element" in the workforce, Briggs decided to engage the services of a Burns Detective Agency "watchman" and an undercover agent. In August the trouble escalated to a rash of hold-ups, and accounts began appearing in the press. One of the Rockefeller foremen, the *New York Times* reported, had fired several workers and hired relatives of his own in their place. The fired workers threatened to "get him," and in a panic he fled "in the night" with his family, after an attempt was made to firebomb his house. Briggs's house was under guard, and the county sheriff had sent in deputies. "It is said that a number of Black Hand men are located at Pocantico Hills," the *Times* continued, adding that the authorities were expecting "trouble to break out among the Italians" momentarily.

At about the same time, nine estate workers were robbed at gunpoint. Then Giuseppe Russo was shot in his vegetable garden, producing front-page headlines. "A veritable Black Hand warfare has broken loose upon the estate of John D. Rockefeller," the *World* declared, claiming the Italian workers were "terror-stricken." Other newspapers reported that Pocantico Hills was "on a martial footing," with "thickset, big-fisted men" questioning all strangers, and in fact the trouble had become serious enough for Briggs to hire fourteen additional armed "watchmen"—like Dunson, blacks from the South. More telling still, Junior decided to interrupt his vacation at Seal Harbor in order to see what he could do himself. One of his objectives was to confer with Detective Burns, with whom he spent an afternoon going over the estate; another was to counteract the grim publicity the events had caused, though his very presence served to fuel rumors. "Son commands Rockefeller Estate Guards," ran one headline, and below it, "Mysterious Man, believed to be Secret Agent, Accompanies Young Mr. Rockefeller."

Hoping to quiet the furor, Junior faced the reporters with a prepared statement. Newspaper accounts of the events were "much exaggerated." The guards were there not to put down trouble but to prevent it. "My father has confidence in his employees and laborers, and the friendliest feeling has always existed between him and them." "A few disgruntled men" should not be allowed, the statement ended, to "intimidate . . . the large number of his men who are loyal and faithful." In answering the questions that followed, Junior said that none of the estate workers belonged to secret societies; that he would not expand on his statement about "jealousy among certain of the men"; that none of the men had been discharged; and that there was no trouble between the men and Briggs. He was also asked about the shooting of Russo, who was, after all, one of the Rockefellers' employees. That had happened, he answered, in an Italian settlement outside of the estate, thereby placing the incident beyond his family's "jurisdiction."

If Junior thought all this would calm matters down, he was wrong. Stories continued to fill the newspapers, including a report that one of the Rockefellers' teamsters, at the end of a day's work, had been held up while a revolver was pointed at his head. By now workers could be seen carrying guns and clubs. Dunson was portrayed as supervising from his rocky ledge with the butt of a rifle sticking out of his pocket, and Briggs was observed walking around with an armed bodyguard. By now, too, attempts were being made to intimidate the Rockefellers themselves.

Just days before minimizing the trouble to the press, Junior had opened a letter from his father's secretary stating, "I deemed it best to say nothing to your father about the receipt of the enclosed letters, bearing on the Italian trouble at Pocantico . . . until I had first referred them to you." Soon newspapers, including the *New York American* and the *Evening World,* informed their readers that Senior and Junior had been threatened with kidnapping or death if they did not pay millions, and with the specter of their $2 million mansion being dynamited. There were also tales of threats to kidnap the grandchildren, two of whom were at the Kent House on the estate, recovering from the measles. According to the stories, the Rockefellers had until September 12 to respond. There were descriptions, as well, of extreme precautions being taken: "The magnificent grounds are to-day bristling with Burns detectives, deputy sheriffs and private watchmen armed with repeating rifles and revolvers, and five savage Great Dane dogs." Junior was reported to be under "heavy guard." The Kent House was cordoned off with guards. The tunnel to the grotto, the *New York Sun* reported, was being used as a secret security base. Both Dunson and Briggs were said to have been threatened with death, "at some convenient time." Meanwhile, no one seemed to know how the threatening letters had been smuggled into the estate by their "eirie [*sic*] couriers." Some were believed to have been mailed, including one from Palermo, but others, according to various accounts, were discovered in such places as the ledge Dunson used to supervise the workers and on the doorstep of Abeyton Lodge.

Despite the "small army" on the estate, the violence continued. When a reputed Black Hander came to collect his "tribute" from John Drago, another estate employee, at his fruit store, both drew guns and a cowboy-style shoot-out ensued in the middle of Tarrytown. It ended when the reputed Black Hander was shot in the leg and limped away while waving his revolver at an excited crowd of bystanders. When the police caught Drago hiding under a barn, he told them that he had had experience with Black Hand agents before, and that it was a case of "give up or shoot." A few days later, one of the guards on the estate wounded an intruder heading for Briggs's house before he escaped and went into hiding.

But this time, like the runaway intruder himself, the whole tangle of violence, threats, rumors, and stories involving the Rockefellers and their Italian workers suddenly began to slip from sight. According to the *New York Times,* the Tarrytown police had been instructed in no uncertain terms to keep the incident involving the intruder under wraps. In answer to speculation that the Rockefeller family was staying away because of the troubles, Sheriff Doyle reported that the grandchildren staying at the Kent House had been taken to Senior's house in New Jersey "for a change of air," adding that stories of armed guards and the Black Hand threats had been "much exaggerated." The *White Plains Record* concluded, too, that though there had been a great many stories, most had "little foundation of fact." In the same vein the *Times* headlined its article about the Rockefellers' absence "Westchester Sheriff Says Threats Do Not Keep Them from Pocantico Hills." Senior and Cettie were at Forest Hill because that was their custom at this time of year, and because Kykuit was not yet finished.

Whatever the truth was—and even now it is hard to tell, for the records preserved in the family papers on the subject are sparse at best—plainly the Rockefellers were determined to minimize the importance of the summer's events. Undercover agents set about questioning all workers with Italian names, but they never publicly came up with much evidence other than identifying one Black Hand agent, a storeowner who suddenly left town. In the end there were only a few arrests. Discussing the estate's regular Italian workers, Senior indicated that some could be promoted to foremen "on our different places," and also that he did not "want the impression to go out" that they were not going to hire Italians or that they were not "kindly disposed" to their loyal workers. By late September Junior was able to report to his father, "We are daily getting new inside information regarding the undesirable Italian element . . . as you can see from the reports . . . there has been no further disorder of any kind for several weeks." In October, when Senior and Cettie, her sister Lute, and their retinue of servants returned to Pocantico from Forest Hill, they were greeted on their way to the Kent House with a fine display of American flags, and when Senior walked around the estate afterward, according to the *Times*, his Italian workers stepped forward, politely doffing their caps. As for the Black Handers, they appeared to have vanished in the mist.

But clearly it was not that simple. Whether masterminded by the Black Hand or not, there had indeed been problems involving the Italian workers on the estate. Some had been threatened with violence, more than a few had been robbed, several wounded, two murdered, and another shot in the stomach and left for dead. For a while, too, the Rockefellers seemed genuinely frightened. Yet Senior's response to bad news about himself and his ventures had always been to proceed as if nothing was wrong and to say, at least for public consumption, as little as possible. Though in time Junior would come to behave quite differently, in this case he chose to do the same, dismissing the events of the summer as little more than a tempest in a teapot, despite all the evidence to the contrary.

Nor did work on Bosworth's forecourt ever stop. All during the turbulence, the wagons continued making their way up to the site, dumping their contents behind the massive stone wall being built to separate the leveled forecourt from the sloping lawns far below. At the same time, too, Bosworth was designing embellishments for the rebuilt entrance facade, which, with its new stone loggia and flattened roofline, needed more and weightier flourishes if it was to be, as Junior said, "the rich end of the house." The irregular stonework of the walls would now be enveloped with applied lime-stone decoration, stretching upward to a heavier, modillioned cornice and a copper roof, blending with those of the garden structures. Also planned were carved, limestone panels above the loggia's arches, wide smooth lime-stone framing for the windows, and a massively adorned pediment filled with reclining classical figures. But perhaps because Bosworth so often found Delano & Aldrich's designs (or their renderings of his) unsatisfac-tory, it was January 1913 before the cuts were made in the exterior walls for the panels, and April before the carving on them was finished.

That was also the month Junior, in an optimistic moment, scheduled the delivery of the furniture to the house, despite the fact that countless de-tails remained to be taken care of inside as well as outdoors. Walls and woodwork needed repainting. Telephones had to be reinstalled, electrical fixtures, push plates, and mirror hooks repositioned, and an improved "an-nunciator" system put in place to direct servants to the rooms where they were needed. Junior and Abby had also continued their visits to "old furni-ture shops," purchasing a pair of tall cabinets supposedly made by John Sheraton for Lord Nelson and a seventeenth-century rug for the music room that had belonged to a "Chinese nobleman." In addition, the trench for the pipes leading from the central heating plant in the coach barn had to be dug, and Bosworth had designed a new, boatlike fountain, with a glass bottom to let in light above the buried service court.

Then there was the statuary Junior and Bosworth continued to collect for the gardens—statuary in traditional, classical style, sparkling with gai-ety in some spots, contemplative in others, with Junior finding as always a deft and sensitive mentor in Bosworth. For a shady niche by the rocky steps that wound down to the grotto room under the classical temple, Janet Scudder created a sprightly bronze Pan. For the niche in the wall backing the orange-tree terrace, Karl Bitter sculpted a "Girl with a Goose." Rudolph Evans, a favorite artist of Bosworth's, who had done several pieces for the Vanderlip estate nearby, was commissioned to fashion something for the inner garden in front of the stone teahouse, an arrangement Junior "drifted into," as he acknowledged to his father when questioned about its cost. He and Abby found Evans's model of a young girl, which the artist proposed to group with a pair of swans, "exceptionally beautiful," but in the end, while the swans were left in place, the female figure was relegated to storage (no doubt in deference to Cettie's feelings because it was nude).

The vast sweep of the newly expanded forecourt had to be appropriately embellished, as well, though as usual Senior's views differed from those of Junior and Bosworth. Studying the plans, he found them overdone. "I clearly recall my own suggestion to Mr. Bosworth, and his favorable response, along the line of treating the forecourt with great simplicity, in part, owing to the fact of the amount of decorations elsewhere in the grounds," he wrote Junior. Yes, Junior agreed, the design for the forecourt should be simple, but because it was now so large and the grounds elsewhere were so elaborate, "it would seem bare and vacant [without] special points of interest." The result, set in rectangular panels of lawn surrounded by nine hundred boxwood bushes, was a pair of pools with fountains flanked by urns on low pedestals and, gracing the entrance of the house, an arrangement of black marble and Tiffany-made glass torches and limestone flower planters.

But most important of all was the eastern end of the forecourt, for which the ever-resourceful Bosworth had "just the thing" in mind: a towering reproduction of a fountain by Giovanni da Bologna in the Boboli Gardens in Florence (illustrated in Wharton's book on Italian gardens). "Monumental" was how Junior described it to his father, and monumental it would be. Standing fully ten feet high, the god Oceanus was to preside over three figures representing the Nile, Euphrates, and Ganges rivers, each holding urns pouring water into a huge granite basin. The basin was to be raised on a seven-and-a-half-foot pedestal, encircled by a marble seat, and bridged at four points over a lower basin. The figures would be sculpted in Europe, and the colossal bowl made from a single piece of granite in Stonington, Maine. Surprisingly enough, considering his argument about simplicity, Senior approved all of this.

Meanwhile, by the summer of 1913, the house itself—if not yet ready for Senior and Cettie—was at least livable enough so that Junior and Abby could go there with their children to enjoy the refurbished surroundings. It was during this time as well that the house acquired the name by which it would be known from then on. Over the years there had been a number of suggestions as to what to call it. "Pocantico Park" was one that had surfaced in 1909, but at that point Junior and Abby were leaning toward something to do with boxwood. "Boxwood House" was proposed, or as an alternative "Boxwood Court," but Junior wrote his mother that he preferred "simply 'Boxwood,' not adding anything else to it," which struck him as "a pretty name . . . not pretentious, but 'homey' and pleasantly suggestive." Perhaps it was the fragility of the boxwood planted in the forecourt at such great expense that eventually killed the idea. "Kykuit," on the other hand, had a long history of being used as a name for the hill on which the house stood, and it related directly to both the view and the land—a true "lookout," as the Dutch word signified. The only difficulty was how to pronounce it, which remains a problem to this day. It also took time to settle on the present spelling. The first recorded use of the word as a name for the house occured in Senior's correspondence rendered as "Kijkuit," which Junior was still using the following year.

Though quieter than the year before, the summer of 1913 was not without problems. On the night of June 30 a fire, starting in the hayloft, severely damaged the coach barn, and earlier that day one of the Italians, Pietro Rebacci, was sentenced to death for a murder apparently related to the previous summer's troubles on the estate. Was there a connection?

Assessing the damage done by the fire, Junior suggested to his father that Bosworth redesign the coach barn to make it more consistent with the house. This time, however, any fresh security measures on the estate were privately handled, and there was little discussion of the fire in the press. But then soon afterward some of the men found a suspicious pile of rags at the Japanese teahouse, and three weeks later the house of Emil Siebern—a sculptor living and working on the estate—was burned down while his wife and children were taking a walk, adding to speculation that an arsonist was at large and prompting the city newspapers once more to send out their reporters. The *New York Times* noted that most of the Italian workers had been "weeded out" after the previous summer's turmoil. Where there had been up to four hundred Italians working on the place, the *Times* recounted, there were now under twenty, though the newspaper failed to note that by then the heavy work on the forecourt had been completed. The *Herald*'s reporter tried to question Kykuit's superintendent, as well as Siebern and the village postmaster, but all were apparently under orders not to talk, indeed not to even admit there had been any fires.

At the same time, in the nation at large labor unrest was gathering momentum among workers of all backgrounds. Growing steadily in strength, the Industrial Workers of the World flatly proclaimed that "the working class and the employing class have nothing in common" and urged workers to "take possession of the earth and the machinery of production and abolish the wage system." Here was a direct and unmistakable challenge to the way people like the Rockefellers habitually handled their employees. Also supporting the workers was the increasingly insistent outcry from sympathizers like the novelist Upton Sinclair. Nor would the Rockefellers escape unscathed from any of this, for within a year labor troubles at Colorado coal mines they owned would bring outraged protestors to the very gates of Kykuit, in response to the deaths of two women and eleven children in the infamous Ludlow massacre.

As fate would have it, too, feelings were nearing fever pitch just as plans were being made for the delivery of the mammoth granite bowl for the Oceanus fountain from Stonington, Maine. Its sheer weight and size alone—more than thirty-five tons in its crate and twenty feet in diameter—would have made moving it a problem. Shipping it down the coast and up the Hudson River was easy enough, but transporting it through Tarrytown involved substantial personal and property liability, requiring negotiations with both the township and the New York Central Railroad, whose tracks would have to be crossed. In the end the Rockefellers were required to provide a $50,000 bond and build a timber and steel bridge across Bedford Road, to protect the Old Croton Aqueduct underneath. But what if the progress of the bowl attracted the attention of protesting "agitators"? A spokesman for George Brown & Company, which handled the bowl's transport, described "alarming rumors . . . prevailing [along with] the actions of a number of lunatics around the Rockefeller Estate" and expressed the hope that before the delivery "these malcontents will have sobered down." Apparently they had not done so, however, for when the bowl reached the dock at Tarrytown, Sheriff Doyle's deputies were called to reinforce the guards after a car rammed Kykuit's gates. More guards were deployed to encircle the "rock" as it embarked along its prescribed route.

Earlier, across the ocean, statuary for the great fountain, copied by European craftsmen, had been packed up in thirteen crates and dispatched to Kykuit via steamer and train, causing still other problems, though none involving labor issues, for Bosworth had misjudged the size of the three "Rivers" as a result of working from a photograph. To Junior's intense annoyance, they had to undergo major alterations, costing over $14,000. Nonetheless all thirteen crates of sculpture were unpacked, waiting for the giant bowl as it made its slow, majestic way, on wooden planks and rollers, up from the dock on the Hudson, over the railroad tracks and the Old Croton Aqueduct, onto the grounds of the estate, and finally through the gates of Kykuit to the end of the forecourt. Watched by clusters of curious onlookers, its journey was a palpable reminder of just how rich and powerful the Rockefellers were, and in the end no angry protests blocked its progress. Yet that hardly meant the peace the family seemed so eager to proclaim had actually dawned.

As imposing as it was, the enormous Oceanus fountain was not the last major piece of sculpture intended for Kykuit. At the end of the garden's north–south axis the "Temple of Love" still stood empty, but Bosworth had long envisioned placing there a particularly beguiling statue of Aphrodite—"certified to be the work of Praxiteles"—that had first captured the attention of New York connoisseurs when it was shown at the National Arts Club in 1905. Himself a member of the club, Bosworth had witnessed firsthand the excitement over the statue. The gallery "was thronged every hour," according to the *New York Herald,* while the *Craftsman* reported, "All literary and artistic New York has flocked to see her . . . with her willowy grace, her satiny gold surface and her dreamy wistfulness of expression." Later, the *New York Times* would recall that it was one of the few artworks "that ever wrought up the people of this town to [such] a pitch of wild and undisciplined excitement." Admirers wrote odes to the statue and placed flowers at its feet. Only the Armory Show of 1913 would cause a greater sensation.

Skeptics tended to attribute the fuss less to the statue's beauty than to its mysterious origins. Was it truly Praxiteles, the famed Athenean of the city's golden age, who had carved it? Or was it, as some experts said, the work of Nikias, a contemporary of Praxiteles? The marble, after all, "undoubtedly" came from the island of Páros, where Nikias lived and worked, and he was known to have used hot gum on his statues to make them more lifelike, which could have produced the Aphrodite's golden color. Yet from the beginning the acting director of the Metropolitan Museum of Art had refused to exhibit the statue, citing its questionable past. A Mr. Cookman had also stepped forward to point out a remarkable resemblance between this work and one he had seen purchased at a fire sale in New Jersey and then boiled in chemical solutions by an insurance adjuster to get rid of its scorch marks, giving it an overall golden hue. There were other theories, as well. Perhaps it was a Renaissance copy of the Medici Venus—or even a modern copy.

What was known for a fact was that the statue had been part of a collection belonging to Augustus C. Linton that was seized by a creditor to settle a $6,000 debt and sold for $100. That was five years before the Aphrodite went on display, and only after Cookman's story began to circulate did Linton discuss the statue's provenance, claiming he had bought it on a boat in Italy from two sailors. Another version of the tale had him going to an Italian ship, moored in the Thames River, to see "a great work of art," which he then bought "after an extended investigation." Beyond those facts he was sworn to secrecy by the seller. In any case, when the New York exhibition was over, the statue was put in storage at the Arts Club.

Yet Bosworth remembered it, and who but the richest man in the world should own such a work, unique for its age and condition, and possibly carved by the hand of the great Praxiteles himself? He took Junior to see the statue, and at some point negotiations were quietly begun through an intermediary with Augustus Linton's son, Charles, who now owned the statue. By the fall of 1909 it had become collateral for a loan to Linton fils, and Junior was confident enough that he could acquire it to ask Bosworth to have it moved to Lincoln Storage. But then new buyers suddenly appeared on the scene, and the statue was whisked away to England to become the property of a pair of British carpet merchants, for an alleged $30,000. Regretfully, Junior had a terra-cotta Flora made up to occupy the empty temple instead.

That might have been the end of it, but in October 1913 Bosworth heard that "with a little careful negotiation" the Aphrodite might still be purchased. A year later, after war had broken out in Europe, he was even more certain of their chances and suggested a price of $70,000. Rumor had it the wife of one of the rug merchants disliked the statue and had consigned it to the basement. Bosworth wrote Junior all this in November 1914, adding that he was sure Junior and Abby would agree it was "one of the great things in the world which is now possible to obtain." Still, Junior proceeded cautiously. "I understood from you the other day that the statue was a white elephant on the hands of the owner, whose wife . . . will not let him take it out of the cellar," he commented dryly.

But as usual Bosworth prevailed, though arriving at a mutually agreeable price took until the end of June 1915. A month later the Aphrodite sailed into New York Harbor on the steamer *Saxonia* and reached her new home above the Hudson River the following day. Her purchase and mysterious history made headlines. Accounts ranged from straightforward narrative to the comic. Ran the headline of the *Evening Mail's* article, "Aphrodite, No Nightie, Bought by John D., Oil Man Mighty." But in a more somber vein, the *Herald* reminded its readers that this was not just any rich man's purchase, for the Aphrodite's eyes, "whose marble wistfulness sent critics into raptures," were about to look out on a world quite different from the one she had known, "totally unfamiliar with the I.W.W.," as she was. Yet perhaps, the article continued, "the goddess of love [could] . . . stand sentry to protect the younger generation of Rockefellers against intruders upon their beautiful grounds."

Meanwhile, up on the hill at Kykuit the statue lingered on its side for another few months, waiting for a temporary pedestal. At that point more than a year and a half had passed since Senior and Cettie moved back into the rebuilt house, and by all accounts they seemed satisfied, a fact the Aphrodite could also have been taken to symbolize. For here was the great gift Junior had wanted to give his parents: classical beauty incarnate, as perfect in its timeless repose as he had dreamed of making Kykuit itself.

Even with the work complete, or nearly so, however, that hoped-for serenity remained at best an elusive entity. The decade of the house's building had seen a constant struggle between Junior and his father over almost everything about the place. How deep was the breach between them, and how was it to be healed? More serious still, visions of timeless repose had also had to confront a world of violence that could not, finally, be shut out of Kykuit's gates. Shootings, fires, robberies, the Black Hand, threats against the family, the IWW, angry protests on every front; as hard as the Rockefellers tried to deny the reality of it all, they could not. At issue, too, whether they saw it or not, was nothing less than the entire capitalist system, which had created not only the great fortune that built Kykuit, but also the conditions that forced immigrant workers to accept—for ten hours of backbreaking, dangerous labor—a mere two dollars a day and to live in constant fear in the disorderly camps to which they were consigned.

Nor was it simply a matter of compassion. When people were injured before their eyes, the Rockefellers could be as compassionate as anyone might wish, as Junior proved during the accident with the steel beams in the autumn of 1911. It was, rather, the larger, more basic issues that seemed to escape them. If the Aphrodite stood for love and beauty, the truth was little enough of either touched the lives of a great many of those who worked to build Kykuit. Yet this was also the place that Junior had hoped would help show that the Rockefellers cared for more than just money and power—a house, as he said, meant to delight not only "those who appreciated fine design and were familiar with beautiful furnishings" but "friends . . . coming from no matter how humble an environment." For all the appeal of that view, however, who could tell where such "friends" were to be found?

On that point the house stood mute, at its side the gentle Aphrodite, but before it the gigantic Oceanus, starkly etched in all its baroque might against the sky—two potent symbols, each with its own meaning, yet radically different from each other: the power of love and compassion versus the power of sheer, unadulterated strength, with figuratively, at least, no common ground to unite them. Bosworth had provided the design, yet the task of finding that common ground lay beyond his art. If it belonged to anyone, it belonged to the Rockefellers—and above all to Junior.

7

Settling Up

According to the nurse who was with her at the time, she departed life "with a look of the most perfect peace and comfort and happiness lighting her face." Her husband and son, both away in Florida, had been assured that her condition was "improving." A specialist had said so, and she herself sent the telegram. She even mentioned the beautiful weather they were having and described an outing, "which does me much good." Much good, but not enough, as it turned out. She died early the following day.

Just six months before, there had been a combined celebration of her seventy-fifth birthday and their golden wedding anniversary. Now there would be no more birthdays or anniversaries to mark the crowded, busy years of their life together. For her, truly, it had all ended.

No doubt if she had had her way it would have happened in that house she had always loved better than any other. But two years earlier her husband, enraged at the extra taxes he was charged because of staying there longer than usual due to her ill health, had declared that he was through with the place. So instead the end came in the new house, the one their son had built for them. And in truth it was probably not a bad place to die. She had come to like it better once it was rebuilt. Still, it could never be what that other house had been, just as the memories the family had of it would now include her hardly at all, except as an invalid, slowly slipping from life.

For all the calm surrounding Cettie Rockefeller's death, which occurred at Kykuit on March 12, 1915, it marked definitively the end of an era for her family. A brief service was held at the house immediately afterward, but because of Senior's tax problems in Cleveland her burial in that city's Lakeview Cemetery had to be postponed for four months. When it finally took place—cloaked in secrecy—Senior, her sister Lute, and her daughter Alta were there to see her into her grave, yet the Rockefellers never again spent time at Forest Hill. Kykuit had become Senior's principal residence; and as if to mark the fact, two years later Cettie's place of places, "dear old Forest Hill," burned to the ground.

Meanwhile, 1915 also saw the work at Kykuit essentially complete, the gardens in the end having taken longer than anything else. For much of the year statuary for them was still being chosen, including the Aphrodite. There were other, smaller details to attend to as well: minor garden ornaments to order, along with bronze fittings for the fountains and winter covers for stone items of all kinds outdoors. Yet basically the job was finished, at least to the point where Junior felt able to send his father final figures for the cost of the entire project.

Doubtless he did so with considerable trepidation, not least because along with his accounting he included a request for a $20,000 payment to Bosworth, over and above what his contract stipulated, for the extra work he had done. But if Senior found that detail annoying, there was, after all, far more in the figures to give him pause than the unanticipated expenditure of a mere $20,000. The total cost of the house and gardens together, as Junior calculated it, was $2,770,603.16. Of that amount, the house accounted for $1,115,555.23; the gardens $1,360,413.19. The remainder, just over $233,000, had been spent on various outbuildings, chiefly the coach barn, the orangerie, and the laundry.

By any calculation these numbers far exceeded anything anyone had estimated beforehand. In the case of the house the final cost stood at almost four times the figure stipulated in the original contract with Thompson-Starrett. It was with the gardens, however, that the overrun reached truly stunning proportions. When the project was still in the planning stages Senior had spoken of spending as much as $30,000 on them. This was a rough guess, hastily made. The reality, however, totaled fully forty-five times that figure.

While the work was going on, Senior had voiced his anxiety about the level of expenses often and at times with genuine anger. The endlessly rising cost of the gardens was a particularly sore subject. In business such reckless extravagance would never have been tolerated. But this was not business, and somehow all Senior's complaints failed completely to change things; as Junior's figures proved, the river of expense had rushed endlessly onward. Even when Senior dug in his heels with the utmost will, as he had done over the curtains for the teahouse, it made no difference. Sooner or later, like everything else, the curtains appeared anyway, just as Bosworth decreed. Indeed, in that mild-mannered landscape architect it almost seemed as if Rockefeller, the battle-scarred veteran of a lifetime spent fighting successfully for control in business, had finally met his match.

The truth was, of course, that Bosworth was not the problem. Junior was. If the ideas—that beguiling vision of an enchanting world stretching out and downward from the house—were Bosworth's, it was Junior who embraced the vision and set it on track to becoming reality. Item by item he had approved it, sending the proposals along to Senior, unfailingly urging their adoption. And in the absence of a detailed, overall plan for the gardens, Senior had found himself in the difficult position of continually confronting a moving target. Just as he took aim at one proposal, another came along, then another, and another after that.

Following the decision to rebuild the house, he had also been much absorbed with his own projects at Kykuit: the service tunnel to the subbasement, switching the heating plant to the coach barn, and adding the baggage cart to the elevator. By then, too, Cettie's health was steadily deteriorating, and given how little she had liked the house initially, he might even have been hoping that larger, ever more elaborate gardens would help reconcile her to the place. As much as he claimed to deplore the expense involved, he never actually did what he had once threatened to do and could easily have done at any moment: simply call a halt to all further garden building at Kykuit.

He did continue to complain, however, and added to all the "needless" expense, he worried about what the cost of Kykuit might do to the family's reputation. In 1910, in a particularly testy letter to Junior about the gardens he ended by declaring, "I should not want the public to know what our expenditure has been." But if that was what worried him, a year later, on May 15, 1911, the Supreme Court handed down its decision upholding the dissolution of the Standard Oil trust. In effect, the people of the United States, acting through the institutions of the federal government, had scuttled Senior's greatest creation, the capstone of his business career. After that, what was there left to fear from the public's wrath, or its dismay at the cost of Kykuit's gardens, if such a thing could be imagined?

Also, as luck would have it, the breakup of Standard Oil mandated by the courts—whatever it did to Senior's pride—injured him not one whit in a material way. Quite the reverse. By the autumn of 1913 the soaring prices of stock in the individual companies spun off from the Standard behemoth had pushed his net worth to $900 million. Meanwhile, the same companies had been paying dividends averaging 53 percent of the capital value of Standard's old stock. A cynic might have pointed out that compared to such figures the expenditure of an extra million or two on Kykuit hardly amounted to a ripple on the surface of a vast sea.

The cynic would have been wrong, however, even if one recognizes that $900 million equals something like $14 billion in today's currency. For ultimately, Senior's constant grumbling over the cost of building Kykuit was only partially about money, as were his criticisms of Bosworth's "luxurious" methods and fondness for "experimenting" at the Rockefellers' expense. Equally upsetting was the kind of place Kykuit had become, and again, Junior, not Bosworth, was to blame for that.

Nor did any of Senior's complaints bear on an entirely different set of issues raised by Kykuit's building—issues that in fact both he and Junior had done their best to ignore. For the violence that had plagued the end of the building process was also part of what the place had cost the Rockefellers, and eventually it too would have to be weighed in the balance.

Early in 1907, Junior had written Charles W. Leavitt Jr., who at that point was being considered as a possible garden-planner at Kykuit, "we do not want anything elaborate or fussy, but rather something simple and dignified." The same phrases could easily have come from Senior's own pen, suggesting that, at bottom, the two agreed about what they hoped to see Kykuit become, and in a sense they did. Where they parted company, and sharply, was over the details of that larger vision. Yet houses and gardens, as they take shape on the ground, are quintessentially collections of details, hundreds upon hundreds of them. Kykuit had first emerged in Senior's design for it, but in the process of making decisions about the myriads of details that design did not include, Junior had produced a place quite unlike the one his father envisioned. This he had done, furthermore, knowing full well what the result of his actions would be.

Invariably he combined his "suggestions" with assurances that though they might be more ambitious and more expensive than what was initially planned, they would make the place better, more comfortable, more pleasing to his parents. In cases where the task of persuading Senior became particularly difficult, he added that the result, grand as it promised to be, was only what his father deserved. Thus he had declared in answer to a letter of Senior's, written early in 1908, complaining about what he considered unnecessary tree planting and masonry work on the north side of the house: "I have felt throughout that in view of the immense amount of money which you are constantly giving away to others and in view of the infinitesimal amount which you have spent for your own pleasure and enjoyment in your life, it was not inappropriate that you should have for yourself and for Mother a place which would give you all the pleasure which could possibly be secured."

Whatever Senior thought of the picture of himself provided with "all the pleasure which could possibly be secured," there was no mistaking the respect and affection his son's words were meant to convey. By the same token, his own remarks about the work, including his perpetual strictures about costs, invariably carried with them warm expressions of gratitude and affection. Even problems like the malfunctioning chimneys in the house as originally built failed to change the pattern. "I know you have given infinite pains and careful attention not only to this but to every other detail of the construction, and have done much better than I could possibly have done," wrote Senior about the chimney problem.

Polite fictions, concocted with an eye to avoiding what could have been a serious rift between father and son? Perhaps, but such statements seem at least as genuine as the rest of what the two had to say to each other. The bonds uniting them were deep and strong. If their remarks were less than wholly candid at times, it is not enough to describe them as polite fictions; they were, indeed, loving fictions. Still, the fact remained that step-by-step Junior had—to put it bluntly—willfully and systematically sabotaged his father's plans for Kykuit.

This at any rate is the story the written record tells. Kykuit itself presents a more ambiguous picture. If it was emphatically not the place Senior had planned, neither did it ever become quite what Junior would have built left to his own devices. Above all, the structure decreed by Senior's original ground-floor plan steadfastly resisted annihilation. Even embellished with Codman's innumerable "touches" and embowered on every side by Bosworth's lavish banquet of gardens, it survived at the center, the essential core of the place, the immutable genome of its identity. So on that level, Senior had in fact prevailed.

But Andrew Jackson Downing's influence had not. At no point could Kykuit have been confused with the sort of relaxed, unpretentious rural villa he had celebrated with such enthusiasm. Ordered and formal, unmistakably a country house, not simply a house in the country, it owed its style forthrightly to the eighteenth century and beyond that to Renaissance classicism. Junior had seen to that, Junior and his designers, Codman and Bosworth.

Inevitably, too, the combination of Senior's plan and Junior's changes and additions had produced some odd effects. With its walls run up another two full stories after 1910 and its front facade thrust forward and stripped of its porches, the house looked taller and narrower than ever, and from some angles even more awkwardly perched on its hilltop site. Then there was the joint appearance, ornamenting the same facade, of the twin groups of basket-bearing cherubs and the great carved eagle, clutching its shield emblazoned with the Rockefeller cipher. Precisely what those pieces of sculpture, together, were meant to convey remains unfathomable. Nor did Bosworth's gardens in their original form always achieve the air of stately repose that makes them so appealing today. On the contrary, photographs taken at the time tend to reveal, at least at some points, precisely the kind of overelaborate fussiness Junior said he wished to avoid. It is the Italian bones of the gardens, minus their more exotic Moorish elements, that continue to work their magic, along with Nelson Rockefeller's brilliantly placed collection of modern sculpture.

Inside the house as well there were some less than wholly successful moments. In most of the ground-floor rooms, Codman's architectural details, if historically correct, seem a bit flat and sparse, especially covered with the dull cream paint used throughout the house. Executed in wood instead of plaster, as they are in the office, they appear to better effect. Also problematic is the music room, only there the combination of the oculus with the mirrored doors and the organ pipes—all encased in garlanded, arched surrounds—proved to be too dense and heavy for the space. (Many of those elements are gone today; though for the sake of historical accuracy, it might make sense to restore them.)

Yet what remains most memorable and attractive about Kykuit is its relatively modest scale combined with the prevailing restraint of its decoration. It is indeed that remarkably *unostentatious* place the *New York Times* would describe in 1994 when the house was first opened to the public. Such aristocratic pretensions as it has pale in comparison with those of dozens of other American houses of the period. There is nothing palatial about its rooms in size, arrangement, or style. Eschewing the French idiom Codman generally preferred, they follow instead English eighteenth-century taste, but they looked for their prototypes not to vast piles like Blenheim or Castle Howard, but to the solid, foursquare houses of the British gentry. There is not an inch of gilt anywhere at Kykuit. Marble appears only in its mantles and a few of its floors. And setting the stage for it all, the entrance hall—even with Codman's vaulted ceiling—remains as it was in Senior's original plan, not particularly wide or long, with no grand stairway to serve as a cynosure. Bosworth's gardens also succeed to an impressive degree in combining formality with looser, more picturesque elements, especially as one moves down the hill, away from the house. As he managed it, too, the union between the two styles is virtually seamless, a tribute to his skill, and one that suggests that as expensive as the gardens seemed, Senior had not, in the end, paid too much for them.

In all of these ways, in fact, it is tempting to think of Kykuit as a compromise between Senior's desires and Junior's, but the terms of the compromise have to be rather carefully drawn. While Junior would doubtless have preferred a larger, grander house, he was no more inclined than his father to favor gilt and marble. It was not keeping up with the Vanderbilts that concerned him, but Ida Tarbell's characterization of Senior as a penny-pinching cretin, oblivious to all that was noble and good in Western civilization. What he had hoped to build was a suitable home for an American gentleman of means, not a palace. Nor was he alone in harboring such hopes, as other American houses dating from those years attest.

A good example is Gwinn, a house built about the same time as Kykuit (1907–09), by William Gwinn Mather, a Cleveland industrialist who had made a fortune in the iron ore business. Located on a bluff high above the southern shore of Lake Erie in the fashionable community of Bratenahl, it was designed by Charles Platt, the author of the pathbreaking book on Italian gardens who went on to design country houses in addition to gardens. Though there was no direct connection between them, Gwinn and Kykuit resembled each other in a number of ways. As at Kykuit, the entrance to Gwinn lay at the narrow end of an elongated, rectangular block. The two houses also had similar ground-floor plans, opening up inside to spectacular views, Kykuit's of the river, Gwinn's of the lake. Like Kykuit, too, Gwinn was surrounded by extensive gardens, formal near the house, and more "natural" moving away from it. By a further coincidence, Gwinn's naturalistic gardens were designed by Warren H. Manning, who had worked at Senior's Pocantico Hills estate in the 1890s. And in yet another connection, at the time Senior was considering rebuilding Kykuit, his daughter Edith McCormick had suggested that he consult Charles Platt, who had just designed a house for her on Lake Michigan. Senior, however, decided to stick with the architects he had.

For William Mather too, building turned out to be a costly proposition. Though his fortune amounted to only a fraction of Rockefeller's, and Gwinn was notably smaller than Kykuit, his original budget of $55,000 rapidly climbed to $80,000, then $146,000, and continued to rise. In 1911 alone he laid out more for garden ornaments, plantings, and paintings than he had once hoped to spend on the entire estate. Yet like Rockefeller he fretted constantly about expenses. "I am afraid of the cost," he wrote at one point. He also declared himself to be not in the least interested in opulence of any sort. "I would be careful not to have it in the slightest degree extravagant," he warned Platt, who at that point was selecting furniture for the house.

Still, for all of Mather's anxiety, Gwinn turned out to be a great success. Not only did it delight him personally, but it was also enthusiastically praised in a wide variety of publications, including several books on American country houses and their gardens. One of the more fulsome notices appeared in the prestigious British magazine *Country Life*, where Platt's creation was described as "full of an aesthetic magnetism" yet done in a "straightforward, wholesome and distinguished manner—a manner as direct as it is unaffected." All of which echoed perfectly what he himself believed a country house ought to be: "built upon models of good tradition . . . having a sense of style . . . as restful as the lines of its suitable and elegant garden."

Measured restraint in all things. That was Platt's message as well as Gwinn's. For like Kykuit, it swept up its skirts and glided serenely by all the more obvious forms of palatial grandeur along with every variety of architectural novelty or quaintness. And for those who might still have missed the point, Platt was ready with a witty description of the opposite of his lofty standard: the typical Victorian house, which he labeled "the dime novel of architecture . . . a much begabled house, prodigal in lattices and window seats, charged upon by a riot of flower beds, and surrounded by nooks and walks."

Places like Platt's typical Victorian house, of course, were exactly what John D. Rockefeller Sr. most admired, and what Kykuit never became. How much, finally, did he care? Given everything left unsaid between him and Junior, it is difficult to know. He may well have seen Gwinn. If so, perhaps it helped reconcile him to the process by which his own architectural preferences were maneuvered farther and farther into the background. But whatever role Gwinn played, it could not have been large. The issues at stake were too complex, and too deeply embedded in the relationship between father and son, to have been resolved by a house on Lake Erie built by someone else.

Yet ultimately a resolution did occur, and it was Senior who took the initiative, for even before the work on Kykuit ended, his complaints had ceased. The critical point may have come as early as the summer of 1913 with the Oceanus fountain. Initial estimates put its cost at not less than $60,000. Gingerly, Junior informed his father, but the very next day the reply came back, with no note of caution, no suggestion that they try something simpler, cheaper, not the least hint of concern. "Do as you think best about the expenditure for a central fountain for forecourt," Junior was told. Considering the amount of money involved, it was an enormous concession. Nor in the months ahead did Senior's attitude change. Except for balking a bit at the cost of the Aphrodite, he posed no further objections to any of Junior's plans for either the house or the gardens. It was as if a curtain had been drawn on the past and the multiple tensions the years of building had entailed.

So Junior had won after all. If Kykuit was not everything he and Abby once hoped it would be, it came close enough. And he had cared enough about building it his way, and not Senior's, to risk all that he risked in the process, including his father's at times quite palpable disapproval, which in turn made of his performance something bold and courageous, indeed as daring in its own way as the sort of coup de main with which Senior had so often astounded the business world. But if there were moments of genuine ruthlessness in the performance—and there were—it was Delano & Aldrich, not Senior, that bore the brunt of most of them.

Junior had also never stopped stressing that what they were doing at Kykuit was the *right* thing to do. Senior might not have agreed, but it was hard to ignore the moral fervor of his son's arguments, and who could say that he was wrong? The world had changed immeasurably since the days when Standard Oil was fighting for control of Cleveland's oil refineries. Practices that had once been considered good business were now condemned, even treated as criminal offenses by the courts. On the other hand, the extravagances of the rich that Senior had always found so deplorable seemed to be more and more accepted, as long as they were thought to be in "good taste," and if he had difficulty understanding what constituted good taste, Junior and Abby were sure they knew.

In sum, battling for Kykuit's soul had been a contest full of meaning for both father and son. By matching Senior's will with an even stronger determination of his own, Junior had proven that he was capable of such behavior and that the sky did not fall, the world did not end, as a result. These were heady lessons, as was their corollary: that for the first time he, and not his father or Frederick Gates or anyone else, had truly taken command. And for Senior's part, accepting Kykuit as it was, without further complaints, amounted to a tacit acknowledgment of his son's achievement.

More important still, what happened at Kykuit proved to be just the beginning. Even before the project was finished, Junior was moving decisively on other fronts to assert his independence, to extend his authority. In 1908, for example, he was accused by Hearst's *New York American* of ordering the construction of a "peonage stockade" to keep the workers of the Corn Products Refining Company, in which he was a shareholder, from escaping, a charge that was patently false. In such situations Senior had followed a policy of silence regardless of the truth of the matter. Yet Junior decided to sue the *American* for libel, and he won.

The year after the libel suit found him again embroiled in legal activities, though of a very different kind. With the "white slave traffic" having become a major issue in New York City politics, he was picked to serve as the foreman of a grand jury charged with investigating the subject. The Tammany forces that had engineered his appointment doubtless expected nothing more than a brief report laced with harmless pieties. Instead— chiefly due to Junior's efforts—the grand jury filed a closely argued, fact-filled presentment that eventually led to fifty-four indictments. "I never worked harder in my life," he remarked later. Nor did his efforts go unnoticed. "He has bumped up against one of the real things of life . . . He has shown himself very much of a man and even more of a good citizen," commented the *Cleveland Leader*.

About the same time the grand jury presentment was filed, Junior also resolved a personal issue of much longer standing in his life. Soon after graduating from Brown, he had accepted a seat on Standard Oil's board of directors, and later he became one of its vice presidents. Yet over the years he had grown increasingly unhappy about his connection with the company his father had founded, especially after he learned of its under-the-table efforts to influence politicians. Finally, in 1910, he decided to resign from the Standard board, along with all but one of his other corporate directorships. Afterward, he would describe this as "one of the most important decisions" of his life. For the most part the press applauded his action, but what he cared most about was his father's reaction. As it turned out he need not have worried. "John," Senior had said when he was told, "I want you to do what you think is right," which was exactly what he had done.

But even when his father was not so accommodating, Junior would go his own way if it mattered enough to him, as he did over what became one of the great passions of his life: collecting Chinese porcelains, a subject that combined the same kinds of questions about money and aesthetic judgment that Kykuit had. By his own admission, prior to 1913 Junior had no hobbies, but that year he bought a pair of Black Hawthorne vases, the beginning of a collection that came to include hundreds of pieces, focusing in particular on porcelains crafted during the Ch'ing Dynasty, in the reign of Emperor K'ang Hsi (1662–1723). Though he bought steadily over the years, the core of the collection was formed in 1915, when he acquired a large number of pieces from the estate of J. P. Morgan. Since the price was high—almost $2 million—he turned to his father for a loan, explaining that he had studied the matter carefully and believed that "such an opportunity to secure the finest examples of Chinese porcelains can never come again."

Unpersuaded, Senior did his best to discourage the purchase. "I feel afraid of it," he wrote. "It would seem to me that it would be wiser not to make this investment now." But Junior was not talking about an investment. Determined to have his way, in an extraordinary letter he poured out his heart to his father: "I have never squandered money on horses, yachts, automobiles or other foolish extravagances. A fondness for these porcelains is my only hobby—the only thing for which I have cared to spend money." Pointing out that collecting porcelain was both "unostentatious and not sensational," he ended by declaring that as much as he wanted "these works of art," he wanted even more to have his father "fully approve" of what he was doing. And evidently his appeal worked, for Senior advanced him the necessary funds, and not as a loan but as a gift.

Yet the year that began with that singular victory was also to test Junior's resolve on far more serious issues, in an arena light-years away from the coolly elegant scenes of Manchu court life depicted on Ch'ing Dynasty vases.

The lone corporate directorship Junior had chosen to hold on to in 1910, when he left Standard's board and the others on which he served, was in Colorado Fuel and Iron. He did so because the Rockefellers owned a controlling interest in CFI, having purchased it with part of the proceeds from the sale of the Mesabi mines to U.S. Steel. At the time it had looked like a promising investment, but to date the company had paid no dividends at all. Equally serious was the abysmal state of its labor relations. Not only were the working conditions appalling, but management steadfastly resisted all attempts at unionization.

In 1913 matters came to a head when the United Mine Workers of America decided to launch a full-scale campaign to organize Colorado's miners. The president of CFI at that point was Lamont Bowers, Frederick Gates's uncle, who had initially supervised Kykuit's construction. An implacable foe of unionization, he responded to UMW's efforts by hiring—with the Rockefellers' approval—armed guards to "protect" the company's interests, and when nine thousand of its workers went out on strike, he declared his intention to resist "until our bones [are] bleached as white as the chalk in these Rocky Mountains." In reality, however, events would rapidly render irrelevant all such pronouncements. The flashpoint came in a tent colony at a CFI mine in Ludlow, Colorado, where open warfare broke out between the miners and National Guard militiamen. Which side fired first would never be known, but when the day was over several strikers lay dead. Worse still, as a result of an attempt by the militiamen to burn the colony down, two women and eleven children—hiding in a hastily dug pit under one of the tents—had lost their lives.

Junior's initial response to the events at Ludlow amounted to a bizarre act of denial not at all unlike his earlier, head-in-the-sand reaction to the difficulties facing Kykuit's Italian workers. Arguing that the women and children had died because of the miners' efforts to protect them, he wrote in a memo for his files: "There was no Ludlow Massacre." But the rest of the world thought otherwise. The public outcry was immense. Led by Emma Goldman, crowds of furious protestors marched on Kykuit, and in the midst of a rally outside the Rockefeller family offices at 26 Broadway one irate speaker demanded that Junior be shot down "like a dog." For the moment he stood firm, at least in public. Yet privately he had begun to waiver, and before long he was rethinking his entire position.

Crucial to that effort was his relationship with Mackenzie King, a former labor minister and future prime minister of Canada. The two had met through the Rockefeller Foundation and eventually became fast friends, though at the moment what Junior needed most was advice on how to handle the situation in Colorado. King's recommendation was emphatic: establish a board "on which both employers and employed are represented" to handle relations between labor and management. In principle Junior accepted the recommendation, but to get to that point he had to contend with the intransigence of both his father and CFI's management in Colorado. He was also compelled to testify on two separate occasions before a specially appointed federal commission on labor relations. Yet through it all King nudged him steadily onward and then joined him in what became the denouement of the affair: a trip the two made together to Colorado in September of 1915.

By then the strike had ended, but the purpose of the trip was to win acceptance by CFI's workers of the "Colorado Industrial Plan," which called for a permanent system of worker representation in dealings with management. To pave the way for the plan's adoption, it became necessary for Junior to fire Lamont Bowers in a particularly unpleasant interview. He also visited every one of CFI's eighteen mines, where he talked openly and informally with the miners, an experience that by all accounts he thoroughly enjoyed, including the time he spent dancing with the wives of the company's employees at one of the camps. The climax came with the adoption of what had now become the "Rockefeller Plan" by an overwhelming majority of CFI's labor force, voting by secret ballot.

In essence, the plan established a company union, which placed it well behind the vanguard of the American labor movement. Yet it did recognize the right of workers to organize and bargain collectively, which had been anathema to both CFI's management and John D. Rockefeller Sr. As for Junior's trip to Colorado, Senior had opposed it and had advised his son's secretary to carry a gun. But when it was all over he seemed to accept the outcome readily enough, quipping, "Yes, it was excellent. I could not have managed it better myself." Junior took a more serious view. For the rest of his life he would consider the Colorado strike a major milestone in his own development as well as "one of the most important things that ever happened to the Rockefeller family." On both counts he was right.

Along with Mackenzie King, Abby had played a central role in shaping Junior's actions. One of her letters in particular stands out. In the autumn of 1914, with memories of the events at Ludlow still painfully fresh, she wrote urging him to "more and more," as she said, "leave to me the petty details of houses, places, etc., and throw yourself into the big, vital questions that come before you . . . No one else can do the big things as well as you can." And while he was in Colorado, she made her meaning even clearer: "If you can help bring about a solution of the labor problem . . . I shall die satisfied . . . I know that this is only one of the first steps . . . but . . . it is in absolutely the right direction."

During the grim days when Junior was trying to forge an adequate response to the events at Ludlow in testimony before the Industrial Relations Commission, Mackenzie King had written him, putting Abby's gentle prompting in even stronger terms: "It seems to me you will have to lead, have to be the example, whether you will or not." There was a time in his life when such advice would have left him numb with terror. Every instinct he possessed would have told him that he was not born to lead. That was his father's role; his was to help in every way he could, to do whatever needed to be done, to smooth the way, to lighten the enormous burden Senior bore and could never lay down.

Happily for his sake the individual who received King's advice was not that person. Events had changed Junior, yet he had also played an important role in the process himself, and it began at Kykuit, where, for the first time, he took tenacious hold of a piece of his father's infinitely complex, endlessly ramifying universe. Granted, it was only a house, a small item in the great scheme of things, yet precisely because that was so, it had been a good point at which to begin, a useful launching platform. Had Junior himself sensed this? If not in the beginning, he certainly seems to have by the end, as did Abby.

Even more puzzling, however, is what Senior thought of it all. That he ended by acquiescing is clear. But why did he? What moved him to accept so much that flew in the face of so many deeply held beliefs? Ultimately two emotions seem to have been uppermost in his mind: concern for his family and concern for Junior in particular. By the beginning of 1905 his only son had reached a state of near total emotional collapse. Something had to be done, and for the moment what Junior himself seemed to want to do more than anything else was build his father a house. So why not let him and see what happened? Senior's own coming-of-age had been marked by building a house for his parents—a neat brick residence that he managed to get built on time and on budget. Could history be made to repeat itself?

As for the Rockefeller family, Senior understood full well the magnitude of the crisis facing its members: the public opprobrium, the near paralytic anxiety it produced in his children, his wife, even, at times, himself. For that reason, too, something had to be done, yet he was astute enough to know he could not do it himself; nor could it be anything like a replay of his career. To attempt such a thing would only make matters worse. It was a new century, a totally different world. If the future of the family was not to be left in the hands of paid employees—with all that implied—Junior would have to take charge and discover for himself what the problems were and where the solutions lay.

Most of all, he would have to decide how, finally, to make the Rockefeller name and fortune stand for something other than unbridled greed, which is exactly what he worked to do both at Kykuit and in Colorado. By going to the mines himself, in person (a month before sending Senior the final figures for the cost of building Kykuit), he managed to bring capital and labor together and assist in the creation of a system that was more than just a response to a single tragic event. Similarly, by proclaiming, as he had through Kykuit (as it grew to be), his allegiance to all "the best" architectural models while steadfastly avoiding the merely grand and opulent, he had produced a memorable result—a house not at all unlike those the architectural critic Herbert Croly hoped wealthy Americans would build, feeling that, as he said, "Unless we are to go back on the whole trend of our civilization, we must find some way of reconciling prosperity with heroism and great wealth with moderation, refinement, and distinction."

But whereas Croly believed the typical American millionaire had to be encouraged to spend less on housing, to build more modestly, Junior's achievement at Kykuit was forcing his father to spend far more than he had ever imagined he would. That achievement could also not have been farther from what Senior had accomplished when he built his parents' house—on time and on budget—or later, as the world's most successful entrepreneur. The unceasing drive to cut costs stood as the cornerstone of his business credo, the very essence of free-market capitalism as he understood it. Nor is it likely that he ever abandoned his convictions on that score, either at Kykuit or afterward, when Junior decided that not only his father's house but New York prostitutes and Colorado miners (not to mention K'ang Hsi porcelains) also had to be rescued from the unmediated operation of the capitalist system. What Senior did come to concede, however, was his son's right to believe whatever he wanted to on such subjects, along with the freedom to act on his beliefs. That was Junior's final victory at Kykuit, and it was to have enormous implications for the future. For increasingly after 1915 the Rockefeller family's affairs would gravitate into his hands, with Senior in most cases content to let him do whatever he wished.

And as Junior himself had decided, for him the great game would be philanthropy, not business. In part it would be institutional, managed through organizations like the Rockefeller Foundation, the board of which he would chair for twenty-three years. Yet there would also be a sizable personal component to it, for the world of taste and beauty that together Abby and Codman and Bosworth had opened for him, would remain a vital part of his life, most notably in the enormous commitment he made to preserving the material remains of the past—at Versailles, at the Cloisters in New York City, at the Agora in Athens, at decaying historic houses along the Hudson River, and at what became the most cherished of all his philanthropies, Colonial Williamsburg. Each of these grew directly from his efforts to ensure that Kykuit became the kind of place it did, and each, with Junior so prominently involved, would join the Rockefellers' broader campaign during the twentieth century to transform the family's role and image in American life. They also spoke unmistakably of Junior's sense—worlds away from anything that had ever occurred to Senior—that such efforts would serve the cause of democracy by educating people, teaching them the value of the higher, nobler human creations that were part of everyone's heritage. If cheap kerosene had brought light to millions of ordinary people, this was a different sort of illumination, but in its own way just as important.

Like Kykuit, too, Junior's work in the field of historic preservation turned out to be costly. On Williamsburg alone he spent more than $60 million. But what would make it all possible was something else that Senior was now prepared to offer his son: money, tens upon tens of millions of dollars of it, transferred to Junior's personal account, beginning in 1916, without caveats, conditions, or stipulations of any sort. It was the first time he had done such a thing for his children, and he did it only for Junior. Evidently he was confident his son would know how to use so vast a windfall, a belief Junior's mother would surely have shared had she been there to see what happened.

Despite all Junior achieved during those years, however, there had been limits to what he attempted. Even as he grew increasingly comfortable departing from his father's views, most often it came to a matter of blunting, tempering, finding a balance among competing imperatives. In Colorado he managed to bring capital and labor together, but through a structure so solidly grounded in capital's camp that in 1935 the New Deal's Wagner Act would outlaw it along with every company union like it. And for all Kykuit's tastefulness and carefully calculated restraint, it remained a very large house, a house too that seemed destined to impose on those who lived there a style of life quite different from the one Senior, at least, was used to. Among other things, scores of people would be needed to staff it. How were they to be managed, and what would their presence and treatment say, in more concrete terms, about the family's commitment to democracy?

Similarly, whatever else was true of the house Junior had labored so long and hard to build, it was indisputably a place set apart from the rest of the world. High on its hilltop, approachable only by a long winding drive leading ultimately to elaborate gates set in thick stone walls, it seemed far better suited to shutting out the curious and uninvited than to democratically welcoming them in. Even the dazzling view of the river, for all its breathtaking openness, had been relentlessly edited—graded, filled, screened with trees—to remove all evidence of any other human presence. Private, closed, exclusive; such appeared to be the logic behind Kykuit's chief physical features. The question was to what extent that logic would control how life was lived there. In the aftermath of Ludlow Junior seemed ready to embrace a more open view of existence. Would that continue? Only time would tell.

For the moment, however, he definitely seemed to be winning on every front—or so Abby thought, which doubtless mattered more to him than anything else. "It all makes me very happy and hopeful," she wrote in the summer of 1915 while he was in Colorado, adding, "I told the children this afternoon what fine, brave things their father was doing."

Interlude

8

Patriarch

They assembled on a sunny morning in July with the air bright and clear, though if any of them were moved to slip off their shoes and feel the fresh grass beneath their feet, they resisted the temptation. Instead they waited patiently, concentrating on what was happening, moving in and out of groups as directed. They had done this before in the same way, for it was an annual ritual, marking yet another year in the family's life and honoring the birthday of its founder.

At first he posed alone, sitting on the porch, then standing in front of a low stone wall, against a background of shrubbery and sweeping tree branches that only slightly obscured the great river toward the far horizon. After that the photographer was ready for the rest of the family, posed in commemorative, multigenerational groupings around him. One of the photographs would show him with his son standing somberly to his right, and his grandson (the only one smiling) holding his son, to the left. The younger men were dressed alike in plain dark suits. In contrast—hand resting on his cane—he wore white pants and a white vest, with a watch chain swagged across it and a light, patterned necktie neatly tucked inside, the entire ensemble crisply set off by his dark jacket.

It was a serious picture, as they all were. There was nothing carefree about the moment, despite the grandson's jaunty smile. This was to be left as part of the record of the occasion—and the place.

Year in and year out the Rockefellers gathered at Kykuit to celebrate Senior's birthday on the ninth of July, and the event invariably began with a series of formal photographs taken in the morning. Afterward the family and guests adjourned to Abby and Junior's Abeyton Lodge for lunch, leaving Senior to rest, but the generations would meet again in the late afternoon, at the "Big House," for the band music and singing he adored. He was particularly partial to a German band, which, dressed in bright red, would play old-time favorites. Occasionally there was even a bit of dancing for the younger generations. In the evening everyone assembled at the table for a formal meal with a large birthday cake, during which they were serenaded by organ music and at least once by a tenor from Radio City Music Hall, singing songs like "Oh, Moon of My Delight" and "Goodbye, Sweetheart, Goodbye." Sometimes, too, after Senior retired, Junior and Abby and their children would stroll through the gardens while they were still lit and the water was playing in the fountains.

Such occasions spoke to the pride the family took in itself, and once the photographs were out of the way the mood was generally happy and informal, though during the first few years, while Cettie was still alive, her health had remained a source of constant concern. By then, confined to her bed or a wheelchair, with nurses around the clock, she was sustained on a diet of gruel and milk. After settling her in the first winter, Senior had left Kykuit to resume his annual routine of golfing in the sun, first in Ormond Beach in Florida, then in the spring, in Lakewood, New Jersey. Not until the following summer would the family fully populate the Pocantico estate again, with Junior and Abby and their children regularly joining Senior for a midday dinner on Sundays. That first year, too, the family had celebrated Senior and Cettie's golden wedding anniversary, for which he had her carried outside to listen to a brass band playing Mendelssohn's "Wedding March."

As ill as Cettie was, Junior had taken care to consult her about the final flourishes for the front facade of the house, including the plaster models of the groups of children holding baskets that would appear above corners of the loggia. "I am wondering," he wrote Bosworth afterward, "whether Mother's criticism may not be . . . met by . . . introducing a ribbon or garland," presumably to cover the children's nakedness at least a bit, which was done in the final, limestone versions. At the same time, the house's complement of furnishings was being rounded out, and because of its sentimental associations Senior added to the library an old family rocking chair from Cleveland, which Junior arranged with Baumgarten to have replaced with one done in a style and upholstery better suited to the room's decor. Then, when the weather turned cold, Senior had traveled south again, leaving Cettie behind. Although no one had expected her to go so soon, when she died early the following spring, even Abby and Junior were away from her side, visiting Senior in Florida.

Meanwhile, outdoors the golden Aphrodite in her temple required a protective glass and bronze cover. Junior also proposed adding curtains "to keep it from prying eyes" (another suggestion of Cettie's?), and it occurred to Bosworth that if the pedestal were made to revolve on demand, the statue would catch the light more dramatically when on show. There were maintenance problems to deal with as well. When the floor of the temple started sagging into the grotto room below, Bosworth replaced "the great Borghese vase" in the room's center with a massive, supporting column and had the Guastavino ceiling tiles repatterned to suggest ancient, overarching palm fronds. The orangerie too was settling badly, causing its walls to push out and its pipes to break. Also, its roof leaked, and over the winter some of the boxwood bordering the forecourt—despite its heavy protective cover of cornstalks (it took twenty acres to produce the 8,500 bundles needed)—fell victim to the raw hilltop winds.

Yet during those first years at Kykuit it was Abby who paid the closest attention to the gardens. Drawing on what she had learned from horticultural books and talking with her father's gardeners at Warwick, she walked through the grounds of Kykuit regularly, viewing them from all angles. Every plant list was subject to her scrutiny. Over time, she seemed to find Bosworth's tastes increasingly fussy and conservative, leading her to value more than ever what had always been her greatest love: the colors and fragrance of flowers, blooming as the seasons came and went, climbing and tumbling over borders and walls. And if Senior was not on hand to see the grounds after a fresh fall of snow or welcome the first signs of spring, Abby and Junior were there to sled down the hills with their children, and later, as the weather changed, to stroll about marveling at the flowering dogwoods. Mainly, though, the house on the hill was quiet during those months— "lonely," as Doris Payne, Senior's housekeeper, put it, writing to thank him for his Christmas gifts and to tell him about using the new, fully electric range to cook the holiday dinner she shared with only the superintendent and his wife for company.

As Doris Payne's presence indicated, even while Senior was away Kykuit was kept open with some staff living there. It was a time when painters and upholsterers could freshen the rooms, while the housekeeper supervised the moving of furniture and made sure any pieces needing repairs went off to Baumgarten's. With the house largely empty, carpets could be taken up, and floors waxed and polished, windows washed, woodwork rubbed down, and rugs cleaned. Junior and Abby pointed out as well that the expensive silk curtains in the ground-floor rooms, instead of being kept tied back as they usually were, should be released to relax their folds and protect the rooms from damaging sunlight. This was the time, too, to clean chimneys, wash chandeliers, and repair boilers, refrigerators, ovens, tanks, and pipelines.

Then on Senior's return to the newly immaculate house it would spring to life again, and through rain or shine he followed the same schedule every day. As Ron Chernow describes it in *Titan:*

> Rising at 6 A.M., he read the newspaper for an hour, then strolled through house and garden from 7 to 8, giving a dime to each new employee and a nickel to each veteran. He then breakfasted at 8, followed at 8:45 by a game of numerica, which gave him time to digest his food properly. From 9:15 to 10:15 he worked on his correspondence, mostly devoted to his philanthropy and investments . . . From 10:15 to 12 he golfed, from 12:15 to 1 P.M. he bathed and then rested. Then came lunch and another round of numerica from 1 to 2:30. From 2:30 to 3 he reclined on the sofa and had mail read to him; from 3:15 to 5:15 he motored, from 5:30 to 6:30 he again rested, while 7 to 9 was given over to a formal dinner, followed by more rounds of numerica. From 9 to 10 he listened to music and chatted with guests, then slept from 10:30 P.M. to 6 A.M.—when the whole merry-go-round started up again.

Despite the rigidity of his schedule—or perhaps because of it—Senior seems to have enjoyed his early years at Kykuit. He loved cruising along country roads during his afternoon drives. Tucked in among his guests, preferably attractive women, in the backseat of his maroon Crane Simplex, he wore driving goggles and caps with "goofy flaps dangling over his ears." Rumor had it that under the lap robe his hands wandered freely to his female companions (one of whom, leaping from the car while it stopped briefly, was supposed to have cried, "That old rooster. He ought to be handcuffed"). Occasionally everyone piled out to linger a bit in the sun; at other times Senior stopped to talk with neighboring farmers, later passing along any useful tips to his superintendent. Along the route, too—still fond of transplanting fully grown trees—he never tired of looking for new candidates for his hobby.

While his mode of living may have been more sedate than the elaborate goings-on in "Society," Senior was anything but reclusive. Friends and relatives came for extended visits, and guests joined him on the golf links, with the women sometimes treated to his mock Charleston after teeing off. Rarely, according to his grandson, did he dine alone. With Fanny Evans, a distant cousin from Strongsville, Ohio, acting as his hostess after Cettie's death (and her sister Lute's two years later), dinners were unhurried and convivial. The conversation was light—never about business—and invariably there was yet another game of numerica. The winners got shiny dimes; losers had to be content with nickels. Impromptu concerts on the player organ often followed, and even more to his liking, singing or humming along to familiar Baptist hymns and the spirituals popularized by Stephen Foster.

Venturing into town on his weekly trips to church, he also made a point of being friendly, bantering with the iceman, one of the village humorists, who reportedly would say at the end of a funny story, "wouldn't that Rockefeller?" Many of those he met were his employees, and some were also guests inside the gates. Dozens more were beneficiaries of his renowned nickels and dimes and the paper vests for motoring in open cars that he handed out as mementos.

To divert Senior at Kykuit, too, there was Junior and Abby's growing family, which eventually included six children—Abby, the oldest, called Babs to distinguish her from her mother, and then in succession, like steps on a ladder (which was how they were often posed for photographs), John 3rd, Nelson, Laurance, Winthrop, and David, the youngest, born in 1915, the year Cettie died. Living below the Big House, at Abeyton Lodge, they cut through the rose garden to join Senior for breakfast or lunch, scrambled everywhere around the grounds and fountains, learned to swim in Bosworth's boulder-rimmed pools, and inside the house acted as "maestros" at the keyboard of the organ.

His grandchildren also found Senior more than willing to play with them on all fours, and although there is no evidence that he entertained them (as he had his own children) by clownishly balancing china plates on his nose at the dinner table, he was not above a game of blind man's bluff or ducking behind the shrubbery outside to play hide-and-seek. And at Sunday lunches with the grandchildren—Babs in her best dress and the boys in their starched white Eton collars and flannel pants—formality often broke down as Senior's stories, punctuated by cracker-barrel moral lessons, merry lyrics, and oft-repeated droll jokes, sent waves of giggles rippling around the room.

For all the "down-home" character of Senior's lifestyle, it was amply supported by a large staff, committed to ensuring his comfort and that of his guests. Nor was there anything the least bit serendipitous about this. The staff had been carefully shaped and trained in ways considered appropriate to the kind of place Kykuit was. For to Junior the house alone had never been enough; it had to be lived in in a particular way as well. To some extent Abby's experience running her father's houses had provided the model, but there were also books and manuals that carefully coached Americans who aspired to live grandly with extensive household staffs. Ultimately such sources looked to the way European aristocrats managed their domestic arrangements and thus were anything but democratic. On the contrary, the chief organizing principles they adhered to can be summed up in two words: *hierarchy* and *distance*—rigid systems of order and rank among those who served and a clear and unbridgeable gulf between them and their employers. All of which promised to work a substantial change in Senior's home life.

Thanks to Cettie's equalitarian attitudes, her servants had customarily been treated as members of the family, a pattern Junior was determined to change. Shortly before his parents moved into the house, he wrote his mother saying frankly that the servants at the Kent House "were never kept up to the mark." As his remark suggested, by then he already had a new system of control in mind. He particularly doubted the competence of Cettie's housekeeper, Miss Wetherby. It was well known that she entertained her friends in the family rooms at the Kent House, and that one of the chambermaids under her jurisdiction did nothing more than take care of her own room and Miss Wetherby's dining room. Her supervision of the cleaning of the front part of the house and the rooms upstairs also left a good deal to be desired. At the suppers Junior had with her during the summer of 1908 he had painstakingly explained the arrangements the new house would require, and after Abby's return from Seal Harbor they both had further talks with her about managing the work. But then when Junior tried reviewing what they expected of her, she interrupted to ask if she could use Senior's office when her friends visited. "She means well, but has no more idea than a cat as to what should be done," he told his mother. While reluctant to hurt Miss Wetherby's feelings, Cettie finally agreed to give her notice, though several versions of her letter were sent to Junior before he judged her "very sweet and friendly" wording clear enough for the woman to realize she was being let go.

By any reckoning, an efficient housekeeper was crucial to running a house as large as Kykuit. She was, in effect, more a prime minister than a servant, ruling in her mistress's (or master's) stead over the household with a firm but just hand. She had command over every polished floor and dusted chandelier, every cupboard and closet. She had to see that every servant was properly trained, that all tasks were clearly delineated, and that each member of the staff lived up to the household's standards regarding appearance, dress, and manner. She had to be sure that everyone was occupied but no one was overworked. When there was a vacancy, she checked references and interviewed applicants. She was also purser and paymaster, purchasing every sponge and bar of soap, as well as keeping the household accounts. At Kykuit she ordered the food for both the Big House and the laundry cottage. Her payroll accounts included the chauffeur assigned to her, the housekeeper of the laundry cottage, and all the housemen and maids living in.

She was the detail person. She kept inventories of valuables and linens. Kykuit's beds and bathrooms were supplied at least once a day with fresh sheets and towels, and each diner was provided with a clean, starched white linen napkin at every meal. The housekeeper recorded the daily turnover of table linens, sheets, and towels before sending them to the laundry cottage and then checked the returns against her list. Everything was checked, as well, for tears or frays, with the offending pieces either sent to the sewing room or replaced.

At Kykuit, too, the housekeeper's importance was reflected not only by her duties, but also in the very architecture of the house. As Abby and Junior pored over Delano & Aldrich's blueprints, they had made sure there was provision for everything the housekeeper would need for her work and her status. Her bedroom—at the top of the house with south-facing windows overlooking the inner garden and the river beyond—was twice the size of the seventeen other female servants' rooms. It was entered through a short hall, off which was a private bathroom. The other women servants were in single rooms directly off the hall and shared three bathrooms. The housekeeper's room had two windows; most others had one. While the

bedroom furniture all came from Grand Rapids, hers was made of ma-
hogany; theirs of oak. Her bed was brass and white enamel, as opposed to
the "institution" beds ordered for the rest.

Aside from having mental acuity, housekeepers had to be well bred.
Senior's housekeeper, Doris Payne, wrote him humorous notes and sat to
his immediate right at the table when she came to visit him at the Golf
House in Lakewood, New Jersey. She was driven by one of the chauffeurs to
the White Mountains during one holiday and went to Cape Cod, Bermuda,
and Europe on others. Yet even though keeping Kykuit immaculately cared
for was due more to her than anyone else, her salary fell below the butler's.
From the housekeeper on down through the ranks, men earned more than
women; both the chauffeur and the houseman earned 50 percent or more
than the cook, who was a woman. The men servants were not called "boys,"
but the women were called "girls." (While talking about her life at Kykuit
later, Happy Rockefeller, Nelson's second wife, referred to them as "the
ladies.")

The housekeeper typically began her day by verifying menus and plans
for lunch and dinner, then conferred with the cook and butler so that their
preparations could begin. Next she made the rounds of the house. "Not a
drawer, dresser, or cupboard should escape her notice," was Mary Elizabeth
Carter's advice in her 1903 manual, *Millionaire Households,* in which she
devoted a chapter to the "Superintending Housekeeper." While making her
rounds she kept notes on anything amiss. If a guest bathroom was not re-
plenished with clean linens, if a fireplace was not laid with firewood and
kindling so that it could be lit at a touch (Kykuit had twenty of those), the
fault had to be brought to the offending staff member's attention immediately. But a wise housekeeper did not visit the pantry until the flurry of
washing, polishing, and putting away china, crystal, and silver after the
noonday meal was over. For there the butler reigned supreme over the disposition of every silver-plated Louis XVI candlestick and soupspoon, every
Chinese Export plate and platter, and every water goblet and finger bowl.

At the Kent House there had been no butler, but Junior and Abby
strongly recommended using one at Kykuit and eventually sent their own
man, Edward, to serve at the new house. The range of his responsibilities
extended well beyond the pantry walls. He supervised the "second man,"
and sometimes a "third man," along with footmen and waitresses, as they
prepared breakfast trays, set the table, and served the meals. While he
handed around the principal dishes, the second man might serve the rest.

As a rule he stood behind his mistress's chair, with his footmen or second and third men behind the others. He was responsible for clearing and cleaning the silver and washing the plates and crystal, though at Kykuit he did not have to worry about the wine, since none was ever served in Senior's or even Abby and Junior's day.

The butler also managed the care of the public rooms, and even more important, he managed access to the family. If the phone rang, he answered it and put the caller off if so instructed. If someone came to the front entrance of the house, he answered the bell, a silver tray in hand to take any visiting cards. For friends and family he opened the door wide, helping them off with their wraps and ushering them into the appropriate reception room. At other times it was up to him to decide who should enter and who should be diverted, thus serving (along with the watchmen, Senior's valet, and his private secretary) to insulate the family from unwelcome encounters. It was a job requiring good judgment, tact, and loyalty to the family. The butler's public role, too, called for identifiable clothing: a suit for the mornings, another with a low-cut waistcoat for the afternoons and evenings.

Despite the essential role they played, all of the servants at Kykuit—and the work they performed—were kept as much as possible out of the way and out of sight. The first three floors of the house were the province of the family and their guests; the servants lived, worked, and spent their leisure time on the top and bottom floors. While open archways provided the family easy access from one public room to another and the stairways they used were both wide and open, servants used separate, narrower hallways and stairs. If their business took them to the family areas of the house, they passed through doors that were otherwise kept closed.

Below the first floor of Kykuit were two service floors: the basement and the subbasement. To spare the family and their guests the smells and clatter of meal preparation, the kitchen was in the basement. When the food was ready it traveled via dumbwaiter to the pantry and was served from there. The basement also contained separate men's and women's toilets, a refrigerator room, three men's bedrooms, a valeting room, a trunk room, a men's hall, the servants' hall—where most of them ate—and a servants' porch. In the subbasement was a room for the central vacuum cleaning system machinery, a cold storage room, two milk rooms, a men's toilet, and a women's toilet. Deliveries were made through the tunnel Senior had insisted on building to the service court on the subbasement level. Breaking the pattern of separating service and family spaces by level, however, was his golf room, fitted out with lockers for family members and guests, on the north side of the subbasement, which was at ground level.

During most of Senior's tenure, Doris Payne and a series of butlers managed the household. They trained the staff well; one of Senior's guests remembered uniformed servants moving around the dining room silently as they served, inquiring in whispers if tea was desired with or after lunch. And much later, after Senior's time, a kitchen maid remembered waitresses and footmen working quietly in the pantry so that they could hear the soft summons of the bell from the dining room. (She also remembered, from taking afternoon walks outside during her breaks, not only the beauty and flawless grooming of the grounds, but the utter silence of the workers as they went about their tasks.)

Working under the housekeeper and butler, each of the servants at Kykuit had clearly spelled-out assignments. For example, a chambermaid's work was confined to the family quarters above the main floor. She began her day cleaning the halls and stairways before the family and guests awoke. Next she picked up breakfast trays from the butler's pantry and carried them upstairs. Only after the bedrooms and bathrooms were vacated did she work on those, cleaning and straightening up, opening the windows wide, removing sheets and spreading blankets over chairs to air, turning the mattresses, brushing or vacuuming the rugs, dry-mopping the floors, and dusting the furniture and objects on surfaces. A chambermaid's arsenal in the broom closet corresponded to her duties. She was equipped with all manner of brooms, brushes, and cloths, each with its own purpose. Thus for cleaning bathrooms, she was armed with chamber cloths for toilets, basin cloths for sinks and soap dishes, and glass towels for water tumblers. In addition to well-cleaned rooms and clean linens, newly arriving guests were meant to find fresh blotting paper, writing paper and ink, a clean bureau scarf and table covers, fresh paper drawer liners, pins in the pincushion, ice water in a carafe on a tray with a glass, and fresh flowers. The chambermaid was also expected to unpack and assist anyone lacking personal servants of their own.

Caroline Reed Wadhams's *Simple Directions for the Chambermaid* (which Abby owned and passed along to her daughters-in-law) dictated not only work tasks and methods but also proper speech. If a maid had a question about an instruction, she was to say "I beg your pardon" instead of

"What?" and then respond by saying "Yes, Madam" instead of "All right." Her uniform included a gingham dress and sometimes a tie, the color keyed to the house, a white apron, cuffs, a collar, and a cap—always clean and in good repair. Typically all female servants had Thursday afternoons and every other Sunday off. On evenings out, women had a curfew.

At Kykuit, a small staff of servants was kept year-round, but with Senior's arrival the household grew by as many as twenty-five additions, since most of his servants moved between houses, keeping the same rotation he did. "The girls who are here for the first time," he once wrote from Lakewood, "seem to be getting over the homesickness . . . Probably they have made some new acquaintances among the young men of this place." Among those traveling between places (which also included the city house) were Senior's three laundresses, personal maids, chauffeurs, and John Yordi, his redoubtable Swiss valet. Some of them accompanied the party as it traveled; others arrived separately. "There will be seventeen," Senior told his housekeeper when informing her which train he, Cettie, her sister Lute, and the household would be arriving on in September 1913. Plans also had to be made to meet the rest of the servants and the trunks arriving on an earlier train. Cettie alone—though a paragon of simplicity and restraint in her dress—had her maid operating out of five or six trunks when staying somewhere for only a few weeks.

If carting people and trunks from place to place was complicated, so too was moving automobiles. On one trip from Ormond Beach to Lakewood, for instance, two cars, the Crane Simplex and an Edison Electric—shipped from Florida to the Clyde Line Pier in New York—were to be picked up by two chauffeurs from Pocantico and driven to New Jersey. But the Lincoln, scheduled to arrive at the same pier two days earlier, had to be met and taken to Pocantico in time for the arrival of Vincent Frasco, Senior's chauffeur, who moved between residences with him. From Pocantico a day later the car was driven down to Lakewood for Senior's use there.

Senior's pleasures may have been comparatively unostentatious, but the miles and miles of country roads he loved to drive along, the healthy milk and fresh vegetables on his table, and his daily rounds of golf at every house he owned all involved complexities barely hinted at by the troops of servants silently circling around him indoors. Also essential to Kykuit's operation were firemen shoveling coal into the furnaces by hand on twelve-hour shifts in the coach barn, masons building stone walls, bridges, and roads, farmers harnessing workhorses to plow and sow corn seed, and scores of other people working on the grounds—all of them lucky to have the wages he paid, or so he thought, even if they never seemed to feel he paid them enough.

As early as 1909 Senior had begun to fear that the growing Pocantico estate was becoming more costly than he had ever anticipated. "We must not continue on anything like the expensive basis of the past," he wrote his superintendent, ordering him to cut the budget by more than half. Still, costs continued to climb. By 1912 the estate covered over two thousand acres and had twenty miles of roads, plus gardens and cut lawns, a golf course, a coach barn for horses and automobiles, greenhouses to provide plants for the gardens and cut flowers for the family houses (flowers for Lakewood and Ormond were delivered to the Rockefeller offices in New York and then taken to Penn Station to travel south by train once a week), the orangerie and palm house, barns, sheds, and livestock pens, in addition to some ninety houses, most of them rented out to estate workers. Following Senior's precept that it was cheaper to have things done by his own (nonunion) men, the Pocantico estate was largely self-sustaining. Included in its outdoor workforce of about two hundred were gardeners, farmers, woodsmen, masons, carpenters, painters, electricians, plumbers, tinsmiths, and blacksmiths. The total cost of running the estate when Senior voiced his concern in 1909 was $109,200; by 1919 the payroll alone, accounting for about half the overall costs, had climbed to $123,628.90.

By then Senior had taken steps to evaluate operations by sending Dyson DeLap, a high school principal and fellow Baptist he was acquainted with in Lakewood, to study all his estates as a covert observer. One result was DeLap's employment, starting in the summer of 1919, as superintendent at Pocantico, a position he would hold for more than two decades. In his first year on the job, he set about getting to know the men and making book-keeping improvements. He understood—possibly through his earlier experience working with modestly paid teachers—the importance of morale. "LET US GET TOGETHER AND PULL TOGETHER FOR THE INTEREST OF OUR EMPLOYER" was the message, spelled out in capital letters, on one set of pay slips during his first year at Pocantico. At Christmas the workers showed their goodwill by signing a letter to Senior giving DeLap credit for building a "contented and interested and therefore efficient" workforce.

Evidently, however, what DeLap liked to refer to as "the arm of friendship" was not always enough, especially when, during the postwar boom, men getting between $2.75 and $4.50 a day, depending on the work they did, were offered double that amount elsewhere. "Several of our best men are inclined to leave us," DeLap warned Senior soon after arriving. Adding that it was time to "establish a morale among our men that will reflect only credit to you," he sent off a schedule of recommended raises for everyone. Senior approved some in July, more in September, but not enough to solve the problem. Entering the fray, Junior wrote his father, "As long as men can get more wages outside, as they can very easily, our men will naturally and properly continue to leave us until the force is so reduced that the place cannot be maintained." And indeed by year's end, almost a quarter of the workers had left.

Early in the new year, DeLap forwarded a fresh set of requests for higher wages to Senior, who was "surprised" at receiving them "so soon." Perhaps DeLap's generous response thus far had "encouraged the men to think that there is no limit to which we will go," he wrote his superintendent. A few months later Junior telegraphed his father that a higher wage scale was crucial to holding their workforce. The estate paid less than jobs on the assembly line at the Chevrolet factory in Tarrytown, and Chevrolet was planning a million-dollar expansion. "Our superintendent . . . is new to the labor problem and we must protect him from impositions of any who take advantage of his kind heart" was Senior's response.

A month later he went further. "Is there not to be some limit to these advances; otherwise we must contemplate sooner or later closing down and letting the men go." DeLap agreed that "labor is going wild," but reported that the men were leaving not just for factory jobs but also to work on neighboring estates, where the wages were up to five dollars a day for unspecialized work. "I have done my best in my work and also to keep the men contented," he wrote, "but I am up against the impossible when industries and other places bid higher than we do for good men." Senior telephoned the next day saying, "Try to hold your men, and say to them that Mr. Rockefeller can afford to pay them as much as anybody." But whatever Mr. Rockefeller could afford to pay, his instructions were to give the men a mere fifty cents more a day, which was as much as he would do.

It was not enough. "Some of our men have been approached in their own homes at night by . . . superintendents offering them $5.50 and $6.00 per day," DeLap warned. Elsewhere, too, men worked an eight-hour day; for Rockefeller they worked nine hours, except during the winter, when the hours were shorter. "When I go out in the morning I don't know whether I am going to have fifty men or forty," DeLap said next, to which Senior replied by phone, "Be of good cheer and persevere and we will get through all those troublesome situations." At that point daily wages at Pocantico were up to $4.50 for common labor, yet Senior was even slower to agree to increases for the foremen and mechanics: "There is some place where we must make a stand." The following fall he asked for estate payroll records so he could compare DeLap's superintendency to the previous one. The results were alarming: for the same ten-month period of the year the totals had almost doubled by 1920.

Then for a short time there was respite, as the economy plunged into a brief recession. After conferring with the superintendents on neighboring estates, DeLap asked his foremen if they would voluntarily accept a cut in their wages and those of their men. They acquiesced, though not without pointing out that earlier, when wages increased, Pocantico had been the last place to raise them. And as Pocantico's mechanics resumed their demands when wages elsewhere began to rise again, DeLap was upset, but not Senior. "I hardly think they would do nearly as well to make a change," he wrote. If they decided to leave after all, so be it. In 1923 the situation was no better. If one of the masons was offered twelve dollars a day plus double wages for overtime elsewhere, at Pocantico the wages for a nine-hour day still hovered below four dollars. Senior finally did concede that they might go to a shorter day, and DeLap and Junior again worked out across-the-board raises for each category of worker—still below what they were being offered on other estates. DeLap reported too that "labor agitators" in the neighborhood were trying to get the estate workers to demand seven dollars for an eight-hour day.

DeLap's ideal for labor relations, as he took care to explain to Senior, envisioned "a perfect organization of the world [with] every man doing his part." Success would come only through the combined efforts of all, a principle he sought to apply to Pocantico. But facing every day the reality of the men's lives, DeLap could not help being sensitive to their situations. If families were hit with hard times, he lent a sympathetic ear and tried to help as best he could, often asking for Senior's aid as well. Exposed to the children's susceptibility to hunger and cold, he reported to Senior when villagers lacked coal and wood. When the children asked him if Santa was coming to the village, he played the role himself, buying oranges and candy for them with his own funds. After the school nurse told him of a family with eleven children, all of whom had been sick during the winter, he and Abby and Junior, knowing that the children's father—an estate worker earning four dollars a day—could not pay the doctor, did what they could and again appealed to Senior. When one of the teamsters (who had seven children) needed a major operation, and the other teamsters contributed to a Christmas collection to pay his expenses, Senior also helped out but asked first for an itemized bill.

His skepticism in this case was typical. When a mason on the estate unexpectedly died, leaving his large family in want, Senior wrote that although he wanted to do the "best thing," it was wiser to wait. "Here is a large family, and foreigners, with many to advise them in the direction of having us look after them," he cautioned DeLap. It was important not to be "humbugged by people who raise a cry for assistance too easily," and who, he said, "cannot, do not, and never have blazed the way and made a success for themselves in life." Nonetheless, it was hard for DeLap, feeling as he did about the importance of everyone working together toward a common end. "I must boil over or get away for a few days," he lamented after having to fire one of the watchmen.

Then there was his own situation. For four years he had resisted asking for a salary increase. When he finally did request one in February 1923, Senior waited for three months before replying, and the answer, when it came, was harsh: a list enumerating the costs of the benefits DeLap had received over the years: rent, coal, farm produce, dairy products, telephone, the use of an automobile, and electricity. Added to the list were the amounts of Senior's Christmas gifts to him, as well as hospital expenses paid when his wife underwent surgery. In presenting the figures, Senior argued that DeLap had, in effect, already been receiving more money in the form of costly benefits. DeLap's first reaction was to ask the office for an open reference. Eventually he got his increase, but it was a hurtful process, requiring Junior's mediation.

Thus despite the beneficence of Senior's philanthropic activities, his actions toward his own servants and workers were at best frugal in the extreme. Some people in the village were shocked, too, when he reduced his Christmas gifts of cash to local officials during the Depression. He cited hard times and the need to help others, yet he was also infuriated by his local tax assessments. In his own mind he was "doing the kindly thing," including saving his pennies for the ills of the larger world, but others closer to home thought he was just plain stingy and mean-spirited.

This, too, despite all the carefully constructed routines and rituals at Kykuit, so many of which seemed designed to present him as kind of a modern-day lord of the manor. While that may have been the role Junior and Abby wanted him to play, clearly there were limits to how far he would go to oblige them. Nor did the family's recent past seem to make any difference in that regard. As he struggled to hold the line on wages at Kykuit, it was as if Ludlow had never occurred, or he had simply forgotten it. Obviously Junior had not forgotten, and between them, he and DeLap did manage to blunt the harshest of Senior's excursions into labor relations. The truth was, however, he remained the hard-driving, cost-cutting businessman he had always been. If part of his persona at Kykuit was supposed to include exhibiting a spirit of noblesse oblige toward his employees there, he would have none of it. Money was money, and it was not meant to be wasted.

Nor were workers' wages the only thing at Kykuit that engaged Senior's cost-consciousness during the 1920s. The house as built contained state-of-the-art systems for central vacuuming, telephone, telegraph, ticker tape, refrigeration, and heating, but some worked better than others. A decade burgeoning with technological advances also offered abundant opportunities to exchange existing systems for newer, more efficient ones. Doris Payne treasured her electric range, and the plumbers and tinners at Pocantico tested new refrigeration and heating equipment alongside the old. Given the coal shortage during and after the war, the high cost of having two "firemen" shovel, rake, and bank coal (817 tons of it in 1919) into boilers sending heat through pipelines stretching from the stable to the house, was especially troubling. About 850 tons of coal were used annually on the estate. Studying the hourly reports for the house, Senior asked that temperatures be lowered for a longer time at night. "If we can save anything with these high prices of coal it is criminal not to do so," he instructed DeLap. A 1920 report on the refrigeration and heating plants at Kykuit recommended installing both refrigerators and automatic rather than hand-controlled thermostats at the house. Over the decade, too, coal was partially replaced by oil—at eight cents a gallon.

Another long-standing problem was the water supply, which did not reach the fourth floor of the house during times when the grounds outside were being watered and the fountains were running. Low water pressure had doomed the Parsons-Wentworth House, as well as much of the coach barn when it caught fire in 1913, and might also have contributed to the failure to stop a fire at the paint shop in 1925, which resulted in the tragic death of one of the chauffeur's sisters, who was living in an apartment above. Senior had intended to have a wider pipe laid between the reservoir and the house, but the project was suspended during the war because of high labor and material costs. Another approach was tried in 1930, when one of the lakes feeding water into the system was enlarged, becoming what was said to be the largest private reservoir in the world.

Some improvements during the decade of the 1920s were driven more by aesthetic considerations than practicality. They ranged from painting the roof and smokestack of Tarrytown's power plant to blend in with the scenery (Bosworth had once suggested rebuilding the water tank to resemble a Chinese pagoda and now suggested a tree of Lebanon as a model) to removing and relocating the New York Central's Putnam Division, a single-track railroad that ran through the estate. The latter project proved to be particularly ambitious, involving the purchase of much of the town of Eastview to provide a new right-of-way, a crew of five hundred to work on the track, and the closing of three stations. The new route opened early in 1931. A fair number of commuters were inconvenienced, but now railroad workers (and who knew who else)—along with the pollution sullying the air—would no longer penetrate the estate's boundaries.

Frederick Law Olmsted's son helped resolve the issue of how to reposition the approach to the house once the Putnam tracks and the railroad station standing on the green opposite the gates to the estate were removed. In the end, too, every house within the fence not lived in by a family member was razed or moved, and a substantial stone bridge carrying Bedford Road over the property was constructed. Olmsted also recommended replacing maple trees that had to be severely pruned each year with dogwoods at the edge of the brook garden, and substituting yews for the troublesome boxwood lining the forecourt, as well as eliminating the rows of clipped bay trees outside the front entrance to simplify the landscaping at that point.

Other parts of the gardens were simplified as well. The great arbor, with its barrel-shaped roof that Junior and Bosworth had long ago had a "séance" over, had to be painted every two or three years. Did Bosworth think—now that the linden trees had matured along the *allée*—that the arbor was still needed? Junior had always found it "very beautiful," but the heavy maintenance it required was a problem. Bosworth suggested taking down the arbor's wings and moving what was left of it to some other place on the estate as a summer house, where, if the paint were removed and it was coated with paraffin, it could be left to weather until it "fell into natural decay." As time went on, the orange trees, so carefully procured from France during the years the gardens were being built, also posed increasing problems. The tubs for each—eleven feet in diameter and weighing three tons—had to be moved one at a time by ten men onto a flatbed truck to be taken from the orangerie to the orange-tree terrace each spring and then moved back again in the fall. By 1935 the trees had also grown so large that they were out of scale with the rest of the gardens and, as Junior confessed, would not be missed if they were gone. It was difficult to find another home for them (other large estates were also trying to rid themselves of similar specimen trees), but in the end they went to the New York Botanical Gardens and the city of Pittsburgh, partly at Junior's expense.

Meanwhile, the maintenance of the estate had become sufficiently complex that a new central office facility was built. There the bookkeeper prepared the monthly farm, dairy, and poultry reports, as well as records for the rentals of some one hundred houses with 109 tenants, the sale of items like livestock, and the payments made for insurance and taxes, which alone consumed up to an estimated two hundred hours a year. In another office a bursar ordered materials and checked bills, while a secretary kept the daily time sheets. Each of the divisions (painting, carpentry, automobiles, etc.) had its own budget and account, with graphs provided to DeLap every month. In addition, the payroll—sent up to the estate from the Rockefellers' New York City office accompanied by armed guards (after a holdup in 1929)—had to be distributed by hand, with each worker presenting an identifying brass token before being paid.

Of the team of nine carpenters, two were assigned to Kykuit and Abeyton Lodge. The six painters and two apprentices rotated among all the houses, though the interior work at Kykuit itself was contracted out. The plumbers and tinsmith took care of repairs and waterlines; at slack times in the winter they shoveled snow. Eighty-five tons of fertilizer were spread annually on fields growing corn, potatoes, oats, hay for the animals, and apples. Eleven horses and one old tractor were used to plow those fields. Vegetables were grown on five acres of field at an operating cost in 1929 of over $6,000, with most of the produce going to the family and the laundry cottage. There were thirty head of cattle requiring two cow barns, two sheds, a dairy, and over twenty-three thousand feet of fencing. The cost of producing a quart of milk was seven cents, but the manure produced annually was valued at $1,000. The poultry operation occupied eleven acres and twenty-nine separate structures, making fresh eggs and chicken at the table a costly luxury.

Aside from the gardens, lawns, golf course, and woodlands, there were now almost thirty miles of roads to maintain on the property. One man with a horse and wagon had the full-time job of collecting the trash—daily at Kykuit, twice weekly elsewhere. There were twelve trucks, most of them Fords, for heavier hauling. In addition to the workhorses, there were ten others used for recreational riding. And guarding all of this was a security force of twelve watchmen, on twelve-hour shifts (with two days off a month), punching time clocks on the half-hour and working with watchdogs plus automatic shotguns (changed to double-barreled breech-loading guns after one of the watchmen accidentally shot and killed one of the other employees in 1921).

Outside the gates, Junior played a prominent part in village affairs. Referred to locally as the "Mayor," he worked toward installing street lighting, organizing the police and fire departments, as well as garbage disposal operations and public road maintenance. He also bought up properties to provide more housing for industrial workers. In earlier years his father might have attended to such things, but by the end of the 1920s Senior had begun absenting himself more and more from the village and his neighbors there.

He also—if the dwindling volume of correspondence with his superintendent is any indication—was increasingly inclined to leave the details of the estate's stewardship to Junior. Nor was this simply a matter of changing roles, since for tax reasons in 1925 Junior had purchased all of Senior's properties, including Kykuit. The truth was, however, that from the beginning Junior had shaped almost everything about life at Kykuit: choosing and organizing the servants, designing the family rituals, mediating between Senior and the outdoor crews to keep wages up to an almost respectable level. Senior's chief role in his son's view had always been to spend his days enjoying himself at the center of the charmed world that had been constructed around him. Yet that was not exactly what happened.

In 1917, at Junior's suggestion, John Singer Sargent went to Ormond Beach in Florida to paint Senior's portrait. He had been reluctant to take on the job; he felt he had done enough portraits and wanted to devote more time to his watercolors. But he was impressed with Senior's "fine, keen aesthetic type . . . and his expression of benevolence." The two also got along well. In the portrait Senior is seated against a plain backdrop, wearing white pants and a white vest with a blue serge jacket—every inch, in short, the quiet, composed gentleman of leisure. The family was delighted with the result, and Sargent came to Pocantico to paint a second version. During the sittings there was much good-natured talk. Senior brought up the vitriolic ill will leveled against him in the past, explaining rather philosophically its inevitability.

Yet it was clear to Sargent that the attacks and threats still rankled. In 1913 a bomb, "presumably" intended for Senior's home, blew up in a tenement on Lexington Avenue, killing four "I.W.W. agitators" but leaving their compatriots at large. After Ludlow, Kykuit had been stormed by Wobblies and anarchists like Emma Goldman and Alexander Berkman, some of whom, eluding the guards, had smashed windows and set one of the barns on fire. Senior had to be persuaded not to talk to the demonstrators; instead, the village fire department turned hoses on them as they tried to climb over the walls. That year the number of guards at Pocantico was doubled, and the gates were "shut tight" after an attack on J. P. Morgan, which, according to the *New York Times*, prompted Senior to cancel a trip to Forest Hill. Not even villagers known by sight were allowed to wander at will over the grounds as they once had been.

Thus as calm and reassuring as Senior had seemed to his family during those trying times, since then Kykuit had become an armed fortress, and he a virtual prisoner, cloistered within it. By comparison, in both New Jersey and Florida the life he led was notably freer, less guarded. In Florida, though his valet Yordi acted as his bodyguard and there were men on watch on the grounds, the house he lived in—in contrast to Kykuit's barbed-wire fences and stone walls topped with razor wire—had only a hedge between it and onlookers. As he walked the streets, he enjoyed being called "neighbor John" and for relaxation he sat on his mother, Eliza's rocking chair in his glassed-in porch, clearly visible to the passersby.

During all the years of Senior's rotation among his three houses, Kykuit was the only one where he kept a year-round staff. It was also the first of the three that he withdrew from—a little at a time at the start and then completely—preferring instead to remain in Lakewood or Ormond Beach. Perhaps as he aged he lost his appetite for Kykuit's formality, a style he had never really wanted in the first place. Certainly his other houses were simpler and more plainly furnished. None of Codman's "pretty things" were to be found in either place, and instead of the Aphrodite or the mighty Oceanus punctuating the view, Senior could content himself with looking at the sky itself.

There may have been another reason as well why he chose the simpler, less complicated life away from Kykuit. Brimming with three generations of his descendants, the house on the hill was anything but restful, and having become obsessed with living until he reached one hundred, he craved tranquillity. By the time he came to Kykuit for his ninety-third birthday, he had begun placing strict limitations on his activities, hoarding his energy as one might save pennies in a bank and avoiding anything that threatened to disturb the hours he spent resting every day. Estate workers were ordered to abandon all work inside the estate's gates at sunset. Armed patrols were still necessary, but the watchmen were instructed to wear rubber soles so they could walk the gravel paths in silence.

The following year, 1934, was the last time Senior celebrated his birthday at Kykuit. Posing in a straw hat with his cane, he looked healthy enough, but the following fall he came down with several severe colds and, much to his consternation, could not go to Florida in time for his annual Christmas party. Instead he spent the holidays at Kykuit, in "extreme quietness," while the rest of the family celebrated at Abeyton Lodge. In February Senior and an entourage of twenty-four left on a private train for Florida. That spring he sent up some rosebushes for the gardens. Perhaps for Abby and Junior's sake he hinted that he intended to come himself later, saying he looked forward to seeing the roses in bloom. But he never did return, choosing instead to remain in the sunshine and tranquillity of Florida.

He was, however, brought back to Kykuit after he died at Ormond Beach three years later. On a beautiful spring day, a small private service, primarily for family members, was held inside the house with the French doors open to the west terrace. His favorite organist played in the music room. For the Rockefellers, Senior had come home: home to Kykuit, which they, at least, thought of that way, even if he did not and perhaps never had.

After his death—and burial by Cettie's side in Cleveland—his other houses would be quickly emptied and placed on the market, but not Kykuit. For Junior, it had always been and would remain "father's house," the place he had built for his parents, appropriate to their position, an expression of their taste and way of life, or what he hoped would become their taste and way of life. He well knew Senior's preference for simpler things, but Kykuit was also, after all, meant to honor him and everything he had accomplished in life as a businessman and public benefactor.

Hereafter, too, it would be the place above all others that anchored the family's memories of him, thanks to all the years they had gathered there in that private domain of beauty and serenity. Such feelings went beyond Delano & Aldrich's architecture, or Codman's interiors, or Bosworth's garden delights—beyond even whatever Senior himself thought of Kykuit. They had become part of the fabric of the Rockefellers' being, of their sense of who they were and how they saw themselves. Logistically it would have been simpler to send Senior's body directly to Cleveland, but Kykuit was the family seat, and his death, for all that it had happened hundreds of miles away in Florida, only deepened the house's identity in that regard. Nor did it matter that much of his life there had been at bottom a kind of performance staged to please his family. However one interpreted it, this was the final act, and there was never any doubt about where it should occur.

9

Family Seat

"Fussy" was how she described the ornaments in front of the house's entrance: the black marble, Vatican-inspired torch bases surmounted by bright orange, flame-like globes, flanking a "spotty" lineup of vases. As a compromise they had the globes painted gray—so they would be "less challenging"—and the smaller vases removed. But her husband was not happy with the changes.

Turning to the individual who had created it all in the first place, he asked for alternative designs, explaining that even though he liked the arrangement ("[it] pleases me greatly, as it always has"), it seemed "to disturb" his wife. Predictably the response that came back was emphatic: the torch bases were "really so fine [that] every adjustment should be made to save them." As for the arrangement as a whole, the glass canopy over the doorway was "so sumptuous" that it had to be supported "by something 'en bas.'" So the husband had the pronouncement he wanted. "In light of your letters," he replied, his wife was "perhaps realizing a little more than she has heretofore the beauty and significance of the marble torches."

In short, nothing would be changed. She had hoped the torches and vases might be eliminated altogether, but perhaps that had never been practical, since they contained crucial elements of the circuitry for the garden lights, a fact both men could be glad of. Yet if she had cared to, she could have pointed out that practicality had never had much to do with either the house or the gardens around it. They aimed at an entirely different standard, and that too would not change.

Abby Rockefeller's appeal to her husband to reconsider the ornaments in front of Kykuit's entrance came in 1942—close to five years after they had begun living in the house themselves, following Senior's death. It was a modest request, which she could have made anytime, but in the beginning, when the house was being built, their tastes had seemed so similar as to be indistinguishable. In forty years that had changed, however. At certain points their aesthetic preferences still coincided, but at others they were diametrically opposed. Mostly it was Abby's taste that had changed—grown, expanded, moved in half a dozen new and different directions; Junior continued to like best what Ogden Codman and William Welles Bosworth, the architect responsible for Kykuit's entrance, had taught him to like.

In some marriages the situation could have caused serious problems, and certainly it produced moments of tension in Junior and Abby's relationship, but it never came to more than that. They also found ways to combine their interests, or at a minimum to negotiate compromises, though as their disagreement over the torches and vases in front of Kykuit proved, sometimes there could be no real compromise. At issue in that case, too, was more than just a handful of ornaments, for over time Junior's view of Kykuit had become increasingly rigid. The ever-tightening security, the carefully perfected family rituals, the hierarchies that dominated the staff indoors and out; more and more those seemed to be what mattered most to him—those and his conviction that whatever else happened, Kykuit must remain as nearly as possible exactly as it was. Thirty years earlier, when the house was being finished, he had made of it a supple and resilient springboard for major changes in his life, but now it was to stand rock solid, immutable, unchanged and unchanging.

What was Abby's role there to be, then? Tirelessly she worked to infuse the place with life and warmth—to counteract Junior's vision of it as a timeless memorial to the finest artistic traditions of human civilization with her sense that it ought to be enjoyed and cherished by a large and growing family of people doing interesting and worthwhile things. Whose vision came out on top? For much of the time hers seemed to, but she then died quite suddenly, well before Junior did, and ironically, like Senior, he ended up spending most of his final years elsewhere.

Even before Kykuit was finished, some differences between Abby's and Junior's tastes were evident. In 1911, in designing their town house (the largest private house in New York City) at 10 West Fifty-fourth Street, Bosworth created a place that reflected Junior's stylistic preferences far more than Abby's. With its stone staircase lined with tapestries, its immense marble reception room, and its multiple settings for displaying Junior's Chinese porcelain collection, it was unrelentingly formal and grand. Between 1911 and 1916, on the other hand, Abby was working closely with *her* favorite architect, Duncan Candler, to enlarge the Eyrie, the couple's rambling sixty-five-room house on the rocky ledges above Seal Harbor in Maine. Reminiscent of a half-timbered, Normandy-style cottage writ large, the Eyrie had giant wings punctuated down the line with peaky gables. Later she would add a brilliant garden—blending Asian sculpture, the landscape of Mount Desert Island, and English perennial borders—designed by *her* choice of landscape architects, Beatrix Farrand (a niece of Edith Wharton's). And just as relaxed and informal as the Eyrie was the architectural hodgepodge of the family's weekend retreat at Pocantico, Abeyton Lodge. All verandas, comfortable chintzes, and sun porches, with doors and windows open to the country air, it proclaimed Abby's instinct for putting things together eclectically and informally. "I have come to the conclusion that I do not want to live with frescoes," she once said. "I prefer a plain wall where I can hang pictures and change them when I want to."

Interestingly enough, as it developed, her concept of a country house was in many ways closer to Senior's than it was to Junior's, and until 1937, when Senior died, it was at Abeyton Lodge that she centered her life and her children's when they were in Pocantico. There, from the stuffed penguin standing in the front hall (a gift from Admiral Byrd) to the friendly fires on cool days and the fresh flowers filling every room, comfort and fun took precedence over formality. "Being less humble and less conscientious than John and harboring in my heart a secret conviction that most worldly success . . . is of a fleeting and uncertain value, I take life more lightly," she remarked at one point. Yet she also worked at giving her children an appreciation of her often distant and stern husband: "Your father is so modest . . . I wonder if you always realize what a tower of strength he is to me and to us all."

Outdoors at Pocantico, the children spent their days picnicking in the woods, sledding down snowy slopes and ice skating in the winter, riding horseback through the estate's woodlands, wading as toddlers in the circular pool in the morning garden, and later swimming in the "grown-up" pool beneath the orange-tree terrace. They rode their bicycles on Senior's roads and, as they grew older, played tennis with their father and drove the "red bugs"—motor-powered buckboards—on the carriage drives. In true Rockefeller fashion, they were required as well to spend part of their time earning money: shining shoes, catching mice, weeding, and, in Nelson and Laurance's case, raising rabbits to sell to the Rockefeller Institute to use for experimental purposes. Inspired by their mother, they also had their own gardens, growing flowers, cabbages, lettuce, corn, and squash to sell to the household staff or to bring to village fetes. After a morning of raking out the winter debris and weeding with the children, Abby wrote Junior, "It rests and refreshes me to come here, you know how much I love it."

Some of their weekend routines never varied. Teatime was for the children, whether in Abby's sitting room or some outdoor spot she chose, reading to them, playing the game of Authors with them, talking with them in her frank and open way about the importance of "fair play" toward others and the obligations they faced because of their particular circumstances. Money, Abby told them, "makes life too easy; people become self-indulgent and selfish and cruel." At Pocantico they also had more access to Junior. A regular feature of their Sundays after church were the long walks he took them on, identifying different trees and flowers, and distributing the maple sugar treats he had stuffed in his pockets.

Abby knew, too, that Kykuit was about more than objects or even the family times they spent together. She reached out to her Pocantico neighbors in ways unlike the rest of the family. She joined the school committee, and from the time she first came, she took an interest in the village women, joining the Pocantico Hills Women's Club, taking her turn serving guests at their socials, chatting about bringing up children and the brutality of war as she sat knitting in their midst, inviting them for evenings at her city house, even learning how to manage the lantern slide projector so she could share with them something of her trip to Asia. Early on in his acquaintance with her, one of the villagers had said to another, "Pay attention to the filly. She's the one really worth watching." It was a prescient remark.

She was always happiest, however, when her children were with her, though as they grew older they needed more space in which to enjoy themselves and be with their friends. With this in mind, she and Junior decided in 1925 to build what the family would always refer to as "the Playhouse." To the tennis courts and outdoor pool already on the estate it would add facilities for sports like squash, played at the prep schools and colleges they were beginning to attend, an indoor pool for swimming laps or playing water polo (difficult if not impossible using Bosworth's circular, grotto-like pool), as well as a gymnasium, a bowling alley, and a billiard room. (In addition an indoor tennis court was added later.) There was already a smaller version of such a place at the Eyrie in Maine, and Abby's father had had one at Warwick that included lounges, a kitchen, and a large room for parties, as the Pocantico Playhouse would.

To plan the structure, they engaged Duncan Candler, who had worked with Abby on both Abeyton Lodge and the Eyrie, and chose a site just north of the lodge, well below Senior's house. For design ideas they studied books on architecture in Normandy, including the recently published *French Provincial Architecture as Shown in Various Examples of Town & Country Houses . . . Adaptable to American Conditions,* by Philip Lippincott Goodwin and Henry Oothovt Milliken. Construction started in the fall of 1925, with the expectation that the building would be closed in by winter, though progress was disheartingly slow, mainly due to Candler's delays in arriving at final designs. At one point Junior suggested that he hire someone like Milliken, the coauthor of the book they had studied, to work with him as a draftsman and a "coadjutor," but Candler (although he did bring in another architect for a while) worked more comfortably alone, drawing, studying, and discarding plans repeatedly before he was satisfied with the results.

There were other problems as well. When it was discovered that several roof lines were out of plumb, they had to be reconstructed and steel beams put in for additional support. It was too damp when the exterior plastering was applied, so it too had to be redone. In 1927 all the workers (who were unionized) went on strike. And due to a delay in getting drawings for the stone overmantles in the main living room, the builders installed the wood paneling without them, causing the fireplaces to be slightly off center, which had to be corrected. All of which added up to the usual hazards of building, yet the results more than justified the frustrations: the building was judged to be a great success.

Decoratively, the interior managed to combine both of their tastes. Ceilings were timbered in oak or vaulted, brackets and lintels were carved with likenesses of rams, wildcats, and wolves, and the great stone fireplaces at the ends of the living room, with French fifteenth- and sixteenth-century sculptures incorporated into their overmantles, were reminiscent of medieval castles. Medieval sculptures from the collection Junior bought from George Grey Bernard were displayed both inside and outdoors, and coaching prints, inspired by his fondness for carriage driving, hung in the card room. The columns with Corinthian capitals surrounding the indoor swimming pool and the room's frieze with its roundels of reliefs also reflected more his interests than Abby's, but the palms between the columns sat in Mexican Talavera glazed pottery urns, and the tin chandeliers and hanging lamps throughout the place, as well as the wooden chargers and boxes decorating many of the rooms, were made in Mexico, the result of her love of that country's handicrafts.

The beds of flowers and trees promising an abundance of bloom—a project she took on about the same time she began to work with Beatrix Farrand at the Eyrie—added to the Playhouse's cheer and whimsy. French ceramic hens and rabbits as well as medieval saints shared the space with pink climbing roses, clematis, and blue and white wisteria. English hawthorns and flowering dogwood and cherry trees, azaleas and laurel abounded; dwarf pines, violets, spring bulbs, and borders of bedded-out annuals ringed the croquet lawn outside the living room's French doors. In a sentimental gesture some of the cuttings came from the Aldrich estate in Warwick.

From the beginning, too, Abby sought opportunities to enjoy the Playhouse with her children and a wide variety of guests. Late in the spring of 1928, just as it was being finished, she spent a Sunday evening there in front of the fire, listening to music on the radio and writing letters with Laurance. "Winthrop is doing up some candy that he is going to sell in school tomorrow," she wrote Nelson, who was away at Dartmouth, "and David is in the kitchen making more candy." A month later, perhaps in response to all the stories published in the newspapers, two hundred residents of Pocantico Hills were invited inside the gates for an afternoon at the Playhouse. Junior and Abby, John 3rd, Nelson, Laurance, and Winthrop led groups around its rooms and facilities, and the pool teemed with swimmers. The villagers danced to the music of a band that had been brought in for the occasion and had dinner at Abeyton Lodge. It was the first time since 1914 that the estate was opened to all, and according to the New York Times reporter covering the event, the villagers were assured that "such gatherings would be frequent."

The Playhouse also came to be used for family gatherings, especially at Christmas, as well as for weekend parties, serving as a center for casual entertaining in contrast to the greater formality of the Big House. On Sundays, the day Junior would have preferred to keep free of all recreational activities, games were permitted, except between the hours of 10:30 A.M. and 12:30 P.M. "Thus no one will have to break up a game to go to church, nor will we as a family seem oblivious of the opportunity and the duty of church attendance." Individual family members could decide for themselves whether or not to go to church, but at least it should not be made difficult for them to do so—hardly a compromise Cettie would have approved of, but one Abby probably told Junior was as much as he could hope to accomplish.

One May after a quiet supper with Junior in the Japanese summer house, Abby wrote her sister Lucy, "It is so beautiful . . . that I greatly grieve that it is not possible for us to spend more time there." Yet they had several beautiful houses to enjoy. For the most part they spent only weekends at Pocantico in the fall, spring, and early summer until just after Senior's birthday. Then they were off to Seal Harbor, where they stayed until sometime in September or October. And after 1928 their time at Pocantico was further limited because of a new venture of Junior's: the restoration of Colonial Williamsburg, a project he embarked on while the Playhouse was under construction.

At first his approach was typically cautious, beginning with small steps after several discussions in New York and tours of the old Virginia capital with William A. R. Goodwin, who had become interested in restoring Bruton Parish Church, following his appointment as its rector in 1903. Over time, he had raised his sights to returning the entire rundown, sleepy town to its "glorious past," and by 1927 he had Junior hooked. He was ready to commission architectural sketches of an overall historical restoration plan and started buying up properties anonymously along the Duke of Gloucester Street, the main thoroughfare of the old capital. Thereafter the restoration of Williamsburg—a place, as Junior saw it, absolutely central to the birth of the American nation—would come to absorb him more than anything in his life ever had or would.

The guiding principle of the project was authenticity: "reverently to preserve every vestige of the old where it survives." Its key sources were a French cartographer's 1782 map showing the shapes and sizes of the buildings on the town's main street, a copper plate discovered in the Bodleian Library at Oxford, depicting the front facades of the College, the Capitol building, and the Governor's Palace, and innumerable pieces of evidence found in property deeds, inventories, and the remnants of foundation walls and broken pottery shards dug up in archaeological excavations. In order to uncover the basement walls of the Governor's Palace and its gardens, twenty-three buildings, including two public schools, plus the tracks of the Chesapeake and Ohio Railroad, had to be removed. For everything there was a continuous flow of plans and maps. Then came the tangible results in the reproductions of the major public buildings and dozens of other structures, like Raleigh Tavern, all utterly captivating to Junior, and all done so future generations of Americans could see and learn from what had been done. "We stuck to absolutely what *was*," he later recalled.

The Williamsburg project also drew Abby in, chiefly through her growing interest in American folk art, and before long they bought a house, Bassett Hall, for their own use. Standing on land abutting the historic park, it was a comparatively simple eighteenth-century, frame, two-bedroom house, to which they made a few small additions. Informally decorated with comfortable furniture and brimming with Abby's assorted collections of chalkware, weathervanes, needlework, and paintings by unknown eighteenth- and nineteenth-century artists, it was much more intimate and unassuming than their other residences. Yet it became their favorite destination for prolonged stays in the spring and fall.

At the same time, however, Abby's interests in artistic expression began to take a startlingly different path from Junior's. Inspired by coming into contact with different cultures, she opened herself to the unfamiliar in art with an instinctive passion that "reached deep into her being," beyond logic. And even if she did not acknowledge the fact to herself, it is possible to see in her tastes (to John she tactfully called them her "fads and fancies") as they developed an antidote to the constraints of being a Rockefeller, at least as they were expressed in Kykuit's scrupulously modulated classicism. For her love of art extended not only to Chinese porcelain and the old masters but also to primitive Mexican textiles, the otherworldly beauty of Asian religious statuary, the canvases and painted wooden panels of unknown early American artists, and eventually and most importantly, to modern art—art that broke completely the mold of conventional "good taste."

Perhaps more than any other single experience, Abby's two-week pilgrimage to art galleries in Vienna and Germany without Junior but in the company of William R. Valentiner, a native German who directed the Detroit Museum of Art, opened her eyes to avant-garde art, beginning with early twentieth-century German expressionism. Especially sensitive to the horrors of the late war, she responded instinctively to the raw relevance in the works of artists like Edvard Munch and Erich Heckels, and back in New York she began collecting in small steps, with an art allowance of $25,000 given her by Junior in 1927. Even when he doubled the amount the following year, it was not enough to buy serious paintings by well-established artists, so she concentrated on prints and the works of younger artists, particularly Americans.

But however hard she tried, she could not interest Junior in modern art. Indeed, he actively disliked it. If to her it seemed spontaneous and excitingly life affirming, to him it appeared brutal and ugly. As a compromise of sorts she was allowed to plan and have built, on the seventh floor of their house at 10 West Fifty-fourth Street, a gallery for her own art. It was designed with sliders on the walls so that paintings and prints could be easily changed and rearranged. There, through gallery talks and over sherry afterward, she could learn more, in the company of a growing circle of like-minded associates. But modern art was banned from the other houses she shared with Junior. Nor would it be permitted anywhere at Kykuit, once it became theirs.

Meanwhile, Junior continued to conjure fresh worlds from the past in his historic preservation projects. Before Williamsburg there had been the monuments of France. In 1923, when that war-torn country was struggling to get on its feet, he and Abby attended a fete at the Palace of Versailles, where more than two centuries earlier the Bourbon monarchy had reigned at the height of its power. Now looking around, Junior discovered leaky roofs, rotting timbers, and broken statuary. And he saw the same at Fontainebleau, the great Renaissance château built by Francis I, as well as at the heavily bombed ruins of the Cathedral of Reims, where kings of France had been crowned and Joan of Arc had met the Dauphin before leading his army against the nation's foes. In the aftermath of the First World War, the French government was in no position to rescue such structures, but if their decay was halted and appropriate restoration carried out, future generations could experience and appreciate them. Suggesting that such a project be set up using a committee composed mostly of Frenchmen, Junior gave it two major donations and saw to it that Bosworth was involved as "Secretaire Générale" of the "Comité pour la Restauration." The entire project proved quite successful, and Junior could remark later, "[That] every detail has been carried out with such conscientious reference to what existed originally adds immensely to my satisfaction."

After France and Williamsburg came the Cloisters in New York, the Agora in Athens, and various historic houses along the Hudson. In every case historical accuracy was the announced goal, but the past Junior was most eager to see restored also tended to have a definite character, as did the message he seemed to hope people would draw from it. For invariably the projects he supported focused on ruling elites—on those with power, those with money, those with "culture." The merchants of ancient Greece, the monks of the high Middle Ages, the courtiers of early modern France, the patriotic gentry of colonial Virginia; they and the elegant places where they lived and worked and the gracefully crafted objects created for their use and pleasure appeared front and center, always. And ineluctably in the very beauty of those surroundings one was invited to see the moral justification for the privileged positions held by such people, the certification of their right to rule. Only dimly present, on the other hand, were the laborers, the poor, the slaves, even what there may have been of a middle class, if indeed they appeared at all. In contrast, the forms of artistic expression Abby most loved could well have stood as a declaration of independence from all this: the meaning imbedded in the objects themselves, regardless of their pedigree. Writing to someone helping her furnish Bassett Hall, she said, "As for myself, I am interested only in furniture that has beauty and charm. The historic side of it doesn't appeal to me as much."

With Abby delving ever more deeply into modern art, and Junior into his historic preservation projects, his energies were suddenly pulled away in a totally new direction that would have major consequences for the future of the entire family. For it was also during this time that Rockefeller Center was born. A project that began originally as a benign civic gesture toward helping create a new home for the Metropolitan Opera as the centerpiece of a major real estate development in midtown Manhattan, it took a dramatic turn for the worse with the financial collapse of 1929. Eventually the opera pulled out of the deal, leaving Junior—who had cosigned the lease on a swath of land, belonging to Columbia University, between Forty-eighth and Fifty-first streets and Fifth and Sixth avenues—holding an enormous hot potato. The main tenant was gone, and no one else was able or willing to develop the property, leaving him on the line for an annual ground rent of $3.3 million. With great anxiety but faith that the economy would ultimately recover, he decided to underwrite and manage the entire development himself, building the buildings and renting out the office spaces created. It was a huge undertaking, but as he said later, "there was no place to run."

By 1931 three major architectural firms were drawing up plans, real estate developers were arranging leases, and Radio Corporation of America had been enlisted as the center's principal tenant. There was also to be a music hall that would be the largest indoor theater in the world. Completing the project eventually cost Junior some $125 million, and throughout, his hand remained firmly on the helm. All policies, management questions, and disputes went through him, as did every item of the design work. However, the endless details—and even more, the worry—exacted a heavy toll, often confining him to a couch for hours on end with severe migraine headaches. Finally in 1931, his doctors insisted that he go to Arizona for a rest (starting a pattern of spending part of each winter away that would continue as long as he lived).

Yet as the buildings began to take shape, the pressure only intensified. The stark, modernistic shafts seemed to onlookers disturbingly brutal. The *New York Herald-Tribune* pronounced them "ugly" and "revoltingly dull and dreary." Declared an editorial in the *New York Times,* "From every source of intelligent appreciation . . . has come a perfect stream of objection, protest, and one may say, wondering malediction." A "graceless bulk" was Lewis Mumford's verdict. But to Junior's credit, the design chosen for the buildings, with its strong Art Deco thrust, represented a striking departure from the past—indeed as close as he would ever come to embracing modernism—which in time critics praised and has since helped make Rockefeller Center one of the best-loved landmarks in the city. And here, too, Abby played a vital behind-the-scenes role. Before the design for the interiors was arrived at, Junior had asked George Vincent, a former president of the Rockefeller Foundation, for his reaction to the different proposals. "The more I ponder the subject," he answered, "the more I find myself in agreement with Mrs. J.D.R., Jr." Doubtless with that in mind, Robert Moses, the all-powerful czar of scores of major New York City building projects, later wrote Junior, "The general public probably did not fully realize how greatly Mrs. Rockefeller contributed to your remarkable achievements, but those of us who had the privilege of knowing her have a dim idea of it."

The designer she particularly favored for Rockefeller Center's interiors was Donald Deskey, whose work included machine-age window displays for Saks Fifth Avenue and whom she engaged to work with Candler designing her seventh-floor art gallery at 10 West Fifty-fourth Street. Deskey's commission at Rockefeller Center was to design the lobbies and hallways of the office buildings and the Music Hall. As a further mark of Abby's influence, one of the painters chosen to work on the project was the renowned Mexican artist Diego Rivera, whom she had supported and befriended. With her son Nelson, also an enthusiast, acting as a mediator, Rivera was asked to produce one of the complex's most important features: a wall painting just inside the main building, facing the plaza entrance.

His ideas for the mural, *Man at the Crossroads,* were accepted on the basis of a sketch he sent to Abby and a synopsis Nelson read of what he intended. "My panel will show the Workers arriving at a true understanding of their rights . . . [resulting in] the liquidation of Tyranny . . . [and] the Workers . . . inheriting the Earth." Here was the spirit that had grown from Ludlow transformed into art—or so one could think. But when the mural was finished, its overt Communist overtones quickly made it the most controversial piece of artwork in Rockefeller Center. Capitalism was depicted by the evils of war and venereal disease, decadent women playing cards, and the brutality of mounted police ready to club workers. Scenes suggesting a Communist utopia took up the other half of the panel: a circle of workers singing and waving red flags, with, most startling of all, Lenin's portrait dominating everything. On behalf of the building's managing directors Nelson appealed to Rivera to at least substitute another likeness for Lenin's. He refused. Fearful that the mural would discourage potential tenants for the center, the directors finally decided to pay Rivera in full and have the mural destroyed, provoking outraged charges of "cultural vandalism." Though Abby never said anything publicly about the episode, she must have been devastated. In the end the conjunction of art, money, family, and politics had proved too powerful for her. Granted, Rivera had misled her; as both his friend and an avid admirer of his work, left to her own devices, she might have been able to find a different solution. Still, it is hard to imagine the directors—or Junior, who would surely have had the final say—letting that happen. From their perspective there was simply too much at stake.

Yet on other fronts Abby's artistic interests led to happier results, most notably in the founding of the Museum of Modern Art. The idea for such a museum had been conceived independently by three women, all of whom deplored the lack of recognition in New York of the modern movement. Lillie P. Bliss's interest in modernism was first sparked by her close friendship with the painter Arthur B. Davies, the person most involved in organizing the Amory Show of 1913. She had met Abby through her association with Adele and Christian Herter, and as early as 1916 she had begun to collect Cézanne watercolors and works by other French Postimpressionists, before moving on to American artists. Mary Sullivan, another friend of Abby's, had taught art before her marriage and, with her husband, collected and championed modern art. Abby herself—the third member of the triumvirate—was a more recent devotee, having been collecting on a modest scale for only a few years.

In the spring of 1929 the three women staged a luncheon at Abby's 10 West Fifty-fourth Street house to ask their guest, A. Conger Goodyear—who had been active in supporting what would become the city of Buffalo's art museum—to chair a committee to organize a museum of modern art in New York. Thereafter, events moved swiftly. By summer three other people had been brought on board, including Paul Sachs, a Harvard professor, and Frank Crowninshield, the editor of *Vanity Fair*. Alfred H. Barr Jr., a young art instructor at Wellesley, was hired as director, and rental space, consisting of six rooms and offices, was found on the twelfth floor of the Heckscher building at Fifty-seventh Street and Fifth Avenue. (It was to be the first of four temporary quarters before a permanent building, designed in the International style by Philip L. Goodwin and Edward Durrell Stone, was constructed in 1939.) Funding came from fifty-four private subscribers, and the museum accepted an initial gift of eight prints and one drawing. In November 1929 it opened to the public with a preview of its first exhibition, featuring borrowed French Postimpressionist works.

The founding of the museum and its early growth were perhaps Abby's greatest—certainly her most courageous—contribution as a patron of the arts. It grew from her fervent belief that art was less to be owned than shared with the public for the good of everyone: "It enriches the spiritual life and makes one more sane and sympathetic, more observant and understanding." The museum was also emphatically her project, not Junior's (though he did contribute later, generously if grudgingly, toward the new building). His lack of interest infuriated her sister Lucy and those of her associates close to the situation. Even Matisse, who tried to persuade Junior of the connections between the art he appreciated and contemporary work, was unable to do so. "Granite indifference" was how Alfred Barr described his attitude. In the same years, on the other hand, the walls of Kykuit acquired, from Joseph Duveen, art dealer to the New York and London establishment, a Hoppner portrait of Miss Judith Beresford of Ashbourne, Derbyshire, costing $136,800, and a portrait of Benjamin Franklin attributed to Benjamin West, presumably with Junior's full approval.

By the late 1930s the Museum of Modern Art's collections had expanded to include architecture, photography, moving pictures, and industrial arts, and plans were also afoot to tear down the Rockefellers' city house, which would eventually provide land for a new museum and its gardens. Meanwhile Abby and Junior moved into an apartment at 740 Park Avenue, and since it was clear that Senior had no intention of returning to Pocantico, they also made plans to lend Abeyton Lodge to Babs and move into Kykuit themselves in the summer of 1937. Then came Senior's death that spring.

With Senior gone, Abby and Junior were free to rearrange things at Kykuit to suit their own preferences, while facing the novel prospect of claiming as their own the house they had created for him. Choosing not to move into his master suite, they decided instead to use the second-floor rooms at the opposite end of the house, above the front entrance, with their bedroom on the northeast corner, Abby's sitting room across the remainder of the front, and Junior's study just behind, overlooking the south garden. Even though by then several of their children had their own places in the country—most on the estate itself—each of them was given a room in the house. Senior's and Cettie's rooms overlooking the river were reserved for John 3rd and his wife, Blanchette; the rooms facing north, above the rose garden, went to Nelson and his first wife, Mary, or Tod, as she was called, and David; Laurance, Babs, and Winthrop and their spouses were given rooms on the third floor. At the time of Senior's death, Abby and Junior had been in the midst of sorting through the furniture from their city house to see what they would keep and what was to be given away. Now, their summer would also be taken up with dismantling Senior's other houses. In all, they had two houses to dispose of and five, counting the Eyrie and Bassett Hall, open in some manner or other. Helping to ease them into Kykuit was Senior's housekeeper, Dora Payne, by now seventy-five years old, who was asked to stay on for a few months until the household could be reorganized. Finally Abby was able to write, "We are . . . safely and peacefully moved into Mr. Rockefeller Sr.'s house, and everything seems to be running smoothly here."

As complicated as all this was, Abby was a veteran of running multiple houses, and fortunately for her sake she had a knack for getting to know her staff as well as the skills to deal with them effectively. Far from being a distant employer, she was a working supervisor and (as she also proved when having to work with the museum staff at MoMA) adept at soothing hurt feelings and giving people needed confidence. To one of her house-keepers facing a particularly heavy day, she remarked, "Come in and laugh with me before we get started on this day. It's going to take some laughing to get through." Strict about the work, she could be forthright when she saw something incorrectly done, "but she always did it in a way that we wanted to make things right," recalled one of her servants. She made a game of showing off her new dresses and hats to the maids and asking them what she looked best in, and she made sure they were shifted from house to house to provide them with variety. She also recruited them to share in the work of her outside projects, for instance, knitting for the sol-diers during the war. "She taught me to love beautiful things, flowers and china and the way the table was set," said one of the waitresses, "and after the guests were gone, she was always hurt if no one had mentioned how nice things had looked or how beautiful the flowers were. 'Just think, Eini,' she would say, 'no one said a single word about all our work.' "

The observations she later made about her southern friends echoed both a bias against racism and her own management ideas: "The women of the South might as well make up their minds now to organize their house-holds on a different basis . . . Negro servants should be given wages that are commensurate with their services . . . they should be treated with not only kindness, but with consideration for their ability." Most of Abby's own maids, on the other hand, were Scandinavian, and servants' wages at Pocantico—though not as miserly as they had been during Senior's day—remained low. While she, too, was a proponent in the abstract of the rights of work-ing women, it was almost certainly true that within her own household, women still earned less than men. Also, after the minimum wage was en-acted nationally, she was relieved to find that the new law did not cover do-mestic help.

Was the spirit of Ludlow fading? No doubt Abby believed her close ties to her servants and concern for their welfare elevated her well above the typical employer of domestic help, and she was right about that. But wages were wages, and there can not have been many of Kykuit's staff who would not have welcomed higher pay.

Quite possibly, too, Abby considered it an added benefit for the staff to be living and working in such a beautiful place. Certainly she felt that way herself. "[Junior], Nelson, David and I simply adore living in this house," she wrote after settling in. "I am not quite sure about Babs, but the little girls have taken to their grandfather's house like ducks to water." Bab's daughters, Abby (called Mitzie) and Marilyn, spent most spring and fall weekends at Kykuit with their grandparents. They had their own bedrooms and playroom at the south end of the fourth floor and were allowed to choose their hand-painted French floral wallpaper. They took drives in the afternoons with their grandparents and had tea with their grandmother. A favorite time was helping her choose her evening dress and accessories for dinner. "Several things were put out and we would choose . . . She would wear a long evening gown every evening, whether it was for guests or just for the two of them. It was a routine beyond belief."

By the end of 1938 there were twelve grandchildren gathering at Kykuit, with six more to follow in the years ahead. As in the generation before, they all dressed up and put on their best manners for Sunday lunches at the Big House, but now Abby and Junior were presiding. "We knew it was a formal occasion, and if we arrived at five to one we used to drive around the [entrance] circle until it was one o'clock," one of them remembered later. "Grandfather did not like people to be early, and he definitely did not like people to be late. It was good to be sort of hovering in the holding zone like an airplane ready to land." In its essentials the ritual never varied: greetings at the entrance; assembling in the library to wait for the butler to open the sliding doors into the dining room; sitting at the table and starting off with clear soup in covered lacquered bowls and ending with finger bowls, a blossom of their grandmother's choice floating in each, followed by dessert topped by heavy whipped cream from the estate. Perhaps remembering his own father, Junior sometimes told jokes at the table, although it is hard to imagine him getting down on all fours to roughhouse with his grandchildren, as Senior had done.

To them, Junior remained a strict, sometimes distant grandfather. He "liked things to be just so," remarked one of the grandchildren later. Yet their grandmother seemed just the opposite: someone who truly enjoyed the disorderliness of children, since it showed her who they were and brought her closer to them. She greeted them with warm embraces—that "enfolded," as one put it—and strove to see the individuality in each, sitting with her daughters-in-law as they watched their children splash in the pool in the morning garden, inviting them to join her for tea in any number of nooks in the gardens she picked at her whim. Two favorite places were under the arbor by the rose garden or looking down at the circular pools in the dappled sunlight.

But if Abby enjoyed spending time with her grandchildren outdoors, it was Junior who was responsible for the maintenance of the grounds. In October 1938 he had the lawns regraded and the golf course redone. He was also determined to keep everything up as meticulously as it had always been. "The whole estate seemed to be in the hands of gardeners," a maid observed from her afternoon walks. "There were head gardeners and there were second gardeners, who drove around on constant reconnaissance in order to tell still other gardeners where to go and what to do next. Each tree and bush was given so much attention that I wondered if any of the Rockefellers knew that in most other places these things just grew." And if what was close at hand received such painstaking care, so too did the views in the distance, including the magnificent five-hundred-foot-high wall of the Palisades across the Hudson River, stretching from New York City up to the Tappan Zee.

Since 1901 the family, along with other wealthy landowners like J. P. Morgan, had contributed toward the preservation of the land beneath the cliffs and the cliffs themselves, which were being quarried and developed as city congestion spread northward. Junior's quiet purchase of parcels of land to give to the Palisades Interstate Park Commission, beginning in the late 1920s, preserved enough of the crest of the cliffs to permit the construction of a scenic road there. Such efforts were not new to him; after a trip to Jackson Hole and the Grand Tetons in Wyoming with Abby and the older boys during the summer of 1926, he worked assiduously to save those sites for posterity, and he did the same for much of the land on Mount Desert Island, in Maine, the redwoods in California, and the tip of Manhattan at Fort Tryon. Part of his concern for the Palisades came from the memories of horseback rides there while he was growing up. It also meant that Kykuit's view to the west (at a cost of approximately $20 million) would be forever saved.

To the grandchildren the estate seemed to stretch on endlessly, yet even outdoors there were rules governing paradise. "Club houses" could not be built by eager young hands at spots where they interfered with their grand-father's views. If young children were sometimes not allowed to wade in garden pools, they were also forbidden to tramp through the garden beds. And if they wanted friends over to play, elaborate arrangements had to be made to get them past the guards at the gatehouses.

Limitations were also placed upon the adults. Each family had just one key to the gates. Some activities could be done spontaneously; others could not. Appointments had to be made at the stables before horseback riding. But if Junior's children occasionally smarted at the control he exercised (in-cluding making them live on allowances that meant out-of-the-ordinary expenses such as vacations or new cars had to be negotiated, a regimen that lasted until 1934, when he was finally persuaded to set up individual trusts for them), life on the estate had definite advantages. Once they established residences of their own in Pocantico, their grounds and gardens were maintained free of charge. They paid nothing for the fuel and electricity they used to heat and light their houses. Each family was given its own watchman. The estate also provided them with milk, cream, fruit and veg-etables, cut flowers, and potted plants. Their mail and newspapers were de-livered by estate workers. Their cars were serviced and garaged (whenever possible), and gas and oil were provided at no cost, as was mechanical work and car painting. They could arrange to use estate trucks for taking things back and forth to the city, and they could use its chauffeurs for tak-ing maids to the Tarrytown station or picking them up. Workmen were supplied to do repair work, but any new construction had to be discussed with Junior beforehand. It was indeed a charmed existence.

The year 1939 was a banner one for both Junior and Abby—a time when their separate efforts produced wide-ranging results. The Museum of Modern Art opened to the public in its new, permanent quarters, and Rockefeller Center was finished. Also, the Cloisters—built to house George Grey Bernard's collection of Romanesque and Gothic fragments, which Ju-nior had purchased and donated to the Metropolitan Museum of Art, along with funding for the building—had just been finished. Perched on a high, rocky promontory overlooking the Hudson River, the building deftly incorporated not only a multitude of smaller fragments but five complete cloisters from French monasteries and a Romanesque tower. Having pro-nounced Rockefeller Center a "graceless bulk," Lewis Mumford had happier things to say in this case: "A little of that ancient peace still broods over this museum . . . you can walk around one of these quiet gardens and even discover whether or not you have a soul."

Abby would have said that you could also find your soul looking at a modern painting at MoMA. She was not closely involved with the Cloisters project, but she certainly was with both Williamsburg and Rockefeller Center, and for his part Junior gave both the land and a sizable cash donation for building "her" museum (making him, in fact, the largest donor to MoMA up to that point). But it was she who was central to the work and decision making, spending countless hours on the telephone, in meetings, and writing letters asking potential donors for money, all of which took time away from Junior, to his great annoyance. According to David, who resented his father for not supporting her interests as fully as she had his, Junior "pressured" her into resigning from MoMA's board. Was it in effect a quid pro quo for his contributions to the new building? Possibly.

That both Junior and Abby were able to carry on so many projects simultaneously was due in no small part to the ample staff employed at the family office, which eventually moved from 26 Broadway to Rockefeller Center. Among other things it was set up to handle a wide variety of requests with previously formatted responses, thereby insulating the family from difficult situations that might have had unpleasant consequences. In many cases it was simply a matter of efficiency—saving their valuable time for more important things—but not always.

In November 1938, Babs received a desperate appeal from Elise Goldstein, a German woman who had worked briefly as her governess when she was nine. The appeal was actually the second one she had sent. Married to a doctor, with two boys, ages eleven and thirteen, she had written a few months earlier asking for help in emigrating from Germany and had heard nothing. "Please, please help us," she wrote this time. "We will certainly not be a bother to you for long. My husband and I are not afraid of work and are entirely healthy." Babs sent the letter to "whoever handles this kind of thing" in the Rockefeller Offices and was told the following February of her family's "definite policy" of not responding to anyone from Germany seeking refuge.

Was Elise Jewish? Did the Rockefellers know? In the abstract, anti-Semitism was abhorrent to both Abby and Junior. In 1923 Abby had written in a letter to her oldest boys, "Out of my experience and observation has grown the earnest conviction that one of the greatest causes of evil in the world is race hatred or race prejudice." Her thinking about the issue was spurred by the lynchings and race riots that were so prevalent at the time, but she included Jews in her remarks. "The two peoples . . . that suffer most . . . are the Jews and the Negroes . . . I long to have our family stand firmly for what is best and highest in life." David, the youngest of her children, and in some ways the closest to her, went to Germany on three different trips during the 1930s. In 1937 he had witnessed firsthand Hitler's goose-stepping troops, the dangerous "frenzied adulation" of the German people toward their leader, and the "flagrant persecution" of the Jews.

Junior, too, seemed to feel strongly about the issue. In 1941, before the United States was officially at war, he wrote, "I would rather die fighting the brutal, barbarous, inhuman force represented by Hitlerism than live in a world that is dominated by that force." Yet apparently he decided to leave unchanged the office policy regarding Jews—or other Germans—seeking asylum in the United States. Thus there was no help available for Elise Goldstein and her family, even though the anti-Semitic riots of "Kristallnacht" (the Night of Broken Glass) had occurred in Germany and Austria just days before her second appeal to Babs, and by the end of January, when Babs was informed of the family's stance on German emigrants, Hitler's policy of exterminating all European Jews had been made manifestly obvious. Yet since Senior's time the family's philanthropic efforts had been directed primarily at addressing large problems requiring the kinds of resources their enormous wealth could provide—not at helping individuals in distress. It was also true that the U.S. government did nothing to help Jewish refugees or to challenge the Nazi regime's policies regarding Jews.

On other fronts, however, Junior and Abby did throw themselves energetically into war activities, concentrating on services for the Allied soldiers such as the USO (United Service Organization). At home, Abby also took up her knitting needles and encouraged her staff to do the same. "I have just finished enough six inch squares to make a very good sized afghan which Eini, our waitress, is putting together for us . . . I have bought . . . hundreds of pounds of wool, which have been knitted into socks, helmets, sweaters, blankets and baby jackets by our Scandanavian [sic] households in Pocantico and here in New York." Her daughters-in-law, too, were knitting along with their households, and as honorary chair of the War Relief Society in the village she gave its members wool to knit "the usual garments for the Red Cross." Among the causes she contributed to were the United Jewish Appeal and the Emergency Relief Fund—both organizations striving to get Jews out of eastern Europe, though most of her efforts in that area were concentrated on rescuing artists like Marc Chagall, Max Ernst, and Jacques Lipchitz from the clutches of the Third Reich. And the wartime project perhaps closest to her heart was organizing the War Veterans Art Center that offered therapeutic classes ranging from drawing and painting to sculpture, metalwork, and weaving to former servicemen suffering from the effects of the fighting.

But primarily Abby's concerns during the war years focused on her boys. John 3rd and Laurance went to Washington, D.C., to take desk jobs for the navy, and Nelson—believing that economic development would help stave off Nazi influence in the southern hemisphere—had persuaded Roosevelt to appoint him coordinator of Inter-American Affairs, placing him in Washington as well. Winthrop had not waited for the United States to enter the war before volunteering and saw combat in the Pacific, and David, enlisting (at his mother's suggestion) in 1942, was assigned to Intelligence and sent to Algiers. With her two younger sons both at the front, Abby monitored the war as closely as she could. Winnie's situation was the most worrisome. Having recovered from a bout of jaundice and pneumonia, he had just rejoined his unit when his ship was struck by a Japanese kamikaze. The officers he was playing cards with died in the blast. Burned on his hands and face, he was sent to a hospital in Guam to recover before rejoining his unit in Okinawa.

There was more to worry about, too, than just the war when it came to the children. Doubtless Abby heard rumors of Nelson's involvement with other women, and she had always been particularly fond of Tod, his wife. Babs's marriage was also floundering. As she confided to Win—the brother she was closest to—David Milton was an inconstant husband, not because of other women but because of his addiction to making deals and not following through. As she said, she never wanted to "save the world"; she did not have that "Rockefeller conceit." All she wanted was a warm and loving home life. They had built a red brick Georgian house at Hudson Pines, property Junior gave them across the road from Pocantico, and for a while her husband had happily taken up farming there with their girls. Yet the farm did not repair the marriage, and in 1943 Babs filed for divorce. There had never been a divorce in the family before. Junior was opposed to it on religious grounds, and it was to David Milton, not Babs, that he finally offered his support. Abby may have ached to say something to her daughter by way of advice, and perhaps she did, but Babs was at heart a private person, not given to confiding in either of her parents. Instead she unburdened her feelings to Win when he took a three-day leave to drive to Reno to see her.

Life at Kykuit was also changed by the war, with cuts in staff outdoors, rationing, and shortages of all kinds. But at last the day came when the fighting ended, and the sons came home to pick up their lives where they had left them. Before they arrived, however, Abby embarked upon a campaign of her own. "My mind is possessed with the idea of having portraits done of all you boys," she wrote Win while he was still overseas. "You will have enough service bars and stripes to make it really exciting." By the time she was done, life-size portraits of everyone in the family hung in the large medieval living room of the Playhouse. Had she purposely chosen a form of memorial common in the English country houses Kykuit seemed in so many ways designed to replicate? Perhaps. But on a more basic level, it was also a simple act of joy that her boys had "made it through."

Yet Abby knew that life would never be the same as it had been before the war. In fact, she had sensed change in the air even earlier. In 1933 Junior had given her plans for a teahouse at Jordan Pond, on Mount Desert Island in Maine, and having gone over them room by room, she sat down to write Grosvenor Atterbury, the architect, a detailed critique. "Mr. Rockefeller said to me . . . that if I had any suggestions . . . he would be glad to hear what they were. Of course it was a very dangerous thing for him to say, for I always have lots of ideas." The "very fine but very elaborate plan," she went on, should be made simpler and more convenient. "It seems to me almost criminal of us not to face the future and to burden the coming generations with equipment which it does not want. The young people who are growing up today don't want to have saddled on them enormous houses, either to live in or to eat in or to play in."

Over the years she had undertaken a variety of projects aimed at providing efficient living quarters for working Americans—including the Grace Dodge Hotel for Women in Washington, D.C., and a model five-room workingman's cottage on a strip of land in Elizabeth, New Jersey, that she had persuaded Standard Oil to donate for the purpose. Equally focused on the practical side of housing were her reactions in 1938 to the architectural drawings for a house John 3rd and Blanchette were planning to build on Butternut Hill at Pocantico. Its size—some 225,000 cubic feet—worried her. "Is it a house that would be complicated to manage? I mean would it require more service because it is spread out over quite a little ground?" she wondered. After the war, even her own beloved Eyrie in Maine had come to seem "a little big and lonely without lots of children in it," as she wrote her friend Olivia Cutting, adding, "I am threatening to push part of it off the cliff."

She and Junior were also spending less time in New York and Kykuit, choosing instead to pass the long winter months away, usually in Tucson at the Arizona Inn, as much for her benefit as his. Her health had become something of a concern, yet she had to be restrained, as she wrote, tongue in cheek, from "going down to the pool where most people congregate." For Junior was afraid if she did she would "become intimate with all sorts of people and will want to talk to them, so generally we eat in what I call the old people's dining room, where he feels I am safer." But when Laurance suggested that they buy a house in Arizona so that the family could visit, she replied, "Certainly I don't wish to acquire another house." She also loved the cozy intimacy of Bassett Hall, in Williamsburg, the smallest of their houses, and wrote to a friend at one point, "I seem recently to have been possessed with a strong desire to live in a small house, a little New England cottage, with green blinds, and room for just John and myself."

But she still loved seeing her grandchildren at Kykuit: "I find our very large family of children and grandchildren so absorbing [that] I have practically seen no one outside the family circle, and spend a great deal of my time trying to become better acquainted." By then all of the children were married, even Winthrop, whose choice of Bobo Sears, the daughter of a Lithuanian coal miner, as a wife was avidly covered in the press. Abby did not know Bobo well, but she was supportive and happy for her son and adored her other daughters-in-law, as they did her. John 3rd, who, among the brothers, had had the most difficulty with his self-confidence, was—thanks to his wife, Blanchette's support—learning to deal with his father's autocratic manner and developing his own philanthropic interests. Nelson was active in Latin American affairs and president of MoMA; he also clearly had political ambitions. Laurance's interests were in venture capitalism and environmental issues. David was rising through the ranks at Chase Manhattan Bank, which he would one day head. And Babs had managed to find happiness with her second husband, Irving Pardee, a neurologist eleven years her senior, who taught at the Columbia University College of Physicians and Surgeons.

Nearer home, the boys were taking on increasing responsibility for the estate. As early as 1934, Junior had turned much of the business management of Pocantico over to John 3rd, who was uncomfortable with his grandfather's view that estate workers should save their meager wages for their old age. "Whatever we have given him," Senior said of one such worker, ". . . has been in the nature of charity. I am sure his family would be much better off to feel that they were independently caring for their own." After a group life insurance plan was adopted by the employees of Rockefeller Center in 1935, John 3rd outlined for his father what the costs would be if the estate were to adopt something similar. But it was not until 1937, when the country as a whole was dealing with the issue of social security (not yet available to employees on private estates), that a general plan covering death benefits, pensions based on salary, age, and years of service was established for the staff at Pocantico. Monthly payroll deductions would be voluntary for current workers, compulsory for new employees.

During his tenure as the estate's administrator, John 3rd also concerned himself—as did Nelson later—with looking for economies and proposed that Kykuit be closed for the winter months. Junior chose, however, to keep the house open, though if he or his sons needed any reminders of the unhappy consequences of extravagance, they had only to look at what was happening to the once sumptuous and massive Rockwood Hall, William Rockefeller's former estate next door. The following year it would be foreclosed and the house torn down. Indeed, estates everywhere were disappearing, making Pocantico itself more of an anachronism all the time, though one most of the family still took for granted.

Even more gratifying to Junior and Abby than the role the boys were playing in managing the estate was the effort they were making to more effectively direct their philanthropic activities. In 1940 they had begun retreating to the Playhouse after Sunday dinners to talk about their shared interests. They asked their father to join them in these "Brothers' Meetings," but he refused, possibly to avoid confronting all of them at once. Abby tactfully declined as well, which left it up to them to decide what to do. Concluding that a jointly supported pool of funds devoted to philanthropic purposes would have more impact than they could hope to have individually, they formed the Rockefeller Brothers Fund, or RBF. Created by a new generation of the family, it promised to continue the Rockefellers' philanthropic principles in an effective manner, an effort Junior would handsomely support by turning over to RBF the note—worth almost $60 million—for the remainder of the funds he had personally advanced to Rockefeller Center.

But what none of them knew during those years was how little time was left to them as a united family. Abby and John returned to New York from Arizona at the beginning of April 1948, and on the following Saturday, Nelson, taking advantage of the time to discuss MoMA affairs, drove his mother to Pocantico, where the family was to gather for a quiet reunion. She wanted to know about who some of the new, promising young artists were and talked of becoming more active again, now that she was home. By temperament given to superlatives, she declared that the time they all spent together that weekend was "perfect." On Sunday she rode back to the city with David, holding her youngest grandchild, Peggy, on her lap, wearing a new dress and hat for the occasion, because, as she said, "I've never been so happy." She stopped on the way to greet her newest daughter-in-law, Bobo, and called her sister Lucy when she got home with all the family news. The next morning, she woke up feeling ill. The doctor was sent for and arrived, but while talking to him, she died suddenly, at the age of seventy-three, of what her doctor, as her son John reported, would call "a tired heart."

It was a devastating blow—most of all for Junior, who was distraught beyond words. Powerless to bring her back, he had her cremated the same day she died. John and Nelson spent the first night with him. Then the letters praising her began pouring in, testimony to all the lives and endeavors she had touched. She *had* achieved great things, but the help she gave others was often intensely immediate and practical. Once during the baptism of the weeping child of one of the family's chauffeurs, Abby had spontaneously taken the child from her mother's arms and pressed the baby's teary cheek against her own to calm her. A small act, but for Abby, it had been instinctive. Perhaps it was such small acts that prompted a family member much later to say she felt Abby had "saved" the family. As one of her friends wrote Junior shortly after her death, "She was like a pure diamond with so many different rays of light that penetrated with clear understanding into so many different hearts." "A great woman," said another, "whom to talk with was to respect, and whom to know . . . was to love her."

Her children, too, reeled with the shock of her unexpected death. As David remarked, her devotion to them had been more sustaining than they realized. "No one else had had a comparable influence on my beliefs, my tastes, and my capacity to enjoy the world around me." In welcoming spontaneous adventure, and in connecting with humanity outside the confining veil of privacy in which Junior tried to envelop them all, she had given her children the capacity to do so as well. The question was to what extent they would continue acting on what she had tried so hard to pass along.

After Abby's death, the family kept coming to Pocantico as they always had. For many it would remain, as one of her grandchildren described it, "perfect," with "an almost magical order and beauty." Yet the same person also found it "hard to imagine living in this amazing house." And among the cousins, some were increasingly uncomfortable with the grandeur and scale of the place. For them Kykuit was rapidly becoming, as one of them put it, "a distant historical site." He preferred spending time at the stable, because he enjoyed riding and visiting Joe, the groom, and his wife, who lived upstairs. "It was more fun, I felt freer there." David Jr. remembered the little door that used to go into the stables, "more of a human scale" than the massive stonework and the lofty ceilings inside where the cars were parked, an almost "sinister" place with its "antihuman" sounds. Others felt Pocantico isolated them from their friends. "The same walls built to ensure privacy and protection also closed out the rest of the world." One cousin, not alone in describing her loneliness, called the estate "a verdant cage." "To us as small children it was a riddle why [the walls] were there and why the guards were there, and why the dogs were there. What did that mean about who was outside?" Some were unwilling to have friends over, not knowing "after they saw the place . . . whether they still cared about us or were just using the means to this luxurious end." Another cousin would remember feeling "extraneous" when her parents gave a birthday party for her at the Playhouse, despite her protests. Above all, though, they had to face the question (as their elders had) of what it meant to be Rockefellers, and in time the Playhouse, as it was for their fathers, became the place where, as "the cousins," they would gather to discuss their shared concerns.

Meanwhile Junior continued his habit of coming for weekends in the spring and fall, but now he had to face being alone up at the Big House. He had never particularly liked to socialize with "miscellaneous people," as he put it once to his biographer, Raymond Fosdick. Instead he used his inner resources and faith to seek what comfort he could, finding solace in hard work and then, three years after Abby's death, in taking a new wife, Martha Baird Allen, the widow of an old college friend. When David was asked what he thought of his father's remarrying, he replied that he remembered his mother had not "thought highly" of Martha—an unfortunate beginning to what became a strained relationship between her and all of Junior's children, with the exception of Nelson.

At the same time Nelson was pressing his father to sell Pocantico to his children so it would be out of his estate for tax purposes, which he finally agreed to do in 1951, for the astonishingly low price of $760,295. And after his remarriage, the boys took firmer hold of the property. Blanchette and her fellow daughters-in-law made up family rules for the Playhouse, to be enforced by a "junior advisory committee" of four of the cousins. More startling than any other change at Pocantico during the 1950s, however, was a new outdoor swimming pool Nelson planned for the Playhouse, along with cabanas and an eating area. Junior visited the site with Nelson's architect, Wally Harrison, in July 1955, in the midst of construction. While the project was "exceedingly unique and fascinating," he wrote his son, it was not at all like the sketches he had been shown beforehand. His tone was actually much milder than his deep visceral dislike of the irregularly shaped, bright blue and white marble pool, with the two boat-shaped hulls projecting from it, and its waterfall, white high-dive platform, and suntrap—all in pronounced dissonance with the surrounding landscape, particularly as viewed from above at Kykuit. What a departure from the Corinthian columns and friezes inside! Somehow, through Nelson's agency, the modernism his father so disliked was making its appearance at Pocantico, encroaching on all he held sacred there. With more respect for his feelings, Abby had never attempted such a thing.

Yet Junior was not at Kykuit very much anymore. Nor did he spend much time in Seal Harbor or at the city apartment. As a result, he saw the family far less frequently during his last years. He had never been as fond as Abby of the disorder and confusion of family life, and David felt that Martha did not want to be with the children and grandchildren. Nor did either of them seem to want to see anyone other than a close circle of employees. As if repeating Senior's pattern of staying away as he grew older, the two of them spent most of their time in Tucson and Williamsburg.

Of all the places available to them, Williamsburg had long since become Junior's favorite. There he was surrounded by the tangible results of the work closest to his heart. There, too, he could move around unobtrusively, almost as an ordinary member of the community. "Sunday Mrs. Rockefeller and I sat in front of the post office for a long time and watched the people passing by," he had written in 1941, while Abby was still alive. "We often do that. And we like to walk home from the movies at night. We look in the windows and we look at the moon and the stars . . . I feel that I really belong in Williamsburg." Back at Kykuit, on the other hand—almost symbolically—the vaulting under the forecourt constructed at such cost during that fateful summer of 1912 to support the giant Oceanus fountain had started to collapse. With the bedrock in some cases a good twenty feet below surface, fixing the problem proved enormously difficult. But it was done; defying the ravages of time, the great fountain survived.

Unlike it, however, Junior proved to be mortal. In 1959 he was diagnosed with prostate cancer and operated on in New York City. Before going to Tucson to recuperate, he refused to talk with his sons about his prognosis. Hurt and angry, they contacted his doctor in Arizona and suggested that they seek a second opinion. The result was a letter, signed by Junior, to David, scolding him in what he considered a "cold" and "hostile" way for interfering with Junior's care and thereby hurting Martha's feelings: "Acutely conscious . . . of the burdens she has carried because of my uncertain health . . . my heart is even heavier at the thought that my own sons should have added by one iota to these strains." Later, David learned from the doctor that the letter was written "in its entirety" by Martha, and that his father had repeatedly refused to sign it before finally capitulating to her wishes. No doubt she thought she was doing the best that could be done—that it would only add to Junior's discomfort to have his sons meddling with his care, or worse, moving him back to New York to undergo treatment there. This way he could at least die in peace.

More upset than ever, David, while on a business trip to Arizona a few weeks later in early April, paid an unannounced visit on his father. He found him very weak and "touched" that David had come, though careful to say how good Martha had been to him during his illness. A month later he died. Presumably in accord at last, his widow and sons arranged to have his body brought back to Kykuit, where services were held and his ashes buried next to Abby's in the plot they had chosen together. Once again, a patriarch had come home to the family seat, having died in a place far away.

What would happen to Kykuit now? If the pool Junior so disliked had become part of the landscape, in almost every other way he had managed to keep the place as it was—to hold at bay all the pressures for change, preserving the house and the estate as he had all those other monuments to times gone by. He had told his biographer, Raymond Fosdick, that he doubted his sons would do the same. Yet no final decision had been made about the future of Kykuit. Legally Martha was free to stay there as long as she wanted. From the first, however, Nelson seems to have set his sights on taking it over, and knowing his son as well as he did, Junior would probably have guessed that he would succeed—as indeed he did.

10

The Prince of Kykuit

"His patrons and collectors were from the American aristocracy," wrote a student of his later, "handsome men and beautiful women that drove up in fine autos and lived in mansions." Still, he was perpetually short of cash. The year of his death found him looking for work as a day laborer to make ends meet.

His life would have been easier if his wife had been less extravagant, but he loved her to distraction, endlessly celebrating her being, her body, in his art. She was a small woman, of striking elegance and beauty, but that was not how he depicted her. Heroically proportioned, with triumphant breasts and thighs, she balances, arms half raised, as if by magic on tiny feet, in what his biographer describes as "the central work of [his] productive life"— Standing Woman or, as it is sometimes called, Elevation.

At the time most people considered his work outrageous, obscene, consisting as it did almost entirely of nude figures, often with distinctly erotic overtones. But it was much admired by those rich handsome men who came in fine autos, one of whom eventually acquired a bronze cast of Standing Woman. In addition, he helped support the sculptor's widow, the beautiful Isabel, though he carefully concealed his identity from her and as a result picked up several major works at bargain prices. (Not for nothing was he his grandfather's grandson.) Later he would make those works, along with Standing Woman, part of his own great creation: one of the world's finest outdoor displays of modern sculpture, which also succeeded in transforming the house and gardens his father had built for his grandfather into something enchantingly fresh and original.

When Nelson Rockefeller met Gaston Lachaise, they were both on the brink of achieving significant prominence in life: Nelson at Rockefeller Center, of which he eventually became president, as well as at his mother's beloved Museum of Modern Art, where he was serving on the Junior Advisory Committee and would soon be made a trustee; and Lachaise in a large retrospective at MoMA in 1935, the first one-man show of the work of an American sculptor (or so described, though he was born in France) ever presented by the museum. As part of a group of young patrons actively promoting Lachaise's work, Nelson was influential in bringing about the retrospective. Lachaise also, during those years, received a pair of commissions for limestone panels above doorways at Rockefeller Center.

Among the other young enthusiasts surrounding Lachaise in the 1930s were Lincoln Kirstein and Edward Warburg. As undergraduates they had helped organize the Harvard Society of Contemporary Art, and both served with Nelson on the Junior Advisory Committee at MoMA. In touting Lachaise's art, they were on thin ice; not all of MoMA's trustees admired the work of the temperamental sculptor, a fact he himself understood only too well. As he wrote his wife, "Warburg said the situation at the Museum was that all the young people like you, but the old ones say 'Why that man with his fat women?' "

Being Lachaise's patron could mean more than just promoting his work, too. Lincoln Kirstein (who, with George Balanchine, later founded the New York City Ballet yet remained passionately interested in sculpture all his life) became the model for *Man Walking,* a two-foot bronze nude, posed in the same position as an Egyptian pharaoh in a diminutive statue that he and the sculptor had found in the Metropolitan Museum of Art. He is also said to have posed with Isabel Lachaise for *The Reclining Couple* (or *Dans La Nuit*), a life-size depiction of a nude couple lying intertwined in sleep. Whether Nelson posed for Lachaise is unclear, but he may have. While the sculptor was working on his second set of panels for Rockefeller Center—which celebrated its builders by showing pairs of men with tools in their hands wearing gauzy tunics that barely concealed their bodies—he wrote his wife, "I am having a debauch of work. I am undressing all my male friends." In any case, Lachaise's panels provoked none of the disastrous controversy Diego Rivera's ill-fated mural did, though he died quite suddenly within months of the MoMA retrospective.

Nelson's payments to Lachaise's widow—$5,000 to help cover her outstanding debts and an allowance of $300 a month for three years—were made through Lincoln Kirstein, who had also encouraged Nelson to commission a work for his garden during the final year of the sculptor's life. According to the contract between Kirstein and Isabel, the money was to be paid back without interest, but it was actually returned to Nelson in the form of sculptures, most notably *Man,* a massive male nude, and a bronze cast of *Dans La Nuit,* the final work done by Lachaise before his death. Both are bold, archetypal pieces that produce the powerful, direct impact Nelson loved in art.

And both would be among the first sculptures he placed in the gardens at Kykuit during the winter of 1962, after he took possession of the house. With snow still covering the ground, he began positioning the larger works he had on hand, including *Man* and *Dans La Nuit,* below the terraces to the west of the house, consulting with MoMA's director, René d'Harnoncourt, as they were moved to their final locations.

Thus began what would remain one of the great passions of Nelson's life: developing Kykuit as a premier setting for the display of modern art. If his father had chosen to let the place harden into a frozen monument to the past, he meant to change all that, and the fact that he refused to wait for the snow to melt before starting was characteristic of the restless energy and drive he would bring to the project. Eventually, too, he placed his sculptures around Kykuit's gardens himself, without bothering to ask anyone for advice. Much as he admired d'Harnoncourt, he was probably impatient even then with the other man's approach to installation, a subject d'Harnoncourt once described as "full of terribly seductive pitfalls," explaining, "You mustn't make things look desirable—dramatization for its own sake must be avoided." D'Harnoncourt may have been right, but for Nelson dramatization, operating hand in hand with his relentless determination to work his will, was everything—in life as well as in art. As for other people's "musts," they existed primarily to be ignored. As Blanchette Rockefeller, his older brother John 3rd's wife, once said of him, "In many ways he was the jewel of the family, in other ways remained a naughty boy. He was just a little out of hand all the time."

The mere fact that Nelson had decided to live in Kykuit was itself a notable piece of self-dramatization. With Junior gone, his widow, Martha Baird Rockefeller, had decided to build a much smaller house next door, and except for Winthrop, all of Junior and Abby's sons, including Nelson, already had houses on or near the Pocantico estate. But Nelson and his first wife, Tod, were on the verge of a divorce, with a new marriage, to Happy Fitler Murphy, in the offing. To begin their life together someplace other than the house he and Tod had shared made sense.

Yet Nelson would have wanted to live at Kykuit whatever the circumstances. He had always loved the place. At one point as a boy, leaving his grandfather's house, he had remarked to his tutor, "I would give three weeks at Seal Harbor any time for three days here at Pocantico." He also believed Kykuit was his by right as the head of his generation of the Rockefeller family. Technically the position belonged to his older brother, John D. Rockefeller 3rd, but "Johnny"—painfully shy and in his early years racked by many of the same doubts and fears that had once plagued Junior—had early on, and with no apparent regret, taken a backseat to his supremely self-confident, charismatic younger brother "Nel."

Inevitably Nelson's desire to take over Kykuit produced a certain amount of turmoil in the family. What right had he to exclusive use of the house? There were those who thought his brother David had designs on it. Yet David's wife, Peggy, had no interest in living there; neither did John 3rd or Laurance. That only left Nelson. A decade earlier, too, while the rest of the family nursed their shock at Junior's remarriage, he had gone out of his way to charm "Aunt Martha" (who was legally entitled to live at Kykuit as long as she liked), and she genuinely enjoyed her special relationship with him. "You and I always 'speak our piece,' don't we, with no aftermath of 'feelings' pro or con," she wrote him at one point. "I think it's wonderful, bless you." Now, when he asked, he found her only too happy to pass Kykuit on to him. She even volunteered to continue paying a good part of the maintenance costs for the house and grounds, just as she would become the family's largest contributor to his perennial political campaigns, giving him more than $10 million before her death in 1971.

So with a minimum of fuss, late in 1961, the family seat became Nelson's. When he took it over, he was fifty-four years old and had already spent three decades renovating, building, and rebuilding more than a half dozen other residences for himself. There was Hawes House, the modest place on the Pocantico estate (formerly occupied by Dyson DeLap) given to him by his parents, which he later much enlarged, as well as a guesthouse and another small retreat he built nearby; his huge apartment on Fifth Avenue in

New York; and the house on Foxhall Road in Washington, D.C., that he acquired when he began his government service there and had redecorated several times. To those he added the Anchorage, a spectacular house perched above the rocky coast of Frenchman's Bay in Seal Harbor, Maine, and a ranch house, built on a hilltop in Venezuela from which it had been necessary to remove an entire cemetery before construction began. Each of these had its distinct character, and Nelson (who had once dreamed of being an architect only to be discouraged by his parents) was intimately involved in planning all of them.

Most of what he built was emphatically modern in style, done in materials that blended with their surroundings, yet boldly assertive in massing and layout. He also invariably used the same architect, Wallace K. Harrison. A leading member of the team that designed Rockefeller Center, "Wally" Harrison had started life as the son of an alcoholic foundry worker in Worcester, Massachusetts. Though less talented than several of the other architects on the Rockefeller Center team, he had considerable charm and the added advantage of being the brother-in-law of David Milton, Babs Rockefeller's husband. He was definitely a comer, the sort of person Nelson—who had introduced himself by offering to help Harrison pin up some architectural drawings—often pulled into his orbit. Before long Harrison was operating as his tutor on architectural issues, a favor he would return not only by hiring Harrison to design his houses but also by inviting him to Washington, where he served as cultural coordinator of Nelson's Inter-American Affairs Office.

After World War II, Harrison worked on the expansion of Rockefeller Center and a score of other high-rise office buildings in the city. At the same time he served as the chief architect for both the United Nations headquarters in New York—built on a site Nelson had persuaded Junior to buy and donate to the organization—and Lincoln Center, which was chaired in its early years by Nelson's brother John 3rd, and where, in addition to heading the board of architects, he designed the Metropolitan Opera House. Following that he turned to Empire State Plaza, the colossal lynchpin of Nelson's campaign to rebuild downtown Albany.

Reflecting on the extraordinary opportunities that came his way in life, chiefly as a result of his friendship with Nelson Rockefeller, Harrison once remarked, "For an architect, it was like being handed a meringue glacé; it was almost too easy." Certainly there were those who would have agreed with that assessment. By and large architectural critics have not been kind to Harrison's work, especially Empire State Plaza, which Daniel Okrent, the author of the definitive study of Rockefeller Center, describes as "one of the most egregious acts of architecture ever committed in the United States . . . a Solenoid Stonehenge rising out of nowhere signifying nothing but the enormity of the ego that called it into being."

As bad as Empire State Plaza was, however, the partnership that Nelson liked to call "the firm of Harrison and Rockefeller" did do some far better work in the smaller, more intimate places built for Nelson's enjoyment as a private person. Ego aplenty there still was (as John Lockwood, the long-time Rockefeller family lawyer, once said, "Nelson *loved* the palaces"), but in this case ambition was tempered by other feelings: a love of nature, a passion for art, and a fascination with fusing the two in exciting structures that were also places to live.

A good example is the Anchorage in Seal Harbor. Nelson chose the site—a rough granite outcrop at the edge of the water with spectacular views in all directions—and according to legend, while exploring it with Harrison he drove pairs of stakes in the ground, telling him they framed the views he wanted to see from the house. The rest he left to the architect. Starting with this "program," Harrison came up with a plan for a wood and fieldstone house consisting of two interlocking crescent-shaped masses, a larger one facing inland, containing the main entrance, the bedrooms, and the service areas, and a smaller one for the living room and dining room turned toward the sea. Cantilevered out from there was a curving balcony for alfresco dining, while in the midst of the house a spiral stairway led from the ground floor up to a tower resembling a lighthouse, which was used to dry sails. And completing the composition outdoors, along the shore, lay a variety of terraces, including one with a swimming pool carved out of the bedrock, filled by the ocean itself, churning around it at high tide.

As good as Harrison's design was, it did not meet with universal approval. The fact that Nelson was building a modern house in the family's much-loved summer retreat had thrown Junior into paroxysms of anxiety, and he made no secret of how he felt. But the reality quite bowled him over. When the house was finished, Nelson invited his parents to lunch, after which Junior went home and wrote him a note full of praise: "As you well know, I have spoken often with some skepticism in regard to your house . . . In view of this attitude on my part I hoped you realized how completely captivated I was by the place and how abjectly I apologized for my skepticism."

The modern house that could charm Junior was indeed a wonder, yet of all the places Nelson and Wally Harrison created during those years, the most provocative for what it revealed of Nelson's taste and aesthetic sense was his apartment at 810 Fifth Avenue. Starting with a one-floor layout in 1934, he added an entire duplex below it three years later to form a truly imposing city residence. But from the beginning he meant to create something totally unlike the typical grand New York apartment. Proposing to combine French, eighteenth-century parquet flooring with a Lachaise mantelpiece in the living room of the original apartment, he managed to shock even his mother when she saw the plans. The Lachaise mantelpiece particularly bothered her. "My own feeling is that nothing else in that room will count. Your furniture will look—in my humble opinion—as if it were trying to associate with people it didn't like," she wrote, adding, "I like being different, but I see no point in sacrificing one's comfort and pleasure on the altar of originality."

Yet mixing works by Lachaise with antique French flooring was exactly the sort of thing Nelson intended to do. As he explained later, "When Wally and I started the apartment, his idea—which we shared—was to do something in the style of Louis XV, with its excitement and beauty, but done in a modern way." Architecturally, modernism was all straight lines and flat, plain surfaces. How to combine it with the swelling curves of Louis XV decorative details and furniture was no easy problem to solve. In practice what it turned out to mean was evident in the vast living room in the duplex, with its rounded corners and its doorway and fireplace openings edged in ogee curves, yet set in perfectly smooth walnut paneling, left in its natural color and polished to a high gloss in the modern manner.

It was the art in the room, however, that gave it its drop-dead panache. To fill the spaces within Harrison's paneling around the fireplaces at either end of the room, Nelson commissioned two murals, one by Matisse and the other by Léger. Matisse painted his—a group of four female figures, their shapes subtly blending with one another, the colors rich and deep—in Paris, working from measured drawings of the space. But Léger actually came over and worked in the apartment. So captivated was Nelson by the result—sinuously curving naturalistic shapes in vivid greens, blues, and yellows—that he asked Léger to stay on and work his magic in the hallways as well as around the central marble staircase and design the ceiling for the master bedroom.

In addition to the murals in the duplex living room, its walls were graced with paintings by Juan Gris, Giorgio de Chirico, and half a dozen other artists, including Matisse and Léger. Jean-Michel Frank, the great French designer, custom-made the furniture, again in simplified Louis XV style, using light woods and modern fabrics, with yellow and blue as the predominant colors, echoing the Léger mural. The lamps were done in gilded bronze by sculptors Alberto and Diego Giacometti, and the carpet was designed by Christian Bérard, with a dark pink background matching the dress of one of the women in the Matisse mural.

"I was always off-beat," Nelson remarked of the apartment at one point, "way ahead of what was going on at the time." He was also only twenty-nine years old when he began transforming the duplex, and it showed. There was an excess of everything in the apartment: of art, of colors, of moods. But Nelson never ceased loving the "warmth" of it all, a warmth that came, he believed, from mixing old and new: "It had elements of the past styled in a contemporary way . . . To me it was ideal." What produced his intense desire to blend the old and the new? In part it was the excitement of trying something new and difficult, the rush of adrenaline triggered by a leap into the unknown, which Nelson would pursue all his life, not always with the happiest of consequences. But experience also played a large role, especially the experience of growing up as Junior and Abby's son.

Like much of what Nelson did thirty years later at Kykuit, the modernism of the Fifth Avenue apartment was an unmistakable reflection of Abby's influence. Thanks to her gentle coaching, he early became someone with whom she could share her passion for modern art. Sending him "an amusing and also very good Daumier lithograph" during his second year at Dartmouth, she had written, "It would be a great joy to me if you did find that you had a real love for and interest in beautiful things. We could have such good times going about together." And a year later she was writing with great excitement about a project that would come to play an enormous role in both their lives: "a new Museum of Modern Art . . . wouldn't it be splendid! It will be ready for you to be interested in when you get back to N.Y. to live."

At that point, Nelson was finishing an economics thesis on Standard Oil (without the talk he had hoped to have with Senior, who declined to discuss

the subject with his grandson), but then instead of continuing with economics he decided to take advantage of a program allowing five Dartmouth seniors to spend their final year free of all regular academic
requirements, studying whatever they wished. The subject he chose was art.
He also began visiting galleries in New York, including his mother's favorite, the Downtown Gallery. "I feel as if I had been introduced to a new
world of beauty," he wrote her afterward, "for the first time I think I have
really begun to appreciate and understand pictures."

In the strongest possible terms, too, he let Abby know how much he admired her activities as a collector and patron. "I sincerely believe you are doing an invaluable piece of work toward the encouragement and advancement
of modern American art," he wrote, and from the first he wholeheartedly
supported her interest in "the new museum," serving on its Junior Advisory
Committee and board of trustees, which he later chaired, and acting as her
agent in behind-the-scenes museum politics. He even tried to persuade her
to chair the board herself, which she resolutely refused to do. He also expressed his commitment to MoMA in a way the Rockefellers often did: in
1934 he pledged $100,000 to the museum. Though he made the pledge
anonymously, he wanted his mother to know that he had done it, as he said,
"in grateful appreciation of all the many, many things" she had done both for
him and for the institution. "If it were not for you the Museum of Modern
Art would be a thing of the past today . . . it is your personality projected into
the Museum that has made it what it is."

If Abby could count on Nelson's moral and financial support for her devotion to modern art, she also had in him what may have mattered even
more: a sympathetic ear to the difficulties her activities posed in her relations with Junior. Her sister Lucy knew of the problem, as did the women
who worked with her to found MoMA, yet even to them it would have
been hard to confide how she felt about it. To Nelson, however, she poured
out her heart freely. "I showed Papa the pictures and the gallery today," she
wrote in 1930, when her rooms on the seventh floor of 10 West Fifty-fourth
Street were finally finished, "he thinks they are terrible beyond words, so
I am somewhat depressed tonight."

Imagining what his feelings must have been on receiving such news and
given the often repeated stories about how cold and aloof Junior was as
a parent, one is tempted to believe that Nelson's own love of modern art
represented, in effect, a covert assault on his father—a playing out of the
age-old Oedipal conflict in the elegant medium of canvasses by Matisse,

Léger, and Picasso and sculptures by Lachaise and Henry Moore, with Fifth Avenue apartments, houses at Seal Harbor, and, for the grand finale, Kykuit itself as the settings for the struggle. Such primal urges could also explain the extraordinary passion and energy Nelson brought to his collecting.

Yet Nelson brought passion and energy to everything he did in life. And if he was so bent on doing battle with his father, why incorporate Louis XV style, a great favorite of Junior's, in the decoration of his Fifth Avenue apartment? Even more to the point, why not simply sweep Kykuit away and replace it with yet another grand house designed by Wally Harrison? If Nelson was doing anything with modern art in relation to his father, he seems to have been trying to find ways of blending his own taste—and Abby's—with Junior's, of forging a rapprochement among competing styles, disparate sets of aesthetic principles. He may not always have succeeded, but there was an earnestness of the effort that is hard to ignore.

Nelson's tastes, too, were anything but narrowly focused on a single kind of art. While becoming a leading collector of modern painting and sculpture, he also acquired important eighteenth-century European porcelains, Chinese ceramics of the Han and T'ang dynasties, Mexican art, and primitive art from around the world. Eventually keeping track of the thousands of objects in his collections became a full-time job, which for many years was handled by Carol Uht, acting as his personal curator, in the family office at Rockefeller Center. Among her duties was attaching paper clips to the pages of the auction catalogs and gallery brochures he loved to pore over, pointing out works that might interest him. He would then mark the pages to indicate whether or not he wanted to make the purchase and how much he was willing to pay. He liked bargains if he could find them. He sold things from time to time, too, and frequently donated others to museums, often having copies made for himself first.

As broad as Nelson's tastes were, however, he did look for particular qualities in art. Above all, he preferred works that engaged him emotionally: "forms of art in which I could feel—feel the artists, feel the material." As his brother Laurance said, "Nelson's reaction to art was visceral," a point echoed by René d'Harnoncourt, who described the euphoric pleasure art gave Nelson as "not unlike benzedrine, a curious combination of excitement and relaxation." Alfred Barr said much the same thing: "Nelson had the most insatiable appetite for art I know. Works of art gave him a deep almost therapeutic delight and refreshment such as other men find in music or alcohol." The art that produced this type of soul-stirring response Nelson repeatedly described as "strong." Art with subtle, symbolic meanings did not appeal to him. Works by Matisse, Braque, Picasso, Léger, Kandinsky, Klee, and later, the American abstract expressionists, Jackson Pollock, Robert Motherwell, and Mark Rothko, formed the core of his collection; missing entirely were works by the surrealists. Increasingly, too, he turned from painting to sculpture, as a yet stronger, more moving form of artistic expression.

Barr also described Nelson's collecting as "exceptionally pure," meaning he collected for none of the reasons people usually did. "Status, competition, investment, pride of possession, pride of taste, even a reputation for being a patron of the arts did not interest him." Yet according to Barr, there was more involved than simply Nelson's personal pleasure: "Beyond his private satisfaction there was a strong desire to share his treasures with others." He was unusually generous in lending works to museums and other institutions, stipulating always that they were to be exhibited without any mention of his name. He also loved giving tours of his collections and would do so at the drop of a hat. But what increasingly fascinated him was the possibility of putting a significant portion of his art permanently on view, in one place. And it was at Kykuit that he would work to bring that project to fruition.

On taking over the house in 1962, Nelson did as his parents had done and had the interior freshened with new paint and draperies and upholstery fabrics. But Happy would remember that it was while he and his three brothers were considering what to do with the furniture in the house that it first occurred to her he was looking ahead to a time when it would no longer be a private residence. "Knowing realistically," she said, "that this would not always be . . . a family home," he dreamed of opening it to the public and therefore wanted to hang on to as much of the furniture as possible. Thus when David Rockefeller suggested dividing the furniture among all the brothers, Nelson became, at least as David reported in his *Memoirs,* "absolutely livid," producing the "first serious confrontation" between the two of them. Here was a telling foretaste of the struggles to come within the family over Kykuit's future, yet for the moment David prevailed.

It was in any case a time when relations among the Rockefellers were severely strained, in large part because of Nelson's divorce and remarriage. Despite Tod Rockefeller's sharp tongue and aloof manner, she was well liked within the family, and Happy Murphy and her first husband, Robin, had been good friends of Peggy and David Rockefeller's. As David said, "[Nelson] had not only torn apart his own family, he had broken up the marriage of two of our close friends." To varying degrees the rest of the Rockefellers shared those feelings, except for Laurance, who had always been the closest of the brothers to Nelson, and in whose living room Nelson and Happy's wedding took place in May of 1963, with none of the other Rockefeller brothers present. Nor, except for Laurance and his wife, Mary, were the members of the extended Rockefeller family often at Kykuit in the years to come. Yet for the first time in the five decades of its existence, the house would have young children living under its roof. Nelson and Tod's children were largely grown, but those from Happy's first marriage spent time at Kykuit, and she and Nelson had two sons of their own soon after they were married.

Nelson had not been much involved in raising the children of his first marriage, but he meant to do things differently with Nelson Jr. and Mark. As family tradition decreed, they kept financial ledgers and had regular chores, like laying fires and polishing their father's shoes. Nelson said morning prayers with them too, but only in the city, not at Kykuit. Kykuit was for fun—for racing over a Big Wheels course that careened across terraces and around fountains and pools, for watching *Kojak* on TV with the family in what had been Senior's office and riding the back of the sofa like a horse, for playing ball on the circular lawn in front of the house and having Halloween parties in the grotto room under Aphrodite's temple, for "hanging out" with the Secret Service men while Nelson was vice president and helping him carry the precious china to set the table in the big dining room. "What if they break it?" people asked. "How else will they learn?" he answered.

With Nelson regularly in Albany through much of the time he served as governor, and the children in school in New York during the week, the family's time at Kykuit was often limited to weekends, but for all of them, Mark Rockefeller would say later, "it really was home." They spent more of the year as a whole there than Senior or Junior had. Nelson also seemed to get more genuine pleasure out of living at Kykuit than either of his forebears. When they were there, Happy recalled, they took time for themselves "to recharge, to fill up, and to rejuvenate." That meant keeping to a minimum the formality of their lives. The staff remained large—as many as twenty-three people indoors in the summer—but Happy wanted no butler hovering behind her chair at meals, and before long arrangements were made to use the dining room only at dinnertime, with lunches served out on the west porch, which in the winter was heated and enclosed with large, removable glass panels. Managing all this fell at first to Mary Hogan as housekeeper and then to the admirably efficient Dorothy Bronson, who began by arranging flowers for parties and eventually became, as Happy said, "the general . . . the administrative assistant of the house."

In another change, Nelson decided to use the rooms at the west end of the second floor for himself and Happy, rather than Junior and Abby's quarters at the east end, which went to the young Rockefeller boys. The view out over the river thus became his, as well as the rooms that had been Senior's when he lived in the house. Was it the view or the symbolism that prompted the change? No doubt a combination of both.

Outside the house there were still other changes, including some that would surely have shocked Junior. In place of the smoothly elegant sunken lawns of the inner garden, Nelson added a pair of swimming pools, one for adults and the other, with a sand "beach" at its end, for children. René d'Harnoncourt liked to refer to them as "reflecting pools," though the truth was they were there for the enjoyment of the family, particularly its younger members. In the summer, Happy remarked, "life revolved around those pools." Also largely for the children's benefit was an even more startling change in the gardens: the installation of a soda fountain in the stone tea-house, Bosworth's Palladian confection, the cost of the curtains for which had so annoyed Senior.

During those years Kykuit, too, was not just a family home; it was a place of business—Nelson's business, the endlessly fascinating, always challenging, sometimes deeply frustrating business of politics and government. Happy recalled that while he was governor, Christmases at the house invariably coincided with the frantic rush to prepare the annual state budget and the state of the state message. Summoned to Kykuit, his aides worked downstairs in the basement, while the family's holiday activities went on upstairs on the ground floor, and Nelson moved back and forth between the two.

Joseph Persico, for many years one of Nelson's speechwriters and the author of a biography of him, recalled that when he and other staff members came to Kykuit to work, things were kept as simple as possible: "No phalanx of servants appeared. The door opening, coat taking, drink mixing, and meal serving were all accomplished by one houseman." Similarly, from traveling with Nelson, Persico knew he had no valet (as Happy had no lady's maid) and packed his own bags. His usual dress at Kykuit was "a forty-year-old sport jacket, shapeless slacks, and scuffed shoes." And though he had thirty-seven restored antique cars in the coach barn, as well as a limousine and a Rolls-Royce convertible he had given Happy, he preferred driving around the estate in a 1965 Mustang.

Yet like the limousines and the Rolls-Royce, Nelson's political entertaining at Kykuit could also be elevated, notch by notch, in elegance and formality to ever-grander heights. Each year while he was governor he and Happy hosted a party for more than eight hundred members of the "Governor's Club," a group made up of those who had contributed five hundred dollars or more to the New York State Republican Party. Drinks and food were served in the Playhouse and, weather permitting, the ground floor of Kykuit and its gardens were open to everyone.

The Rockefellers also entertained important political figures from around the world as their personal guests at Kykuit, including the Lyndon Johnsons, the Richard Nixons, and the Gerald Fords, Egyptian president Anwar el-Sadat and his wife, the shah of Iran, the queen and prince of Denmark, the emperor and empress of Japan, President and Mrs. Echeverría of Mexico, and President and Mrs. Somoza of Nicaragua, as well as people like Frank Sinatra, Lord Mountbatten, and Jackie and Ari Onassis. On occasion, too, they loaned the smaller houses on the estate to friends and associates, like the Henry Kissingers, for periods lasting as long as several months.

The single grandest event at Kykuit during those years—and one that had political as well as social implications—was a dinner dance, given on June 9, 1967, to celebrate Happy's fiftieth birthday. The guest list included both old friends, like Wally Harrison and his wife and the Edward Warburgs, and social lions like Brooke Astor, the William Paleys, and Jean Vanderbilt. The Robert McNamaras attended, and since it was his birthday too, his name was on the cake with Happy's. The arts were represented by Alfred Barr, René d'Harnoncourt, George Balanchine, Josh Logan, Richard Rodgers, Truman Capote, and Philip Johnson (who as a favor to Nelson designed the lighting for the party). George Plimpton, Cardinal Cushing, and Kitty Carlisle were there, along with political figures like Robert Kennedy, Jacob Javits, Kenneth Keating, Mayor Robert Wagner of New York, U.S. senators Hugh Scott and John Sherman Cooper, and the governors of Massachusetts, Rhode Island, and Delaware. Also attending were at least twenty CEOs of major U.S. corporations.

The largest single group present, however, came from the media. The heads of both AP and UP were there, as were the chairmen of Hearst Corp. and Time, Inc., Kay Graham, the owner of the *Washington Post,* Jack Howard of the Scripps-Howard newspapers, Dorothy Schiff, the publisher of the *New York Post,* and Arthur Ochs Sulzberger, the publisher of the *New York Times* (along with the paper's executive and managing editors, and three other members of its staff). The nonprint media were represented by the chairmen of ABC and CBS. In addition, more than a dozen columnists, commentators, and reporters attended, including Joseph and Stewart Alsop, Walter Cronkite, Chet Huntley, and Howard K. Smith.

On arriving at Kykuit, guests passed through the hallway of the house into the music room, then out onto the west terrace. Having been greeted by the Rockefellers, they were free to roam the gardens until members of the orchestra, playing as they went, led them to dinner in a huge green-and-white-striped tent lined with pink silk, where dinner was served at forty round tables with ten places each. Above hung white iron baskets from which cascaded arrangements of blue hydrangeas lit by soft pink lights. Beginning with cold salmon and sauce *verte,* the meal progressed to chicken sauced with champagne, followed by strawberry sherbet with fresh strawberries and tiny white-frosted cakes. After the guests sang "Happy Birthday"—first to Happy, who according to the newspapers was "radiant" in a long chartreuse skirt and lime green top, and then to Robert McNamara—the dancing began.

Altogether it was a memorable evening. At one point Cardinal Cushing was heard to remark that he had never seen anything like it before, to which the person he was talking with replied, "John, nobody here has." "It was probably the most beautiful party ever given" was Emmet Hughes's verdict. Certainly there had been nothing to compare with it at Kykuit before. Nor would there be again.

For gathered under the vast silk-lined tent in extraordinary numbers that night were the members of the American Establishment—the men and women who exercised the lion's share of economic, political, and cultural power in the nation. Relying on a sturdy network of institutional ties, they governed secure in the belief that their actions benefited not only themselves but all mankind. Yet just as the guest list for the party included few if any people of color, or poor people, or people with radical political views, right or left, the Tet Offensive had not occurred in Vietnam, Martin Luther King and Robert Kennedy had not been assassinated, the riots had not exploded outside the Democratic Convention in Chicago, and Richard

Nixon had still to be elected president. But all that lay only a year away. The world was about to change radically, and one consequence of the change would be a steady erosion in the power of the American Establishment.

For Nelson Rockefeller, too, the summer of 1967 would prove to be a pivotal time. Despite all the predictions to the contrary, it seemed the turmoil in his personal life had not ended his political career. The previous November he had won a third term as governor by almost four hundred thousand votes. In part, the dinner dance was meant to celebrate that victory, yet more than anything else in the world Nelson wanted to be president of the United States. If the past was any guide, the people there that night would be crucial to his success, and when the time came he had the support of most of them (including the usual $1 million contribution from Brooke Astor). But in the fractured political world of 1968 it made no difference. Once again the Republicans denied him the prize; the party's nomination went instead to Richard Nixon on the first ballot.

Afterward all the usual reasons were offered for Nelson's defeat: his personal life had indeed alienated many voters; he was too liberal, too far east, too rich, too much of a Rockefeller. Whatever explained it, most observers, including most Republicans, thought the death knell had sounded for his loftier political ambitions. Perhaps he had chosen the wrong party, though later that year, when Hubert Humphrey offered him the chance to run for the vice presidency on the Democratic ticket, he refused, commenting, "I'm terribly flattered. But I've been a Republican all my life. I can't change now." Yet events had a way of playing odd tricks during those years. In 1974, following Nixon's resignation, Gerald Ford offered Nelson the vice presidency, and this time he accepted, only to discover what an empty honor the office could be. To win the Senate's approval, he had to lay bare the details of his personal finances and those of the Rockefeller family, and most of his time as vice president seemed to be spent attending the funerals of deceased heads of state. But the cruelest cut of all came when Ford decided to bump him from the Republican ticket in 1976.

All the while, too, his political sympathies were moving steadily to the right. Before Watergate he had even developed a grudging admiration for Nixon's position on international issues, including Vietnam, and after Nixon's reelection in 1972 he invited the president to Kykuit. Describing the visit, Happy Rockefeller would remember the moment when Mrs. Nixon asked not to be taken to a room where she knew Nixon was meeting with H. R. Haldeman and John Ehrlichman, saying, "Those men are going to destroy my husband." Then there was Attica. In 1971 the prison had been seized by a group of inmates holding guards as hostages, and rather than negotiate, in what proved to be a devastating blunder, Nelson had chosen to use force, which left twenty-nine inmates and ten guards dead. Two years after that he sponsored the infamous New York State Drug Law, mandating life in prison for anyone convicted of trafficking in hard drugs. First announced in a staff meeting at Kykuit, the law drew the opposition of every liberal group in the nation but passed anyway.

Even with the darkening clouds of his disappointed hopes and mounting conservatism gathering around him, however, Nelson kept up his usual activities at Kykuit. In 1971 he and Happy hosted four major events there (two within days of the tragedy at Attica): the annual Governor's Club party, a cocktail party for Chase Manhattan Bank executives, a reception for the Advisory Commission on Intergovernmental Relations, and the annual Rockefeller family Christmas luncheon. But more and more during those years, it seemed, he found his deepest satisfaction—and solace—in the works of art he continued to bring together at Kykuit.

Along with placing his Lachaises and several other large sculptures outdoors in the snow, Nelson also, in the winter of 1962, began planning where to display art inside the house. For the most part he meant to keep what was already there: the paintings, the engravings in the frames Codman had made in France, and Junior's Chinese porcelains. Since the organ in the music room was no longer playable, Martha had decided to have it taken out, and Nelson went on to simplify the room's plasterwork and remove its wall sconces and mirrored doors, both to open the house up and to create more space for hanging pictures. One of his first additions to the room was a portrait of his ancestor Senator Nelson Aldrich, which was eventually joined by several large modern canvases, including Joan Miró's striking *Hirondelle Amour.*

Two other early additions on the ground floor were a seventh-century, T'ang Dynasty marble bodhisattva, placed in the alcove room in front of the large window overlooking the river, and a portrait of Abraham Lincoln, hung in the library across from a Gilbert Stuart painting of George Washington. A stunningly beautiful sculpture combining elements of Chinese, Indian, and Greek style, the bodhisattva had belonged to Abby, and according to Nelson was the first work of art that caught his eye as a boy. Later he asked her to leave it to him in her will, which she did. The idea of adding the portrait of Lincoln was Happy's. Done by Joseph Alexander Ames in 1865, it is one of only a handful of Lincoln portraits painted from life.

As important as these additions were, they barely scratched the surface of what Nelson hoped to do at Kykuit, but from the first he had to deal with the fact that the amount of available wall space was severely limited. There were too many doors, too many windows, too many architectural flourishes preventing him from doing what he had done on Fifth Avenue—filling the rooms with modern art—unless he gutted the house and completely redid its interior, an option he never seriously considered. He wanted a blend, but a different kind of blend from the one he had achieved in New York. This time there would be the house Senior and Junior had built, with their things in it, *plus* his art. But where would the art go? If bronze sculptures could be left outside to brave the elements, paintings could not.

One possibility was building a separate structure somewhere near the house, and Nelson may have discussed the idea with Philip Johnson, but between them they came up with a very different solution: using the long corridors lining the south side of the basement under the house. "Walls!" Nelson had said to Happy—those corridors had walls, and with their handsome Guastavino tile ceilings, they could be repainted and relit, in a design devised by Johnson, to become attractive galleries with ample space for displaying paintings and other art objects. Leading off them, there was also a large room that originally held the machinery for the organ on the floor above, which could be furnished with couches as well as various pieces of art.

In those spaces hung a constantly shifting selection of paintings, etchings, and lithographs by dozens of different artists. Today, they include works by Toulouse-Lautrec (four examples), Picasso (five), Braque (four), Léger (two), and Chagall. Among the American artists represented are Robert Motherwell and Andy Warhol, whose paired portraits of Nelson and Happy are prominently displayed. (Nelson never liked the portrait of him, but it hangs there still.) There are also sculptures by Louise Nevelson, Alexander Calder, Henry Moore, Amadeo Gabino, Francesco Somaini, and many others. Nor did the eclectic character of the galleries end there. Next to the chair Nelson often used to make telephone calls hangs a finger painting, done by Nelson Jr. when he was a toddler, and standing at the entrance to the galleries is a handsome display case filled with old glass bottles dug up by the boys around the estate and arranged by Nelson with all the painstaking care he always brought to placing art anywhere.

At the other end of the basement galleries hangs a group of large tapestries, based on paintings by Picasso. Among the more unusual objects in Nelson's collection, they appealed to him in part because of cost. Over the years Picasso's paintings had risen steadily in price to hundreds of thousands, sometimes millions of dollars. Yet Nelson discovered that even though Picasso himself provided the designs for the tapestries and approved their colors, they could be had for as little as $12,000. The first one he bought, *Guernica*, in 1955, was followed by seventeen others, most of them copied either from his own collection or from MoMA's, including works like *Three Musicians, Night Fishing in Antibes, Girl with Mandolin,* and *Harlequin.*

Though the two never met, Nelson was captivated by the idea of working with Picasso. He even claimed his admiration for the artist grew after discovering that each time an order for a new tapestry was sent from New York to the weaver in France, Madame J. de la Baume Dürrbach, she actually produced three of them: one for Nelson, one for herself, and one for Picasso, all, in effect, paid for by Nelson. "That Picasso sure is a good businessman," he is supposed to have said when he found out. Alfred Barr, on the other hand, was less taken with the tapestries and fussed endlessly over the colors, which he sometimes felt were dead wrong. Contrary to Nelson's instructions, too, with every order the tapestries grew larger, principally because—or so Carol Uht believed—Madame Dürrbach was paid for her work by the square centimeter. "My own feeling is that she is making a killing on these things," Uht wrote in 1975.

Were the tapestries great art? Probably not, but they were big, bold, and eye-catching. Perhaps in ordering them Nelson also thought of the works of famous Renaissance painters that had been copied by European tapestry makers to adorn the walls of royal palaces, not to mention the stunning Unicorn Tapestries, the acquisition of which had been Junior's single greatest coup as an art collector. Here was Nelson's entry in that long tradition, and again a way—his way—of following in his father's footsteps.

There were other points at which the art he brought to Kykuit touched what Junior had left there. To the K'ang Hsi porcelains his father had loved so, he added his own, much earlier, Han and T'ang pottery figures: horses, warriors, and a double-humped camel in the library, all rendered with stark force, in contrast to Junior's delicately detailed Ming vases and figures, yet products of the same civilization. Like Junior, too, Nelson was deeply concerned with how objects were displayed. (To ensure that everything remained exactly where he put it, the staff used photographs of his tabletop arrangements.) Lighting was especially important, and to better show off the portraits and porcelains in the dining room, he installed a crystal chandelier, lit by candles and surrounded with dozens of small electrical fixtures, recessed in the ceiling.

Glowing in the dramatic light thus produced was one of Nelson's most striking additions to Kykuit's interiors: three massive white ceramic birds, modeled by Johann Joachim Kandler at the Meissen porcelain works in the early eighteenth century. The largest of them, an eagle, occupies a table in the room's bay window; the other two, a pair of vultures, stand on the sideboard beneath Sargent's portrait of Senior. Caught with heads bowed, their talons gripping the stumps beneath them, they convey an air of great power momentarily at rest, which their whiteness seems to emphasize. They also bear an uncanny resemblance to Senior as Sargent painted him, which can hardly have been lost on Nelson.

In contrast to the Meissen birds, the large dining table is decorated today with a delicate cut-glass epergne and pairs of Bow and Meissen shepherds and shepherdesses, though on special occasions Nelson used one of the extraordinary early Worcester, Spode, or Chinese export dinner services he, as well as Abby and Junior, collected. So fond was he of the services that he had several small rooms on the north side of the ground floor combined into a single "china room," with lighted glass cases for displaying various pieces from the collection. According to Happy, it was Laurance who suggested creating the china room, and also at his suggestion the room was regularly used for cocktails.

Nelson made other, smaller changes inside the house, and additional artworks arrived all the time, particularly after he left the Governor's Mansion in Albany in 1973. But it was the size of the sculpture collection outside that continued to grow most dramatically and more and more claimed the largest share of his attention.

Today the published guide to Kykuit's outdoor sculpture collection lists ninety works, seventy-one of them brought there by Nelson. They come in all sizes and are made of every conceivable material, from stainless steel and bronze to plastic. In some cases they are richly colored; in others it is their very blankness that commands attention. They were created by fifty-five artists. Four of them—Reg Butler, Gaston Lachaise, Aristide Maillol, and Elie Nadelman—are represented by three works each. Among the other sculptors included are Jean Arp, Constantine Brancusi, Alexander Calder, Alberto Giacometti, Jacques Lipchitz, Henry Moore, Louise Nevelson, and Isamu Noguchi. There is also a soaring totem pole, its creator listed simply as "Thlingit Tribe."

The collection reflects virtually every major trend in twentieth-century sculpture. In mood and spirit it runs the gamut from dark and somber, even frightening, to whimsically humorous. There are works stunning in their massiveness and grandeur, like Henry Moore's *Knife-Edge, Two Piece*, and others that charm by their airy delicacy, like Brancusi's *Grand Oiseau* and David Smith's *The Banquet*. Some are raised on bases, like Max Bill's *Triangular Surface in Space*; others sit flat on the ground, like Lachaise's *Dans La Nuit*. Some had belonged to Nelson for decades, but well more than half were created or cast after he took over Kykuit, and he was still purchasing new works as late as 1974. Some of what he acquired he bought from dealers. In other cases it was a question of having casts made from existing works. Several times, too, he dealt directly with the artists, which he especially enjoyed, or if they were dead, with their families.

All three of the large works by Elie Nadelman at Kykuit were purchased after the sculptor's death in 1946, two from his widow and one from his son. Cast in bronze, they depict nude women in various poses and were grouped with Lachaise's *Standing Woman* and two works by Maillol, *Torso* and *Bather Pulling Up Her Hair*, around the new swimming pools in the inner garden. In acquiring them, Nelson again worked with Lincoln Kirstein, who—as he had done in the case of Isabel Lachaise—was looking after Nadelman's widow. Thanking Nelson for buying another large sculpture from her in 1951, he had written, "You must realize how grateful I am, and Mrs. Nadelman is [for] your continuing interest. She has a hard time making two ends meet . . . this will pay for her taxes for this year."

In addition to encouraging Nelson to purchase the works by Nadelman, Kirstein supervised their casting in bronze. In his opinion simply by having that done Nelson rendered an invaluable service. In their original state, as they had come from Nadelman's hands and as Nelson purchased them, they were made of materials like plaster, papier-mâché, and *galvanoplastique*— all quite fragile and impermanent. Thus not only had he "helped a very decent woman in a very generous way," he had also, as Kirstein wrote, "preserved from certain deterioration the work of a great sculptor."

Among the artists from whom Nelson personally commissioned works for Kykuit were Henry Moore and Alexander Calder. He already owned several sculptures by Moore, but nothing large enough to place outdoors in the gardens. His solution was to ask Moore, an old friend, if he had anything available that might be suitable. He responded with a pair of suggestions: *Nuclear Energy* and *Knife-Edge, Two Piece.* Nelson bought them both. A monumental work, formed of two opposing, roughly rectangular masses, *Knife-Edge, Two Piece* would be called by MoMA's William Lieberman "one of the sculptor's most splendid achievements." It stands today on the open lawn beyond the rose garden. *Nuclear Energy,* a model for a piece commissioned by the University of Chicago, though smaller than *Knife-Edge, Two Piece,* is still a work of great power: a dense mushroom cloud, frozen in bronze.

Nelson also already had a number of smaller works by Calder, but again nothing appropriate for the gardens at Kykuit. In this case, however, he knew exactly what he wanted and felt he knew Calder well enough simply to ask him for it. In 1942 he had done an aluminum stabile, twenty-six inches high, called *Spiny,* which Nelson owned and loved. Gently humorous, it depicts four (or perhaps only two?) figures with elongated "necks" and small "heads," which could be stylized giraffes or horses—or simply a collection of abstract shapes. Nelson's idea was to have Calder create a much larger version of it, which the artist was delighted to do. Constructed of steel finished in black and titled *Large Spiny,* it stands over twelve feet high, on the lawn to the west and north of Kykuit. With the broadly curving sweep of the river behind it, it manages to look simultaneously grand and amusing. In 1969 it was chosen for the cover of the catalog of MoMA's exhibition of Nelson's collection and is probably the single most photographed sculpture at Kykuit.

The placement of *Large Spiny* followed a broad pattern that Nelson developed over the years. Works that were more representational, like the Lachaises, Nadelmans, and Maillols, were placed near the house; less representational, more abstract works farther away. The farther one moved from the house, too, the larger the works tended to become. The logic of this arrangement reflected the nature of the settings themselves. Works near the house were of a size consistent with its architecture; those farther away reflected the scale and grandeur of the surrounding landscape.

The arrangement also traced, in a rough way, the prevailing trend in modern art—at least during the first sixty years of the twentieth century—toward increasingly abstract, nonrepresentational forms of expression. For those who cared to follow it, Nelson was offering a short course in recent art history, in which one could progress from the easily recognized, if exaggerated, contours of Lachaise's *Woman Standing*, out across the terraces and lawns to James Rosati's vast, vivid orange *Lippincott II*, a composition of stacked, hard-edged geometric shapes that meant whatever the viewer wanted it to mean, or to Tony Smith's *Wandering Rocks*, five huge, irregular, stainless steel blocks, which Nelson constantly rearranged, as the work's title commanded.

But whatever his broader goals may have been, the issue that most preoccupied him, always, was finding the right place for each individual work in his collection. At any given moment the intensity of his concentration on "Where to put that"—that painting, that particular sculpture—could be awesome to behold and over the years produced dozens of stories, with the wonder of it all compounded by the complexity of the logistics involved. Huge pieces of stone or metal, weighing many hundreds of pounds, were not easily moved, and the fact that Nelson thought not just in terms of "a foot more" here or there but had everything calibrated in his mind down to a matter of inches made it all the more difficult.

Perhaps the most memorable story in the ongoing saga of "where to put that" involved Henry Moore's *Knife-Edge, Two Piece*. As the guides at Kykuit tell it today, David Rockefeller was playing golf with a group of Chase Manhattan executives when a helicopter suddenly appeared overhead, trailing Moore's gigantic bronze sculpture, which was being moved to the place Nelson had chosen for it. David, in the middle of a putt at that point, angrily assumed the entire incident was simply a case of Nelson grandstanding as usual. But later, speaking before the Westchester County Arts Council, Nelson explained this was not the case: "The day before . . . it had rained and the helicopter couldn't come. And then somehow we didn't stop." All of which provided, he quipped, "insights into the joy of having a collector in the family."

Over time Nelson and his staff developed a regular system for moving sculptures around the gardens. Working on weekends with Joe Canzeri—a political advance man he had put in charge of Greenrock Corporation, which had been created in 1960 to manage the estate—he would pick the place where he imagined a particular piece of sculpture might go. With bamboo poles marking the spot, he then viewed it from every angle. If he liked what he saw, Canzeri would arrange to have a plywood model of the work set up for Nelson to check the next time he was at Kykuit. Only then would the final decision be made and plans worked out for moving the sculpture into place.

As orderly and precise as this process seemed, what drove it finally was Nelson's intuition plus a goal that not even those closest to him fully grasped. "He seemed to have an eighth sense," Happy remarked; "I don't remember him ever measuring," to which Laurance Rockefeller added, "There was great therapy . . . great joy to it." But when Laurance said to Nelson, at one point, "In a way you remind me of a shepherd with a flock of sheep. You gradually move [your sculptures] around [and around]," Nelson replied that Laurance missed the point entirely. "Nothing could be farther from the truth. I am looking for the ultimate position for each one with the thought of never moving it again."

The ultimate position! It conjures up images of camels passing through the eye of a needle, of developing the perfect golf swing, of constructing an Italianate Eden on top of a craggy, New World knoll, of building Rockefeller Center and making it pay, of being the grandson of the richest man in the world and becoming president of the United States—high-stakes games all. Some of them had been winnable; others had not. What would be the outcome in this case? As one strolls through Kykuit's gardens today, it truly seems that Nelson did win. It is hard to imagine a more interesting, better-placed group of modern sculptures, or a more stunning setting for them. In a way that never quite happened elsewhere in his life, everything comes together here, caught in reality as it was in his ever-fertile imagination: the right things in the perfect place.

Around his great achievement, however, Kykuit continued to change, and there remained, always, the question of what to do with it all in the future.

When Nelson chose Joe Canzeri to head Greenrock, his instructions were characteristically emphatic: "My father built this place for his father. There is nothing like it anywhere in America. Keep it that way." Joe Persico described Canzeri, who had been in the hotel business before becoming a political advance man, as "a dark-haired, compact dynamo" who could display all "the sledgehammer authority of a sergeant in an army of occupation." Yet his competence was unsurpassed, and he also had, much of the time, an appealingly impudent manner. Nelson's charge to him would require all of those qualities, plus considerable mental dexterity. For to "keep it that way" in the case of Kykuit and the estate was simply not possible any longer. The cost of doing things as they had always been done had grown too great. Economies had to be made.

Having almost doubled in the three decades after 1930, the cost of running the estate during the 1960s remained more or less constant at roughly $1.25 million annually. But in 1971 Martha Baird Rockefeller died, and thereafter the substantial portion of the costs that she had been paying (over $160,000 in 1968) had to be made up by the brothers. Most of those costs, too, were generated by Kykuit and its gardens; therefore, the logical person to cover them was Nelson. Yet his finances were stretched to the limit. To pay for his political campaigns and purchases of art, he had cut deeply into the principal of his trusts and thus had both less capital and less income than his brothers. Also, due to an agreement reached in 1954 that had given him the largest share in the ownership of the Park area (which contained Kykuit), he was already paying more than any of his brothers for the estate's upkeep. To help him out they agreed, in 1972, to equalize their ownership of the Park and apportion the costs of the estate's upkeep accordingly. But while that did reduce Nelson's burden a bit, there was the inflationary spiral that began in 1973 to take into account, as well as the generally flat stock market of those years.

Ever since Senior's time, estate managers had been admonished to watch costs constantly but still to keep everything running smoothly and the place looking as wondrously perfect as it had been designed to look. The ghost of Dyson DeLap hovered constantly at Joe Canzeri's side, yet now it had become a question of finding major savings, even if it meant doing less, chipping away at standards, perhaps letting some things go altogether. In May 1971, four months after Martha Rockefeller's death, Canzeri produced a densely packed memorandum listing twenty-one areas in which cuts could be made, beginning with lawn mowing and ending with having the main gate electronically opened and closed from a central location rather than having a guard at the gate to do it (a saving of $50,000). In some cases, like lawn mowing and leaf removal, he recommended making no changes. Those areas where he thought the largest savings could be achieved were flower production—no longer growing plants in the greenhouse to set out in the gardens in spring and summer and buying them from commercial growers instead (a saving of $83,000); reducing the Playhouse staff ($43,000); cutting the number of horses stabled on the estate (up to $42,000); and "plowing under all greens, tees, traps, and 'other parts of the game' " on the golf course—in short eliminating it ($57,000).

In total, the savings Canzeri listed amounted to $490,000. Doing away with the golf course, he knew, was never a realistic option (Nelson, David, and Laurance all played regularly), but putting it on the list at least let the brothers see the cost of their pleasures relative to other estate expenses. Canzeri's own choices among the items listed were closing the greenhouse, reducing the number of horses, cutting back on the Playhouse staff, and lowering the level of care in the estate's wooded areas. He also pointed out that it would take a while for the savings to materialize, assuming the brothers had no intention of letting large numbers of the staff go, or cutting wages. Nor was Canzeri interested in going to a system of seasonal employment. "It takes a certain type of man to perform well in the type of job we have," he wrote. "I feel we would not be able to give the family the type of service they now received from Greenrock if the element of seasonal employment were inserted in the picture."

If it seemed Canzeri's "picture" amounted to a curious mixture of hard-headed capitalism and something approaching medieval feudalism, he understood perfectly the people he worked for. The Rockefellers were determined to save money, but in an enterprise where more than three-fourths of the costs (by Canzeri's estimate) went for labor, they wanted no one treated badly—had no intention of going to the extent Senior had to keep labor costs on the estate down. They also wanted to feel they knew the people working for them. There were to be no sudden layoffs and no strangers within the gates of the estate. Noblesse oblige was what they aimed at, even if by some lights it was a luxury they could no longer afford. Like Canzeri, too, the family was eager to ensure that whatever budget cuts were made had "the least visible effect" possible.

In the end, some of Canzeri's recommendations were accepted (with the labor savings allowed to occur gradually over time, as staff members died or retired), and others were not. No one seemed interested in economizing on the Playhouse, and seven years later the horse issue was still being debated. The care of the wooded areas and fields was cut back, however, and the estate did go out of the greenhouse business, but with Nelson insisting on having as many flowers planted as always, the savings were reduced from a projected $83,000 to between $40,000 and $50,000.

In each of those cases the brothers decided as a group whether or not to approve the proposed cuts. On routine matters involving Kykuit Canzeri dealt with Nelson alone, though to Nelson nothing about Kykuit was ever routine. Usually the two of them spent several hours each weekend walking over the grounds around the house. Making notes as they went, Canzeri would produce afterward a typed list of everything to be done. Technically, as head of Greenrock, he worked for all of the brothers, and they were not always happy about the amount of time he spent doing things for "the governor." But if Nelson loomed large in Canzeri's schedule, he loomed large everywhere else on the estate. He was, after all, the master of Kykuit.

In his own mind that also made it his responsibility to determine its future. Discussions of the subject had begun as early as 1960 in the "brothers' meetings" held periodically to discuss issues in which they shared an interest. From the beginning Nelson's position would remain the same: eventually the house should be opened to the public. To his brothers, however, this was by no means self-evident, and though they agreed to consider the matter and spent a good deal of money hiring consultants to study it, opinions among them continued to vary.

Nelson's position began with the assumption that no one would want to take over Kykuit when he was gone, which doubtless was true. Yet that hardly settled the issue if the family's history was any guide, for the Rockefellers had disposed of at least as many houses as they had built over the years, usually by simply tearing them down. That had been the fate of Senior and Cettie's house on Euclid Avenue in Cleveland, of both their house and Junior and Abby's on West Fifty-fourth Street in New York, of Abeyton Lodge on the Pocantico estate, and the Eyrie in Seal Harbor. Indeed none of the places where the brothers had lived as boys was standing by 1962. Overlarge, no longer practical or wanted by anyone in the family, they had been eliminated, not without a certain amount of sadness presumably, but because in every case it had seemed the sensible thing to do.

If Kykuit was to be preserved, then, it would become the exception to the rule, and opening it to the public would be an even more striking departure, given how closely the Rockefellers had always guarded their privacy. Yet that was what Nelson wanted to do. As for why he felt as he did, the surviving record reveals little. He did make clear from the start that he meant to keep the art he had placed in and around the house there as an integral part of what people would see when they came, which lent weight to the conviction within the family that, at bottom, the entire scheme was merely another example of his ungovernable penchant for self-aggrandizement.

True, no doubt. But was that all there was to it? If so, why take such pains to preserve what his parents and Senior had made of the place, their Kykuit, along with his own? It would seem that what he wanted people to discover there was not just Nelson Rockefeller but the Rockefeller family as a group of complex, interesting individuals, each with his or her own interests, tastes, and personalities, a family, in short, not so very different from most American families. Because of all he had done to the place since taking it over, it would also be clear that Kykuit had changed through the years. And if Kykuit had changed, so by implication had the Rockefeller family, reconstituting itself anew with each generation, just as every American family did, indeed as the nation itself did—ever fluid, constantly evolving, dynamically democratic.

But on a deeper level still, Nelson was also proposing something that in effect would bring both the family and Kykuit full circle. Junior had begun by hoping the house would make a statement about the strength of the Rockefellers' determination to devote their wealth to higher ends, but he had also, over the years, seemed to work ever more tirelessly to protect the privacy of the place. Each decade had brought new gates, more guards, higher fences and walls. At the same time, with the railroad and much of the village that originally stood near the house swept away, it had moved farther and farther from the ordinary realities of American life (just as under Junior's eagle eye Colonial Williamsburg had). Often Junior's stated concerns were aesthetic, but eventually privacy for its own sake seemed to gain the upper hand. Now Nelson wanted to take down that cordon sanitaire and let the world in. Moreover, so eager was he to see his plan implemented that he was prepared to contemplate the unthinkable: actually leaving Kykuit himself to help bring it about.

In the early 1970s he and Happy had decided to build a Japanese-style house at the end of the Japanese garden, which was being reworked and enlarged. To design the house he brought Junzo Yoshimura from Tokyo to Pocantico, along with eight carpenters to work on the project. Built for a comparatively modest $650,000, the Japanese House was occasionally used for distinguished visitors. Nelson's announced plan, however, was to move there himself with Happy, making it their home, and in the summer of 1978 Greenrock was already working out the details of the move.

Would he have actually gone through with it? Certainly it is hard to imagine him leaving Kykuit, with all its countless associations, yet for someone with his love of drama, what an extraordinary Zen-counterpoint living in the Japanese house would be to the rest of his life, to the crowded rush of events and the equally crowded settings in which he had endeavored to stage those events. More important, once he left Kykuit, the pressure on his brothers to decide the house's fate would be that much greater. Also, everything that he had brought to the place would remain there: his collections, the art that had given him so much pleasure. But was he truly prepared to live without it physically surrounding him, so that he could touch things, lift them, move them to another, better place? Only he could answer that question.

But then suddenly, time ran out.

Legacy

11

The Gift

He died as he had lived, in memorable circumstances. Late in the evening of January 26, 1979, he suffered a sudden heart attack in the town house where his parents had lived as newlyweds, and which he had owned for a number of years, using it, in the words of one of his brothers, "as an informal club." Ostensibly he was there to work on a series of art books he planned to publish, but he was not alone. An attractive young assistant was with him, and her presence, added to the fact that following his attack roughly an hour passed before any assistance was summoned, inevitably led to questions about what had happened. A story obscuring the facts was hastily concocted, but it did not stand; the truth came out soon enough.

What did stand, however, was his final will and testament and the vision it contained of what should be done with the family home. Most of his relatives did not like the vision at all, but it was of a piece with the rest of his life—bold, expansive, simultaneously generous and self-promoting. Essentially it was about breaking down barriers, which many family members claimed they thought was a good idea. Yet here was the last and most sacrosanct barrier of them all. Ought it not to be left standing, at least for a while longer?

That was certainly the view of some of his relatives, which he already had ample cause to understand when he signed the will. But evidently he decided to go ahead anyway and let the chips fall where they would.

For his extended family, Nelson Rockefeller's death came down to yet another way in which he had shed unwanted attention on them. First there had been his divorce from Mary Todhunter Clark and the scandal surrounding his marriage to Happy Murphy, then all the less attractive aspects of his political career, including the revelation of so much about his personal finances and those of the rest of the family at the time of his appointment as vice president, and now this. Returning on the Chase Manhattan Bank plane from an interview with the sultan of Oman, David Rockefeller was met at the airport by his wife, who explained the more awkward aspects of the situation just as they were about to become public. He can hardly have been pleased at what he heard, but time heals most wounds, and in his *Memoirs* he described his brother's death simply as a "sad ending for a man whose career had been so distinguished."

What David Rockefeller could not forgive, however—what he would still, after two decades, angrily describe as "Nelson's Revenge"—were the provisions in Nelson's will regarding Kykuit. Despite the fact that he had lived in the house for almost twenty years, legally it was not his to dispose of, for it remained part of the much larger, and as yet undivided, Pocantico estate that he owned jointly with his brothers. Nonetheless his will instructed his executors to convey to the National Trust for Historic Preservation his one-quarter interest in the "Park" section of the estate—the fenced-in area that included Kykuit—in the hope that the house with its furnishings would be, as he said, "preserved as nearly intact as may be practicable" and opened to the public. Also part of the gift were most of his artworks inside the house as well as his sculpture collection outdoors. At the same time the will provided no financial support for any part of this bequest.

In explaining his feelings about what Nelson had done, David Rockefeller focused first on money. "Nelson's final gesture would cost me, and to a lesser degree Laurance, many millions of dollars and even more headaches over the next fifteen years." About the headaches he had nothing further to say. But he did offer a reasonably detailed account of the circumstances leading up to Nelson's bequest, and family papers and interviews make it possible to fill in the gaps. The story is complex, involving many different issues, of which Kykuit's future was only one. For with the three-quarter mark of the twentieth century approaching, the Rockefeller brothers had begun drawing together the multiple strands of their far-flung interests in hopes of shaping them into a permanent memorial to their generation's achievement, and yet at almost every turn divisions arose—often surprisingly deep—pitting brother against brother.

Fate also lent a hand. Two of Junior and Abby Rockefeller's six children, Winthrop and Babs, were dead by 1976, but that still left four of their sons alive. Then in the summer of 1978 John D. Rockefeller 3rd was killed in a freak automobile accident, and within another six months Nelson was dead. Had either or both of them lived longer, much that happened afterward might have turned out differently, or so it is often claimed. And perhaps on some issues a deft compromise or two could have been worked out; but not on others, and almost certainly not on Kykuit.

During the years while Nelson was busy filling the house and its gardens with art, the Pocantico estate—as a legal entity—had continued to evolve under the terms of Junior's sale of it to his sons in 1952. The purpose of the sale had been to shelter the property from taxation on his death. But for the brothers to have passed the estate along to their children in the same manner would not have worked. The next generation of the family was too large and the situations of its members were too diverse to make joint ownership feasible. Nor did it make sense to have the trust funds Junior had settled on the brothers acquire the estate. That had been done to solve the tax problem in the case of Rockefeller Center, but unlike the Center, the estate had no potential to add to the income from the trusts, which the brothers counted on to meet expenses.

Some changes were made, however. After a number of years the cumbersome system (set up by Junior at the time of the 1952 sale) that had Hills Realty Corporation holding the title to the estate, while in turn the brothers owned Hills, was abandoned. Also, Winthrop Rockefeller, having moved to Arkansas, decided that he no longer wanted to own his share of the property, and the other four brothers—John 3rd, Nelson, Laurance, and David—agreed to buy him out.

In each case these arrangements were easily and amicably made. Yet they contributed nothing to resolving the long-term future of the estate. On that point—chiefly in response to Nelson's desire to see Kykuit eventually opened to the public—the brothers agreed to do what the Rockefellers so often did: they hired experts to advise them, in fact a whole string of them. Between 1962 and 1985 no fewer than twenty-two studies of the

Pocantico property were produced. Most conceived of it as divided into two parts: a central core, the Park, which included Kykuit and was also referred to as "the historic area," and the land outside it, a medley of meadows and forests known as the "open space." Commercial uses for both parts of the property were considered, but, as Nelson hoped, it was generally assumed that Kykuit would be turned into a national historic site, with guided tours emphasizing the Rockefellers' activities in behalf of "the public good." Similarly, the usual plan for the open space saw the pubic being given access to at least a portion of it for recreational activities like walking and bike riding.

In those cases where the public was to be admitted, the plan was for the brothers to donate the property to nonprofit organizations, thereby eliminating the tax bite on their estates and providing them in the bargain with handsome tax deductions. The organizations most often mentioned in this connection were Sleepy Hollow Restorations, the National Park Service, and the National Trust for Historic Preservation. There was also talk of incorporating into the historic area some sort of institute dealing with important social questions. Crucial issues left unresolved were when the transfer of various parts of the property would occur, how the portions of the estate open to the public would be demarcated from those still being used by the family, and who would pay the attendant costs, including the very considerable annual bill for maintaining Kykuit and its gardens.

Among the various consultants who produced plans for the estate, the land-use specialist Hideo Sasaki and his associates had the greatest impact on the early stages of the process. But the individual who worked most closely with the Rockefellers on the project over the years was the family's chief attorney, Donal O'Brien. As skilled lawyers do, he excelled at defining options and recommending the best choices among them to achieve the results his clients wanted. He was also discreet and loyal. In dealing with the Pocantico estate, he would need every one of those attributes, plus, it turned out, preternatural patience and persistence.

As a legal matter, O'Brien concentrated on how the brothers' wills should be written to produce the type of outcome they appeared to agree on, at least in principle, for the disposition of the estate. Since almost certainly they would die at different times, it seemed wise for them to take several steps jointly yet leave a number of points vague in order to preserve maximum flexibility. Thus, while O'Brien recommended that they all include provisions in their wills indicating their desire to have a sizable part of the estate turned over to appropriate nonprofit organizations, he advised them not to name the specific recipients or to attach precise time frames to what was to be done. That would leave their executors free to work out the details, depending on how many other brothers were still alive when any one of them died, and whether there were surviving widows whose life tenancies in the property needed to be protected.

Then there was the ticklish question of money. Nelson held out the hope that public funding would be available to underwrite a significant share of the costs if either the National Park Service or the National Trust were involved. But prudent soul that he was, O'Brien thought it best to plan on at least some of the funds coming from the family and suggested a formula to that end. Under it, peripheral parcels of land could be sold to raise money and each of the brothers would agree to include in his will a bequest of $5 million to go toward endowing the upkeep of the rest of the property. If more was needed, perhaps it could come as a grant from the Rockefeller Brothers Fund. In the worst case, the grant might have to be as high as $15 million, given the $38 to $45 million usually mentioned as the amount needed to endow the historic area alone.

Through the middle 1970s public financing remained a distinct possibility, though in retrospect the notion that the federal government would fund a program to open the estate of America's richest family to the public, while at the same time that family (albeit perfectly legitimately) was using the property to substantially reduce its tax liabilities, seems bizarre, to say the least. Nonetheless "the Pocantico Plan," as it had come to be called, continued to move forward, with the tacit consent of all the brothers. But then early in 1976 one of them—John 3rd—began to have doubts, especially about the part of the plan involving Kykuit. As he saw it, there were three problems: the amount of money required, the fact that turning the house and gardens into a museum appeared, as he confided to his diary, "a bit like building your own memorial," and finally Nelson's modern sculpture, which, John wrote, "now so permeates the whole area" and about which he had "real reservations." In his opinion it was "more a museum collection than what one might expect in terms of home and garden decoration."

As his remarks suggested, the oldest of the Rockefeller brothers had scant use for modern art. In that respect he was very much his father's son. Like Junior, too, after an anxious, doubt-ridden start in life, he had grown increasingly confident over the years and could point to significant achievements as board chair of the Rockefeller Foundation, as well as in new areas he pioneered on his own, like working to improve relations between Asia and the United States and focusing greater public attention on the problem of worldwide population growth. He had also played a leading role in developing Lincoln Center in New York City and had taken on within the family growing responsibility for acting as—in the phrase the authors would use for the title of his biography—"the Rockefeller Conscience."

Yet despite all his earnestness and hard work John 3rd remained simply one of the Rockefeller brothers, not the family's leader as he might have been. That position still belonged to Nelson, though his involvement in politics had considerably reduced his role in family affairs. By 1976, however, his political career appeared to be ending. The same year, too, another event took place that deeply affected all the Rockefellers, and that was the publication of yet another book about the family, one that in its own way was every bit as critical as Ida Tarbell's series had been all those years ago.

The book in question, *The Rockefellers: An American Dynasty*, was written by Peter Collier and David Horowitz, two West Coast authors and self-styled Marxists who edited *Ramparts* magazine. Lively and eminently readable, it covered all four generations of the family, from Senior through "the cousins," and became an instant best seller. And whereas Tarbell's series had focused mainly on Standard Oil, Collier and Horowitz leveled their sharpest barbs at the Rockefellers as individuals.

Given its subject matter, reading the book was bound to be a difficult experience for the family. But for the brothers' generation it went deeper than that, for much of the criticism of them was based on information provided by their own children. Afterward the cousins would claim that Collier and Horowitz had misled them about their intentions, which seems to have been true. It was also a time when many parents and children in America found themselves locked in conflict across "the generation gap," and the Rockefellers were no exception. Still, the damage done to trust and goodwill within the family was enormous. More than two decades later David Rockefeller could still recall how "very painful" he had found reading Collier and Horowitz's book.

Understandably so. In the pages of the book one could discover that David's wife, Peggy, "despised" her brother-in-law Nelson, information that almost certainly came from her children. Then there was the way David's daughter Abby described her father's reaction to Nelson's marriage to

Happy Murphy: "The remarriage was the most distressing thing to him that ever happened in the world." In a different, even more personal vein, Laurance Rockefeller's daughters, Laura and Marion, offered such remarks about their father as: "I feel sad for him, in a way. He missed the boat! Daddy could have been creative," and "He's always getting off one jet and on to another; hasn't got time for anything especially for understanding himself." Other judgments were less harsh but still guarded. Observed Mary, Nelson's daughter, "My father, well, I love him for his warmth. But he stands for power, and I think it's very important how one relates to power. It stands as a warning."

As striking as their comments about their parents was the candor with which the cousins described their own lives—lives that, according to Collier and Horowitz, were mainly devoted to freeing themselves from the burden of being Rockefellers. Some rebelled openly; at least one changed her name; another remarked, "You need an exorcism." Yet for all the cousins' candor, Collier and Horowitz's assessment of them was hardly admiring or congratulatory, dismissing their attempt "to recapture a personal identity from the family" as "too tentative and stumbling, and finally too mundane to seem a heroic enterprise."

But it was the brothers who remained Collier and Horowitz's chief targets, though the question of what to do about it left them confused and divided. As would happen so often during those years, Nelson and John ended up at opposite ends of the spectrum, with Laurance and David somewhere in the middle. Nelson was so outraged that he never fully forgave the cousins for what he saw as their attack on the family and on him personally. John, on the other hand, began searching almost at once for ways to draw the family back together. He spent hours lunching with his children and his nieces and nephews, trying to fathom how they saw the future and their role in it. Much of what he discovered confirmed what he already knew or had found out by reading Collier and Horowitz's book. Not only were the cousins' values and goals different from those of their parents'; the lives they led were worlds apart from their parents' lives. As for carrying on the family's commitment to philanthropy—something that particularly concerned John 3rd—most tended to favor smaller, more sharply focused ways of doing good in the world. Few seemed interested in involving themselves in the great family foundations.

Ultimately John's researches persuaded him that it was best to dismiss the Collier and Horowitz book as "water over the dam." He also believed the cousins would welcome the opportunity to work more closely with the brothers in the future. He reported, too, that they appeared "relaxed" about the plans for Kykuit, though that may or may not have pleased him, given his own generally negative views on the subject.

In any case, in November of 1975 an important step toward implementing those plans was taken when President Gerald Ford came to Kykuit to designate "the John D. Rockefeller Estate" as a National Historical Landmark. Both the designation and the president's visit—largely engineered by Nelson—had been the subject of elaborate planning for months. In addition to the ceremony itself, there were various dinners and luncheons; the president played two rounds of golf with David, Nelson, and Laurance Rockefeller; and everyone attended a service at Union Church in Pocantico Hills, after which the president and Mrs. Ford bought pastries at a bake sale organized by the church's youth group. By all accounts the Fords' visit went well. Surrounding it, however, was a distinct aura of poignancy, for less than a month earlier the president had been defeated in his bid for reelection by Jimmy Carter. Nor was he the only one about to lose high office; the end of his term would mark the end of Nelson's vice presidency.

While not much was known about Nelson's plans, he had made it clear that he would be coming home, and never one to do things by halves, he chose to mark the occasion by holding the annual Rockefeller family Christmas luncheon at Kykuit. In recent years, because of its size, the luncheon had taken place in the coach barn. Moving it to the Big House was thus a break with tradition, but John 3rd thought it a great success, with "an amazing number of family members there" (eighty-three out of ninety-three), which he felt "really was a tribute to Nelson."

A week earlier, however, John had gone to see Nelson "to talk with him about the family," and it had not been a promising session. Though he was pleased to find his brother willing to discuss "the gradual transfer of responsibility from the brothers to the cousins," Nelson had also taken the opportunity to vent his "quite strong feelings" about the cousins' part in the Collier/Horowitz book. According to John, it was "the one time he really showed emotion in our two-hour discussion," and as a result John went away convinced there were "some real problems ahead."

All families construct legends about themselves, but the Rockefellers are particularly prone to doing so, perhaps because so many legends had been constructed about them. In any case, Nelson's behavior on his return from Washington quickly became a legend of towering proportions. The relevant pieces can all be found in John 3rd's diary, and his biographers would scrupulously follow the same line, as did David Rockefeller in his *Memoirs*. "Appalling" was the term he used to describe Nelson's conduct, echoing the judgments of still other contemporaries, which fairly bristled with words like "irascible" and "imperious," "destructive," driven by "power" rather than "principle," "self-interest" instead of the "public interest."

In essence, the heart of the legend can be summarized easily enough: his political hopes shattered, Nelson returned home to reclaim the only kind of power left to him—control over the Rockefeller family—and in the process arrogantly ran roughshod over the feelings of almost everyone in the family, as well as not a few people outside of it. With so much testimony confirming this version of the story, it would be difficult to refute. The truth is, however, the facts do not always support it. The relentless uniformity of the testimony also raises doubts. It almost seems as if everyone was reading from the same script, and perhaps in a sense they were.

One thing John 3rd's diary makes clear is that the Rockefeller brothers no longer spent much time together or even appeared to know one another very well. They continued to gather in "brothers' meetings," but those occurred on no set schedule and tended to focus on specific issues. Otherwise the contacts among them were few and far between. Shortly before the Fords' visit, for example, John wrote of a golf game with Nelson and David, "We have not played together for years, and perhaps the strain was too much for us." At about the same time he described being shown around Kykuit by Nelson to see the changes he had made "since taking over the house after father's death," suggesting at a minimum that John was not a regular guest at Kykuit and had not been for a long while, though his own home was barely a mile away.

Absorbed in their busy lives, yet facing a series of important issues requiring their cooperation, the brothers were thus left to navigate the perilous terrain of family relationships as best they could. Ironically, however, there was one guide available to them all. In the pages of Collier and Horowitz's book they could find their siblings described in painstaking detail: their activities; their personalities; how other people, including their own children, saw them; their hopes, their dreams, their shortcomings, their failures. It was all there, laid out in chapter after chapter.

To have relied on this material in fashioning the family legend that so demonized Nelson—in effect allowing art to transform itself into life— would have been natural enough to do. Certainly the ingredients were there. For Collier and Horowitz the central element of Nelson's personality was his insatiable lust for power, which grew, in their words, "like some devouring metabolic disorder," made even more ravenous by his mounting "bitterness . . . as the presidency receded from his grasp." The anxious thoughts John confided to his diary at the time of Nelson's return from Washington suggest that he was already expecting his brother to behave in exactly this way, and when matters came to a head six months later, he lost no time in producing an interpretation of what happened that could have come straight from the pages of Collier and Horowitz's book.

It is equally true, on the other hand, that Nelson returned home with a definite agenda in mind. Above all, he wanted to see three issues addressed: the family office, the changing character of the Rockefeller Brothers Fund (RBF), and the future of Kykuit. By general agreement, the family office at Rockefeller Center, which, with its staff of scores of highly competent individuals, handled the countless, day-to-day practical details that made it possible for the Rockefellers to live as they did, needed overhauling, and Nelson volunteered to take the lead in working through the problem. RBF, the foundation that over the years had managed much of the brothers' charitable giving, presented more complicated issues: chiefly what the fund's long-term future would be and what kind of ongoing relationship the family would have with it. On the first question Nelson proposed a broad study similar to one he had supervised for RBF in the 1950s; on the second he was adamant: at least for the present the brothers should continue to play the dominant role in managing the fund.

Nelson's position on Kykuit was already well known, but he came back eager to move the project along as rapidly as possible. John 3rd continued to register doubts, however, and in a memorandum to the brothers written in March 1977 Donal O'Brien reminded them that they had yet to agree either on how to fund the Pocantico Plan or on what should be done to protect the life interests of Nelson and Laurance's wives in their homes on the estate. But then in June, representatives of the National Park Service came to Kykuit to review for the brothers the service's impressively ambitious plans for the estate. With reassuring certainty (and more than a touch of what the service's staff probably learned from Vice President Rockefeller's office on the subject), the report declared that "the John D.

Rockefeller Estate meets all criteria for inclusion in the National Park System," adding:

> In itself, the estate reflects the best qualities of land use and exemplifies one way of "man living with nature." It is physical evidence of the Rockefeller family's attitude and philosophy, which has characterized their positive good works in virtually every segment of American society for the past seventy years. It is a fitting and logical testament that this estate, in its entirety, belong to the people as part of the National Park System for the use and benefit of future generations.

Equally encouraging was the recommendation regarding funding, which called for the passage of federal legislation "authorizing . . . the appropriation of monies for development, operation, and maintenance of the park." In short, the news could not have been better, and for a change even John 3rd seemed positive about the project, noting in his diary, "All of us were very pleased with the Park Department's approach."

Unfortunately that gratifying moment of consensus among the brothers ended all too soon, for after the meeting with the Park Service people that Saturday there followed a series of sessions on other topics, which extended into the next weekend and came to involve the cousins as well as the brothers, all the while becoming steadily more acrimonious. Initially the brothers focused on the family office, then they turned to RBF, yet on both subjects the difficulties appeared all but impenetrable, thanks to months of intense maneuvering beforehand by John 3rd as well as Nelson.

Though John liked to think of himself as a novice at the game of politics, the reality belied his modest pretensions. In meeting after meeting, arranged at his request, with various family members and RBF staff people, he listened patiently and sympathetically to all that was said, yet his primary goal was winning support for his own position: Nelson's "power grab" had to be stopped; the cousins had to be given more of a role both in managing the family office and on the board of RBF; the brothers needed to intervene less in such areas not only for the sake of maintaining harmony within the family but also to preserve its "character" and reputation.

Predictably, Nelson disagreed with every one of these points, but he did make several attempts to placate John, the most important of which was to suggest that the two of them sign a memorandum agreeing to certain basic principles regarding the running of RBF. John refused to sign, however, arguing that what he particularly opposed were prior agreements among the brothers on RBF matters, which Nelson in fact thought ought to be a regular practice and which the memorandum he was proposing would itself constitute. "I cannot help believing," John wrote, "that decisions reached in advance by the brothers would make it difficult for the RBF Trustees to arrive at decisions as objectively and independently as they should."

Nelson also assured John that he had no interest in heading RBF's board, though John felt that was simply because the current chair, Laurance Rockefeller, blindly followed Nelson's lead. To counteract Nelson's influence, John had tried to interest David Rockefeller in the chairmanship, but he was willing to serve only if Laurance wanted to step down, which he did not. John's talks with David had convinced him, too, that David sided with Nelson, as did Laurance, on the importance of maintaining the brothers' control over RBF.

All of which appeared to leave John out in the cold, as in fact it did throughout that first weekend. Reflecting afterward on those "two somewhat wearing days," he concluded that with Nelson and David "so used to power" and Laurance "completely in Nelson's hands," the odds were against him from the start. What he failed to consider was that his brothers might have taken the positions they did less as a power play than as a matter of honest conviction. In any case, his views were to find more support the following weekend, when the cousins joined the brothers in what proved to be a shatteringly tumultuous series of encounters.

As the brothers had been doing for decades, the cousins had begun gathering as a group several years earlier. This time, with the meeting planned for Sunday and dinner the night before to be preceded by cocktails with the brothers and their wives, the occasion seemed as if it would at least begin on a convivial note. Friday night, however, Rodman Rockefeller, Nelson's oldest son, hosted a dinner, attended by his father and several of the cousins, at which Nelson took the occasion to spell out his plans for the family office and also to express in no uncertain terms his anger at those cousins who had helped Collier and Horowitz with their book, a performance that left everyone present thoroughly annoyed.

Caucusing the next day, the cousins unanimously rejected Nelson's proposals for the office, but the real fireworks came at a meeting Sunday

Junior, Senior, and
Nelson A. Rockefeller,
holding his son, Rodman,
photographed at Kykuit
(Courtesy of the Rockefeller
Archive Center)

Senior celebrating his
ninetieth birthday at
Kykuit (Courtesy of the
Rockefeller Archive Center)

Senior enjoying himself with his golfing friends in Florida (Courtesy of Michael S. Rockefeller)

The house on West 54th Street, designed by Welles Bosworth for Junior and Abby. Built next to Senior's house, it was the largest private residence of its day in New York. (Courtesy of the Rockefeller Archive Center)

The young Rockefellers swimming in the pools below Bosworth's terraces at Kykuit (Courtesy of the Rockefeller Archive Center)

The Playhouse as it looked soon after its completion during the 1920s (Courtesy of the Rockefeller Archive Center)

Abby with three of her grandchildren (Courtesy of the Rockefeller Archive Center)

Abby's art gallery, tucked away on the seventh floor of the house on West 54th Street, in space previously used as the children's nursery (Courtesy of the Rockefeller Archive Center)

The five Rockefeller brothers with their father at Kykuit soon after World War II: from left to right, Laurance, Winthrop, Junior, Nelson, John, and David (Courtesy of the Rockefeller Archive Center)

Gaston Lachaise next to his monumental *Standing Woman* (A. E. Gallatin, courtesy of the Philadelphia Museum of Art)

Happy and Nelson Rockefeller (Courtesy of the Rockefeller Archive Center)

A Picasso tapestry from Nelson's basement art galleries at Kykuit (Courtesy of the National Trust for Historic Preservation, Nelson A. Rockefeller Bequest, Pocantico Historic Area)

Large Spiny, by Alexander Calder, commissioned by Nelson in 1966 for the gardens at Kykuit (Courtesy of the Rockefeller Archive Center)

A crew of Pocantico groundsmen working with a hefty piece of sculpture being moved into place by helicopter (Courtesy of the Rockefeller Archive Center)

John D. Rockefeller 3rd,
seated beneath an
early portrait of Senior
(Courtesy of the
Rockefeller Archive Center)

David Rockefeller,
October 1987 (Courtesy of
the Rockefeller Archive Center)

The Rockefeller family gathered for their annual Christmas luncheon in 1976, held that year at Kykuit, at Nelson's invitation. (Courtesy of the Rockefeller Archive Center)

morning, which he had called with all four brothers and the cousins' executive committee present. To chair the office board, the cousins had settled on Laurance, knowing full well that Nelson wanted the job himself. Furious, he demanded an explanation, which one after another the cousins gave him, expressing, as John described it afterward, "their strong reservations as to the way Nelson had handled himself in relation to the office, the RBF, and the family since his return." Nelson fought back with a will, but the cousins, including his own son Steven, who chaired the group, refused to back down.

Confronted with a crisis of the first order, the brothers withdrew to the Playhouse to consider what to do next, while the cousins gathered around the swimming pool to plot strategy. Both David and Laurance "felt strongly," according to John, that Nelson should chair the office board, but John continued to hang back. Finally, after an hour-and-a-half discussion, with Nelson out of the room part of the time, John relented. Still, at least two of his objectives had been achieved that day, or so he mused later in his diary: "the cousins had, as a group, come of age," and perhaps even more important, people's feelings about Nelson had been brought "out in the open."

In his *Memoirs* David would recall Nelson's reaction when the cousins announced their opposition to his chairing the office board: "[he] was as angry as I had ever seen him." Yet the next day John found him anything but angry or glum. Not even when John solemnly stressed the "depth of the feeling about him by the cousins" did Nelson appear at all "down or depressed," which John supposed was due to his long experience in politics: "In public life one has to quite frequently accept major defeats and still move forward." Yet the fact was Nelson had gotten what he wanted in the case of the family office, and if it took a dramatic display of anger to do it, such indeed were the wiles of politicians. As he outlined his plans, too, his management of the office promised to lead to significant cost savings and increases in efficiency, as in fact it did.

The issues involving RBF were not so easily resolved. By June Nelson had managed to get two of his candidates—Henry Kissinger and Nancy Hanks—elected to "nonfamily" slots on the RBF board and had joined the group himself. But at the same time he was trying, with less success, to win funding for a pet project of his: the establishment of a school of osteopathic medicine at the New York Institute of Technology, an idea conceived by Dr. Kenneth Riland, who had been treating him for back pain for years. John strongly disapproved of this sort of personal use of RBF funds, and apart from Nelson no one else, either in the family or on RBF's staff, supported it. The staff was also becoming increasingly uncomfortable with the acrimony among the brothers. "Absolutely ghastly" was how William Dietel, the able and compassionate president of the fund, would remember that time; and John 3rd's diary records Dietel as letting it be known quietly that if a position somewhere else were offered to him, he might well consider accepting it.

As if all this were not enough, two other events, one late in June, and one in July, further complicated matters at RBF. On June 23 a lengthy article appeared in the *New York Times* detailing the turmoil at the fund, with a wealth of facts backed up by extensive quotations from privately circulated memoranda. To have the conflict thus aired in public produced a veritable firestorm. The information in the article had to have come from somewhere, after all, and given its accuracy, the only imaginable source was someone on the inside, though all of the principal players formally declined to be interviewed by the *Times*.

The second event to muddy the waters at RBF was the resignation from its board of John Gardner, former secretary of health, education, and welfare and the founder of Common Cause. One of the small number of non-family trustees, Gardner had been assiduously cultivated by John 3rd, who considered him an ally. David Rockefeller, on the other hand, was convinced that Gardner had "played a role" in leaking the RBF story to the *Times*. He would also describe later a stormy session in which Laurance lashed out at Gardner for opposing Nelson's position on family control, implying that this was the reason for Gardner's resignation.

As for whether Gardner had been the source of the leak to the *Times*, opinions continue to differ. Nelson at one point accused William Dietel of being the culprit, which infuriated Dietel, who was definitely not guilty, though someone else on the RBF staff may have been. An even likelier source was John 3rd's staff, or perhaps even John 3rd himself. At a minimum, it is possible to imagine him wishing aloud—after the manner of Henry II—that the story *would* break, so convinced was he of the correctness of his position. But correct or not, John 3rd was still facing the united opposition of his brothers. Wrestling with how he might tip the balance, in July he finally decided to try a forthright, no-holds-barred statement to Nelson, laying out the whole case in terms at once more sweeping and more personal than anything he or anyone else had attempted up to then.

If the result fell short of being a full-fledged declaration of war, it did not do so by much. Nelson's entire connection with the family was reviewed, beginning when he first took the lead among the brothers "many, many years ago." At that point he had appeared to "care deeply" about the family and put its interests above his own. "Then," wrote John, "came your remarriage and the years away." During that period Nelson had lost one of the two great ambitions of his life: "the presidency of the U.S.A." Now he was in danger of losing the second: "the leadership of a united Rockefeller family." And the fault was his own, for he insisted on playing "power politics [which] just are not appropriate on the home front." The result? "To be perfectly frank with you, as I see it, you are on trial within the family. To me it is tragic, but I realize you may well look at it quite differently." To rectify the situation Nelson would have to change his position on the brothers' role at RBF and immediately withdraw his "osteopathy item." Only that way could he show that he accepted "what the family stands for" and was willing to compromise "for the good of the whole." "Please believe me, Nel," John concluded, "time is running out."

In response to this salvo, a flood of messages welled up from Nelson's side, some sent, some not, some on paper, and others delivered over the phone. His initial response, which was also his angriest, survives only in draft form and was probably not sent. It described John's letter as "intemperate in tone and, in the main, inaccurate," and accused him of confusing "candor with invective." More significant, if less harsh, was a phone call he made several days later suggesting that John "withdraw" his letter lest it become public as other family documents had in the recent *New York Times* article on RBF. John agreed to withdraw the letter but then delayed sending any written confirmation long enough that Nelson felt moved to write a lengthy letter of his own, which went through multiple drafts, denying outright every one of his brother's charges. Yet in tone Nelson's letter was civil enough, and with its assurances—"[of] my respect and admiration for you as a person"—it did succeed in producing a reply from John formally withdrawing his own letter, which in due course made its way from Nelson's office, down the hallways of the Rockefeller family headquarters, back into John's hands.

Nelson also asked to have his latest letter to John returned. But interestingly enough neither one of them chose to take the next step and destroy the letters in question to keep them from prying eyes—the reason Nelson had given for initiating the withdrawals. On the contrary, the entire correspondence survives to this day in their papers at the Rockefeller Archive Center, testifying to just how deeply invested their emotions were in the ongoing struggle between them. Having approached the brink, however, the two brothers did retreat thereafter to gentler, less impassioned exchanges. They continued to disagree, especially about RBF, but the truth was that by the end of 1977 they had fought to a draw on the issues that had claimed most of the brothers' attention up to then, the fund and the family office.

That still left Kykuit to be dealt with, however.

Despite the positive response that greeted the unveiling of the National Park Service's plan for the Pocantico estate in the summer of 1977, problems had begun to surface almost at once. In a long memorandum to the brothers written in September, Donal O'Brien mentioned that some of them as well as a number of the cousins were concerned about the potential tax losses to local communities. More telling still was anxiety among the brothers as to whether they could "financially afford to commit . . . virtually all of [their] Pocantico holdings" to park-making, as the Park Service seemed to assume they would.

After a meeting with representatives of the service, O'Brien was able to clarify several points, the most important being that before anything could be done the brothers would have to specify the minimum amount of land they were willing to commit to creating a park. "This Minimum Plan," according to O'Brien, "would then be submitted to the Park Service to determine if it is viable from the Service's standpoint," and only if the determination was positive would Congress be approached for funding. The Park Service's representatives also made clear that the Rockefellers would have to contribute at least some money to the effort. O'Brien thus urged the brothers to consider these matters and if possible agree about how to handle them. Recognizing, however, that they might not be able to agree, he proposed an alternative: partition—dividing the Pocantico property they currently owned as "tenants in common" into individual holdings. New York state law permitted any one of them to request partition, and it could be done either by mutual agreement or by the courts. The advantage would be that each of them would then be able to do whatever he wished with the resulting shares.

In asking the brothers to consider partition, O'Brien was acknowledging that, as he remarked to John 3rd in October of 1977, "the Brothers are maybe farther apart [with respect to Kykuit] now than they have been for some time." Nelson himself conceded as much by announcing a few days later at a brothers' meeting that while he had long dreamed of Kykuit becoming "a beautiful and significant historic site open to the public," he felt there was opposition to this in the family and was going to "relax and try to go along with what others want." However, according to John, it then slipped out that Nelson had changed his will, leaving only Kykuit for public purposes, with his share of the open space going to Happy. He also claimed to be negotiating with Marriott to build a major hotel and conference center on land he owned adjacent to the estate and said he was considering, as well, selling part of his sculpture collection in the gardens at Kykuit.

Suddenly dropping this particular bombshell in his brothers' midst—for so it must have seemed to them—may well have been a ploy on Nelson's part to get their attention in hopes of compelling them to agree to his vision for Kykuit. At a minimum it presented a dramatic preview of what partition might look like. It also highlighted the fundamental division among the brothers regarding the future of the estate.

Nelson's primary interest had always been in Kykuit. But he was also eager to raise money for himself and his family. (He had even started a business to merchandise reproductions of some of the artworks in his collection.) Selling off his share of the open space of the estate, or leaving it to Happy so she could do so, would help considerably in that regard. In the opposing camp, on the other hand, were those brothers whose chief concern was turning over to the public as much of the open space as possible, and who remained skeptical or downright hostile to the idea of preserving Kykuit as a museum. Ideologically Laurance—having made a national reputation for himself as a dedicated environmentalist—belonged in that camp, yet his long-standing loyalty to Nelson complicated his position. So it had become John 3rd who embraced most wholeheartedly this side of the dispute.

Kykuit versus the open space; Nelson versus John—once again. But undaunted, Donal O'Brien continued to try to bring the brothers together, while Nelson busied himself with embellishing his plans for Kykuit. He talked of moving the house in which Senior had been born from Richford, New York, to the estate as well as developing a carriage and automobile museum in the coach barn. With both ideas John saw problems. He did, however, urge Nelson not to remove any of his sculpture collection from the gardens, though the reason he gave was hardly encouraging: "Our problems in relation to the future of the estate are already of such magnitude that we must not do anything to add to or complicate them."

Meanwhile Donal O'Brien's chief strategy for getting the broader plan for the estate back on track was to organize yet another study of the subject. A committee was appointed, to be cochaired by himself and Harmon Goldstone, an architect and historic preservationist already well known to the Rockefellers. The fact that the group spent much of its time visiting historic houses around the country suggests its principal mission was to reassure John that Kykuit could become a worthwhile historic site, offering genuine benefits to the public. And in fact after the report appeared in May of 1978 John lost no time in declaring his "general agreement" with it and warmly thanked Goldstone and O'Brien for all their hard work at a time "when the boat seemed to be rocking somewhat precariously."

Packed with detail, the report ran to over a hundred pages, but its major recommendations were straightforward enough: the bulk of the estate should be donated to the National Park Service, with the service administering the open space and Sleepy Hollow Restorations managing the historic area. In anticipation of these recommendations, Interior Secretary Cecil Andrus and his wife had visited Kykuit the preceding month, because, as John 3rd remarked, "a decision with the government will take time, and it is essential to carry out negotiations during one administration."

But as it turned out, time was not all the situation required. John continued to fret about the details of the plan. One problem for him was a seemingly peripheral issue involving their great-uncle William Rockefeller's old estate, Rockwood Hall, which through a circuitous route had come into Laurance Rockefeller's hands, and which he had decided to develop commercially. John thought Rockwood Hall ought to be included in the Pocantico Plan, and when Laurance rejected his suggestion, he persuaded David that the two of them should try to buy the property from Laurance. Furious, Laurance refused to discuss the matter, and as David remembered it later, "essentially pushed us out the door."

The entire episode was curious because all of the brothers owned parcels of land bordering the estate, and except for Rockwood Hall there was never any suggestion that they be added to the Pocantico Plan. It is tempting to think that John may have targeted Laurance out of frustration at his continuing support for Nelson. In any event, tempers soon cooled, though even as they did John hung back from taking the final steps needed to implement the Pocantico Plan. He also continued to oppose a grant from RBF to endow the historic area, and even more serious was his failure to incorporate in his will the $5 million bequest that all of the brothers were supposed to make as the core of the Pocantico endowment. He did ask his lawyers to draft appropriate language for such a bequest, yet version after version left him dissatisfied. Perhaps in time the right combination of words might have been found, but it never was. On July 10, 1978, the car in which John 3rd was being driven to catch a train to New York from the country was hit head-on by a Volkswagen sedan, instantly ending his life.

For all the Rockefellers, John 3rd's death stood as a milestone. The oldest surviving member of the family was gone. Half of Junior and Abby's children were now dead, with all that implied for those who remained. The cousins generation, too, had particular cause to mourn John's passing, having found him of all the brothers the most eager to see them move ahead to positions of power and responsibility within the family. He liked to think of this as a matter of principle, but among his nieces and nephews he also won the allies he needed to confront his brothers, with whom he felt increasingly at odds.

As the chief target of John's alliance-building, Nelson doubtless imagined he would now have freer rein to do as he wished. But if so, he quickly discovered otherwise. On the plane returning from his ranch in Venezuela, he had begun making notes for the eulogy he assumed he would deliver at his brother's memorial service in Riverside Church, only to be told by Blanchette and Jay Rockefeller—John's widow and oldest son—in what surely must have seemed a deliberate slap in the face, that he was not being asked to speak, whereas his son Steven, a great favorite of John's, would be delivering a few remarks. Worse still was John's failure to include the $5 million for the Pocantico Plan in his will, which left Nelson "beside himself," David wrote later. "As the pertinent provisions were read to us, I could see [his] eyes harden with anger." From that point events moved inexorably on to the denouement of the drama: Nelson's own death six months later and the provisions in *his* will regarding Kykuit.

Though he had his will rewritten immediately after John's death, Nelson waited until December to tell his brothers what it contained. As he had threatened to do earlier, in the new will he abandoned the whole idea of joint action on Pocantico, choosing instead a scheme that mandated partition. The key was naming specific recipients for his bequests, which under O'Brien's plan the brothers were to avoid doing. Thus his portion of the open space would go to Happy, and the National Trust for Historic Preservation would receive his share of the Park, plus most of his art collection, both inside and outside of the house. Also, as John had done, he left out the $5 million that was supposed to accompany his bequests.

In this bundle of changes, one item requires additional explanation, and that is Nelson's choice of the National Trust as the recipient of his share of the Park and Kykuit. He had, after all, been the chief instigator of the plan to use the National Park Service in this way, and the agency remained interested in acquiring the estate. The problem was that its representatives had made it clear that they expected, over time, the lion's share of the property to go to the Park Service, which would have precluded selling off sizable portions of the open space, something that was definitely on Nelson's mind. The Park Service also wanted a significant level of financial participation from the Rockefellers, which Nelson was eager to avoid. The National Trust, on the other hand, cared only about Kykuit and its outbuildings, and Carl Humelsine, who chaired the trust's board of trustees, had assured Nelson that it would shortly be receiving, through congressional action, millions of dollars from the sale of offshore oil rights, and so would have no difficulty handling the cost of maintaining Kykuit.

For all of these reasons Nelson chose the National Trust over the Park Service, yet none of them made a dent in the stony wall of anger and opposition that greeted him when he told his brothers of his plans. He pointed out that they could still salvage the old Pocantico Plan by agreeing to buy Happy's share of the open space after his death and falling in with his choice of the National Trust to receive and administer Kykuit, but as David wrote later, "I was outraged and told Nelson so." When he saw how angry his brothers were, "he retreated a bit," David noted, saying that his will was not final. Yet a little more than a month later Nelson lay dead, with the will unchanged.

Such was "Nelson's Revenge." But in his view what he did had been provoked by what he surely saw as "John's Revenge"—his failure to include the $5 million bequest for the original Pocantico Plan in his will. Then and later many of those familiar with the situation believed that had either brother lived longer, calmer councils would have prevailed, and the offending wills would have been changed. Yet this is to suppose that the two were behaving like a couple of naughty boys throwing stones at each other, or more aptly, perhaps, like a pair of demented elephants, blindly crashing together in the dark, when in fact the depth of passion revealed by their behavior indicates something far more basic at work than temporary fits of pique or even rage.

More basic and also more complicated, for every now and then gestures of genuine kindness broke through their quarreling: John's telling Nel at one point how much he liked his photographs of the sculptures in the gardens at Kykuit, for example, or the "beautiful arrangement" of flowers Nelson and Happy sent "Johnny" when he was recovering from surgery. Whatever else was true, these were people who cared about each other—brothers who, all things being equal, would rather not have spent their days locked in combat.

Yet all things were not equal. The issues that divided Nelson and John Rockefeller were of grave and abiding importance, for they went to the very essence of who they were both as individuals and as Rockefellers, and of what to leave on earth as memorials to themselves and the family that had simultaneously enriched their lives with such stunning opportunities and imposed upon them such heavy burdens of responsibility. And right there, in a sense, lay the rub, because for Nelson the opportunities had always mattered most, while for John the responsibilities loomed largest. To be a Rockefeller to Nelson meant using money and the power that went with it to shape the world as he thought it ought to be, which could mean anything from managing the future of the nation to finding the perfect place for a wonderful piece of sculpture. To John, however, being a Rockefeller meant serving, nurturing, giving others the chance to do what they dreamed of doing.

Both strains were solidly imbedded in the family's heritage from Senior's time on. In Junior's life they had contended constantly, with duty winning for the most part, but not always. Abby in her gracious but firm way usually came out on the side of power. She was also inclined to think that being a Rockefeller could be fun, that it did not have to be quite so serious a matter as Junior imagined. Nelson was her son; John was Junior's. But if the two strains mingled in the lives of Junior and Abby, what had caused them to divide so sharply in the experience of their two oldest sons? Part of it, certainly, was personality and temperament. Yet even more important seems to have been a sense both brothers had that with their generation a great deal that had once characterized the Rockefeller family would be ending. Henceforth there would be both less money and less power. Nor, if Collier and Horowitz's book was to be believed, would power and duty ever be the principal points around which the cousins charted their lives. Their concerns were more personal, more intimate, less public.

With so much ending, it was only natural to want to sum things up, to make clear once and for all who the Rockefellers had been and what they had achieved over the years. Which is exactly what Nelson and John were trying to do. The problem was they each wanted to have the last word, and they could not agree about what it should be. Had the stakes not been so high, chances are they would have found a way to compromise, to muddle on through. For ironically they did agree about one all-important point: they both believed that keeping the Pocantico estate the closed, intensely private refuge it had become would be wrong; that it was time to give it a broader, more democratic significance. But by the end they were too angry at each other to recognize that bond.

So it seems unlikely they would ever have agreed about what, finally, to do with Kykuit—the consummate emblem of the family's power, the intractable core that could not be bargained away. Yet after all there was something fitting about that. For seventy-five years earlier Junior and Senior had battled over the same ground. In that case it had been Junior who emerged victorious; this time it would be Nelson. His will left a dozen or more loose ends to be raveled up somehow; but the house and gardens, with his brilliantly placed sculpture collection, would survive, and the public would be welcomed in to enjoy it all. His brothers, he knew, would be furious about his will, yet he also knew that once its terms became public they would have no choice but to find a way of making his vision work, of giving up that wondrous haven that had meant so much for so long. It would not be easy, but ultimately the world would demand nothing less of them.

12

Going Public

"Quite a titanic kind of struggle" was how he would come to describe the events of those years. But fortunately for everyone's sake, he had a genius for compromise and the grace to let it seem to happen naturally. His legal training may have helped, though much of his early career was spent in the gentler world of academe, and moving from there to become head of a philanthropic foundation meant following a well-traveled path. Many college presidents had done the same. Yet few if any of them had to face, so early in their tenures, the grinding dilemmas he did, especially over a house.

What emerged most clearly from his conversation about it later was a sense of the strength of the personalities involved—of a collection of individuals, each bent on single-handedly controlling what happened in a situation where that was simply not possible. Something had to give, and it fell to him to figure out what.

In the end he succeeded brilliantly, as effective mediators always try to do, by letting everyone walk away with at least part of what they wanted. As one person at the center of the negotiations would remark later, "He was just, he was masterful." Were the ghosts of the family he had served so well gathered somewhere in the mists singing anthems of praise to him? Certainly they should have been. At a moment when the ship was foundering, when those left to carry on had lost their way, he stepped in and guided them safely back on course.

By the time Colin Campbell took over as president of the Rockefeller Brothers Fund in 1988, almost a decade had passed since Nelson Rockefeller's death, and despite the terms of his will not a single member of the public had been admitted to Kykuit. Nor, as matters stood, did that seem likely to change anytime soon, though the intervening years had seen a steady proliferation of plans, studies, proposals, counterproposals, divisions of property, and articles in the newspapers, all having to do with Kykuit. Yet none of it resolved what had been from the start the overriding issue: how to open the house and grounds to the public in a way that other members of the Rockefeller family—principally Nelson's two surviving brothers, David and Laurance, and his widow, Happy—would accept.

Their acceptance was essential because of the one item Nelson's will had not included to carry out his plans for Kykuit: money. He had continued to hope the National Trust would be receiving federal revenues from offshore oil leases, but that never happened, so the trust lacked the means to do much of anything with his lavish gift. The Rockefellers, on the other hand, had set aside funds to finance at least part of the project, but they resolutely refused to let go of them, at least to the National Trust.

The funds had come from two sources: a surprising (because she had never liked Kykuit) $1.5 million bequest from Abby ("Babs") Rockefeller Milton Pardee Mauzé—the brothers' only sister—which had been left to RBF to administer, and a $15 million grant from the fund itself. The grant had been approved in the autumn of 1978, shortly after the death of John 3rd, who had always opposed taking such a step. Over time, too, RBF's "Pocantico Fund" grew substantially, totaling more than twice the original $16 million by 1988—almost enough to pay the cost of endowing Kykuit's maintenance, as the people at the National Trust pointed out more than once. Yet all to no avail: the money remained at RBF.

With the trust powerless to carry out Nelson's intentions regarding Kykuit, the refusal of the Rockefellers to provide the necessary funds could have seemed like an outright campaign to block the terms of his will, and often it amounted to exactly that. Yet in the long run the family's objectives were more complex than this implies, though because they rarely bothered to explain themselves, events constantly appeared to be careening uphill and down with no clear destination in sight. In a nutshell, that was the problem Colin Campbell would face: how to slow down and give purpose and direction to all that ceaseless motion. To succeed, however, he first had to understand not only the decadelong history that preceded his appearance on the scene but also the goals and interests of the principal actors in that history.

In part, the Rockefellers' difficulty with the National Trust stemmed from their view that it was neither a very well run organization nor a particularly effective one, a judgment even some of its own trustees would later confirm. Established by Congress in 1949, it had been patterned on the eminently successful British National Trust, but Congress in giving it life neglected to fund it, and through the 1950s its growth was modest at best. Though it did manage to acquire a small collection of historic properties and at least the beginnings of an endowment, membership rose slowly, reaching only 4,500 at the end of the decade, compared to the British National Trust's 300,000. But then during the 1960s and '70s membership did increase, growing to 160,000 by 1979. Also, in 1966 the trust began receiving a small federal appropriation annually, and the following year it launched a campaign to quadruple its $5.7 million endowment. In light of all that happened later, an interesting consequence of that effort was a $500,000 grant from the Rockefeller Brothers Fund.

From 1980 on, however, the organization's problems multiplied steadily. As part of the Reagan administration's crusade to cut the "frills" from the federal budget, the trust's $4.4 million appropriation came under fire. Thanks to Democratic majorities in Congress it survived, but by then costs were rising and membership had begun to fall. Even more serious was a rapidly developing change in the entire historic preservation movement in the United States. Where once the "historic house," usually of some "important" person, had been the movement's principal icon—and the trust's mainstay—the focus was shifting to preserving the material world of ordinary Americans: seaport dock areas, urban neighborhoods, small-town main streets, as well as early industrial buildings and communities. To its credit, the National Trust did its best to keep abreast of the latest trends in historic preservation, creating both the National Mainstreet Center and a $1 million revolving fund to protect endangered historic buildings of all kinds. Its public statements also stressed that historic preservation was "working for lower income people . . . not just for the wealthy." Yet by 1982, with income flat and membership still falling, hard choices had to be made. Reluctantly, the organization announced that it would close four of its fourteen historic houses for an indefinite period.

Given the difficulties facing the trust, the Rockefellers' anxiety about seeing it take over Kykuit was understandable. For the same reason providing it with the more than $16 million Pocantico Fund seemed problematic. As one observer later remarked, "If you haven't hedged a fund legally so they can't grab it, any institution is bound, if it's starting to drown like the proverbial drowning man, to grab anything that floats, and you're now talking about 17 or 18 million dollars." Equally troubling was the trust's program of closing historic houses. Kykuit itself was a historic house, after all.

By the time the closings occurred, however, it had begun to seem that Kykuit's future might not involve the National Trust after all, for its trustees had been asked to consider "gifting over" Nelson's bequest to Sleepy Hollow Restorations (SHR). Founded a generation earlier, SHR operated three historic Hudson Valley properties that Junior, somewhat reluctantly, had agreed to purchase and restore. All three—Washington Irving's Sunnyside and Philipsburg and Van Courtland manors—were near Kykuit, and even though Junior was much involved with Williamsburg at the time, each had been in dire need of "saving." Turning Kykuit over to SHR would rescue the National Trust from the embarrassment of owning a house it could neither maintain nor show to the public, or so ran the argument. For its part, SHR stood to acquire a valuable property, plus RBF's Pocantico Fund, which, with barely the blink of an eye, its trustees voted to pass along to SHR, something they had never been willing to do for the National Trust.

But as it turned out, the plan to have SHR take over Kykuit proved unworkable. Though it was a sound organization with a $20 million endowment of its own, its trustees concluded after a year and a half of study that even with the addition of RBF's Pocantico Fund SHR lacked the resources needed to shoulder such an ambitious project. So the Pocantico Fund went back to RBF, and RBF compensated SHR for the expenses of its study, which a report from SHR set at more than $1.3 million.

Thus ended the first chapter of the saga. Five years had already passed since Nelson's death, yet the abortive attempt to transfer Kykuit to SHR had established a pattern that would prove remarkably durable. If the Rockefellers considered the National Trust ill equipped to take on Kykuit, in truth the trust was neither smaller nor notably less well supplied with resources than SHR. But SHR was—as the trust was not—an organization the family controlled; it had been founded by Junior, and both David and Laurance Rockefeller served on its board of trustees. Evidently whatever happened to Kykuit, the Rockefellers meant to keep control of it and had decided that the surest way of doing so was to remove it from the trust's hands and find some other institutional home for it, one that would be duly attentive to the family's wishes. That would not change.

Yet as central as the issue of control was to the entire episode, it also had about it a puzzling air of almost willful miscalculation. SHR could not afford to take on Kykuit. It was a matter of simple arithmetic, and surely David and Laurance were in as good a position as anyone to have anticipated the problem—and to have solved it with a timely donation of additional funds to SHR, which they chose not to do. On the other hand, the net effect was to keep Kykuit exactly as it was, to stave off the avalanche of change Nelson's bequest threatened to unleash upon it, which appears to have been precisely what the Rockefellers intended. Nor would it be the last time they resorted to such tactics.

Meanwhile, the closing months of 1983 saw two new developments that would significantly alter the future of the entire Pocantico estate. The first was the donation of a sizable portion of its "open space" to create a New York state park for activities like hiking and bicycling. The second was an agreement between David and Laurance Rockefeller and the National Trust enabling the brothers to lease the historic area, including Kykuit, for a period of three years. During that time, according to the agreement, the trust was to draft a plan to utilize the site, which the brothers would then consider, with the option of either approving the plan or, failing that, purchasing the historic area from the trust at fair market value.

As a necessary preface to these developments, a complicated series of agreements had split the Pocantico property into separate parcels and divided them among David, Laurance, and the estates of John and Nelson. As a result, John's estate ended up with parcels only in the open space, while Nelson's estate (and through it the National Trust) received eighty-six acres in the Park area, plus Kykuit, the coach barn, the orangerie, and the greenhouses, with the remainder of the property going to David and Laurance. In effect these arrangements cleared the way for implementing *both* of the quite different visions of the estate's future that John and Nelson, battling to the end, had carried to their graves. Beyond dividing the property, however, they mandated nothing. It would be up to those who held the various parcels to determine their fate.

Because the issues involving the open space were simpler, they were settled more quickly. The creation of "Rockefeller State Park" had been previewed in 1981 by Laurance Rockefeller, speaking of the projected facility's "superb recreational potentials" at a ceremony on Rockefeller Point, overlooking the Hudson River. Two years later, at Pocantico Hills School, Governor Mario Cuomo formally accepted the Rockefellers' gift of land for the park and praised their "generosity of spirit." New York State park commissioner Orin Lehman also spoke, as did David Rockefeller, who described the occasion as "historic and sentimental . . . for our family." In addition, Blanchette Rockefeller, John 3rd's widow, presented Commissioner Lehman with two checks, totaling more than $3 million, to endow the park.

Almost all the 743 acres transferred to New York at the 1983 ceremony had come from John 3rd's estate, with the balance provided by David Rockefeller. He and Laurance also promised to add more land in the future. And true to John's wishes, the creation of the state park had nothing at all to do with Kykuit. Yet that did not mean the house had no place in the celebratory moments surrounding the event. At Rockefeller Point in 1981, Laurance Rockefeller had noted that Kykuit "would be added to the responsibilities of Sleepy Hollow Restorations" (as then envisioned), and two years later, when the land for the park was transferred to the state, the National Trust's president, Michael Ainslie, was quoted as saying that the house would "eventually be available for public exhibition," adding, "it might also be given other uses, as the site of international meetings, for example." As for when any of this might happen, however, all David Rockefeller would say was "That's difficult to answer: I'm feeling pretty healthy," a remark hinting at a problem that would loom steadily larger in the years ahead.

The *New York Times*, which gave front-page coverage to the Rockefeller State Park story, also never missed an opportunity to bring up Kykuit. Still, almost everything about the house's future remained unsettled. The 1983 lease agreement between the Rockefeller brothers and the National Trust, while resolving some of the uncertainty, had offered no hard-and-fast solutions, or even any very clear sense of how the parties involved might eventually reach an agreement. The most it did was give the trust a chance to try to prove to David and Laurance that it could mount an acceptable program for opening Kykuit to the public.

The person chosen to direct that effort was George H. Bohlinger III, a former deputy associate attorney general of the United States, whose primary area of expertise, according to the *New York Times*, was "running correctional institutions." If the appointment seemed an odd one, Bohlinger argued that his new assignment, while "not analogous to running prisons," would nonetheless require substantial "organizational and management skills." The major challenge in the case of the Kykuit study, as he saw it, would be to "tie the property in with the preservation goals of the National Trust and with the public spiritedness of the Rockefeller family," which was at least a diplomatic way of describing some of the problems he would face.

To assist Bohlinger, the trust selected an eleven-member "Pocantico Planning Project Advisory Board," including both its own president and the chair of its trustees, as well as New York State park commissioner Orin Lehman and several individuals with ties either to the Rockefellers personally or to organizations close to them. Yet no members of the family itself were slated to serve on the advisory board, possibly to avoid conflicts of interest, though that in itself might have seemed a less-than-hopeful portent of things to come.

In any case, over the next thirty months Bohlinger and his small staff labored diligently to produce a plan for "the ultimate use" of Pocantico's historic area. Among other things they reviewed all of the previous studies of the property, hired, at various times, ten consultants, and worked with a specially appointed Pocantico Institute Committee to investigate ways of using the historic area beyond public visitation. They also analyzed a large amount of data from Greenrock Corporation on managing the physical fabric of the estate, and later, in their report, they would thank both the Rockefeller family office and David Rockefeller personally for his "guidance and encouragement." The expenses of the study, which by the middle of 1987 had reached $777,198, were paid out of income from RBF's Pocantico Fund, and William Dietel, RBF's president, reported regularly to its trustees on the progress of the effort. RBF's staff also undertook a separate study of their own on the possible creation in the historic area of an institute related to philanthropy.

As promising as much of this seemed, both the RBF study and the tenor of some of Dietel's remarks appeared to indicate a certain anxiety about what the Bohlinger group might come up with. The anxiety was real. As it happened, however, Kykuit was only part of its cause, for during the past several years RBF had also been undergoing a period of intense change. Faced with the brothers' advancing age, its trustees had decided to make a series of sizable "capital grants" to nineteen organizations that the brothers had consistently supported through the fund—places like Rockefeller University, the Sloan-Kettering Institute, and the Museum of Modern Art—with an eye to ending smaller, annual donations to those organizations, thereby freeing RBF to devote its resources to new initiatives. Ultimately $85 million was used in this way, all money well spent, by general agreement. (Even John 3rd and Nelson, while disagreeing over some of the details, had joined in supporting the basic plan.) But as William Dietel reported to RBF's trustees in 1984, the resulting hole in the fund's endowment had reduced it to thirty-ninth in total assets among American community and private foundations, whereas in 1960 it had ranked ninth.

For the future, Dietel believed it was essential for RBF to broaden both its mission and its capital base, and in this respect he saw the fund's association with Kykuit posing, simultaneously, a danger and an opportunity. Highlighting the danger, he declared, "Nothing would be more foolish than for the Fund to become deeply involved at Pocantico Hills in order to give meaning to the effort to preserve and present to the public that elegant piece of land." But properly used, the estate could, he felt, enhance RBF's program by providing a place for studying broad issues related to philanthropy and by encouraging "wider fourth and fifth generation participation" among the Rockefellers in the work of the fund: in short, by bringing in fresh energy and new money. Yet a few months later, stressing the danger again, he reported to RBF's board that he "consistently said in his conversations about Kykuit that the Fund does not have the resources to rescue the project."

Dietel's sense of the risks Kykuit posed for RBF was shared by its staff as well as by several of the cousins on its board, particularly Nelson's son, Steven Rockefeller, whose attitude reflected more than a trace of John 3rd's distaste for "building monuments to oneself." And with Nelson gone, even Laurance Rockefeller was rapidly losing whatever taste he once had for turning Kykuit into a museum, to the point where he confided to his brother David that he believed the best solution was simply to tear the house down. Said another family member later, paraphrasing Laurance's thoughts on the subject, "It's a beautiful place. Send it back to nature. It's done its thing. The family doesn't need to shine a light on itself."

Still, no one was about to suggest that the National Trust abandon its study of public visitation at Kykuit. What did claim increasing attention, on the other hand, was the notion of an institute in the historic area as a supplement to opening the house for public tours. With both the Bohlinger group and RBF's staff working on the possibility, it had clearly become a serious matter, though the two efforts were moving in different directions: RBF's toward a "Center for the Advancement of Philanthropy," while the Bohlinger group favored a "Pocantico Institute for Science, Technology, and International Affairs," which David Rockefeller strongly endorsed as well. The idea of a center of some sort also had considerable appeal to several of the cousins.

Most of the Bohlinger group's energies, however, went into creating what its members hoped would be an acceptable way of handling the general public at Kykuit. The result, finally unveiled in October 1986, in an eighty-three-page "Plan for Pocantico," described a series of carefully controlled guided tours of the house and gardens, with strict limits on the number of people in each tour group. The National Trust would conduct the tours, which would begin at a reception area in the coach barn, and the emphasis would be on "the attributes of the setting and the interpretation of the property, rather than on the lives of the owners." At a projected level of fifty-seven thousand visitors a year, the program would bring in nearly $550,000, more than enough to cover its operating expenses. Not included in those figures, however, was the cost of maintaining the property or the funds needed for renovations before the tours could begin.

In addition to the description of "Estate Visitation," the "Plan for Pocantico" included a section on "The Pocantico Institute for Science, Technology, and International Affairs," another addressing the highly sensitive issue of "Family Use," and a third titled simply "Specifications." Based on longstanding philanthropic interests of the Rockefeller family, the Pocantico Institute, as proposed, would function as "a private institution of the highest quality devoted to the international development and application of science and technology for the benefit of mankind." To fulfill this mission it would sponsor collaborative projects with other institutions, organize meetings of interested people around the globe, and develop studies of specific topics in a wide variety of areas—tasks that would require a staff of "about thirty" administrators, scientists, and science and technology policy scholars—all to be paid for, presumably, by the Rockefellers.

With regard to "Family Use," the report presented information from Greenrock Corporation detailing the size, location, and type of the sixty-four events various Rockefeller family members had sponsored at Pocantico during the two years from 1984 to 1986. More than 80 percent involved the Playhouse, which was not among the trust's holdings (having gone to David in the division of the estate), and which the report recommended should remain in the family's hands, to be used as its members wished. Significantly, nothing was said about family access to Kykuit itself, but the point hardly needed elaboration. Once the house was opened to the public, it would be closed to the Rockefellers, at least for the kinds of uses they were accustomed to making of it.

An even more sensitive issue the plan raised was the loss of privacy those living on the estate would face once the public appeared within its gates. Crucial, too, was the matter of timing. From the beginning "the senior Rockefellers"—Laurance, David, and Nelson's widow, Happy—had assumed that they would be able to live out their lives at Pocantico before tours of Kykuit began. In line with that hope, the 1983 agreement with the National Trust gave the two brothers the option of securing "Life Estates" in the historic area if they wished. Under the heading "Specifications," however, the Bollinger report recommended a schedule that had them renouncing that option as soon as the plan for public visitation was accepted. Six months later the National Trust would begin construction to accommodate public tours, and thirty-six months after that a "phased program" of tours would begin. In five years the "Estate Visitation Program" would be in full operation.

Thus, if the Bohlinger plan went into effect, in less than four years the Rockefellers stood to lose the privacy that had been as much a part of their experience at Pocantico as the ground beneath their feet. And the "Specifications" section of the report was equally forthright about money. Implementing the plan would require $36.9 million from "the Interested Rockefeller Parties" as an endowment to maintain the historic area. Presumably RBF's Pocantico Fund—transferred to the National Trust—would make up most of that sum. The Rockefellers were also expected to provide the $5.684 million needed for initial construction, plus, again, the cost of running the Pocantico Institute.

<hr/>

For the trustees of the National Trust the Bohlinger group's plan presented no particular difficulties, and they approved it promptly, though one of them remarked later, "We were not real players . . . it wasn't going to make a lot of difference what we did, because it was going to be determined elsewhere." "Elsewhere," of course, meant by the Rockefellers themselves, and their response to what had now officially become the proposal called for in the 1983 lease agreement with the trust took shape more slowly. It also shifted over time; nor, until late in the day, did any sort of consensus emerge within the family. On the contrary, individual interests and personalities continued to tug in different, sometimes diametrically opposed directions.

In Laurance and David's case there remained the basic issue of whether Kykuit should be preserved at all. Laurance, the dedicated environmentalist—and, some thought, the wisest and most reflective of all the brothers—continued to think it should be torn down. He also owned a house within the Park area and thus had more reason to be concerned about protecting his privacy than David, who lived across the road from the estate. Yet David, the youngest of the brothers, had spent more time at Kykuit than the rest of his generation and had been a particular favorite of his grandfather's. His career as a banker, too, had given him a different perspective from his siblings on Kykuit. As he remarked at one point, "The Rockefeller family has been on the national scene in important ways for over 100 years; Kykuit has been occupied by four generations of the family, and there is no other house or place of which that is true." He also pointed out that it was a place "where a great many important and interesting people from around the world have been entertained." Not to preserve the house, he believed, would be an enormous mistake. "Absolutely appalling" was his verdict on Laurance's notion that it should be torn down. As for what should be done with it, David was much taken with the idea of an institute for science and international affairs; indeed it seems to have originated with him. He was also eager to involve Rockefeller University in the project. Opening the house to the public he found less appealing, but if it was to occur, he wanted it put off until after his generation had passed from the scene.

Given their conflicting opinions, David and Laurance had agreed to apportion the cost of maintaining the house and gardens (which they were obliged to cover under the 1983 agreement) unequally, with David paying two-thirds and Laurance one-third, but they continued to bicker about the issue, to the acute discomfort of those around them. As one person described such an exchange later, it went from "No, David, this is your project," to "Well, Larry, we have to do this together," with David usually carrying the day, at least about the money. Yet two successive presidents of RBF—William Dietel and Colin Campbell—both came to feel that what actually divided the brothers was not money at all but the future of the Rockefeller family. And there they saw a fundamental split between what Campbell calls "the dynasts" in the family and "the people who did not have that approach." Should the Rockefellers remain a united family play-ing, collectively, a major role in the larger world? Laurance, "the epitome of the nondynast side," thought not; David, the quintessential dynast, dis-agreed and saw keeping Kykuit intact as a vital means of holding the fam-ily together.

But for other family members the puzzle Kykuit presented was not so easily defined. Happy Rockefeller respected and honored Nelson's desire to open the house to the public, yet of all the family she lived closest to it, in the Japanese-style house that she and Nelson had built together, which stood at the end of the Japanese garden, a site the Bohlinger report pro-posed using for one of the National Trust tours. She had also, like Nelson, long been close to Laurance and relied on him to keep her informed about the negotiations over Kykuit and to represent her interests, even though the two of them disagreed about what to do with the house.

Equally complex was the position of the cousins, many of whom had traveled a considerable distance emotionally and intellectually since the furor over the Collier and Horowitz book. Among them, three individuals would play particularly prominent roles in shaping the future of Kykuit: Nelson's son, Steven Rockefeller; David Rockefeller Jr.; and Laura Chasin, Laurance's eldest daughter. All three served at various times as RBF trustees, with David Rockefeller Jr. taking over from his father as chair of the board just as the negotiations over Kykuit were reaching their most critical point.

Steven Rockefeller, who also later chaired the RBF board, was the oldest of the three. A committed environmentalist who had sided with his uncle John on a variety of issues, he was adamant about limiting the fund's in-volvement with Kykuit as much as possible. More relaxed on that score, David Rockefeller Jr. and Laura Chasin were attracted to the idea of an in-stitute on the property, though not the Institute of Science, Technology, and International Affairs that the Bohlinger report recommended and David's father favored. Eventually their thoughts resulted in a report pro-posing "a composite idea" they called "the Bedrock Institute," which fea-tured both an advisory council of scientists and technologists and an advisory council of family members, overseeing a "Bedfellows Institute," so named, as David Jr. explained later, because their goal was "getting people of all kinds to come together in a beautiful place." In this way they hoped "to buy a piece, if you will, of the action"—to play a significant role as a new generation of Rockefellers and also to announce, as David Jr. put it, referring to Kykuit: "This is not a mausoleum. This is not a memorial to the family. This is a center of activity—ongoing activity—in which the family is engaged."

Such were the Rockefellers' visions of Kykuit's future—a medley of ideas little calculated to harmonize with one another—though they did have one thing in common: all of them departed significantly from the National Trust's "Plan for Pocantico." But under the circumstances, a cautious initial response seemed best. In conveying the plan to RBF's board in November 1986, David Rockefeller reviewed the events that had led to it and pointed out that RBF's trustees would now have to decide whether or not to make its Pocantico Fund available to the National Trust to carry out the plan. He explained that Donal O'Brien had recommended, if that was done, creating a separate charitable trust to keep the funds secure, which David supported. Beyond that, he offered his fellow trustees no advice. He did mention, however, that the time available for making a decision was short, only 180 days, and William Dietel added that he and David had already begun negotiations with the trust over "some changes" they wanted to see in the plan—a statement that proved to be the most telling clue of all to what lay ahead.

As it turned out, the 180-day deadline came and went with no resolution of any of the subjects under negotiation between the Rockefellers and the National Trust. On the contrary, they only multiplied, making it necessary to extend the deadline repeatedly. Meanwhile, the Rockefeller forces turned to devising alternatives to put in place of the trust's plan, for the plain truth was it was not acceptable to the family, as David Rockefeller made clear in describing the first of the alternatives in April of 1987. Once again it called for the National Trust to give up ownership of the historic area, including Kykuit, this time to Rockefeller University, which in turn would assume responsibility for both the Pocantico Institute and a public visitation program to begin at some unspecified time in the future. RBF's Pocantico Fund would also be turned over to the university, and David himself would provide any additional money needed.

The reasons given for removing Kykuit from the trust's hands varied depending on who was presenting them. Speaking to his fellow RBF trustees, David Rockefeller, who had played a major role in shaping the plan, stressed the inadequacy not only of the trust's financial resources but also its "human resources," particularly for managing the proposed Pocantico Institute. Shortly afterward, in a memorandum summarizing for Laurance and

David the state of the negotiations over Kykuit, Donal O'Brien cited a broader range of issues, including privacy and security, "public values," endowment, governance, operations, and "interaction between the National Trust and Rockefeller interests." Of these, he particularly stressed privacy and security. In agreeing with Nelson's executors to partition the Pocantico estate, David and Laurance had reserved the right, O'Brien claimed, "to live out the balance" of their lives in their homes and "to enjoy 'the Park' in a private and secure manner." The National Trust's plan would terminate that right. Because of this and the other concerns he mentioned, "the Rockefeller parties" had met and concluded that "both sides, acting in good faith and with great diligence, were struggling . . . to force a solution that was not the right one." What they needed to do instead was find "a different kind of stewardship" for Nelson's bequest.

Hence the plan to turn Kykuit over to Rockefeller University. A scientific research institution of great distinction, it had begun life as the Rockefeller Institute in 1901 and remained closely tied to the family, with David counting it as one of his two favorite philanthropies (the other being the Museum of Modern Art). Also, for administrative purposes the university had already taken under its wing the Rockefeller Archive Center, housed next to Kykuit, which held, among other things, the family papers. In short, it was a place the Rockefellers both admired and trusted. As O'Brien said, "It has a continuous history of Rockefeller family leadership, a distinguished board, administration and faculty, a strong endowment and demonstrated convening powers." By the end of 1987 both the university and RBF had tentatively approved the arrangement, and RBF was ready to pass its Pocantico Fund along to the university. Initial inquiries also suggested that the plan would be acceptable to the National Trust.

But then, just when everything seemed settled, the Rockefeller forces abruptly changed course, switching the proposed recipient of Kykuit from Rockefeller University to RBF itself, in a move so surprising that even some of the RBF's own trustees seemed puzzled by it. Steven Rockefeller wondered who had suggested it and was not at all sure the fund's board ought to approve the plan. Yet there was nothing capricious about the change. What had caused it was the sudden appearance in the deck of a wild card, in the person of Robert M. Bass, who in October 1987 became chair of the trust's board of trustees, and who from the beginning, unlike his fellow trustees, conducted himself as very much a player on the issue of Kykuit, and a determined, hard-driving one at that.

A member of an enormously rich Texas family that ironically, like the Rockefellers, owed its wealth to oil, Bass had earned a reputation in the business world as a skillful deal maker. For the most part he avoided the hostile takeovers typical of that time, and he did not always emerge victorious from the fray, but more often than not he got what he wanted. In 1987, for example, he bought the Plaza Hotel in New York City and sold it a year later to Donald Trump for a profit of more than $100 million—all without putting up any money of his own. Yet the year before that he had lost out to another buyer in attempting to acquire Outlet Communications, a major investor in radio and TV stations. The seller in that case had been Rockefeller Group, Inc., which was primarily engaged in managing the Rockefeller family's personal trusts.

As Bass's deals had grown in size and scope, so had his social profile. Reported the *New York Times* in the fall of 1988: "On September 28, Robert and Anne Bass will preside over a dinner-dance marking completion of the restoration of Union Station . . . The occasion will be a coming out of sorts for the 40-year-old billionaire, who has been quietly restoring a historic Georgetown house." Along with chairing the National Trust's board, Bass was a member of the Collectors' Committee of the National Gallery of Art and had contributed to both the restoration of Blair House, the presidential guesthouse, and the furnishing of the Diplomatic Reception Rooms at the Department of State. With so much of his attention focused on Washington, rumor had it that he hoped to become a major power broker there. But a close friend of Bass and his wife, who had a strong interest in urban planning, disagreed: "They both are extraordinarily earnest, serious people . . . They don't talk in terms of wielding power and influence. They talk about making a contribution."

All of which made them sound rather like the Rockefellers. Coincidentally, both families also summered at Seal Harbor in Maine, and Robert Bass served with David Rockefeller on Rockefeller University's board of trustees. Yet those ties had not stopped the Rockefeller Group from turning down Bass's bid for Outlet Communications. Nor would they stop Bass from doing everything he could to thwart the Rockefellers' plans for Kykuit. For as he saw it, letting the family walk off with Nelson's bequest without providing anything in return was a deal he wanted no part of. Either the National Trust would keep what had been given to it, or there would have to be some sort of compensation—a quid pro quo, and a large one—which the arrangement with Rockefeller University did not include. Also, whatever else happened, the public had to be admitted to Kykuit, and soon. That was Bass's position, which he appeared to have no intention at all of changing.

It was at this point that Colin Campbell entered the story, having left the presidency of Wesleyan University in Middletown, Connecticut, to become president of RBF in place of William Dietel. Shortly before that, in another important change at RBF, David Rockefeller Jr. had replaced his father as chair of the board of trustees.

On arriving at RBF in September 1988, Campbell focused at first on the fund's regular activities, waiting for a number of months before turning to Kykuit. When he did so, however, the full measure of the difficulties he faced became all too apparent. By then Bass had made his position abundantly clear, and what David Rockefeller told Campbell about the family's views seemed to leave little if any room in which to maneuver. Most of its members were steadfastly opposed to letting the National Trust keep Kykuit, did not like the idea of public visitation, and were not about to let RBF's Pocantico Fund pass into the trust's hands. A candid assessment of the situation would also have indicated that if the Rockefellers had failed thus far to win their points, they had at least managed, by insisting on them so relentlessly, to keep Kykuit as it was, a result with which they had every reason to be pleased.

Still, both David and Laurance did say they wanted the matter settled, and Campbell brought with him a large supply of natural optimism, plus an open mind and less anxiety about Kykuit than his predecessor. He would also have in the new head of RBF's board a useful ally. David Rockefeller Jr. had headed the search committee that brought Campbell to the fund, and he offered a fresh perspective on Kykuit. Operating outside the customary family orbit, he had developed a career of his own in the field of classical-music management in Boston, and though in recent years he had moved closer to family concerns in New York, he kept his principal residence in Massachusetts. By the same token he knew and understood his father's views about Kykuit but did not always agree with them. Thanks to his influence and that of the other cousins, by the end of 1987 the Institute of Science, Technology, and International Affairs, which the trust's proposal included and his father favored, was essentially a dead letter. And that in turn made the connection between Kykuit and Rockefeller University seem less logical, thus smoothing the way for the next alternative to the National Trust's plan: the proposal that saw RBF itself taking over Kykuit.

Even though skeptics like Steven Rockefeller continued to doubt the wisdom of such an arrangement, Campbell, whose idea it was, genuinely believed it offered RBF "an exciting challenge." "Let me make you a proposal," he had said to David Rockefeller when the idea first came up, and David had encouraged him to go ahead, with good reason. From the family's standpoint, RBF had even more to recommend it as the potential owner of Kykuit than Rockefeller University. Smaller and closer to the family, it offered a more private setting in which to hammer out Kykuit's future. (Robert Bass was not among RBF's trustees.) Indeed for the family's "dynasts," having Kykuit in RBF's hands promised to bring everything—the place, brothers and cousins, philanthropic mission, and public outreach— together in the closest imaginable way. It also amounted to an ideal circling of the wagons in the face of danger, namely Robert Bass and the topic he had turned into a red-hot issue: the question of compensation.

What, if anything, should the National Trust be paid for giving up Nelson's gift to it? Within the family there was a good deal of ill-tempered talk about "having to pay through the nose for your heritage," and Donal O'Brien argued that no payment was necessary since RBF, in assuming responsibility for maintaining the property and financing the programs there, would be relieving the trust of obligations it lacked the means to fulfill. In theory Colin Campbell agreed with O'Brien, but he was too astute to go empty-handed to Bass and the National Trust. There were issues on which he was prepared to make concessions, including compensation.

Technically the concessions were part of a formal offer, made by RBF, to "acquire" from the National Trust "those parts of the Pocantico Historic Area that were deeded to the Trust under Nelson A. Rockefeller's Will." Conveyed in a letter from Campbell to Bass dated December 15, 1989, the offer was accompanied by an account of how RBF planned to use the property, including a description of a public visitation program not unlike the one the trust had proposed. Tours would be limited in size, available by reservation only, and closely monitored. About the same number of visitors was projected, with operating costs covered by ticket sales. In RBF's version of the program, however, Historic Hudson Valley (HHV)—as Sleepy Hollow Restorations had been renamed—would be conducting the tours, not the National Trust. Also, there would be no regular tour of the Japanese garden, and instead of having visitors park and begin their tours at the coach barn, HHV planned to have them arrive at a visitors' center more than two miles away at Philipsburg Manor and bus them to Kykuit. All of which would help ensure that, as the proposal put it: "at no time will the visitors be allowed to roam around the grounds or through the house on their own," thereby protecting "the right to privacy of those individuals who continue to reside in the Park area."

In addition to the visitation program, RBF proposed to operate a conference center, located in the coach barn, that would bring together groups related to its continuing interest in improving the human condition on a large scale or small, here or abroad. With an agenda no more specific than that, the center sounded rather like "the Bedrock Institute" proposed by Laura Chasin and David Rockefeller Jr. The fund also committed itself to providing the National Trust with a series of preservation easements guaranteeing the maintenance of the historic area and its collections in their current state.

Though the Rockefeller forces considered the easements a concession of sorts, there were two other, far more important issues on which they were willing to give way. While the proposal itself was silent on the subject, correspondence between RBF and the National Trust made it clear that members of the family were prepared to provide the trust with a $5 million charitable donation. This was the compensation it was to receive for relinquishing Kykuit to RBF, but delicacy (and quite possibly a concern for tax issues) kept the offer out of the proposal as a simple quid pro quo. Campbell also feared the amount in question might fall short of "the level hoped for by the National Trust." Yet if that was so, the Rockefellers' next concession was all but guaranteed to please the trust. Provided everything went as planned, public tours of Kykuit could begin as early as "the spring of 1992," in other words in less than three years.

This was indeed a major concession, for which Colin Campbell had argued strongly. Not to have broken the logjam on the point would have left the Rockefellers in the untenable position of appearing to wage an all-out war to keep the public out of Kykuit, when Nelson's will clearly called for admitting them. Fully a decade had gone by since his death. The National Trust had come up with what was at least a respectable plan for public visitation and was now, under Robert Bass's leadership, digging in on this and other key issues. Plainly the string had run out. As disconcerting as it would be to find strangers inside the gates at Pocantico, at least they would be kept under strict control; a catastrophe it would not be.

RBF's proposal, in short, was a serious one, and no doubt in the past it would have been accepted. Twice before, the National Trust had been on the verge of agreeing to give up Nelson's bequest, first to Sleepy Hollow Restorations, and more recently to Rockefeller University. This time, too, the trust was being offered far more in return. But who could tell how Robert Bass would react?

Predicting Bass's reactions might have been easier if his motivation in the battle over Kykuit had been clearer, but to this day what led him to do what he did remains a puzzle. At least one member of the National Trust's board at the time believed that anger over the Outlet Communications sale was an important factor. David Rockefeller Jr.'s impression (which he feels his father shares) was that Bass thought he had found "a financing opportunity" for the National Trust, a way of "getting a chunk of money into the National Trust's coffers by having the Rockefeller family buy back Kykuit." Nor does David Jr. seem to harbor any rancor toward Bass on that score. "You can't blame him. He's a dealmaker [and] saw an opportunity to make a good deal." Yet other people tend to give less weight to Bass's "entrepreneurial posture," as David Jr. calls it. Certainly the National Trust needed money, but Colin Campbell believes Bass was at least as concerned with having the trust play the role Nelson had envisioned for it. "We have agreed that this property would be open to the public," says Campbell, paraphrasing Bass's position, "and that has to be a requirement of anything that's done with it."

But whatever Bass's motives were—and it was not his style to reveal them—he let the entire winter of 1990 go by without replying to RBF, which left Campbell frustrated and annoyed. Meanwhile, in yet another wrinkle in the situation, Campbell's wife, Nancy, had joined the National Trust's board, though as it turned out all he gained was a place to vent his anger. "This is unconscionable," he recalls blurting out to her at one point. "At least we should have an answer to the letter." Yet apparently Bass meant to take his time, nor was Nancy Campbell able to be much help, since due to her marital relationship she was excused from board meetings whenever Kykuit was discussed.

In effect what Campbell was waiting for was a response to the basic trade he had offered Bass: opening Kykuit to the public in return for the sale of the property to RBF. When Bass's reply finally came in May of 1990, it was graciously cordial, praising many aspects of RBF's proposal. On the essential point, however, his answer was an unequivocal no—the National Trust would not sell Kykuit. But seasoned dealmaker that he was, Bass was not about to let the negotiations end there. He had a proposal of his own to offer, one in which he too conceded several important points. As he outlined his plan, Kykuit would be operated under a "co-stewardship agreement," in which the National Trust would retain title to the property while RBF gained actual "possession" of it, and with possession would go control over any and all programs in the historic area, including public visitation. In specific terms, Bass accepted virtually all of the programmatic aspects of RBF's latest proposal: Historic Hudson Valley could manage the public tours using Philipsburg Manor as a starting point; the conference center was approved as described; Greenrock Corporation would continue caring for the property; the house would be opened to the public within three years.

With regard to funding, Bass also followed RBF's lead, with one major exception. As proposed, the Rockefellers and RBF would foot the bill for maintaining the historic area and making the various changes that were needed to it. Yet that was all they would be required to pay. Since there was to be no "transfer" or sale of the property, no compensation was necessary. Bass turned down what he called "the unrelated grant of $5 million to the National Trust"—the payment the Rockefellers had offered for Kykuit. He did suggest, however, that they contribute $600,000 as "an endowment payment for on-going National Trust supervision" of the property.

So much for Bass's "entrepreneurial posture." If the deal he offered was any indication, his chief priority truly seemed to be fulfilling the terms of Nelson's will, not pumping up the National Trust's endowment. Or was it simply that the price the Rockefellers had offered to pay for Kykuit was too low? Would he have let it go for $10 million? Or $15 million? The numbers David Rockefeller Jr. remembers being bandied about were $20 million, or even as much as $50 million, which was certainly more than the family would have paid. It was also more than they could afford to pay, given their other obligations.

So Bass's deal-making had compelled the Rockefellers to acknowledge the limits of their wealth. They did not hold all the cards, and getting them to concede that fact may even have struck him as something of a victory in the perennial American contest between new money and old. (He himself would contribute generously to the National Trust over the years.) Or perhaps it was enough that he had seen a means of cutting through the gnarled tangle of issues littering the ground the Rockefellers and the National Trust had been crossing and recrossing for the past decade. Yet before any real progress could be made on that front, legions of details had to be resolved, and there once again it fell to Colin Campbell to lead the way.

Bass's talk of "co-stewardship" had a fine ring to it, but what did it mean exactly, and how was it to be implemented? Those were the primary questions Campbell had to answer, both to the Rockefellers' satisfaction and to his own. He had no intention of letting RBF become mired in a fuzzy, ill-defined relationship with the National Trust. The "Kykuit problem" had already consumed an extraordinary amount of his time and energy as well as the staff's. That could not continue. But Bass's letter did seem to offer grounds for hoping the end might just be in sight.

Legally, co-stewardship would take the form of a lease in which RBF, for a stated period of time, acquired the use of Kykuit, its collections, and the other property held by the National Trust, with carefully spelled out conditions and responsibilities on both sides. In negotiating those conditions and responsibilities, Campbell repeatedly stressed three things: the National Trust must not become "an intrusive landlord," there had to be clear limits to RBF's financial exposure, and the Pocantico Fund would remain in its hands. RBF also had to be able to exit the arrangement (taking the Pocantico Fund with it) should it decide that it was necessary to do so. That was Campbell's view of what "co-stewardship" meant, and slowly, patiently, detail by detail, he managed to translate it into a series of legal agreements that all parties were willing to sign.

It took time, however—sixteen months from the date of Robert Bass's reply to Campbell; this, too, with no major stumbling blocks, just a collection of issues that continued to require very careful handling. By and large the notion of leasing Kykuit "back" seemed acceptable to the Rockefeller parties. Richard Parsons, a canny nonfamily member of RBF's board, said he found the National Trust's refusal to sell the property "not a terribly disappointing response," and Steven Rockefeller agreed, having never wanted RBF to own Kykuit. Still, there were those family members who remained anxious about letting go of what some continued to think of as the family seat. Yet gently, firmly Campbell kept the focus on reality, on the options that actually existed, not those that were gone, let alone those that had never had much substance. Insisting on family ownership of Kykuit was bound to be "a deal-breaker." There was simply no way to make it happen.

For Robert Bass, on the other hand, the central issue, as Campbell summed it up in a single word, was "trust." Just how hospitable to the public was RBF really prepared to be? Bass wanted the agreement to include an explicit commitment to have "more than 25,000 visitors a year," because, as he told Campbell, "he felt that if visitation was fully under the control of the family through the Rockefeller Brothers Fund, they would keep visitation down, and he wanted to see it up." Campbell did his best to persuade Bass that RBF would in fact fulfill its part of the bargain, that it "wanted to do it right . . . to get people there." Still, Bass's 25,000-visitor minimum became part of the final agreement, his assurance that the Rockefellers would indeed perform everything they promised to perform in the deal that would now make them *all*—the family, RBF, the trust, and Bass himself— partners in Kykuit's future.

The press release announcing the agreement between the National Trust and RBF included statements by Bass and both David Rockefellers, Senior and Junior, reflecting on what was about to happen at Kykuit. With Bass declaring he thought they had "found the ideal way to serve the best interests of the visiting public, carry out the spirit of the bequest and fulfill the mandate of the National Trust," and David Jr. stressing the dual nature of the programs planned for the historic area—public visitation plus "the enhancement of [RBF's] international and domestic grant making" through the use of the coach barn as a conference center—it fell to David Sr. to speak to the significance of the agreement to the family, and in particular to his generation: "Laurance and I share Nelson's enthusiasm for the preservation and commitment to public uses of this historic landmark that has meant so much to our family during the past century." If little in this pronouncement could be described as true, at least it put a pleasant face on the occasion, which did, after all, mark a new beginning for Kykuit. And unlike the painful moment when the quarrel between John 3rd and Nelson over RBF found its way into the *New York Times,* none of the awkward struggle over Kykuit's future that filled the past twelve years ever became public knowledge. This time there were no leaks to the press, and in his *Memoirs* David Rockefeller would say nothing at all about the subject.

Perhaps he felt it reflected unfavorably on the family or on him. Or possibly he found it too upsetting to deal with in his usual, magisterially confident manner. In the battle between John 3rd and Nelson, he had remained largely neutral, a crafter of compromises, which, as he remembered it later, drew the cousins closer to their elders. But the denouement as it took shape in Nelson's will had truly infuriated him. Twenty years later his eyes still flashed with anger when he spoke of it and, as he said in his *Memoirs,* the "many millions of dollars" that the will had cost him, chiefly in payments for Kykuit's upkeep through all those years—payments that were not even tax deductible.

He also genuinely disliked the idea of having Kykuit in the hands of the National Trust, given the sundry weaknesses of the organization, and did not want the house opened to the public during his lifetime. Nor had his plan to have Rockefeller University take over Nelson's bequest been simply a way of preventing those things from happening, at least according to Colin Campbell: "He saw this as a place for some very high level science." But the costs had turned out to be, as Campbell said, "beyond the pale," and the idea had little appeal to the rest of the family. Then Robert Bass became chair of the National Trust's board, and everything changed. All of which left David with no plan for Kykuit's future. Still, among "the interested Rockefeller parties" he was sure to carry the greatest weight in determining what happened to the place, as both his son and Colin Campbell recognized. They could suggest, present options, negotiate; in the end it was David Sr. who would decide—who did decide. What finally tipped the balance? Campbell thought money was the crucial factor, the huge sums David and Laurance laid out each year to maintain the historic area "right down to every rose," though he also saw David as deeply sentimental about Kykuit and everything associated with it: "He was the one who truly loved the house and the setting and all that."

David's sentimentality about the family's houses had already manifested itself dramatically at least once before. Shortly after Junior's death, he and Nelson, who by then had become joint owners of the property, decided to have the Eyrie, in Seal Harbor, torn down. It was simply too large to use any longer. But it had been a special favorite of Abby's, so as a kind of memorial to his mother, David decided to have it all photographed while it was still standing. The difficulty was that Martha, Junior's second wife, had extensively redecorated the house. So on David's orders, the entire place was redecorated yet again, this time to put it back to the way it had been in Abby's day. When the work was finished, the house was filled with flowers and fires were lit in the living room and dining room, "just as my parents had done on foggy days when we were children," wrote David in his *Memoirs*. Only then, "when everything was ready," did Ezra Stoller, "the great architectural photographer," carry out the mission that had been given him. Later at Kykuit, too, David would have the second-floor rooms that had been his parents' quarters returned to the way they were in Junior and Abby's time. And he was proud that during the years when the house's future remained unsettled, he had entertained President and Mrs. Ronald Reagan there, as Nelson had the Nixons and the Fords.

But as sentimental as David could be about some things, like all the men of the first three generations of the Rockefeller family he was driven by an irresistible need to control whatever touched his interests. Senior, Junior, the brothers; they all marched to the same drumbeat in that regard, and David's years at the helm of Chase Manhattan Bank, one of the nation's leading financial institutions, had only strengthened his will to command. But they had also taught him the uses of charm, and increasingly in the years to come his charm would be what people noticed most. He lived on to become a regular at New York charity balls. He even initiated an ambitious preservation scheme on his own estate in Pocantico, refurbishing, for public tours, its stone barns, complete with an expensive restaurant, to which there was also talk of adding a high-end housing development, a spa, and a luxury hotel—ideas that provoked considerable controversy both within the family and among the residents of Pocantico Hills. His favorite project, however, remained the restaurant. If it turned out to be as good as he imagined, he commented, "it would be quite a temptation to go there often—even though we have quite a good cook at home."

David (whose personal fortune at that point was estimated at $2.5 billion) continued to be generous in other ways as well, in 2005 setting aside $100 million for Rockefeller University and an equal amount for MoMA to mark his ninetieth birthday. Celebrated at multiple galas, the event itself was hailed in highly flattering terms by both the *New York Times* and the *New Yorker,* which lauded him as "Modern at Ninety" in sharp contrast to the decidedly cool profile of him the magazine had run forty years earlier. And with Laurance's death the year before, he had acquired the added distinction of being the last surviving member of his generation of the Rockefeller family.

If willing it alone—or charm or generosity—could have settled the issue, David would surely have kept Kykuit under the sole control of the Rockefellers. But he was also a realist and knew, as Senior would have been the first to point out, that you only own what you own, and the National

Trust held the title to Kykuit; the Rockefellers no longer owned it. At least the house would be preserved and not torn down as Laurance wished, but somehow between Nelson's will, Bass's deal-making, and Colin Campbell's deftly sensitive mediation it had slipped through the family's fingers, and there was nothing anyone could do about that. Already, by November of 1993, the *Times* was describing the changes being made throughout the historic area in anticipation of the house's opening to the public. Architects, contractors, and curators had been hired, and Charles Granquist, a former assistant director at Thomas Jefferson's Monticello, had been engaged to supervise it all: the conversion of the carriage barn into a conference center and the top-floor rooms in the main house into bedrooms for conference attendees, and the construction needed to accommodate tours, along with the special features required for the handicapped, plus the cataloging of all the thousands of objects that made up Kykuit's "collections"—everything from Junior's K'ang Hsi porcelains to the old bottles Nelson's sons had dug up on the estate—each item numbered, recorded, and put in its assigned place.

Then there was the house itself, every part of which had to be cleaned, repaired, and polished. Yet as a whole it would remain what it had always been: a place, as the architectural critic Paul Goldberger would so aptly put it, "slightly at odds with itself," one that seemed "to want to be grand and to disappear at the same time . . . a country house in a corset." That, too, along with all the oddly assorted notes struck by the objects in and around the house—the cacophony of Rockefeller family tastes—would be there for the public to experience and learn what they could from it.

But there were some things people coming in the vans from the visitor's center at Philipsburg Manor would not find. Inside the house the tours would go only to the first floor and the basement galleries. Its upper stories and the service areas in the basement and subbasement would remain off-limits to visitors. Presumably the occupants of the house had slept somewhere. Surely, too, life in so large a place required servants as well as spaces where they lived and worked. But none of this would the public see, leaving people to think what? That the Rockefellers had been fed and their rooms cleaned by troops of invisible elves and fairies—or almost as unlikely, that they did the work themselves? At other great houses open to the public, Biltmore, for example, much had always been made of the whole, intricately choreographed, "upstairs/downstairs" routine of service and servants without which life in such places would have been unimaginable. Even at Mount

Vernon, by this date, the guides were discussing George Washington's slaves. But at Kykuit there were to be no such concessions, despite the fact that at least one director of a major American outdoor museum strongly advised including the kitchen, pantries, and servants' quarters on the tours.

Why leave the servants out of the story? No explanation was offered, but surely they posed the single greatest challenge at Kykuit to any easy assumption about the compatibility of wealth and democracy. As restrained and tasteful as the place was, the fact that more than two hundred people had been employed there year in and year out to serve the Rockefellers set the place light-years apart from the experience of ordinary Americans. Junior had hoped it would justify itself by offering the public useful lessons in the art and culture of the past. Nelson too embraced that hope, though unlike his father he felt the only way to teach those lessons was to let people actually see the house and gardens, not just pictures of them in magazines. Yet John 3rd and Laurance seemed to think that the risk was too great; that all of it, including the servants, would be misunderstood.

David, on the other hand, appeared surprisingly relaxed on the servant issue. Or at any rate in his *Memoirs* he described with something approaching glee the Rockefellers' annual progress to Seal Harbor when he was a boy: "The family and household staff filled an entire Pullman sleeping car. In addition to Mother, Father, and the six children, there were nurses, personal secretaries, Father's valet, waitresses, kitchen maids, parlor maids, and chamber maids—each a distinct vocation—to take care of some one hundred rooms in the Eyrie." Yet David was also careful to explain, only a page later, that his parents considered life in nearby Bar Harbor "too flashy and ostentatious."

It was, after all, precisely such finely drawn distinctions that had always hedged 'round the Rockefellers' world. Great wealth might be a problem in a democracy, but their wealth was good wealth, just as their taste was good taste, and they were good people—which Junior had believed Kykuit would make clear. But then, transfixed by the beauty and the magic of it all, plus the caution he could never quite banish from his mind, he had drawn the cordon of security ever more tightly around the place, cutting it off from the rest of humanity. And when Nelson set about trying to break through the charmed circle, it had very nearly shattered the family. At least it had until Robert Bass and Colin Campbell appeared on the scene: Bass to confront them all with a measure of reality, and Campbell to show them how to deal with it. For both men knew, even if the Rockefellers did not, that by the end of 1991 the string had indeed run out. The family had delayed as long as it decently could honoring Nelson's wishes. The time had come to let the people in.

In making that point, Bass and Campbell had also been able to count on a singularly powerful ally: the great bull market of the end of the twentieth century. With stock prices depressed through the 1970s and early 1980s, funds were too tight everywhere to do much about Kykuit. But then slowly, surely, the market began to rise, lifting the Rockefellers' own fortunes and even more dramatically the value of RBF's Pocantico Fund with it. Moreover those increases would continue, making Kykuit what it remains to this day: the best-endowed historical property in the United States. And though by the 1990s the bill for the changes needed to open the house and grounds had also grown (to more than $8 million), the senior Rockefellers— primarily David—paid it readily enough, something made more palatable, no doubt, by the fact that the money could be cycled through RBF as a charitable donation, thereby earning a tidy tax deduction.

All of which seemed to prove yet again what had so often seemed true in the Rockefellers' case, though few of them cared to admit it: that to be rich in America offers its own salvation. Perhaps, too, as Nelson had believed, the loss of Kykuit would be repaid by the goodwill that opening the house would earn the family. Yet obviously during all those years David Rockefeller worked to hold on to it, he had seen the matter in a different light, and possibly some of what was on his mind may have occurred to the *New York Times* reporter who compared the opening of the house, when it finally occurred, to the opening of Buckingham Palace. Long a potent symbol of royalty, the palace had always been a closely guarded, private preserve entered by few people, and then only by invitation. As such it had excited enormous public curiosity, and in turn, as a place full of mystery, it served as an invaluable prop to the majesty and power of the monarchy. What the *Times* reporter did not consider—either in the case of Kykuit or Buckingham Palace—was what would happen when the mystery was swept away.

The Rockefellers were scarcely royalty. Their power depended on their bank accounts and trust funds, not their bloodlines. Still, through much of the twentieth century they had been widely assumed to be America's richest family, and as was true of Britain's royals, their private lives were elaborately shielded from public view. Inevitably the effect was to create around them an aura of mystery, which the passage of time only seemed to augment. Part of the reason may have been that where once the Rockefellers, like the royals, lived not so differently from other very wealthy people, less and less was that true, until at the end they stood virtually alone in choosing to maintain the lifestyle they did. In any case, the net effect was to increase, sometimes mightily, the perception of their power by others. So what was the family now to become in the eyes of the world if anyone with price of admission could tour "the Rockefeller Family Home"?

Kykuit the grand and mysterious versus Kykuit the redeemingly restrained and accessible (and servantless); what should people be allowed to see—and not see? Nelson had wanted them to see it all; John 3rd and Laurance wanted the house wiped from the landscape. David wanted it preserved but closed to the public, at least until after his death. There was no consensus among them. Yet their failure to agree went to the very heart of the sharply contradictory impulses that, as a family, the Rockefellers had followed for more than a century. Were they the open, humane, democratic benefactors of mankind they often seemed to want to be, or were they as aloof, distant, and heavily defended as their manner of living suggested?

Kykuit offered no clear-cut answer. Itself a great puzzle, densely layered, full of contradictions, it mirrored all too precisely the minds of the individuals who had built it and lived there. But for that very reason, perhaps there never had been, or ever would be, a better picture of the Rockefellers and their protean ambitions for the enormous fortune Senior had settled upon them. Junior had hoped that building the right kind of house would address what many people at the time saw as the fundamental incompatibility between wealth and democracy; in the next generation it often seemed Kykuit did more to amplify that problem than solve it. Yet outside its gates the larger world continued to change, and ironically by the end of the twentieth century Americans in general appeared to be far less troubled than they once had been by economic inequality. With a rapidly rising share of the nation's wealth in the hands of a steadily shrinking segment of its population, serious protest was nowhere to be found. Senior should have been so lucky!

Where, then, did that leave Kykuit? Whatever else was true, the opening of the house marked a beginning as well as an end. Only time would tell what its ultimate meaning might be—time and all those people about to start winding up the long drive to the top of the hill to hear about Sunday dinners with the grandchildren and games of numerica; to see Senior's golf room and Junior and Bosworth's Aphrodite, Codman's coolly correct Georgian interiors and Nelson's paintings and tapestries in the basement galleries; to stand before Sargent's portrait of Senior and Abby's bodhisattva, the towering Oceanus fountain and Lachaise's *Dans La Nuit*; to smile in surprise at the soda fountain in the stone teahouse and stare in wonder at the breathtaking sight of the Hudson, rounding the hills to the north and west for its last, long run to the south and the sea beyond—to discover, in short, what it had once really been like to be "rich as Rockefeller."

Numbers

During the twelve years between 1994 and 2005 more than half a million people—542,560 to be precise—visited Kykuit, which puts the average annual visitation at just over 45,213. By comparison, roughly a million people a year visit George Washington's Mount Vernon, and about half that number see Thomas Jefferson's Monticello. In recent years Kykuit's numbers have been falling. The high was reached in 1996, with 57,073 visitors; by 2005 the figure stood at 33,367. Many other historic houses have experienced similar declines in visitation.

A three-season visitor survey, done in 2001 for all of the properties managed by Historic Hudson Valley, revealed that 95 percent of the visitors to Kykuit were adults unaccompanied by children; that close to 70 percent of them came from either Westchester County or the metropolitan New York–New Jersey area; that 60 percent of them earned at least $75,000 a year; that 66 percent of them were over fifty years old; that 65 percent of them were women; that 43 percent had gone beyond college to graduate school; that 87 percent described themselves as white/Caucasian; and that over 50 percent of them had visited at least three other historic sites. As for the experience they had at Kykuit, 75 percent gave it a 9 or 10 rating on a scale of 10. An even larger number (82 percent) said they found the tour "interesting," and 34 percent claimed they might come back again. The best-liked part of the tour was the gardens, to which 75 percent gave a rating of "very high" (as opposed to 44 percent for the house). Of the things they found disappointing, 22 percent said they would have liked to see more of the house; 33 percent said (not necessarily as a criticism of the tour) that they wanted to learn more about the Rockefellers.

In addition to tours of the house and gardens, the larger plan that saw Kykuit opened to the public called for the creation of what came to be called the Pocantico Conference Center of the Rockefeller Brothers Fund. Broadly speaking, its mission is to provide accommodations and support facilities for conferences on topics related to RBF's interests and activities. Located in the lower portion of the coach barn, it also, when necessary, houses attendees in rooms on the upper two floors of Kykuit itself. Between 1995 and 2005 the center hosted 579 conferences, an average of slightly more than 51 a year. To look more closely at a single year, in 2005 a total of 56 conferences brought 1,479 people to Pocantico. Nineteen of those conferences were sponsored by the Rockefeller Brothers Fund, thirty-seven by other nonprofit organizations; twenty-nine were wholly funded by RBF, two were co-funded by RBF, and twenty-five were funded by outside sources. The total amount of funding provided for the fifty-six conferences was $418,000. A majority of the programs lasted for three days (with two overnights), while four lasted for more than three days. The topics covered (as designated by RBF's general program themes) included "democratic practice," "sustainable development," "peace and security," and New York City, with, as well, one conference apiece on South Africa and China as other "pivotal places." Fourteen programs fell in the "miscellaneous" category.

For 2005, the amount budgeted for "Pocantico Operations"—including maintenance of the property (the largest single item) and administrative and capital costs—was $3,398,000. Actual expenses represented a 5.24 percent rate of spending relative to the $64,582,000 average market value of RBF's Pocantico Fund.

On November 21, 2006, the *New York Times* informed its readers that David Rockerfeller was planning to make a $225 million bequest to RBF. The gift—to support programs in sustainable development, poverty eradication, and international trade and finance—would raise to $900 million his charitable donations and bring to over a billion dollars RBF's total assets.

ACKNOWLEDGMENTS

Having grown up in Cleveland, Ohio, we owe our first encounters with the Rockefellers to our families' memories of them. One of our grandfathers played golf with Senior and later negotiated, on behalf of the City of Cleveland Heights, of which he was mayor at the time, the transfer of part of the Forest Hill estate to the city as a public park. An uncle, his son, received several of the famous Rockefeller dimes. On the other side of the family a grandmother spoke bitterly of Senior's having said at one point that someone ought to find her husband a job—true enough, as it turned out. (She also claimed that Senior was a notorious "fanny patter.")

Like all the myths and legends of the Rockefellers that lingered in Cleveland, these bits of information did not tell us much, but they do suggest how powerful an aura the family left in its wake. Later, when we came to know several family members ourselves—a colleague and his wife at Yale and a student at Williams—and twice attended functions at the Pocantico estate, we found that aura continued to eddy through such experiences. But nothing about them suggested we might one day want to write about the Rockefellers. That came much later, as we were finishing our book on Mount Vernon and thinking about what our next project might be.

At the outset one of us was more intrigued with the idea of "doing" Kykuit and the Rockefellers than the other. What clinched the case was actually seeing the house on an individual tour that McKelvin Smith, Marketing Director of Historic Hudson Valley, was kind enough to arrange for us. At the same time we met and talked with Harold Oakhill, who was closely connected with both Kykuit and the Rockefeller Archive Center, and soon afterward, Peter J. Johnson, who was engaged in various projects at the Rockefeller family office. Each of them has continued to help us in a variety of ways, including arranging interviews for us with members of the Rockefeller family.

For generously sharing their time and memories, we owe all the people we interviewed a great deal. Often the information they gave us we could have found in no other way. Among them were David A. Doheny, former council for the National Trust for Historic Preservation; Charles Longsworth, former board member of the National Trust and president of Colonial Williamsburg; Richard Moe, president of the National Trust; Robert Snyder, the former president of Greenrock Corporation; Ted Taylor, also a former National Trust board member and president of the Kresge Foundation; and David Rockefeller.

Four other interviews that proved absolutely crucial to our thinking were those we had with Happy Fitler Murphy Rockefeller, who talked with us for a period of several hours, while she took us through Kykuit from top to bottom; Colin Campbell and William Dietel, both past presidents of the Rockefeller Brothers Fund, who explained the complex role they and the fund played during the decade and a half between Nelson's death and the opening of the house to the public, a period about which there is as yet little information available in the family papers; and David Rockefeller Jr., who covered the same ground with admirable candor and insight.

With the exception of those last few years, our chief source of information about Kykuit and the Rockefellers has been the collection of materials that constitute the Rockefeller Family Archives at the Rockefeller Archive Center in Sleepy Hollow, New York. Full of interest, it is an extraordinary resource—as is the center's staff. Because the materials arrived at different times and from multiple sources, there is no overall catalog or finding system. With the excellent guidance we received from the staff, however, we were able to move from topic to topic with reasonable efficiency. Two individuals in particular who went out of their way from the beginning to help us were Darwin H. Stapleton, executive director of the center, and Thomas Rosenbaum, a longtime member of the staff, now retired. More than just a guide, Tom also became a mentor and friend, gently nudging us onward, sometimes in surprising new directions.

Others who assisted with the research in important ways are Cynthia Altman, Kykuit's able and dedicated curator; Charley Bradley, active both at the Archive Center and as a guide at Kykuit; Robert Snyder, who opened Greenrock Corporation's archives to us with a minimum of fuss; Charles

Grandquist and Judy A. Clark, Director and Associate Director, respectively, of Pocantico Programs at RBF, who made available information about the operations of the Pocantico Conference Center between 1995 and 2005; and Susan Tischler Greenstein, Director of the Kykuit Program at Historic Hudson Valley, who provided us with visitation figures for Kykuit between 1995 and 2005 as well as the results of the 2001 visitor survey.

While most of our research was done at or near the Rockefeller Archives Center, at Columbia University's Avery Architectural & Fine Arts Library—thanks to Janet Parks, Curator of Drawings and Archives—we saw a number of interesting items relating to Kykuit, including a complete set of Ogden Codman's designs for the interiors of the house. Additional information regarding Codman's role came from Pauline Metcalf's research files on him, to which she graciously gave us access. And Michael Rockefeller kindly shared with us his large collection of Rockefeller family memorabilia, photographs and postcards, which contains many images not available at the Archive Center.

We are also grateful to Christine Ménard, Rebecca Ohm, Walter Komorowski, and Lori DuBois, members of the Research and Reference Services staff of the Williams College Sawyer Library for providing innumerable pieces of information over the years. Our calls on their skills were frequent, yet unfailingly met with care and patience. Alison O'Grady often came to our rescue, as well, by obtaining materials from other libraries so expeditiously.

Many people have read all or part of what we have written, offering comments and suggestions that challenged us to do more, work harder, and saved us from innumerable blunders. Any errors that remain are wholly our responsibility. The list of readers includes Professor James Wood, of the Williams College History Department, Pauline Metcalf, Larry Pearson, William Lilley III, Robert H. Rodgers, two of our sons, Fred and Jeffery Dalzell, one a professional historian and the other an architect, and Dorothy Rudolph. Joseph Ellis, professor of history at Mount Holyoke College, has been good enough to read both early versions of several chapters and later, the manuscript in its entirety. Free with sage advice as we knew he would be, he has helped make this a notably better book than it would have been otherwise. Equally important in that regard has been the remarkable generosity of Fred Rudolph, Professor Emeritus of History at

Williams College, who read, reread, and reread yet again everything between these covers. His insight, wisdom, and enthusiasm for the project have been of inestimable value to us both.

In Geri Thoma of the Elaine Markson Agency, our agent, and Jack Macrae of Henry Holt and Company, our editor, we were lucky enough to find two other people who shared that enthusiasm. At every stage of the project they were ready with useful suggestions and hearty encouragement. We are also indebted to the rest of the efficient staff at Holt who worked on the book, and to Linda Saharczewski of the Williams College Faculty Secretarial Office, who transformed the material we gave her into a remarkably error-free set of computer files.

The expenses involved in doing the research and writing were paid for through the generosity of Peter Willmott and the Willmott Family Third Century Professorship, which carries with it a substantial fund for such purposes. Also, the trustees of Williams College approved two sabbatical leaves at various points that speeded the pace of the work.

Finally, the debt we owe each other as collaborators is immense. While it may not always be true that the family that writes together stays together, we thoroughly enjoy working as partners and like to think it produces better books, even if it isn't necessarily the most efficient way of getting them done.

NOTES

Abbreviations used in the notes

AAR	Abby Aldrich Rockefeller	LCSR	Laura Celestia Spelman Rockefeller
CC	Colin Campbell	LSR	Laurance Spelman Rockefeller
D & A	Delano & Aldrich	NAR	Nelson Aldrich Rockefeller
DR	David Rockefeller	OC	Ogden Codman
DR Jr.	David Rockefeller Jr.	RAC	Rockefeller Archive Center
JDR	John D. Rockefeller	RBF	Rockefeller Brothers Fund
JDR Jr.	John D. Rockefeller Jr.	RBFA	Rockefeller Brothers Fund Archives
JDR 3rd	John D. Rockefeller 3rd	RFA	Rockefeller Family Archives
HFMR	Happy Fitler Murphy Rockefeller	SHR	Sleepy Hollow Restorations
HHV	Historic Hudson Valley	WWB	William Welles Bosworth

All interviews, unless otherwise noted, were conducted by the authors.

INTRODUCTION: *SIC TRANSIT . . .* DECEMBER 1991

1 "It was an extraordinary evening": Rockefeller family member, unnamed, quoted in Mary Louise Pierson and Ann Rockefeller Roberts, *The Rockefeller Family Home, Kykuit* (New York, 1998), 50. This book, along with its thoughtful text, contains dozens of remarkable color photographs taken by Mary Louise Pierson of Kykuit and its gardens.

1 "just thinking how sad": Rockefeller family member, unnamed, quoted in ibid.

1 The three *New York Times* articles: May 1, 5, and 6, 1994.

1 "more or less akin": Ibid., May 6, 1994.

2 "Oddly restrained": Ibid.

2 "You know it really was": Ibid., May 4, 1994.

2 "a simple ceremony": Pierson and Roberts, *Rockefeller Family Home,* 50.

2 "until there was a ring": Ibid.

3 "a hermitage": Dell Upton, *Architecture in the United States* (New York, 1998), 30–38.

4 "incredible shower": Rockefeller family member, unnamed, quoted in Pierson and Roberts, *Rockefeller Family Home,* 50.

1: HEIR APPARENT, 1902

10 The most complete account of the fire, based on a letter from JDR Jr. to LCSR written September 23, 1902: Albert I. Berger, "My Father's House at Pocantico:

Kykuit and the Business Education of John D. Rockefeller, Jr.," 1985, unpublished manuscript, RAC.

10 Tarbell's articles in *McClure's Magazine* were subsequently republished as *The History of Standard Oil* (New York, 1904).

10 Tarbell's early career and the series on Standard Oil: Ron Chernow, *Titan: The Life of John D. Rockefeller, Sr.* (New York, 1998), 435–61.

10 Rockefeller's income in 1902: Ibid., 504.

10 The building of Forest Hill and the Rockefeller family's life there: Raymond S. Fosdick, *John D. Rockefeller, Jr.: A Portrait* (New York, 1956), 5ff.

11 Tarbell's criticism of JDR's "cult of the unpretentious" extensively quoted and discussed: Clive Aslet, *The American Country House* (New Haven, Conn., 1990), 52–54.

11 JDR's reaction to Tarbell's indictment of him: Chernow, *Titan*, xxi–xxii.

11 "a monument of cheap ugliness": Tarbell, quoted in ibid., 54.

11 JDR Jr.'s early years in the family office: Fosdick, *John D. Rockefeller, Jr.*, 83–103.

12 The fullest account of Gates's life and his role in the Rockefellers' affairs: Frederick Taylor Gates, *Chapters in My Life* (New York, 1977).

12 JDR Jr.'s stock market losses: Fosdick, *John D. Rockefeller, Jr.*, 89–92.

12 JDR Jr.'s dealings with Morgan and his parents' reaction to them: Ibid., 105.

12 The profit from the sale of the mining properties to Morgan: Chernow, *Titan*, 192–93.

12 "American Beauty Rose Speech" and the storm of protest it produced: Fosdick, *John D. Rockefeller, Jr.*, 130–31.

12 "A rose by any other name": Reverend Charles D. Williams, sermon at St. Bartholomew's Church in New York, quoted in ibid., 131.

12 JDR Jr.'s Bible study class: Ibid., 125–33.

13 "With his hereditary grip": *Pittsburgh Press*, November 15, 1904, quoted in ibid., 126.

13 "This work has meant": JDR Jr. to "a few members of the class," July 11, 1905, quoted in ibid., 128.

13 JDR Jr.'s role is establishing the General Education Board: Ibid., 116.

13 JDR's early charitable giving: Chernow, *Titan*, 50–51, 237–42, and 298–329.

14 JDR's wealth at the turn of the century: Ibid., 343–44.

14 JDR's views on philanthropy spelled out at length: John D. Rockefeller, *Random Reminiscences of Men and Events* (Garden City, N.Y., 1916), 137–88.

14 "Two courses are open": Frederick T. Gates, to JDR, June 5, 1905, quoted in Fosdick, *John D. Rockefeller, Jr.*, 119.

14 "Mr. Gates's letter to you": JDR Jr. to JDR, June 21, 1905, quoted in ibid., 119–20.

14 JDR's gifts made during this period to the General Education Board and other family trusts, as well the total amount contributed over his lifetime: Ibid., 120–22.

15 "I believe this is a great thing": JDR Jr. to JDR, June 29, 1905, quoted in ibid., 120.

15 "My breath was completely taken away": JDR Jr. to JDR, January 13, 1902, RFA2.Z.II, B6 F69.

15 The moral atmosphere of the Rockefeller home while JDR Jr. was growing up: Chernow, *Titan*, 119–28 and 181–96.

15 "Is it right": JDR Jr., address, Dutch Treat Club, New York, March 11, 1924, quoted in Fosdick, *John D. Rockefeller, Jr.*, 43.

16 "the trouble and expense": JDR Jr. to JDR, February 14, 1992, in Joseph W. Ernst, ed., *"Dear Father"/"Dear Son": Correspondence of John D. Rockefeller and John D. Rockefeller, Jr.* (New York, 1994), 8.

16 "Be assured": JDR to JDR Jr., February 17, 1992, in ibid., 9.

16 JDR Jr.'s years at Brown: Fosdick, *John D. Rockefeller, Jr.*, 45–82.

16 "How very thankful we are": LCSR to JDR Jr., June 28, 1897, quoted in ibid., 81.

16 "I have been in many homes": JDR Jr. to LCSR, July 4, 1897, quoted in ibid., 81.

16 "all the *savoir-faire*": JDR Jr., interview by Fosdick, September 23, 1952, RFA.2.Z.V, B57 F503.

16 "began thoroughly to enjoy": Ibid.

17 The most complete treatment of AAR's life: Bernice Kert's admirable *Abby Aldrich Rockefeller: The Woman in the Family* (New York, 1993). See also Mary Ellen Chase, *Abby Aldrich Rockefeller* (New York, 1950).

17 JDR Jr.'s protracted courtship of AAR: Kert, *Abby Aldrich Rockefeller*, 63–80; see also Fosdick, *John D. Rockefeller, Jr.*, 97–101.

17 "Marriage either makes or breaks": JDR Jr. "to the author," quoted in ibid., 99.

17 "Never shall I forget": JDR Jr., "Recollections of My Father," quoted in ibid., 91.

17 "All right, John, don't worry": JDR, quoted in ibid.

17 "Because of your forbearance": JDR Jr. to JDR, November 11, 1919, in Ernst, *"Dear Father"/"Dear Son,"* 19.

18 "Why, the girls in the office": JDR, interview by Fosdick, April 2, 1953, RFA2.Z.V, supplement A, B57 F503.

18 "I lived in a sort of vacuum": JDR Jr., interview by Fosdick, September 23, 1952, ibid.

18 "a fairly nice time": Ibid.

18 "Of course you love Miss Aldrich": LCSR, quoted by JDR Sr. in an interview by Fosdick, April 2, 1953, ibid.

18 The wedding of JDR Jr. and AAR: Kert, *Abby Aldrich Rockefeller*, 80–87.

18 "each day is happier than the last": JDR Jr. to LCSR, June 15, 1902, RFA2.Z.II, B4 F38.

18 "She seems a wife made to order": LCSR to JDR Jr., June 22, 1902, ibid.

19 "I won't": AAR, quoted in Chase, *Abby Aldrich Rockefeller*, 28.

19 "instead of speaking of it": AAR to JDR Jr., August 14, 1907, quoted in Kert, *Abby Aldrich Rockefeller*, 114–15.

19 "the only woman present": JDR Jr. to JDR, no date, quoted in Fosdick, *John D. Rockefeller, Jr.*, 118.

19 The West Fifty-fourth Street house and its history and decoration: Chernow, *Titan*, 219–20.

20 The taste AAR would have favored at the time, presented in detail, along with a scathing indictment of the "eclecticism" that preceded it: Edith Wharton and Ogden Codman's pathbreaking *The Decoration of Houses* (New York, 1897). See especially 1–30.

20 AAR and JDR Jr.'s losses in the fire: Kert, *Abby Aldrich Rockefeller*, 103.

21 The refitting of the Kent House for the senior Rockefellers: Ibid., 103–4.

21 "on a little business matter": JDR Jr. to Chester Aldrich, RFA1.L, letterbook 74, 59.

21 Chester Aldrich's background and training: Peter Pennoyer and Anne Walker, *The Architecture of Delano & Aldrich* (New York, 2003), 13–18.

21 Further details about Rockwood Hall: Harold G. Gulliver, "Rockwood Hall on the Hudson," *Country Life,* March 1923, 7–10, and April 1923, 8–11, sales advertisements sponsored by the heirs of William Rockefeller, who had died in 1922, RFA2.I, B50 F505.

22 "his ideal for a summer house": JDR Jr. to LCSR, October 6, 1902, RFA1.L, letterbook 253, 141.

22 "so indefinite": JDR Jr. to Chester Aldrich, November 7, 1902, RFA1.L, letterbook 74, 113.

23 "a residence so outwardly simple": JDR Jr., quoted in Fosdick, *John D. Rockefeller, Jr.*, 196.

2: TITAN, HUSBAND, FATHER

24 JDR's description of the removal of the tree: Rockefeller, *Random Reminiscences*, 28–29.

26 The fullest description of JDR's early years in the oil industry: Chernow, *Titan*, 73–117 and 129–82. For another, spirited, if highly selective account, see Rockefeller, *Random Reminiscences*, 55–112.

27 "None of us ever dreamed": Ibid., 60.

27 JDR's explanation of the Mesabi iron ore development: Ibid., 115–32. See also Chernow, *Titan*, 382–93.

27 "for receiverships are very costly": Rockefeller, *Random Reminiscences*, 119.

28 The "Cleveland Massacre" and its aftermath: Chernow, *Titan*, 133–48.

29 JDR on the benefits of industrial combination as opposed to competition: Rockefeller, *Random Reminiscences*, 55–71 and 144–45. And for a thoughtful reflection on those views, see Chernow, *Titan*, 148–55.

29 "The greatest, wisest, and meanest monopoly": Henry Demarest Lloyd, "Story of a Great Monopoly," *Atlantic Monthly*, March 1881, 329.

29 "The Standard has done everything": Ibid., 322.

30 The mounting political problems facing JDR and Standard at the time: Chernow, *Titan*, 208–15, 288–98, and 331–34.

30 The growing pressures on JDR to give more money for humanitarian purposes and how he felt about the issue: Ibid., 299–301, and Rockefeller, *Random Reminiscences*, 137–62.

30 The Rockefeller family's travels during the 1880s: Fosdick, *John D. Rockefeller, Jr.*, 36–37, and Chernow, *Titan*, 234–37.

31 "Such care in small things": JDR Jr., "Recollections of My Father," quoted in Fosdick, *John D. Rockefeller, Jr.*, 109.

31 JDR's discovery of golf and his love of the game: Chernow, *Titan*, 398–401.

32 JDR's retirement: Ibid., 342–44.

32 JDR's hair loss: Ibid., 407–9.

33 JDR's original land purchases at Pocantico: Berger, "My Father's House," 50–74.

33 Early landscaping work at Pocantico: Ibid., 75–96.

33 JDR's gift to JDR Jr. and AAR of the house eventually known as Abeyton Lodge: Kert, *Abby Aldrich Rockefeller*, 103.

34 JDR Jr.'s letter to Aldrich on JDR's lack of interest in building a new house: November 7, 1902, RFA1.L, letterbook 253, 141.

34 "comes to the point": JDR Jr. to Chester Aldrich, February 9, 1903, ibid., letterbook 76, 221.

34 "They were all much pleased": JDR Jr. to Chester Aldrich, August 6, 1903, ibid., letterbook 79, 105.

34 "talks from time to time of building": JDR Jr. to Chester Aldrich, December 8, 1903, ibid., letterbook 81, 36.

35 "a house at Pocantico Hills": JDR Jr. to Lamont Bowers, June 10, 1904, ibid., letterbook 84, 81.

35 "various architects of standing in the city": JDR Jr. to Percy Rockefeller, ibid., letterbook 84, 380. Dunham Wheeler's career is detailed in Hugh J. McCauley, "Visions of Kykuit: John D. Rockefeller's House at Pocantico Hills, Tarrytown, New York," *Hudson Valley Historical Review*, September 1993, vol. 10, no. 2, 43–44.

35 "crude and mongrel": JDR Jr. to AAR, July 25, 1904, RFA2.Z.II, BI F5.

36 Bowers's background and early career: Chernow, *Titan*, 386.

36 "The world is full of Sham": JDR to LCSR, January 20, 1872, quoted in Clarice Strasz, *The Rockefeller Women: Dynasty of Piety, Privacy and Service* (New York, 1995), 73.

36 "They had no civic or social relations": JDR Jr., interview by Fosdick, January 20, 1953, RFA2.Z.V, B57 F503.

37 LCSR's increasing distance from JDR's business activities and the changing character of their correspondence: Chernow, *Titan*, 234.

38 JDR Jr.'s emotional problems and eventual nervous breakdown in 1904–5: Kert, *Abby Aldrich Rockefeller*, 108–13.

38 JDR Jr.'s lobbying activities on behalf of Standard Oil and his growing anxiety about them: Fosdick, *John D. Rockefeller, Jr.*, 141.

39 "no responsibility on Mother": JDR to JDR Jr., August 2, 1904, RFA1.L, letterbook 212, 128.

39 JDR's suggestion that Bowers could choose the architect: JDR to JDR Jr., June 29, 1904, ibid., letterbook 212, 30. JDR Jr.'s reply: JDR Jr. to JDR, June 30, 1904, ibid., letterbook 84, 227.

40 "interior plan of the house" and JDR's other thoughts on the subject: JDR to JDR Jr., August 2, 1904, ibid., letterbook 212, 128.

40 "I think you are wise": JDR Jr. to JDR, August 4, 1904, ibid., letterbook 84, 410.

40 "make any suggestions": JDR Jr. to Chester Aldrich, August 5, 1904, RFA2.I, B22 F206.

40 "I have seen Chester Aldrich": JDR Jr. to AAR, August 22, 1904, RFA2.Z.II, B1 F4.

40 "I am sorry": AAR to JDR Jr., August 23, 1904, ibid.

40 "Would you object": JDR Jr. to JDR, telegram quoted in JDR Jr. to William Delano, August 23, 1904, RFA1.L, letterbook 85, 6.

40 "Think utility and convenience": JDR to JDR Jr., telegram, quoted in ibid.

41 "agreeable": Ibid.

41 "Mr. Delano spent several hours": JDR Jr. to AAR, August 27, 1904, RFA2.Z.II, B1 F4.

41 "I stopped in to see Mr. Delano": JDR Jr. to AAR, August 29, 1904, ibid.

41 "My father's mind": JDR Jr. to William Delano, September 15, 1904, RFA1.L, letterbook 85, 170.

42 JDR Jr.'s continuing emotional difficulties: Kert, *Abby Aldrich Rockefeller*, 113.

42 JDR's request to have the plans for the house sent to him in New York City: Berger, "My Father's House," 123–24.

42 "the biggest criminals in the country": Theodore Roosevelt, quoted in Chernow, *Titan*, 521.

3: KYKUIT RISING I

47 Description of JDR's siting of the house: Chernow, *Titan*, 523.

48 D & A's dislike of hilltop sites: Pinnoyer and Walker, *Architecture of Delano & Aldrich*, 23.

48 "essential parts of the architect's work": D & A, "For You to Decide," quoted in ibid., 23.

48 "Bitter": Ibid., 21.

49 The awkward and protracted negotiations necessary to terminate Wheeler's services: Berger, "My Father's House," 122–23 and 155–58.

49 A usefully detailed analysis of the background, training, and social and artistic milieu in which the "gentlemen architects" practiced their profession: Mark Alan

Hewitt, *The Architect and the American Country House, 1890–1940* (New Haven, Conn., 1990), 25–67.

50   D & A's rank among designers of American country houses: Ibid., 43.

50   The role New York clubs played in D & A's work: Pennoyer and Walker, *Architecture of Delano & Aldrich*, 17 and 43–50.

50   The social significance of changing tastes and styles in country–house architecture and the growing fashion at the turn of the century for large, monumental designs: Hewitt, *Architect and the American Country House*, 10–14 and 69–76. Other sources of useful information on the subject: Aslet, *American Country House*, and Richard Guy Wilson, *The American Renaissance, 1876–1917* (Brooklyn, N.Y., 1979).

51   On Biltmore: Aslet, *American Country House*, 3–17, and Hewitt, *Architect and the American Country House*, 1–9.

51   The role of Alva Vanderbilt's Fifth Avenue mansion in winning her a place in New York society: Aslet, *American Country House*, 4.

51   "the ancestral seat of one line of Vanderbilts": *New York Evening Telegraph*, quoted in ibid., 3.

52   An excellent source on English country houses and the multiple functions they have performed over the centuries: Mark Girouard, *Life in the English Country House: A Social and Architectural History* (New Haven, Conn., 1978).

52   Biltmore's failure to live up to the English ideal: Aslet, *American Country House*, 15–17.

52   The growing number of publications devoted to American country houses and the life associated with them: Hewitt, *Architect and the American Country House*, 13, and Aslet, *American Country House*, 71.

53   "To erect palatial abodes": E. L. Godkin, "The Expenditure of Rich Men," *Scribner's*, October 1896, 495–501.

53   Croly's work and evolving point of view as a critic of country house architecture: Hewitt, *Architect and the American Country House*, 14–23.

53   "Americans do everything": William Herbert (a pseudonym under which Croly wrote), *Houses for Town or Country* (New York, 1907), 78.

53   "In regard to the houses": Ibid., 87.

54   "one of the spoils": Ibid., 67.

54   "no conception of art or beauty": JDR Jr., interview by Fosdick, September 26, 1952, RFA2.Z.V, B57 F503.

55   "a great public park": "John D. Rockefeller's Pocantico Estate," *Country Calendar*, November 1905, 633.

55   "Anything is good enough": JDR, quoted in ibid.

55   "but when it will be begun": Ibid.

55   "He seeks not to play": Ibid., 636.

55   "Here, if anywhere": Ibid., 637.

55   The best analysis of Downing's work, philosophy, and influence: William H. Pierson, Jr., *American Buildings and Their Architects: Technology and the Picturesque* (Garden City, N.Y., 1978), 349–431.

56   The 1959 inventory of JDR Jr.'s library: RFA2.Z.II, B16 F132.

56   "In our republic": A. J. Downing, *The Architecture of Country Houses, Including Designs for Cottages, and Farm Houses, and Villas, With Remarks on Interiors, Furniture, and the Best Modes of Warming and Ventilating* (reprint, New York, 1969), 257.

56   "For it is in such houses": Ibid., 258.

56   "age after age": Ibid., 268–69.

56   "the home of the individual man": Ibid.
57   McKim, Mead & White's early houses discussed, analyzed, and pictured in detail: Samuel G. White, *The Houses of McKim, Mead & White* (New York, 1998), 9–171. See also Richard Guy Wilson, *McKim, Mead & White, Architects* (New York, 1983), and Vincent Scully Jr., in Antoinette F. Downing and Vincent Scully Jr., *The Architectual Heritage of Newport, Rhode Island, 1640–1915* (New York, 1967), 153–75.
57   "The dark shingles": Ibid., 164.
57   The Ogden Mills and Frederick William Vanderbilt houses: White, *Houses of McKim, Mead & White*, 172–81 and 190–97.
57   "imperial, with no concession": Ibid., 192.
58   "many interviews": D & A to JDR Jr., July 13, 1907, RFA2.I, B22 F206.
58   Floor plans of Kykuit: RAC contains a complete set of blueprints done as early as 1906. Nothing done before that date survives. For a modern version, see "Kykuit, Historic Buildings Survey," http://hdl.loc.gov/loc.pnp/hhh.ny1715.
59   Downing's plans and rationale for his "Lake or River Villa for a Picturesque Site": Downing, *Country Houses*, 343–52.
60   "billowing tablecloth of roof": Aslet, *American Country House*, 56.
60   "delicious curve": Downing, *Country Houses*, 345.
60   "Common quarry stone": Ibid., 351.
62   "revise them or plan": JDR Jr. to JDR, March 7, 1906, RFA1.L, letterbook 95, 481.
62   "the most comfortable": JDR Jr. to JDR, April 2, 1906, ibid., letterbook 96, 328.
62   "We are now digging": JDR to Lamont Bowers, May 9, 1906, ibid., letterbook 97, 264.
62   On Thompson–Starrett's previous experience in the construction business: McCauley, "Visions of Kykuit," 40–41.
62   The details of the contract with Thompson–Starrett to build Kykuit: Berger, "My Father's House," 148–49.
63   "I do not feel we are justified": JDR to JDR Jr., April 3, 1907, RFA1.L, letterbook 220, 160.
64   JDR Jr.'s dealings with the president of U.S. Steel: Berger, "My Father's House," 150–51.
64   JDR Jr.'s objections to Thompson–Starrett's charges: Ibid., 154–55.
65   "I am crazy to hear about the house": AAR to JDR Jr., July 24, 1906, RAC2.Z.II, B1 F4.
65   Bessie Rockefeller Strong's death and the federal government's commencement of antitrust proceedings against Standard Oil: Chernow, *Titan*, 526–30.

4: "FOR THE SAKE OF HARMONY"

67   D & A's letter to JDR Jr. protesting the hiring of Codman: December 10, 1906, RFA2.I, B22 F206.
68   "nice quiet talk": JDR Jr. to AAR, August 20, 1906, RFA2.Z.II, B1 F4.
68   There are no early plans by D & A for Kykuit's interiors. Working drawings, dated 1906, showing floor plans and elevations primarily, with some interior detail, are available at the RAC.
68   Undated catalog of books shelved at 10 West Fifty-fourth Street house: RFA2.I, B137 F1369.
68   "[He] had been at great pains . . . how to replace him": Quoted in Pauline C. Metcalf, "Ogden Codman, Jr., Architect–Decorator Elegance without Excess" (unpublished master's thesis, Graduate School of Architecture and Planning, Columbia University, 1978), 45.
68   "by a superficial application": Wharton and OC, *Decoration*, xix.

68   The details of Wharton and OC's pronouncements on proportions: Ibid., especially 31ff.

68   "more strongly developed in those races": Ibid., 34.

68   "There is no question": AAR to DR, August 31, 1944, quoted in Kert, *Abby Aldrich Rockefeller*, 99.

69   JDR Jr.'s response to D & A: December 19, 1906, RFA2.I, B22 F206.

70   "We had thought of": Ibid.

70   On Codman: The only full-length biography of OC is Florence Codman, *The Clever Young Boston Architect* (Augusta, Me., 1970). See also, Pauline C. Metcalf, ed., *Ogden Codman and the Decoration of Houses* (Boston, 1988), especially Metcalf's "From Lincoln to Leopolda," 1–47, and Richard Guy Wilson, "Edith and Ogden: Writing, Decoration, and Architecture", 133–84.

70   "Do write me": OC to Sarah Bradlee Codman, January 29, 1884, quoted in Metcalf, "From Lincoln," 7.

70   "dreary": Ibid.

70   OC's work for Edith Wharton in Newport: Wilson, "Edith and Ogden," 138–146, in Metcalf, *Ogden Codman.*

71   "I wish the Vanderbilts": Edith Wharton to OC, April 17, 1896, quoted in ibid., 149.

71   "You would scarcely recognize me": OC to Arthur Little, April 17, 1896, quoted in Metcalf, "From Lincoln," 8.

71   "she considers me too frivolous": OC to Sarah Bradlee Codman, March 13, 1901, quoted in ibid., 21.

71   Friends attending OC's wedding to Leila Griswold Webb: *New York Times,* October 9, 1904.

72   OC's proposed changes to D & A's plans: JDR Jr. to OC, December 21, 1906, RFA1.L, letterbook 101, 445.

72   "certain points": JDR Jr. to D & A, February 5, 1907, quoted in Albert I. Berger, "Kykuit Design and Construction, 1902–1915: Time Line and Summary of Correspondence" (1984), unpublished manuscript, RAC.

72   A contemporary description of Kykuit's interiors as designed by OC: "The Country Home of John D. Rockefeller, Esq.," *House Beautiful,* June 1909, 1–10.

73   "as extensive and as comprehensive": JDR to Harry Shelley, March 12, 1907, RFA1.L, letterbook 120, 160.

73   D & A's request for additional compensation to JDR Jr., April 12, 1907: RFA2.I, B22 F206.

73   "broad, liberal spirit": JDR Jr. to D & A, April 26, 1907, RFA, ibid.

74   "Many of these changes": D & A to JDR Jr., July 13, 1907, RFA, ibid.

74   "I do not hesitate": JDR Jr. to D & A, July 22, 1907, RFA1.L, letterbook 277, 58.

74   Choice of wallpaper for bedroom: JDR Jr. to LCSR, July 30, 1908, RFA2.Z.II, B4 F39.

74   JDR Jr.'s changes to OC's designs: JDR Jr. to OC, March 18, 1908, RFA1.L, letterbook 110, 122; Baumgarten to JDR Jr., April 27, 1908, RFA2.I, B17 F165; Baumgarten to OC, June 22, 1908, RFA, ibid.

74   Examples of OC's carelessness and inattention to detail: JDR Jr. to OC, January 16, 1908, RFA1.L, letterbook 108, 150; JDR Jr. to OC, January 26, 1908, RFA, ibid., 108, 299; JDR Jr. to OC, February 15, 1908, RFA, ibid., 109, 55; JDR Jr. to OC, March 4, 1908, RFA, ibid., 109, 375; JDR Jr. to OC, April 7, 1908, RFA, ibid., 110, 445; JDR Jr. to OC, April 17, 1908, RFA, ibid., 111, 124.

74   "success had done nothing": F. Codman, *Clever Young Architect,* 17.

75   JDR Jr., asking OC to review furniture selections in Baltimore: JDR Jr. to OC, March 7, 1907, RFA1.L, letterbook 104, 273.

75   Shopping for more furniture in April: Berger, "Kykuit Design," 17.

75   Bargaining for lower prices: JDR Jr. to Koopman & Co., March 9, 1908, RFA2.I, B30 F281; JDR Jr. to Koopman & Co., April 11, 1907, ibid.

75   JDR Jr.'s practice of asking for returns without penalty: JDR Jr. to Koopman & Co., March 7, 1908, ibid.

75   "He thinks these very beautiful": JDR Jr. to Koopman & Co., January 2, 1908, ibid.

75   JDR Jr. asking OC about the mantle question and other unresolved issues: April 13, 1907, RFA1.L, letterbook 105, 347.

76   Details of contract with Baumgarten: Berger, "My Father's House," 299.

76   List prepared for the New York Telephone Company: August 27, 1907, RFA2.I, B36 F350. Description of construction process: Berger, "My Father's House," 229–34.

76   Misplacement of staircase: JDR Jr. to D & A, October 30, 1907, RFA2.I, B22 F206.

77   "rather more girlish": JDR Jr. to OC, May 11, 1908, RFA1.L, letterbook 112, 2.

77   Delays in the production of the carpets: Berger, "My Father's House," 252–62.

77   "The changes will take all the style": OC to R. and L. Hamot, July 16, 1908, quoted in ibid., 255.

77   JDR Jr. putting furniture in place: JDR Jr. to AAR, July 25, 1908, RFA2.Z.II, B1 F5.

77   "because 'the other client' ": JDR Jr. to AAR, July 29, 1908, ibid.

77   "I particularly . . . fully occupied": JDR Jr. to OC, July 30, 1908, RFA1.L, letterbook 121, 341.

78   "see the house and possible locations": JDR Jr. to LCSR, August 25, 1908, RFA2.Z.II, B4 F39.

78   "Mrs. Rockefeller and I feel": JDR Jr. to OC, September 14, 1908, RFA1.L, letterbook 115, 225.

78   JDR Jr. questions OC on progress: September 21, 1908, RFA1.L, letterbook 115, 367.

78   JDR Jr.'s requests for items to give "that homelike touch": JDR Jr. to OC, September 14, 1908, RFA1.L, letterbook 115, 225. See also JDR Jr. to OC, September 21, 1908, RFA1.L, letterbook 115, 367; JDR Jr. to OC, October 6, 1908, RFA1.L, letterbook 116, 152.

78   "based on some of the most beautiful models": OC to JDR Jr., July 7, 1908, quoted in Berger, "My Father's House," 257.

78   "complete or elaborate": JDR Jr. to OC, July 25, 1908, RFA1.L, letterbook 115, 24.

78   "while the designs are so much more interesting": OC to JDR Jr., July 7, 1908, quoted in Berger, "My Father's House," 257.

78   JDR Jr. writing about umbrella stand: JDR Jr. to OC, October 3, 1908, RFA1.L, letterbook 116, 375.

78   "pretty things a bit out of the common": OC to JDR Jr., September 26, 1908, Pauline Metcalf research files.

79   "one soon forgets": Ibid.

79   "all perspiration and prayer": Comment made by OC to F. R. Church and quoted in a letter from Florence Codman to Mr. McKibbin, May 31, 1967, F. Codman, *Clever Young Architect,* 17.

79   "As a rule my clients": OC to JDR Jr., October 20, 1908, PM research files.

79   "as handsome as possible": OC to JDR Jr., October 12, 1908, ibid.

79   Examples of JDR Jr.'s civility: JDR Jr. to OC, July 27, 1908, RFA1.L, letterbook 114, 296; JDR Jr. to OC, September 21, 1908, ibid., 115, 367.

79   "Mr. and Mrs. John D. Rockefeller": "The Country Home of John D. Rockefeller, Esq.," *House Beautiful,* 2.

79   "the palace of a Croesus": Ibid., 1.

79   "entirely removed from the elaborate": Ibid., 4.

80 "A series of rooms": Ibid.
80 On OC's motto: Metcalf, *Ogden Codman,* preface, x.
80 "gave to the renaissance its life": JDR Jr.'s art history class notes, 1896, Brown University, RFA2.Z.II, B37 F319.
80 "changes in manners": Wharton and OC, *Decoration,* xxi, xxii.
80 "When the rich man": Ibid., 5.

5: "THE FRUITS OF THE SPIRIT"

83 "the look of being put up": Lamont M. Bowers to JDR Jr., February 12, 1907, RFA2.I, B36 F345.
83 On the sport of motoring: Joseph Tracy, "Common Sense in Automobile Driving," *Country Life in America,* November 1907, 35–38, 102; D. Enville, "The Confessions of an Anti-Motorist," ibid., 39–40; Harry B. Haines, "Putting Up a Car for the Winter," ibid., 64.
83 "the furniture question": JDR Jr. to AAR, August 20, 1906, RFA2.Z.II, B1 F4.
83 "After this great landscape architect": John D. Rockefeller, *Random Reminiscences,* 24–25.
83 On the two styles of gardens: Karson, *The Muses of Gwinn,* 7–11.
84 "I am afraid that I do not think": Frederick Law Olmsted to William Platt, February 1, 1892, quoted in ibid., 18.
84 "return to a state of nature": Charles A. Platt, "Where We Get Our Ideas of Country Places in America," *Outing,* June 1904, quoted in ibid.,19.
84 "the American landscape has no foreground": Edith Wharton to Sally Norton, 1905, quoted in Max Griswold and Eleanor Weller, *The Golden Age of American Gardens: Proud Owners; Private Estates, 1890–1940* (New York, 1991), 13.
84 On country house and design, including that for Herbert Croly: Sherwin Hawley, "Good Taste in Country Houses: Two Dozen American Country Houses Chosen by Four Successful Architects . . . ," *Country Life in America,* October 1906, 611–19.
84 On the characteristics of country house landscape features: Griswold and Weller, *Golden Age of Gardens,* 18.
84 "sinning against their own opportunities": William Herbert, *Houses for Town or Country* (New York, 1907), 212.
85 JDR Jr.'s request to Charles Leavitt: April 10, 1907, RFA1.L, letterbook 105, 295.
85 On JDR Jr.'s introduction to WWB: WWB, "Time with Mr. Rockefeller," December 1961, 1–2, RFA2.Z.H, B49 F356.
85 "I hope that you and I": Adele Herter to JDR Jr., Summer 1907, RFA2.AA, B3 F34.
85 On WWB's background and experience: F. S. Swales, "Master Draftsman IX: Welles Bosworth," *Pencil Points,* 1925, 59–64; Adolf K. Placzek, ed., *Macmillan Encyclopedia of Architects* (New York, 1982), vol.1, 261–62; "Master of '*Villa Marietta,*'" Marietta College Alumni Magazine, August 1958, RFA2.Z.H, B49 F356.
86 On WWB's initial ideas for Kykuit's landscaping: WWB, "Time with Mr. Rockefeller," 2–3.
86 On carrying a pencil: Interview of JDR Jr. by Raymond Fosdick, c. 1953, RFA2.Z.V, B57 F503.
86 Example of WWB's sketches: WWB to JDR Jr., June 17, 1909, RFA2.I, B18 F169.
87 Publication of WWB's drawings: Swales, "Master Draftsman," 60–64.
87 "It was seven years": WWB, "Mens Sana in Corpore Sano," *Architectural Record,* August 1911, 151.
87 "stick a few pins at random": WWB, "The Garden at Pocantico Hills," *American Architect,* January 4, 1911, 2.

87   "how to make each part perfect": WWB, "Mens Sana," 158.

87   Enlistment of Turner: WWB, "Time with Mr. Rockefeller," 3–4.

88   "natural disposition": WWB, "The Garden at Pocantico," 4.

88   "as all gardens should be": Ibid., 3.

88   "inverted oyster shell": Ibid., 4.

88   "As compared with the plans": JDR Jr. to JDR, April 24, 1908, RFA1.L, letterbook 111, 251.

88   a "true" garden: WWB, "The Garden at Pocantico," 3.

89   WWB's conditions for undertaking the work: WWB to JDR Jr., June 17, 1907, RFA2.I, B21 F192.

90   "They are enchanting": JDR Jr. to AAR, July 12, 1907, RFA2.Z.II, B1 F5.

90   Stonework and masonry on the gardens: JDR Jr. to AAR, July 30, 1907, ibid.; WWB, "The Garden at Pocantico," 5.

90   JDR Jr.'s modifications: Berger, "My Father's House," 211. JDR Jr. to WWB, July 24, 1907, RFA1.L, letterbook 227, 87; JDR Jr. to Thompson-Starrett, August 16, 1907, ibid., 330.

90   Purchases of statuary: JDR Jr. to William Baumgarten & Company, February 14, 1908, RFA1.L, letterbook 109, 71; JDR Jr. to Day & Meyer, January 7, 1908, ibid., 107, 472.

90   On acquiring plantings: WWB, "The Garden at Pocantico," 4.

91   On Senior's request for a flagpole: JDR Jr. to WWB, July 3, 1908, RFA1.L, letterbook 113, 378.

91   On garden features: WWB, "The Garden at Pocantico," 6–8.

91   Progress of construction: Berger, "My Father's House," 196; photograph, March 3, 1908, R.W. Grange Album, RFA 1006.

91   Arrangements with Wadley & Smythe: memo, October 23, 1908, RFA2.I, B32 F319.

92   Specifications for tiling: JDR Jr. to WWB, September 17, 1908, Berger, "Kykuit Design," 43.

92   "the great Borghese vase": WWB, "The Garden at Pocantico," 7–8.

92   "dreamy and delightful": Ibid., 8.

92   Description of the orangerie: Pierson and Roberts, *Rockefeller Family Home*, 100.

92   Building the Japanese garden: Robert Snyder, "The Japanese Garden of the Rockefeller Family," March 1978, RFA2.I, B36 F348.

92   On Japanese gardens for Americans: Eleanor Bartlett, "A Natural Japanese Garden," *Country Life in America*, March 1905, 493; O. Tsuji, "A Japanese Garden Six Feet Square," ibid., 495.

93   "materially increase the difficulty": JDR Jr. to JDR, August 27, 1908, RFA1.L, letterbook 115, 67.

93   Progress on gardens: JDR Jr. to AAR, July 24, 1908, RFA2.ZII, B1 F5.

93   "séance" with WWB: JDR Jr. to AAR, July 27, 1908, ibid.

93   "Mr. Bosworth came up after lunch": JDR Jr. to AAR, June 30, 1908, ibid.

93   "It might be a diversion": JDR Jr. to AAR, July 29, 1908, ibid.

93   "I think they are both foolish": AAR to JDR Jr., May 25, 1909, ibid., F6.

94   JDR Jr. to LCSR advising delay: September 14, 1908, ibid., B4 F39.

94   "practically completed": JDR Jr. to Fred Manpoting, June 14, 1910, RFA2.I, B32 F319.

94   "it was quite like fairyland": JDR Jr. to LCSR, August 8, 1910, RFA2.Z.II, B4 F41.

94   "Those little brooks": JDR to a friend, no date, quoted in Tom Pyle and Beth Day, *Pocantico: Fifty Years on the Rockefeller Domain* (New York, 1964), 123.

94   JDR's conversation with Turner about WWB: WWB, "Time with Mr. Rockefeller," 4.

94   "I am not in the least afraid": JDR Jr. to JDR, September 7, 1907, RFA1.L, letter-book 278, 39.

94   About the disadvantages of halting the work: JDR Jr. to JDR, January 5, 1908, ibid., 119, 86.

95   "It seems to me": JDR to JDR Jr., April 21, 1908, RFA1.L, letterbook 223, 109.

95   "I like Mr. Bosworth increasingly": JDR Jr. to JDR, April 24, 1908, RFA1.L, letterbook 111, 254.

95   "simply reflections": JDR to JDR Jr., April 25, 1908, ibid., 223, 129.

95   "My thought was that": JDR to JDR Jr., September 11, 1908, ibid., 224, 349.

95   "I can hardly understand": JDR to JDR Jr., April 17, 1909, ibid., 226, 308.

95   "It was conceded by his architectural friends": JDR to JDR Jr., January 11, 1910, ibid., 229, 194.

96   Gift of the fur coat: Chernow, *Titan*, 505.

96   "not having definite ideas at the outset": JDR to JDR Jr., January 11, 1910, RFA1.L, letterbook 229, 195.

96   Sketches of cross sections: WWB, "The Garden at Pocantico," 3.

97   "Long ago we ceased to regard you as": JDR Jr. to WWB, February 11, 1913, RFA2.H, B48 F354.

97   "My work with you and Mrs. Rockefeller": WWB to JDR Jr., February 14, 1915, ibid.

97   Photograph of JDR Jr. in bedroom: WWB to JDR Jr., February 6, 1931, ibid.

98   Covering expenses for WWB's operation and house alterations: Renée Bosworth to Janet Warfield, October 23, 1958, RFA2.H, B49 F356.

98   "artistic apartments": JDR Jr. to LCSR, January 21, 1909, RFA2.Z, B4 F40.

98   JDR Jr.'s hunt for Holt's book: JDR Jr. to WWB, December 4, 1928, RFA2.H, B48 F354.

98   "I miss you very much": WWB to JDR Jr., May 24, 1934, ibid.

98   Association between WWB and JDR Jr.: WWB to JDR Jr., November 20, 1920, ibid.; WWB to JDR Jr., June 3, 1937, ibid.; WWB to JDR Jr., November 12, 1956, ibid., F356.

98   Gift of piano for new house: WWB to JDR Jr., October 23, 1916, RFA2.H, B48 F354.

98   Babs and family as first guests: WWB to JDR Jr., September 2, 1936, ibid.

98   Trip to Williamsburg: Ibid.

98   Bosworth's recollections of assistance: WWB to Janet Warfield, October 12, 1958, RFA2.ZII, B49 F356.

98   "I am trying to entertain her": WWB to JDR Jr., March 25, 1929, ibid., F354.

99   "Every hour spent with you": WWB to JDR Jr., February 14, 1915, ibid., F359.

99   "Our country is still too immature": WWB to JDR Jr., November 12, 1956, ibid., F356.

6: KYKUIT RISING II

100   Accounts of the shooting of Russo: *New York Evening World*, August 26, 1912; *New York Tribune*, August 26, 1912; *New York American*, August 27, 1912.

101   "It is beautiful and convenient": Entry from LCSR's diary, October 8, 1908, RFA1.SL, B2 F10.

101   Plans for more closet space: JDR to JDR Jr., December 5, 1910, RFA1.L, letterbook 232, 337.

101   Advantages of heightened ceilings and LCSR's displeasure: JDR Jr. to JDR, March 8, 1911, ibid., 293, 245–46; Berger, "My Father's House," 268–69.

101 JDR's displeasure with noise made by dumbwaiter: RFA1.L, letterbook 232, 271–72.

101 Noise from elevator and plumbing: JDR Jr. to Chester Aldrich, October 27, 1908, ibid., 116, 428.

101 Noise from coal car: Berger, "My Father's House," 272.

101 Uneven heat: JDR to JDR Jr., December 14, 1910, RFA1.L, letterbook 232, 280.

101 Water running from the chimney: Berger, "My Father's House," 272.

102 Downdrafts from chimneys: JDR to JDR Jr., June 13, 1910, RFA2.I, B22 F206.

102 Placing blame on architects and contractors: JDR to JDR Jr., June 13, 1910, ibid.; JDR Jr. to D & A, October 27, 1908, RFA1.L, letterbook 116, 428.

102 "What can now be done": Ibid.

102 "Let us spare no expense": JDR to JDR Jr., June 12, 1908, ibid., 223, 361.

103 Consultation on and experiments with chimneys: Berger, "My Father's House," 273.

103 On chimney extensions: JDR Jr. to Chester Aldrich, July 5, 1909, RFA2.I, B22 F206; D & A to JDR Jr., August 31, 1909, ibid.; JDR Jr. to Chester Aldrich, May 23, 1910, ibid.; D & A to JDR Jr., May 25, 1910, ibid.

103 "So desirous am I": JDR to JDR Jr., June 13, 1910, RFA2.I, B22 F206.

103 "roof rooms": JDR Jr. to Chester Aldrich, June 14, 1910, ibid.

103 JDR Jr.'s request of Chester Aldrich: JDR Jr. to Aldrich, June 14, 1910, ibid.

103 "I am glad to hear": OC to C. A. Wulff, July 20, 1910, PM research files.

103 Projection of east wall: JDR to JDR Jr., August 12, 1910, RFA1.L, letterbook 231, 303.

104 D & A's objections to a flat roof: D & A to JDR Jr., August 31, 1910, RFA2.I, B17 F165.

104 Instructions on forwarding plans: Ibid.

104 JDR Jr. urging his father to reach decision: JDR Jr. to JDR, October 3, 1910, RFA1.L, letterbook 138, 106.

104 Suggestion for Platt as consultant: Ibid., 463.

104 Instructions to proceed: JDR Jr. to JDR, November 10, 1910, RFA2.I, B17 F165.

104 Senior's suggestions for second floor: JDR Jr. to Chester Aldrich, November 22, 1910, RFA1.L, letterbook 232, 292; JDR to JDR Jr., December 5, 1910, ibid., 337.

104 On the addition of a freight elevator: JDR to JDR Jr., January 26, 1911, RFA1.L, letterbook 233, 124; JDR Jr. to JDR, January 27, 1911, ibid., 291, 113.

104 On the extension of the west porch: L. W. Eisinger to JDR Jr., January 12, 1911, RFA2.I, B21 F193; JDR Jr. to Eisinger, January 16, 1911, ibid.

104 On the new plan: JDR Jr. to OC, February 25, 1911, RFA2.I, B17 F177.

105 Proposal of new plan to Senior: JDR Jr. to JDR, March 8, 1911, RFA1.L, letterbook 293, 245.

105 Senior's acceptance and suggestions: JDR to JDR Jr., March 11, 1911, ibid., 233, 275.

105 Five contractors: JDR Jr. to JDR, February 10, 1911, ibid., 292, 322.

105 Problematic past experience on city house with Thompson-Starrett: Stan J. Murphy to JDR Jr., November 9, 1908, RFA2.I, B22 F206; Thompson-Starrett to JDR Jr., November 18, 1908, ibid.; memorandum by JDR Jr., November 25, 1908, ibid.

105 Dismantling the house: JDR Jr. to LCSR, April 13, 1911, RFA2.Z.II, B4 F41; "Articles Removed from the New Pocantico House," April 27, 1911, RFA2.I, B26 F234.

105 Addition of house contents: JDR Jr. to OC, May 18, 1910, Pauline Metcalf research files; JDR Jr. to OC, February 18, 1911, RFA1.L, letterbook 292, 401.

105   Description of inner garden: WWB, "The Garden at Pocantico," 5; Pierson and Roberts, *Rockefeller Family Home*, 148.

106   "the most artistic furniture ever executed": William Baumgartner & Co. to WWB, December 16, 1910, RFA2.I, B36 F346.

106   Senior's objections to the cost of the teahouse curtains: JDR to JDR Jr., January 3, 1911, RFA1.L, letterbook 232, 487.

106   JDR Jr.'s response to his father's objections: JDR Jr. to JDR, January 17, 1911, ibid., 140, 437–38.

106   JDR's suggestion for a heating system in the coach barn: JDR to JDR Jr., May 18, 1911, ibid., 234, 106.

106   JDR Jr.'s response to JDR's suggestion: JDR Jr. to JDR, June 14, 1911, ibid., 296, 174.

107   Hargreaves's idea for a tunnel: JDR to JDR Jr., May 18, 1911, ibid., 234, 106.

107   "busy surveying something": AAR to JDR Jr., May 20, 1911, RFA2.Z.II, B1 F6.

107   Senior busily surveying for a tunnel: JDR to Dr. I. Dever Warner, June 17, 1911, quoted in Berger, "My Father's House," 327.

107   "It would be costly"; JDR Jr. to JDR, June 14, 1911, RFA1.L, letterbook 296, 174–75.

107   "feasible and easier than [he] had expected": JDR to JDR Jr., June 17, 1911, ibid., 234, 235.

107   Junior's objections to tunnel and to hiring Howatt: Berger, "My Father's House," 327–28.

107   Junior's wish that D & A confer with Munn and WWB "at each step": JDR Jr. to JDR, June 21, 1911, RFA1.L, letterbook 296, 261.

107   "Mr. John does not sympathize": JDR to M. A. Munn, June 23, 1911, quoted in Berger, "Kykuit Design," 111.

107   "to do one of the finest pieces of work": JDR to WWB, June 23, 1911, RFA1.L, letterbook 234, 271.

107   Senior urges Junior to stay away longer: JDR to JDR Jr., July 18, 1911, Berger, "Kykuit Design," 113.

108   Consultations with Howatt: JDR to WWB, June 23, 1911, RFA1.L, letterbook 234, 271; JDR to D. E. Howatt, July 20, 1911, Berger, "Kykuit Design," 114.

108   "so that Mr. John will have no necessity of complaining": JDR to WWB, July 20, 1911, Berger, "Kykuit Design," 114.

108   "These I have mentioned to father": JDR Jr. to WWB, July 3, 1911, RFA2.I, B21 F193.

108   "father's project": JDR Jr. to D & A, December 4, 1911, in Berger, "Kykuit Design," 126.

108   Recommendation not to blast: Howatt to JDR Jr., December 15, 1911, RFA2.I, B31 F302; JDR to JDR Jr., August 24, 1911, in Berger, "Kykuit Design," 119.

108   Preference for adding pit for elevator: JDR Jr. to Howatt, December 15, 1911, RFA2.I, B31 F302.

108   Orders to stop blasting: Berger, "My Father's House," 331–32.

108   "in order that the house and gardens": JDR Jr. to William Delano, June 12, 1911, RFA2.I, B21 F193.

108   Delano's acquiescence: Delano to JDR Jr., June 14, 1911, ibid.

108   Tour of house fronts in the city: JDR Jr. to AAR, August 10, 1911, RFA2.Z.II, B1 F6.

108   WWB's work on designs: JDR Jr. to Chester Aldrich, September 25, 1911, RFA2.I, B21 F193; Berger, "Kykuit Design," 123–26.

109   Account of accident: "Narrow Escape for J. D. Rockefeller, Jr.," *New York Times*, September 16, 1911.

109   JDR's opposition to a "thoroughfare": JDR to WWB, December 26, 1911, RFA2.I, B18 F169.

109   WWB's preference for central axis: WWB to JDR, December 22, 1911, ibid.

109   "I had not given this matter much thought": Memorandum of phone conversation between WWB and JDR, December 18, 1911, ibid.

109   "The 'best thing'": WWB to JDR, December 22, 1911, ibid.

110   "very simple" forecourt: JDR to WWB, December 26, 1911, ibid.

110   Approval to begin preparing the site: JDR Jr. to JDR, April 9, 1912, ibid., F170.

110   Consultation with "[his] friend Platt": WWB to JDR Jr., June 26, 1912, ibid.

110   JDR's proposal using steam: Typescript of telephone message from JDR to JDR Jr., April 15, 1912, ibid.

110   Description of Catskills project: Alfred D. Flinn, "The World's Greatest Aqueduct," *Century Magazine*, September 1909, http://www.catskillarchive.com/aqueduct, accessed July 18, 2005. On average wages, see Charles Heytt to Frederick Briggs, April 15, 1912, RFA1.L, letterbook 303, 144; JDR Jr. to JDR, April 16 and 17, 1912, RFA2.A, B54 F435.

110   Italian immigration and *padrone* system: Paola A. Sinsi-Isolani, "Italians," *A Nation of Peoples: A Sourcebook on America's Multicultural Heritage* (Westport, Conn., 1999), 294–95; *The Italian American Experience: An Encyclopedia* (New York, 2000), 321–29; Gunther Peck, "Divided Loyalties; Immigrant Padrones and the Evolution of Industrial Paternalism in North America," *International Labor and Working-Class History*, Spring 1998, 49–68; Gunther Peck, "Reinventing Free Labor: Immigrant Padrones and Contract Laborers in North America," *Journal of American History*, December 1996, 848–71; Humbert S. Nelli, "The Italian Padrone System in the United States," *Labor History*, Spring 1964, 153–67; Robert F. Harney, "The Padrone and the Immigrant," *Canadian Review of American Studies*, 1974, 101–18.

111   On Kensico: http://www.co.westchester.ny.us/wcarchives/Kensico, accessed July 18, 2005.

111   On the Black Hand: Thomas Monroe Pitkin and Francesco Cordasco, *The Black Hand: A Chapter in Ethnic Crime* (Totowa, N.J., 1977); Arthur Woods, "The Problem of the Black Hand," *McClure's Magazine*, May 1909, 40–47.

111   "I knew [the Black Hand] before I could even talk": Statement of Stanislas Pattenza at his trial for kidnapping, quoted in Sydney Reid, "The Death Sign," *Independent*, April 6, 1911; "Italian Problem," *Harper's Weekly*, July 3, 1909, 5.

111   Discovery of Black Hand account book: *New York Times*, October 25, 1906.

111   "especially out on the line": "Italian Problem," *Harper's Weekly*, July 3, 1909, 5.

111   Press speculations about secret squad: "New Secret Service to Fight Black Hand," *New York Times*, February 20, 1909.

112   On Kensico workers arming themselves against the Black Hand: "Italian Problem," 5; "NYC Watershed Retrospective," http://reflector.net/watershed, accessed July 19, 2005.

112   Report of Cadenza's murder: *New York Times*, January 31, 1907.

112   Referral to "Italian troubles": Berger, "My Father's House," 350.

112   Account of the beating of the bank manager: *New York Times*, February 11, 1911.

112   Account of murder of Tony Ditto: Ibid., March 3, 1911.

112   On the Italian who was jailed: Berger, "My Father's House," 351.

112   On the waste pipes: Munn to JDR Jr., May 31, 1912, RFA2.I., B13 F166; JDR Jr. to Munn, June 3, 1912, ibid.; D & A to JDR Jr., August 14, 1912, ibid.; JDR Jr.'s reply, August 26, 1912, ibid.; D & A to JDR Jr., August 28, 1912, ibid.

112   Added workforce: Berger, "My Father's House," 340.

113   Wages for workmen: Heydt to Briggs, April 15, 1912, RFA1.L, letterbook 303, 144; JDR Jr. to JDR, April 16 and 17, 1912, RFA2.A, B54 F435.

113   Dunson's job: Berger, "My Father's House," 341.

113   Told not to fraternize: World, September 3, 1912.

113   "do what you think best": JDR to Briggs, July 8, 1912, RFA1.L, letterbook 238, 417.

113   "bad element": Ibid.

113   The Times account of summer's troubles: New York Times, August 17, 1912.

113   Robbery: New York American, August 27, 1912.

113   "A veritable Black Hand warfare": World, August 26, 1912.

113   "on a martial footing": Berger, "My Father's House," 343–44.

113   Fourteen additional watchmen: World, September 3, 1912.

114   "Son commands": "Son Commands Rockefeller Estate Guards," RFA1.M. Scrapbooks, 4.

114   JDR Jr.'s remarks: New York Sun, August 28, 1912, RFA1.M. Scrapbooks, 4.

114   Report of robbery of teamster: New York Times, August 30, 1912.

114   Armed workers: New York Sun, August 28, 1912, RFA1.M. Scrapbooks, 4.

114   Description of Dunson: World, September 3, 1912.

114   Briggs with armed guard: New York American, August 27, 1912.

114   "I deemed it best": Unsigned letter from Rockefeller office to JDR, August 21, 1912, RFA1.L, letterbook 239, 239.

114   Reports of threats against Rockefellers and mansion: World, September 3, 1912; New York American, September 3, 1912.

114   "The magnificent grounds are to-day bristling with Burns detectives": Evening World, September 3, 1912.

115   Kent House guards: World, September 3, 1912.

115   Security base: New York Sun, September 6, 1912, quoted in Berger, "Kykuit Design," 171.

115   "at some convenient time": Evening World, September 3, 1912.

115   "eirie[sic] couriers": World, September 3, 1912.

115   Account of Drago incident: New York Times, September 4, 1912.

115   Intruder wounded: Ibid., September 8, 1912.

115   Sheriff William Doyle's report: Ibid., September 14, 1912.

115   "little foundation of fact": White Plains Record, September 12, 1912, RFA1.M. Scrapbooks, 4.

115   Sheriff William Doyle's report: New York Times, September 14, 1912.

116   Investigation on workers with Italian names: Berger, "My Father's House," 349–50; Heydt to W. H. Dorsey, September 20, 1912, RFA1.L, letterbook 306, 254; JDR Jr. to Briggs, September 28, 1912, ibid., 306, 361.

116   "on our different places": JDR to Briggs, August 27, 1912, ibid., 279, 259.

116   "want the impression to go out": JDR to JDR Jr., September 10, 1912, ibid., 239, 318.

116   "We are daily getting new inside information": JDR Jr. to JDR, September 25, 1912, ibid., 306, 311.

116   Account of JDR's return: New York Times, October 5, 1912.

116   "the rich end of the house": JDR Jr. to E. F. Caldwell, July 2, 1912, RFA1.L, 305, 132.

117   On WWB's conflicts with D & A: JDR Jr. to Chester Aldrich, April 13, 1913, RFA2.I, B21 F194; JDR Jr. to JDR, October 14, 1913, RFA1.L, letterbook 177, 585.

117   On progress of east facade: Berger, "My Father's House," 363.

117 Date for furniture delivery: Instructions for housekeeper, Berger, "Kykuit Design," 187.

117 On painting and installations of telephones: JDR Jr. to JDR, June 5, 1913, ibid., 193, 195; Clark, MacMullen & Riley to WWB, January 2, 1914, RFA2.I, B18 F170.

117 On the purchases: Furniture inventory, RFA2.I, Kykuit Housebooks, 159.

117 WWB's fountain: L.W. Eisinger to JDR Jr., October 30, 1911, RFA2.I, B18 F169.

117 Statuary: Illustrations and captions, Pierson and Roberts, *Rockefeller Family Home*, 158, 152.

117 On choosing the Evans statue: JDR Jr. to JDR, February 21, 1913, RFA1.L, letterbook 309, 312.

118 "I clearly recall": JDR to JDR Jr., November 22, 1912, ibid., 240, 164.

118 "it would seem bare": JDR Jr. to JDR, November 21, 1912, ibid., 317, 334.

118 Proposal for "just the thing": JDR Jr. to JDR, May 20, 1913, ibid., 159, 138–39.

118 Suggestions for naming the house: JDR Jr. to LCSR, February 25, 1909, RFA1.L, letterbook 212, 122; March 1, 1909, RFA2.Z.I, B4 F40.

119 "Kijkuit": JDR to D. E. Howatt, September 29, 1913, RFA1.L, letterbook 243, 420.

119 Events of June 30: Berger, "Kykuit Design," 126.

119 Choice of WWB to redesign coach barn: Pierson and Roberts, *Rockefeller Family Home*, 98.

119 Discovery of rags: *New York American and Evening Journal*, August 20, 1913, quoted in Berger, "Kykuit Design," 201.

119 *Times* report: *New York Times*, July 22, 1913.

119 *Herald*'s report: Berger, "Kykuit Design," 198.

119 "the working class": "Industrial Workers of the World," *Encyclopedia of the American Left* (New York, 1998), 356–57.

119 Reports of IWW agitation: *New York Times*, May 4, June 1, and June 8, 1914.

120 Requirement for bond: Pocantico estate's acting superintendent to John J. Wirth, May 1, 1914, RFA2.I, B30 F298; Berger, "My Father's House," 389.

120 "alarming rumors": George Brown & Co. to J. Alva Jenkins, May 12, 1914, RFA2.I, B30 F298.

120 Account of stone bowl's progress: *New York Times*, June 8, 1914.

120 Junior's annoyance: JDR Jr. to WWB, February 9, 1914, RFA2.I, B30 F298.

121 "certified to be the work of Praxiteles": *New York Herald*, August 1, 1915, ibid., F187.

121 "was thronged every hour": Ibid.

121 "All literary and artistic New York": *Craftsman*, April 1905, quoted in ibid.

121 "that ever wrought up": *New York Times*, August 2, 1915, ibid.

121 Theories of Aphrodite's origins: *New York Herald*, August 1, 1915; *New York Times*, August 2, 1915, ibid.

122 Early negotiations: Berger, "My Father's House," 381–82.

122 Sale allegedly for $30,000: Henry W. Earle to WWB, October 31, 1913, RFA2.I, B20 F184.

122 Terra-cotta Flora: Berger, "My Father's House," 384.

122 "with a little careful negotiation": Earle to WWB, October 31, 1913, RFA2.I, B20 F184.

122 "one of the great things in the world": WWB to JDR Jr., November 19, 1914, ibid.

122 "I understood from you the other day": JDR Jr. to WWB, November 18, 1913, ibid.

122 Purchase of Aphrodite: Berger, "My Father's House," 395–400.

122 "Aphrodite, No Nightie": *Evening Mail*, August 2, 1915, RFA2.I, B20 F187.

123 "whose marble wistfulness": *New York Herald*, August 1, 1915, ibid.

123 "those who appreciated fine design": JDR Jr., "Father's House at Pocantico Hills," January 1940, 2–3.

7: SETTLING UP

125 LCSR's death and burial: Chernow, *Titan*, 594–96.

126 JDR Jr.'s accounting to JDR of the total cost of the house and gardens: JDR Jr. to JDR, October 14, 1915, RFA1.L, letterbook 177, 583.

127 "I should not want the public": JDR to JDR Jr., January 11, 1910, ibid., letterbook 229, 194.

127 The Supreme Court's decision in the Standard Oil case: Chernow, *Titan*, 553–55.

128 The impact of the Supreme Court decision on Rockefeller's wealth: Ibid., 555–57.

128 "we do not want anything elaborate": JDR Jr. to Charles W. Leavitt Jr., April 10, 1907, RFA.1.L, letterbook 105, 295.

129 "I have felt throughout": JDR Jr. to JDR, January 5, 1908, ibid., letterbook 199, 89.

129 "I know you have given": JDR to JDR Jr., June 16, 1909, ibid., letterbook 227, 126.

130 The *New York Times* article on the absence of ostentation at Kykuit: May 6, 1994.

131 The creation of Gwinn, focusing primarily on its gardens but providing as well an account of the design and building of the house: Karson, *Muses of Gwinn.*

131 Charles Platt's career as a landscape designer and architect: Ruth N. Morgan, *Charles A. Platt: The Artist as Architect* (New York, 1985). On Gwinn, see 110–12.

132 Manning's career and work at Gwinn: Karson, *Muses of Gwinn*, 21–28, 43–51, 67–106, and 121–35.

132 Platt's work on Edith Rockefeller McCormick's house on Lake Michigan: Morgan, *Charles A. Platt*, 113–20.

132 The escalation of costs at Gwinn: Karson, *Muses of Gwinn*, 57.

132 "I am afraid of the cost": William G. Mather, quoted in ibid., 58.

132 "full of an aesthetic magnetism": *Country Life*, May 1916, quoted in ibid., 5.

132 "built upon models": Charles A. Platt, "Where We Get Our Ideas of Country Places in America," *Outing*, June 1904, quoted in ibid., 19.

132 "the dime novel of architecture": Ibid.

133 "Do as you think best": JDR to JDR Jr., May 23, 1913, RFA1.L, letterbook 242, 126.

134 The Corn Products Refining Company case: Fosdick, *John D. Rockefeller, Jr.,* 135–36.

134 "I never worked harder in my life": JDR Jr., quoted in ibid., 137.

134 "He has bumped up against": *Cleveland Leader*, May 9, 1910, quoted in ibid., 139.

135 "one of the most important decisions": JDR Jr., quoted in ibid., 141.

135 "John . . . I want you to do": JDR as quoted by JDR Jr. in ibid., 142.

135 JDR Jr.'s collecting of Chinese porcelains: Ibid., 333–36. See also JDR Jr., interview by Fosdick, 1952, RFA1.Z.V, B57 F503.

135 "such an opportunity": JDR Jr. to JDR, January 28, 1915, quoted in Fosdick, *John D. Rockefeller, Jr.,* 334.

135 "I feel afraid of it": JDR to JDR Jr., January 28, 1915, quoted in ibid., 334.

135 "I have never squandered money": JDR Jr. to JDR, January 29, 1915, quoted in ibid., 334–35.

136 Colorado Fuel and Iron and the early stages of the strike: Chernow, *Titan*, 571–78.

136 "until our bones [are] bleached as white": Lamont Bowers, quoted in ibid., 575.

136 The Ludlow massacre: Ibid., 576–78.

136 "There was no Ludlow Massacre": JDR Jr., quoted in ibid., 578.

136 The demonstrations at Kykuit and 26 Broadway: Ibid., 579–80.

137 JDR Jr. turns to King for guidance on labor issues: Ibid., 581–83.

137 "on which both employers and employed": Mackenzie King to JDR Jr., August 6, 1914, quoted in Fosdick, *John D. Rockefeller, Jr.,* 160–63.

137 JDR Jr.'s trip to Colorado: Mackenzie King to AAR, October 6, 1915, RFA2.AA.II, B3 F38. See also Fosdick, *John D. Rockefeller, Jr.,* 160–63, and Chernow, *Titan,* 588–90.

137 "Yes, it was excellent": JDR, quoted in ibid., 590.

137 "one of the most important things": JDR Jr., quoted in Fosdick, *John D. Rockefeller, Jr.,* 167.

138 "more and more . . . leave to me": AAR to JDR Jr., date unclear, "probably" October 4, 1914, RFA2.Z.II, B1 F7.

138 "If you can help bring about": AAR to JDR Jr., September 27, 1915, ibid.

138 "It seems to me": Mackenzie King to JDR Jr., February 9, 1915, quoted in Fosdick, *John D. Rockfeller, Jr.,* 159.

139 "Unless we are to go back": Harry W. Desmond and Herbert Croly, *Stately Homes in America: From Colonial Times to the Present Day* (New York, 1903), 280.

140 JDR Jr.'s work in historic preservation: Fosdick, *John D. Rockefeller, Jr.,* 272–301 and 349–68.

140 JDR's gifts of money and securities to JDR Jr., which caused his net worth to rise from $20 million to $500 million in five years: Chernow, *Titan,* 621–24.

141 "It all makes me very happy": AAR to JDR Jr., September 27, 1915, RFA2.Z.II, B1 F7.

8: PATRIARCH

146 Songs like "Oh, Moon": AAR to Lucy Truman Aldrich, July 10, 1935, RFA2.AA.I, B4 F53.

146 Description of wedding anniversary celebration: Chernow, *Titan,* 593–94.

146 "I am wondering": JDR Jr. to WWB, April 16, 1914, RFA2.I, B20 F179.

146 Replacement for rocking chair: JDR Jr. to Émil Baumgarten, December 28, 1916, ibid., B17 F166.

147 "to keep it from prying eyes": WWB to JDR Jr., October 7, 1915, ibid. B20 F184.

147 Bosworth on revolving pedestal: WWB to JDR Jr., September 10, 1917, ibid.

147 Replacement of vase with supporting column: Correspondence between JDR Jr. and WWB, Spring 1916, ibid., B36 F351.

147 Boxwood care: "Pocantico Hills Estate," May 13, 1930, 5–6, ibid., B35 F344.

147 Abby's love of flowers: W. G. Woodger to AAR and JDR Jr., June 1, 1916, ibid., B32 F319; Chase, *Abby Aldrich Rockefeller,* 65; Kert, *Abby Aldrich Rockefeller,* 237–40.

147 "lonely": Doris Payne to JDR, December 27, 1921, RFA2.A, B55 F438.

148 Handling curtains properly: JDR Jr. to LCSR, January 25, 1909, RFA2.Z.I, B4 F40.

148 JDR's daily schedule: Chernow, *Titan,* 502.

148 "goofy flaps": Ibid.

148 "That old rooster": Quoted in ibid, 635.

149 Dancing a mock Charleston: Ibid., 634.

149 "wouldn't that Rockefeller?": Editorial, *Tarrytown News,* June 7, 1937, RFA2.H, B56 F416.

149 Description of Sunday lunches: Chernow, *Titan,* 628–29.

150 "were never kept up to the mark": JDR Jr. to LCSR, September 28, 1908, RFA2.Z.I, B4 F39.

150   "She means well": JDR Jr. to LCSR, January 25, 1909, ibid., F40.

151   "very sweet and friendly": JDR Jr. to LCSR, February 11, 1909, RFA1.L, letter-book 120, 399.

151   Servants' furniture: "Furniture and Fixtures for New Pocantico House," RFA2.I, B26 F236.

152   Doris Payne's visits: Doris Payne to JDR, August 1919, RFA2.A, B54 F432; Payne to JDR, August 1921, ibid.; Payne to JDR, 1922, RFA2.H, B55 F439; Payne to JDR, January 1923, RFA2.A, B54 F438; Payne to JDR, April 11, 1925, RFA2.H, B55 F432.

152   Wage discrepancies: Household payroll for 1936, RFA2.I, B33 F329.

152   "the ladies": HFMR interview.

152   "Not a drawer": Mary Elizabeth Carter, *Millionaire Households and Their Domestic Economy with Hints upon Fine Living* (New York, 1903), 44.

152   Installation of a butler: JDR Jr. to JDR, March 24, 1908, RFA2.Z.I, B1 F14; JDR Jr. to LCSR, January 7, 1914, ibid., B4 F44.

154   Silent service at dining room table: "Sculptured Bust of Mr. R. (Sr.) from Jo Davidson," *Between Sittings: An Informal Autobiography* (New York, 1951), 2, RFA2.I, housebooks.

154   Kitchen maid's recollections: Anne Marie Rasmussen, *There Was Once a Time of Islands, Illusions, and Rockefellers* (New York, 1975), 19.

154   Wadham's books passed along: Lists of books from 10 West Fifty-fourth Street given to children, RFA2.I, B137 F1368.

154   Instructions for speaking to supervisors: Caroline Reed Wadham, *Simple Directions for the Chambermaid* (London, 1917), 6.

155   "The girls who are here": JDR to M. A. Hargreaves, July 26, 1913, RFA1.L, letter-book 250, 111.

155   "There will be seventeen in the party": JDR to M. A. Hargreaves, September 18, 1913, ibid., 89.

155   Laura's trunks: LCSR to JDR Jr., August 2, 1912, RFA2.Z.I, B4 F41.

155   Car arrangements: JDR to D. F. DeLap, March 19, 1930, RFA2.A, B54 F432; JDR to Delap, April 11, 1930, ibid.

156   "We must not continue": JDR to N. C. Ailes, January 26, 1910, RFA1.L, letter-book 229, 301.

156   Size of estate: JDR Jr. to G. B. Dorr, April 9, 1912, ibid., 303, 51.

156   Escalating costs: W. S. Mitchell to JDR, November 5, 1920, RFA2.A, B55 F437.

156   "LET US GET TOGETHER": DeLap to estate workers, November 8, 1919, ibid., B54 F436.

156   "contented and interested": The employees on this estate to JDR, December 25, 1919, ibid.

157   "Several of our best men": DeLap to JDR, January 9, 1919, ibid.

157   "establish a morale": DeLap to JDR, June 25, 1919, ibid.

157   "As long as men can get more wages": JDR Jr. to JDR, October 28, 1919, ibid.

157   Turnover rate: "Pocantico Hills Ledger," 14–15, RFA1.F, 1919.

157   "surprised": JDR to DeLap, January 13, 1920, RFA2.A, B55 F437.

157   Need for wage increases: Telegram from JDR Jr. to JDR, March 4, 1920, ibid.

157   "Our superintendent": JDR to JDR Jr., March 5, 1920, ibid.

157   "Is there not to be some limit": JDR to DeLap, April 27, 1920, ibid.

157   "labor is going wild": DeLap to JDR, April 26, 1920, ibid.

157   "I have done my best": DeLap to JDR, May 18, 1920, ibid.

157   "Try to hold your men": Confirmation of telephone message from JDR to De-Lap, May 19, 1920, ibid.

157 "Some of our men": DeLap to JDR, May 20, 1920, ibid.
158 "Be of good cheer": Telephone message from JDR to DeLap, May 1920, ibid.
158 "There is some place": JDR to DeLap, June 8, 1920, ibid.
158 Payroll figures: W. S. Mitchell to JDR, November 8, 1920, ibid.
158 Volunteer pay cut for foremen: DeLap to JDR, February 10, 1921, ibid., F438.
158 "I hardly think": JDR to DeLap, February 5, 1923, ibid., F439.
158 Wage situation in 1923: DeLap to JDR, April 4, 1923, ibid., F440.
158 Wage increases: DeLap to JDR, April 10, 1923, ibid.
158 "labor agitators": DeLap to JDR, April 18, 1923, ibid.
158 "a perfect organization of the world": DeLap to JDR, October 5, 1922, ibid., F439.
158 DeLap as Santa: DeLap to JDR, December 1922, ibid., F439.
158 Aid to family with eleven children: DeLap to JDR, May 3, 1920, ibid., F437.
159 Senior's request for itemized bill: JDR to DeLap, January 9, 1923, ibid., F439.
159 "best thing": JDR to DeLap, April 6, 1922, ibid.
159 "humbugged by people": JDR to DeLap, February 23, 1921, ibid., F438.
159 "cannot, do not, and never have": JDR to DeLap, March 5, 1923, ibid., F439.
159 "I must boil over": DeLap to JDR, March 1, 1923, ibid., F440.
159 Senior's response to DeLap's request for wage increase: JDR to DeLap, May 16, 1923, ibid.
159 Request for reference: DeLap to Mr. Houston, ibid.
159 Junior's mediation: JDR Jr. to JDR, May 21, 1923, ibid.
159 Cuts on Christmas list: JDR to DeLap, December 13, 1930, ibid., B54 F430.
159 Village resentment at Senior's stinginess: New York Times, June 5, 1910.
160 1919 coal consumption report: DeLap to JDR, June 22, 1920, RFA2.A, B55 F442.
160 "If we can save": JDR to DeLap, December 28, 1920, ibid.
160 Report on heating and refrigeration: George Runscline of the Knickerbocker Ice Co. to DeLap, September 14, 1920, ibid.
160 Price of oil: Salesman for General Oil Burner Sales Corporation to DeLap, August 19, 1921, ibid.
160 Low water pressure: DeLap to JDR, June 15, 1925, ibid., F441.
161 Construction of reservoir: New York Times, April 15, 1931.
161 Relocation of Putnam Division: Ibid., March 30, 1930, and March 16, 1931.
161 Enlistment of Olmsted office: JDR Jr. to F. L. Olmsted, August 10, 1931, RFA2.I, B31 F300.
161 Olmsted's help with landscaping: F. L. Olmsted to JDR Jr., June 25, 1934, ibid., B32 F316; JDR Jr. to F. L. Olmsted, October 5, 1934, ibid.
161 "very beautiful": JDR Jr. to WWB, March 29, 1932, ibid., B18 F170.
162 "fell into natural decay": WWB to JDR Jr., April 12, 1932, ibid.
162 Annual movement of orange trees: Description of Kykuit in a forthcoming history of Westchester County by Lewis Historical Publishing, April 1, 1925, 3, ibid., B30 F296.
162 Decision to dispose of orange trees: JDR Jr. to F. W. Smythe, July 9, 1935, ibid., B32 F318.
162 Description of estate and its administration: Survey of estate, May 13, 1930, ibid., B35 F344.
163 "Mayor": New York Times, May 24, 1937.
164 "fine, keen aesthetic type": Quoted in Chernow, Titan, 613.
164 Conversations during sittings: Ibid.
164 Bomb incident: New York Times, July 5, 1914.
164 Kykuit stormed: Chernow, Titan, 579.
164 Kykuit "shut tight": New York Times, July 5, 1915.

164   Description of JDR's life at Ormond: Chernow, *Titan*, 611.
165   Need for quiet and rest: *New York Times*, July 2, 1932.
165   "extreme quietness": Ibid., December 21, 1933.
165   Departure from Kykuit: Ibid, February 16, 1934.
165   Roses for the gardens: Ibid., May 7, 1934.
165   Description of funeral at Kykuit: AAR to Lucy Truman Aldrich, May 28, 1937, RFA2.AA.I, B4 F54; DR, *Memoirs* (New York, 2002), 4.

9: FAMILY SEAT

167   Debate about the ornaments at the front entrance: JDR Jr. to WWB, October 5, 1942, RFA2.I, B21 F195; WWB to JDR Jr., October 11, 1942, ibid.; JDR Jr. to WWB, October 27, 1942, ibid.
169   "I have come to the conclusion": AAR to Lucy Truman Aldrich, *Abby Aldrich Rockefeller's Letters to Her Sister* (New York, 1957), 304.
169   Descriptions of Abeyton Lodge interiors: DR, *Memoirs*, 28; Kert, *Abby Aldrich Rockefeller*, 163.
169   "Being less humble": AAR to Charles Eliot, May 9, 1921, RFA2.AA, B2 F29.
169   "Your father is so modest": Quoted in Chase, *Abby Aldrich Rockefeller*, 44.
169   Children's activities at Pocantico: Kert, *Abby Aldrich Rockefeller*, 163; AAR to JDR 3rd, April 8, 1922, RFA2.AA.I, B4 F60.
170   "It rests and refreshes me": AAR to JDR Jr., March 19, 1922, RFA2.Z.I, B1 F8.
170   "fair play": AAR's frequent use of expression described in *The Delineator*, May 1927, RFA2.AA.II, B13 F157a; AAR to JDR 3rd, LSR, NAR, ibid., I, B3 F45.
170   Money "makes life too easy": AAR to LSR, March 23, 1923, quoted in Kert, *Abby Aldrich Rockefeller*, 208.
170   Sunday walks: JDR Jr., interview by Fosdick, March 24, 1953, RFA2.Z.V, B57 F503.
170   Abby's relations with village women: Kert, *Abby Aldrich Rockefeller*, 102–3; AAR to JDR 3rd, March 6, 1922, RFA2.AA.I, B4 F60.
170   "Pay attention": Ibid., ix.
170   Warwick playhouse: Kert, *Abby Aldrich Rockefeller*, 81.
171   Study of Goodwin and Milliken's *French Provincial Architecture* for Playhouse: JDR Jr. to Duncan Candler, April 8, 1926, RFA2.I, B33 F321.
171   Suggestion for a "coadjutor": JDR Jr. to Candler, September 28, 1926, ibid.
171   Candler's process: Candler to JDR Jr., October 2, 1926, ibid.
171   Building problems: William Crawford to JDR Jr., October 4, 1926, ibid.; Candler to JDR Jr., June 16, 1927, ibid.; AAR to NAR, January 1927, RFA2.AA.I, B5 F64.
171   Description of Playhouse interior: Pierson and Roberts, *Rockefeller Family Home*, 122–33.
172   Description of Playhouse grounds: Ibid.
172   "Winthrop is doing up some candy": AAR to NAR, May 1928, RFA2.AA.I, B5 F65.
172   "such gatherings": *New York Times*, June 21, 1928.
173   "Thus no one will have to break up a game": JDR Jr. and AAR to Babs and David Milton, JDR 3rd, NAR and Mary Todhunter Clark Rockefeller, LSR, Winthrop Rockefeller, and DR, May 5, 1930, RFA2.I, B33 F321.
173   "It is so beautiful": AAR to Lucy Truman Aldrich, May 24, 1923, *Abby Aldrich Rockefeller's Letters to Her Sister*, 130.
173   Restoration project at Williamsburg: Fosdick, *John D. Rockefeller, Jr.*, 272–301.
173   "reverently to preserve": Guiding formula quoted in ibid., 296.
174   "We stuck to absolutely what *was*": JDR Jr., interview by Fosdick, June 15, 1954, RFA2.Z.V, B57 F503.

174 "reached deep into her being": Kert, *Abby Aldrich Rockefeller*, 215.
174 "fads and fancies": AAR to JDR Jr., February 22, 1923, RFA2.Z.I, B1 F9.
174 Pilgrimage to art galleries in Vienna and Germany: Kert, *Abby Aldrich Rockefeller*, 218–19.
175 French restoration project: Fosdick, *John D. Rockefeller, Jr.*, 352–57.
175 "[That] every detail": JDR Jr. to his children, July 6, 1923, quoted in ibid., 356.
176 "As for myself ": AAR to Edith G. Halpert, July 18, 1931, RFA2.AA.I, B6 F81.
176 Rockefeller Center project: Fosdick, *John D. Rockefeller, Jr.*, 262–71.
177 "there was no place to run": Quoted in ibid., 266.
177 Rest cure: AAR to NAR, February 12, 1931, RFA2.AA.I, B4 F63.
177 "ugly": Quoted in Fosdick, *John D. Rockefeller, Jr.*, 268.
177 "From every source": Ibid.
177 "graceless bulk": Ibid.
177 "The more I ponder": George Vincent to Arthur Woods, March 23, 1932, quoted in Kert, *Abby Aldrich Rockefeller*, 352.
177 "The general public": Robert Moses to JDR Jr., April 21, 1948, RFA.AA.VII, B37 F339.
177 Abby's role: Kert, *Abby Aldrich Rockefeller*, 353.
178 "My panel will show": Ibid., 355–56.
178 "cultural vandalism": Quoted in Fosdick, *John D. Rockefeller, Jr.*, 267.
178 Founding of the Museum of Modern Art: Kert, *Abby Aldrich Rockefeller*, 267–86; "Beginnings of Museum of Modern Art," RFA2.AA.I, B7 F98.
179 "It enriches the spiritual life": AAR to NAR, quoted in Kert, *Abby Aldrich Rockefeller*, 254.
179 Reactions to JDR Jr.'s lack of interest: Lucy Truman Aldrich to AAR, March 7, 1934, RFA2.AA.I, B1 F12; DR, *Memoirs*, 442–44.
179 Matisse's attempt to persuade: Kert, *Abby Aldrich Rockefeller*, 303–4.
180 "Granite indifference": Alfred Barr to AAR, September 6, 1930, quoted in ibid., 283.
180 Purchases of paintings from Duveen: RFA2.I, housebooks.
180 Arrangements to move into Kykuit: JDR Jr., office memo, April 26, 1937, RFA2.I, B33 F329.
180 Allocation of rooms in house: Pierson and Roberts, *Rockefeller Family Home*, 21.
180 Arrangements with Doris Payne: Office memo for JDR Jr., April 30, 1945, RFA2.I, B31 F308.
181 "We are . . . safely and peacefully moved": AAR, quoted in Pierson and Roberts, *Rockefeller Family Home*, 21.
181 Abby's relationship with household servants: Chase, *Abby Aldrich Rockefeller*, 36–37.
181 "Come in and laugh with me": Ibid., 36.
181 "but she always did it in a way": Ibid., 37.
181 Recruiting servants to knit for soldiers: AAR to Fanny Evans, October 14, 1940, RFA2.AA.I, B2 F29.
181 "She taught me to love beautiful things": Chase, *Abby Aldrich Rockefeller*, 37.
181 "The women of the South": AAR to DR, November 17, 1944, quoted in Kert, *Abby Aldrich Rockefeller*, 446–47.
181 Most servants were Scandinavian: AAR to Robert Gumble, July 19, 1941, RFA2.I, B30 F283.
181 AAR's feelings about minimum wages for household servants: AAR to Lucy Truman Aldrich, August 4, 1933, *Abby Aldrich Rockefeller's Letters to Her Sister*, 207.
182 "[Junior], Nelson, David and I": AAR to Minnie MacFadden, October 4, 1937, RFA2.AA.I, B3 F40.

182 "Several things were put out": Abby O'Neill, quoted in Pierson and Roberts, *Rockefeller Family Home*, 23.

182 "We knew it was a formal occasion": DR Jr., quoted in ibid.

182 Sunday lunches: Ibid., 24.

182 He "liked things to be": DR Jr., quoted in ibid.

183 "enfolded": Ibid.

183 Favorite places for tea: Ibid., 25.

183 Lawns and golf course work: AAR to Lucy Truman Aldrich, October 1, 1937, RFA2.AA.I, B4 F54.

183 "The whole estate": Rasmussen, *There Was Once a Time*, 31.

183 Preservation of the Palisades: Fosdick, *John D. Rockefeller, Jr.*, 322–24.

183 Restrictions for the children: Pierson and Roberts, *Rockefeller Family Home*, 27.

184 Limitations for adults: Stasz, *Rockefeller Women*, 275.

184 Advantages from living on estate: JDR Jr. to Babs R. Milton, NAR, and JDR 3rd, March 31, 1934, RFA4.H, B32 F382.

185 "A little of that ancient peace": Lewis Mumford, quoted in Fosdick, *John D. Rockefeller, Jr.*, 341.

185 "pressured": DR, *Memoirs*, 444.

185 "Please, please help": Elise Goldstein to Babs R. Milton, November 15, 1938, RFA2.IV, B4 F43.

185 "Out of my experience": AAR to JDR 3rd, NAR, LSR, February 8, 1923, ibid., AA.I, B3 F45.

186 "frenzied adulation": DR, *Memoirs*, 86.

186 "I would rather die fighting": JDR Jr. to Arthur Hays Sulzberger, April 1941, quoted in Fosdick, *John D. Rockefeller, Jr.*, 408.

186 "I have just finished": AAR to Fanny Evans, October 14, 1940, RFA2.AA.I, B2 F29.

186 Wartime projects: Kert, *Abby Aldrich Rockefeller*, 449–50.

187 Rockefeller sons during WWII: DR, *Memoirs*, 105–7; Kert, *Abby Aldrich Rockefeller*, 434–39, 459.

187 Babs's divorce: Kert, *Abby Aldrich Rockefeller*, 440–41.

188 "My mind is possessed": AAR to WR, quoted in Chase, *Abby Aldrich Rockefeller*, 99.

188 "Mr. Rockefeller said to me": AAR to Mr. Atterbury, October 2, 1933, RFA2.AA.I, B1 F2.

188 "Is it a house": AAR to Blanchette and JDR 3rd, June 20, 1938, ibid., B4 F61.

189 "a little big and lonely": AAR to Olivia Cutting, July 31, 1946, ibid., B2 F25.

189 "going down to the pool": AAR to Lucy Truman Aldrich, March 11, 1947, *Abby Aldrich Rockefeller's Letters to Her Sister*, 286.

189 "Certainly I don't wish": AAR to May Coleman, March 5, 1947, RFA2.AA.I, B2 F25.

189 "I seem recently": AAR to Olivia Cutting, July 30, 1947, ibid.

189 "I find our very large family": AAR to Olivia Cutting, ibid.

190 "Whatever we have given him": JDR to DeLap, July 18, 1922, RFA2.A, B55 F439.

190 1935 proposal: JDR 3rd to JDR Jr., January 15, 1935, RFA2.I, B31 F310.

190 Adopted plan: JDR 3rd to JDR Jr., "Pocantico Estate Industrial Relations," April 13, 1937, ibid.

190 Proposal to close down Kykuit for winter: JDR 3rd to JDR Jr., "Pocantico Estate Economies," ibid., B33 F328.

190 Birth of RBF: DR, *Memoirs*, 139–42.

191 Abby's last days and death: Kert, *Abby Aldrich Rockefeller*, 471–72; DR, *Memoirs*, 180.

191   Description of baptism: J. Homer Nelson to JDR Jr., April 8, 1948, RFA AA.VII, B37 F339.
191   "She was like": Ellen Milton to JDR Jr., July 25, 1948, ibid.
191   "A great woman": L. U. Noland, April 15, 1948, ibid.
191   "No one else": Ibid., 181.
192   "perfect": Pierson and Roberts, *Rockefeller Family Home,* 24.
192   "a distant historical site": Ibid., 26.
192   "more of a human scale": Ibid., 27.
192   "The same walls": Ibid.
192   "a verdant cage": Ibid.
192   "To us as small children": Ibid.
192   "after they saw the place": Ibid., 27–28.
192   "extraneous": Ibid., 28.
192   "miscellaneous people": JDR Jr., interview by Fosdick, June 15, 1954, RFA2.Z.V, B57 F503.
193   not "thought highly": DR, *Memoirs,* 182.
193   Nelson and the sale of the estate: Ibid., 143.
193   Family rules for the Playhouse: Laura Rockefeller, Sandra Rockefeller, Steven Rockefeller, and DR Jr., "Playhouse Rules," April 1953, RFA2.I, B33 F321.
193   "exceedingly unique": JDR Jr. to NAR, July 5, 1955, ibid., F323.
193   Staying away: DR, *Memoirs,* 183.
193   "Sunday Mrs. Rockefeller and I": Fosdick, *John D. Rockefeller, Jr.,* 429.
194   Underpinning Oceanus: Report, June 24, 1958, RFA2.I, B35 F341.
194   "cold": DR, *Memoirs,* 184.
194   "Acutely conscious": JDR Jr. to DR, quoted in ibid.
194   "touched": Ibid.
195   Junior's doubt that sons would keep up the grounds in the same way: JDR Jr., interview by Fosdick, May 11, 1954, RFA2.Z.V, B57 F503.

10: THE PRINCE OF KYKUIT

197   NAR's early activities at MoMA and his association with Kirstein and Warburg: Cary Reich, *The Life of Nelson A. Rockefeller: Worlds to Conquer, 1908–1958* (New York, 1996), 101–5. For Lachaise's connection with the group, see George Nordland, *Gaston Lachaise: The Man and His Work* (New York, 1974), 42–48 and 52–56.
197   "Warburg said the situation": Lachaise, quoted in ibid., 46.
197   Kirstein's posing for Lachaise: Ibid., 46–47.
197   "I am having a debauch": Lachaise, quoted in ibid., 48.
197   An early appeal by Kirstein to NAR for help for Lachaise: Lincoln Kirstein to NAR, April 4, 1935. NAR's reply: NAR to Lincoln Kirstein, April 5, 1935. The contract with Isabel Lachaise: April 26, 1938, RFA4.C, B15 F135.
198   Arrangements for the "purchase" of *Man:* Doris Levine ("Secretary to Mr. Lincoln Kirstein") to Elizabeth Phillips ("Office of Nelson Rockefeller"), October 26, 1938, ibid. Payment for the casting of *Dans La Nuit:* Note (no sender's name) accompanying a check from NAR addressed to Doris Levine, ibid.
198   Description of NAR's initial placement of sculptures at Kykuit: Carol K. Uht to Mordechai Omer, November 6, 1970, RFA4.C, B15 F133.
198   "full of terribly seductive pitfalls": René d'Harnoncourt, quoted in Bethany Newbauer, "René d'Harnoncourt," *American National Biography* (New York, 1991), vol. 6, 540.
198   "In many ways he was the jewel": Blanchette Rockefeller, quoted in Reich, *Nelson A. Rockefeller,* 114.

199   "I would give three weeks": NAR, quoted in Zenos R. Miller to AAR, April 5, 1921, RFA2.AA.I, B3 F40.

199   JDR 3rd's early years and relations with NAR: John E. Harr and Peter J. Johnson, *The Rockefeller Conscience: An American Family in Public and in Private* (New York, 1991), 3–13, 22–27, and 201–8.

199   "You and I always 'speak our piece' ": Martha Baird Rockefeller to NAR, RFA18, B15 F306.

199   Martha Baird Rockefeller's contributions to NAR's political campaigns: Harr and Johnson, *Rockefeller Conscience*, 208–9.

199   NAR's various houses: Samuel E. Bleecker, *The Politics of Architecture: A Perspective on Nelson A. Rockefeller* (New York, 1981), 223–58. The book includes a large number of superb photographs by Ezra Stoller and additional commentary by George A. Dudley.

200   Wally Harrison's career and relationship with NAR: Reich, *Nelson A. Rockefeller*, 119–21 and 398–400.

200   Harrison's later career: Ibid.

201   "For an architect it was like": Wally Harrison, quoted in ibid., 121.

201   "one of the most egregious acts": Daniel Okrent, *Great Fortune: The Epic of Rockefeller Center* (New York, 2003), 152.

201   "Nelson *loved* the palaces": John Lockwood, quoted in Reich, *Nelson A. Rockefeller*, 397.

201   The Anchorage: Ibid., 152–53. See also Bleecker, *Politics of Architecture*, 222, 225, and 228–37.

201   "As you well know": JDR Jr. to NAR, August 21, 1944, RFA4.H, B31 F378.

202   "My own feeling is that": AAR to NAR, July 6, 1935, ibid., B32 F388.

202   "When Wally and I started the apartment": NAR, quoted in John Loring, "Nelson Rockefeller's Fifth Avenue Apartment: Recalling the Residence of the Notable Politician and Philanthropist," *Architectual Digest*, April 2001, 102. The article also contains excellent color photographs of the apartment taken by Horst and Elizabeth Heyert.

202   Matisse and Léger's work in the apartment: Ibid., 118.

203   Artworks in the living room of the apartment: Ibid., 110–18.

203   "I was always off-beat": NAR, quoted in ibid., 114.

203   "It had elements of the past": NAR, quoted in ibid., 118.

203   "an amusing and also very good": AAR to NAR, January 7, 1928, RFA2.AA.I, B5 F65.

203   "a new Museum of Modern Art": AAR to NAR, April 14, 1929, ibid.

204   NAR's changing academic interests at Dartmouth: Reich, *Nelson A. Rockefeller*, 59–65.

204   "I feel as if I had been introduced": NAR to AAR, January 2, 1928, RFA2.AA.I, B5 F65.

204   "I sincerely believe": NAR to AAR, April 26, 1929, ibid.

204   NAR's attempt to persuade AAR to chair MoMA's board: NAR to AAR, April 22, 1933, ibid., B4 F63.

204   NAR's pledge of $100,000 to MoMA: NAR to AAR, April 5, 1934, ibid., B5 F6.

204   "in grateful appreciation": Ibid.

204   "I showed Papa the pictures": AAR to NAR, no date, probably May 1930, ibid.

204   JDR Jr.'s coldness as a parent: The point is made in a number of places, but most forcefully by DR in his *Memoirs*. See especially 14–20.

205   An overview of the range of NAR's artistic interests: Joseph Persico, *The Imperial Rockefeller: A Biography of Nelson A. Rockefeller* (New York, 1982), 174–83.

205   Carol Uht's role as NAR's curator: Ibid., 178.
205   "forms of art in which I could feel": NAR, quoted in Marion Oetinger Jr., *Folk Treasures of Mexico: The Nelson A. Rockefeller Collection* (New York, 1990), 61.
205   "Nelson's reaction to art": LSR, quoted in ibid., 63.
205   "not unlike benzedrine": René d'Harnoncourt, quoted in ibid.
205   "Nelson had the most insatiable": Alfred Barr, quoted in ibid.
206   "exceptionally pure": Alfred Barr, quoted in ibid.
206   "Beyond his private satisfaction": Alfred Barr, quoted in ibid.
206   NAR's plans for Kykuit's future: HFMR, interview.
206   "absolutely livid": DR, *Memoirs*, 193.
207   "[Nelson] had not only torn apart": Ibid., 192.
207   NAR as a parent: Persico, *Imperial Rockefeller*, 152–57.
207   NAR's younger sons at Kykuit: Pierson and Roberts, *Rockefeller Family Home*, 32–33.
207   "What if they break it?": HFMR, interview.
207   "it really was home": Mark Rockefeller, quoted in Pierson and Roberts, *Rockefeller Family Home,* 32.
207   "to recharge, to fill up": HFMR, interview.
207   Changes made by HFMR at Kykuit: Ibid.
208   "the general . . . the administrative assistant": Ibid.
208   "reflecting pools": René d'Harnoncourt, quoted in ibid.
208   "life revolved around": Ibid.
208   NAR at Kykuit at Christmastime moving back and forth between political meetings and family activities: Ibid.
208   "No phalanx of servants": Persico, *Imperial Rockefeller,* 93.
209   "a forty-year-old sport jacket": Ibid., 95.
209   The annual Governor's Club party at Kykuit: Ibid., 92.
209   Prominent people entertained at Kykuit during NAR's time there: Joseph W. Canzeri to Nina Jones, January 24, 1977, Greenrock Corporation Archives.
209   Guest list for HFMR's birthday party, June 9, 1967: RFA4.A, B72 F609.
209   Details of the party: *New York Post,* June 10, 1967.
210   "John, nobody here has": Undated, unsigned note, RFA4.A, B71 F609.
210   "It was probably the most beautiful party": John Emmet Hughes, quoted in *New York Post,* June 10, 1967.
211   NAR's 1966 gubernatorial campaign: Persico, *Imperial Rockefeller*, 56–59.
211   The 1968 presidential campaign: Ibid., 64–81.
211   The election and its aftermath: Ibid., 84–87.
211   "I'm terribly flattered": NAR, quoted in ibid., 81.
211   NAR as vice president and Ford's decision to eliminate him from the ticket in 1976: Ibid., 260–69.
211   Pat Nixon at Kykuit: HFMR, interview.
212   NAR and Attica: Persico, *Imperial Rockefeller*, 137–40.
212   The New York State Drug Law: Ibid., 140–45.
212   Planning for major social events at Kykuit in 1971: RFA4.A.
213   AAR's acquisition of the bodhisattva and her bequest of it to NAR: NAR, "Speech to the Westchester Council of the Arts," December 16, 1977, RFA4.M, B2 F17.
213   HFMR's suggestion that there be a portrait of Lincoln at Kykuit: HFMR, interview.
213   "Walls!": NAR, quoted by HFMR in ibid.
213   The creation of the basement galleries: Ibid.
213   Artworks in the basement galleries: *Kykuit,* a published catalog of the artworks on view in and around the house, no date.

214   The Picasso tapestries: RFA4.C.2 contains voluminous material on the subject; see especially boxes 27 and 28.

214   Dürrback's production of extra copies of the tapestries NAR ordered: Persico, *Imperial Rockefeller*, 178–79.

214   "That Picasso sure is": NAR, quoted in ibid., 179.

214   Barr's concern about the colors used in the tapestries: Alfred H. Barr Jr. to Madame Petro van Doesburg, February 10 and 20, 1952; Barr to NAR, February 20, 1956; Barr to NAR, November 21, 1962, RFA4.C.2, B28 F239 and B27 F227.

214   "My own feeling is that she": Carol Uht to "Ann," February 12, 1975, RFA4.C.2., B27 F228.

215   NAR's relighting of the dining room at Kykuit: HFMR, interview.

215   The creation of the "china room": Ibid.

215   The outdoor sculpture collection at Kykuit, complete lists: *Kykuit,* catalog of all the artworks in and around the house, and *Kykuit Sculpture,* a list indicating locations, materials used, and dates created and/or cast, when known, as well as dates of the sculptors' lives. There are some discrepancies between the two listings. Where they occur, we have relied on the *Kykuit Sculpture.*

216   "You must realize how grateful": Lincoln Kirstein to NAR, March 15, 1951, RFA4.C.2., B20 F179.

217   "preserved from certain destruction": Kirstein to NAR, September 6, 1951, ibid.

217   "one of the sculptor's most splendid achievements": William Lieberman, "The Nelson Aldrich Rockefeller Collection," in *Twentieth Century Art from the Nelson Aldrich Rockefeller Collection,* exhibition catalog, the Museum of Modern Art (New York, 1969), 33.

217   Calder's *Large Spiny:* NAR, "Speech to the Westchester Council of the Arts," December 16, 1977, RFA4.M, B2 F17.

218   "The day before . . . it had rained": NAR, ibid.

218   NAR's placement of sculptures at Kykuit: Pierson and Roberts, *Rockefeller Family Home,* 35–37.

219   "He seemed to have an eighth sense": HFMR, quoted in ibid., 35.

219   "There was great therapy": LSR, quoted in ibid.

219   "In a way you remind me": LSR, quoted in ibid.

219   "Nothing could be farther": NAR, quoted in ibid.

219   "My father built this place": NAR, quoted in Persico, *Imperial Rockefeller,* 91.

219   "a dark-haired compact dynamo": Ibid., 74.

220   Canzeri's memo on possible areas of cost-saving at Pocantico: Joseph W. Canzeri to J. R. Dilworth and D. C. O'Brien, May 19, 1971, Greenrock Corporation Archives.

221   "It takes a certain type of man": Ibid.

221   Cost-cutting measures eventually agreed upon: Joseph W. Canzeri to NAR, July 1, 1971, ibid.

222   NAR's weekly tours of the estate with Canzeri: Pierson and Roberts, *Rockefeller Family Home,* 35.

223   The building of the Japanese House: Persico, *Imperial Rockefeller,* 95.

223   Nelson's plans to move to the Japanese House: Robert Snyder, interview.

11: THE GIFT

228   "sad ending for a man": DR, *Memoirs,* 354.

228   "Nelson's Revenge": Ibid., 352.

228   The terms of NAR's will regarding Kykuit: *New York Times,* February 10, 1979.

228   "Nelson's final gesture": DR, *Memoirs,* 353.

229   The various legal changes the Pocantico estate and Kykuit underwent between 1952 and 1977: Harr and Johnson, *Rockefeller Conscience,* 17–18 and 493–99.

229   Summary of studies of Kykuit and the Pocantico estate: "The Plan for Pocantico, Pocantico Planning, Final Report, Oct. 16, 1986," appendix B, RBFA, RBF document of record no. 14102.

230   O'Brien's recommendations with regard to Kykuit and the Pocantico estate: Donal O'Brien to JDR 3rd, NAR, LSR, and DR, July 14, 1976, RFA5.1.2, B26 F108.

231   O'Brien on the possibility of additional funding from RBF: Donal O'Brien to JDR 3rd, NAR, LSR, and DR, May 27, 1976, ibid.

231   "a bit like building your own memorial": JDR 3rd, diary, June 4, 1976, RFA5.1.1, B13 F89.

231   "now so permeates the whole area": Ibid.

231   JDR 3rd's early life and philanthropic activities: Harr and Johnson, *Rockefeller Conscience,* 3–197.

232   The impact of Collier and Horowitz's book on the Rockefeller family: Ibid., 483.

232   "very painful": DR, *Memoirs,* 322.

232   "despised": Peter Collier and David Horowitz, *The Rockefellers: An American Dynasty* (New York, 1976), 434.

232   "The remarriage was the most distressing thing": Ibid., 348.

232   "I feel sad for him": Ibid., 404.

233   "He's always getting off one jet": Ibid.

233   "My father, well": Ibid., 587.

233   "You need an exorcism": Ibid., 510.

233   "to recapture a personal identity": Ibid., 626.

233   JDR 3rd's efforts to reach out to the cousins: JDR 3rd diary, March 11, April 6, May 26, August 26, October 20 and 28, and December 16, 1976, RBFA5.1.1, B13 F89 and 90.

233   "relaxed" attitude of the cousins toward plans for Kykuit: Ibid., April 6, 1976, B13 F89.

234   Gerald Ford's dedication of Kykuit as a National Historical Landmark: *New York Times,* November 21 and 22, 1976. See also *Washington Post,* November 22, 1976.

234   "an amazing number of family members": JDR 3rd, diary, December 18, 1976, RBFA5.1.1, B13 F90.

234   "to talk with him about the family": Ibid., December 11, 1976.

234   NAR's behavior on returning from Washington in 1976: Harr and Johnson, *Rockefeller Conscience,* 484–86 and 533; DR, *Memoirs,* 336–38; Persico, *Imperial Rockefeller,* 299.

235   "We have not played together": JDR 3rd, diary, September 11, 1976, RFA5.1.1, B13 F90.

235   "since taking over the house": Ibid., July 22, 1976.

235   "like some devouring metabolic disorder": Collier and Horowitz, *The Rockefellers,* 531 and 526–27.

236   NAR's positions on the family office and RBF: Harr and Johnson, *Rockefeller Conscience,* 531 and 526–27. See also DR, *Memoirs,* 345–47 and 340–42.

236   O'Brien's memo directing the brothers' attention to outstanding issues regarding Kykuit: Donal O'Brien to JDR 3rd, NAR, LSR, and DR, March 7, 1977, RFA5.1.2, B26 F102.

236   "the John D. Rockefeller Estate meets": National Park Service, Department of the Interior, "Study of the John D. Rockefeller Estate," RBFA5.1.2, B49 F303.

236   Proposed plan for public funding: Ibid.

237   "All of us were very pleased": JDR 3rd diary, June 11, 1977, RFA5.1.1, B14 F92.

237 JDR 3rd's alliance-building in opposition to NAR's "power grab": Ibid., March
     28 and 31, April 11, 13, 16, and 28, May 26, and June 3, 6, 8, 11, 12, and 16, 1977,
     B13 and 14 F91 and 92.
237 NAR's proposal to JDR 3rd regarding RBF: NAR to JDR 3rd, April 18 and 22,
     1977, RFA4.A, B160 F177.
237 "I cannot help believing": JDR 3rd to NAR, April 20, 1977, ibid.
238 JDR 3rd's attempt to convince DR to accept the chairmanship of RBF's board of
     trustees: JDR 3rd, diary, May 28 and June 5 and 12, 1977, RFA5.1.1, B13 and 14
     F91 and 92. See also DR, *Memoirs*, 343.
238 JDR 3rd's conviction that DR and LSR sided with NAR on RBF: JDR 3rd, diary,
     June 12, 1977, RFA5.1.1, B14 F92.
238 "two somewhat wearing days": Ibid.
238 NAR's behavior at his son's dinner party: DR, *Memoirs*, 346.
238 "their strong reservations": JDR 3rd, diary, June 19, 1977, RFA5.1.1, B14 F92.
     Also: DR, *Memoirs*, 346–47.
239 JDR 3rd agrees to accept NAR as head of the family office: JDR 3rd, diary, June
     19, 1977, RFA5.1.1, B14 F92.
239 "the cousins had, as a group": Ibid.
239 "[he] was as angry": DR, *Memoirs*, 346.
239 "depth of feeling about him": JDR 3rd, diary, June 10, 1977, RFA5.1.1, B14 F92.
239 "In public life": Ibid.
239 Nelson's plans for the family office: DR, *Memoirs*, 345.
239 Henry Kissinger and Nancy Hawks elected to RBF's board of trustees: *New York
     Times*, June 23, 1977. See also JDR 3rd, diary, June 16, 1977, RFA5.1.1, B14 F92.
239 NAR's osteopathy proposal: Harr and Johnson, *Rockefeller Conscience*, 537.
239 "Absolutely ghastly": William Dietel, interview.
239 JDR 3rd's statement that Dietel might consider leaving RBF if offered a position
     elsewhere: JDR 3rd, diary, June 29, 1977, RFA5.1.1, B14 F92.
240 The *Times* article on RBF's problems: *New York Times*, June 23, 1977.
240 JDR 3rd's feelings about Gardner and his resignation from RBF's board of
     trustees: JDR 3rd, diary, June 16 and July 12, 1977, RFA5.1.1, B14 F92.
240 DR on Gardner's resignation and the likelihood that it was Gardner who had
     leaked the information about RBF to the *Times*: DR, *Memoirs*, 343–44.
240 NAR's accusation that Dietel had been the source of the leak to the *Times*:
     William Dietel, interview.
240 "many, many years ago": JDR 3rd to NAR, July 15, 1977, RFA4.1, B160 F177.
241 "intemperate in tone": NAR to JDR 3rd, "Draft," July 18, 1977, ibid.
241 "[of] my respect and admiration": NAR to JDR 3rd, August 17, 1977 (preceded
     by five drafts, the first in longhand and several with comments indicating that J.
     Richardson Dilworth, the head of the Rockefeller family office, did some of the
     drafting), ibid.
241 JDR 3rd's note "withdrawing" his letter of July 15, 1977, to NAR: JDR 3rd to NAR,
     August 15, 1977, ibid. Nelson's reply: NAR to JDR 3rd, August 18, 1977, ibid.
242 O'Brien's September memo on Kykuit issues: Donal O'Brien to JDR 3rd, NAR,
     LSR, and DR, September 19, 1977, RFA5.1.2, B26 F102.
242 "financially afford to commit": Ibid.
242 "This Minimum Plan": Ibid.
242 O'Brien's description of the partition option: Ibid.
242 "the Brothers are maybe farther apart": JDR 3rd, diary, November 2, 1977,
     RFA5.1.1, B14 F92.
242 "a beautiful and significant historic site": NAR, quoted in ibid.

243 NAR's plans to change his will and his negotiations with Marriott: Ibid.

243 NAR's financial situation: Harr and Johnson, *Rockefeller Conscience*, 530.

243 "Our problems in relation to the future": JDR 3rd to NAR, January 10, 1978, RFA5.3.2, B40 F229.

244 List of places studied by the Goldstone group: Harmon Goldstone to Donal O'Brien, September 1, 1977, RFA5.1.2, B49 F303.

244 "when the boat seemed to be rocking": JDR 3rd to Donal O'Brien and Harmon Goldstone, June 5, 1978, RFA5.1.2, B4 F231.

244 "a decision with the government": JDR 3rd, diary, April 17, 1978, RFA5.1.1, B14 F93. The schedule for Secretary Andrus's visit: Donal O'Brien to JDR 3rd, NAR, LSR, and DR, April 7, 1978, RFA5.1.2, B49 F303.

244 JDR 3rd's attempt to persuade LSR to add Rockwood Hall to the Pocantico Plan: DR, *Memoirs*, 350.

244 JDR 3rd's failure to include the $5 million bequest in the Pocantico Plan in his will: Harr and Johnson, *Rockefeller Conscience*, 501. See also DR, *Memoirs*, 350.

245 Further details of JDR 3rd's death: Harr and Johnson, *Rockefeller Conscience*, 548–49.

245 NAR told that he would not be asked to speak at JDR 3rd's memorial service: Ibid., 550.

245 "beside himself": DR, *Memoirs*, 352.

245 NAR's new will: Ibid.

246 Carl Humelsine's prediction that the National Trust would be receiving enough funds from the federal government to finance the portion of the Pocantico Plan involving Kykuit: Ibid.

246 "I was outraged": Ibid.

246 JDR 3rd on NAR's pictures of the sculptures in the gardens at Kykuit: JDR 3rd to NAR, January 10, 1978, RFA5.1.2, B40 F229.

247 "beautiful arrangement": JDR 3rd to "Nel and Happy," May 11, 1978, RFA4.A, B160 F178.

12: GOING PUBLIC

250 Notice received by RBF of the pending payment of Abby R. Mauzé's $1.5 million bequest to be used for the realization of the Pocantico Plan: Minutes, annual meeting of RBF Board of Trustees, June 15, 1978, RBFA. Creation of RBF's Pocantico Fund: Minutes, special meeting of the RBF Corporation and Board of Trustees, October 5, 1978, RBFA.

250 Growth of RBF's Pocantico Fund: RBF, "Annual Report, 1989: Portfolio Composition by Manager," April 30, 1990, RBFA. The total given for the fund: $30,480,000.

251 The Rockefellers' generally unfavorable opinion of the National Trust: Various interviews.

251 The establishment of the National Trust for Historic Preservation: *New York Times*, December 21, 1952. The launching of the campaign to increase the trust's endowment: Ibid., September 20, 1967. RBF's $500,000 grant to the trust: Ibid., January 26, 1968.

251 Attempts to cut the National Trust's federal appropriation: Ibid., April 11, 1981, and March 27, 1982.

251 Changing goals of the historic preservation movement: Ibid., April 13, 1980, and October 9, 1980.

251 The shifting focus of the National Trust's programs: Ibid., December 3, 1978, and March 27, 1982.

251   "working for lower income people": Michael L. Ainslee, quoted in ibid.

251   The closing of the National Trust houses: Ibid., January 24, 1982, and January 5, 1984.

252   "If you haven't hedged a fund": William Dietel, interview.

252   JDR Jr.'s restoration of the Hudson Valley houses: Fosdick, *John D. Rockefeller, Jr.*, 350–51.

252   History and activities of SHR: *New York Times*, September 12, 1982.

252   Plan to transfer NAR's bequest to SHR: Minutes, RBF Executive Committee meeting, February 19, 1981, and RBF Corporation and Board of Trustees meeting, March 20, 1981, RBFA.

252   SHR's decision not to go ahead with the plan, the return of the Pocantico Fund to RBF, and SHR's compensation for its study: Minutes, RBF Corporation and Board of Trustees meeting, November 18, 1983, RBFA. See also "Report on Negotiations with Sleepy Hollow Restorations, Inc., Re Kykuit Historic Park Project," January 24, 1984, RBF document of record no. 13,834, and minutes of RBF Executive Committee meeting, February 2, 1984, both RBFA.

253   Initial announcement of the state park project by Laurance Rockefeller: *New York Times*, October 25, 1981. Subsequent *Times* articles dealing with subject: October 26 and November 15, 1981, and August 29, 1982.

254   The agreement between DR, LSR, and the National Trust, dated December 7, 1983: "The Plan for Pocantico, Pocantico Planning Project, Final Report, Oct. 16, 1986," appendix A, RBF document of record no. 14,102, RBFA.

254   The division of the Pocantico estate: Harr and Johnson, *Rockefeller Conscience*, 560.

254   The 1983 ceremony at Pocantico Hills School, including selections from the remarks of Mario Cuomo, Orin Lehman, and DR: *New York Times*, December 22, 1983.

254   "would be added to the responsibilities": LSR, quoted in ibid., October 25, 1981.

254   "eventually be available": Michael Ainslee, quoted in ibid., December 22, 1983.

254   "That's difficult to answer": DR, quoted in ibid.

254   "running correctional institutions": Ibid., August 26, 1984.

255   "not analogous to running prisons": George H. Bohlinger III, quoted in ibid.

255   The full membership of the Pocantico Planning Project Advisory Board: "Plan for Pocantico," RBFA, V.

255   "guidance and encouragement": Ibid., viii.

255   RBF's payments to the Bohlinger group: Minutes, RBF Executive Committee meeting, February 2, 1984, and RBF Board of Trustees annual meeting, June 27, 1986, RBFA.

255   The development of the capital grant program, or the "Creel grants," as they were known, after Dana Creel—the president of RBF prior to William Dietel—who first suggested the program: Harr and Johnson, *Rockefeller Conscience*, 523–41.

256   Dietel's thoughts on RBF's changing role and position: "President's Report to the Trustees," November 29, 1984, RBFA.

256   "Nothing would be more foolish": Ibid.

256   "wider fourth and fifth generation": Ibid.

256   "consistently said": Dietel, quoted in minutes, RBF Executive Committee meeting, April 16, 1985, RBFA.

256   LSR's belief that Kykuit should be torn down: DR, *Memoirs*, 348.

256   "It's a beautiful place": DR Jr., interview.

257   "the attributes of the setting": RBFA, "Plan for Pocantico," 31, RBFA.

257 The "Plan for Pocantico"'s projections of numbers of visitors and income: Ibid., 48–51.
257 "a private institution of the highest quality": Ibid., 60.
257 Greenrock's data regarding family use of estate and conclusions drawn from them: Ibid., 69–75.
258 Timetable for the implementation of the "Plan for Pocantico"'s public visitation program: Ibid., 81–82.
258 Funding for proposed plan: Ibid., 80.
258 "We were not real players": Charles Longsworth, interview.
259 "The Rockefeller family has been": Minutes, RBF Board of Trustees meeting, November 11, 1986, RBFA.
259 "Absolutely appalling": DR, interview.
259 DR's fondness for the Institute for Science and International Affairs proposal and for involving Rockefeller University in the Pocantico project: CC and DR Jr., interviews.
259 "No, David, this is your project": LSR, quoted by CC, interview.
259 "the dynasts": Ibid. On the same subject, see also William Dietel, interview.
260 "a composite idea": DR Jr., interview.
261 DR's initial statements about "The Plan for Pocantico": Minutes, RBF Board of Trustees meeting, November 11, 1986, RBFA.
261 "some changes": Ibid.
261 DR's announcement of the plan to have Rockefeller University take over Kykuit: Minutes, RBF Executive Committee meeting, April 14, 1987, RBFA. The plan itself: RBF document of record no. 14,168, June 26, 1987, RBFA.
261 "human resources": DR, quoted in ibid.
262 O'Brien's list of the issues dividing the National Trust and the Rockefellers: Donal O'Brien, memorandum to LSR and DR, May 21, 1987, RBF document of record no. 14,107, 6–7, RBFA.
262 "to live out the balance": Ibid., 3.
262 "both sides, acting in good faith": Ibid., 8.
262 DR's connection with Rockefeller University and its importance as a center for research: DR, *Memoirs*, 145–48 and 488–89.
262 The creation of the Rockefeller Archive Center and its connection with Rockefeller University: Harr and Johnson, *Rockefeller Conscience*, 487–90.
262 "It has a continuous history": Donal O'Brien, memorandum to LSR and DR, May 21, 1987, RBF document of record no. 14,107, 9, RBFA.
262 Announcement of the plan to have RBF take over Kykuit: Minutes, RBF Board of Trustees meeting, November 18, 1988, RBFA.
262 The response of Steven Rockefeller to the new plan: Ibid.
263 Robert Bass's deal-making activities, including his acquisition of the Plaza Hotel: *New York Times*, September 25, 1988.
263 The Outlet Communications sale: *Wall Street Journal*, February 6, 1986.
263 "On September 28,": *New York Times*, September 15, 1988.
263 "They both are extraordinarily earnest": Unnamed source, quoted in ibid.
264 The Rockefellers' position on Kykuit as described by DR to CC: CC, interview.
265 "an exciting challenge": Ibid.
265 "Let me make you a proposal": Ibid.
265 "having to pay through the nose": Various interviews.
265 O'Brien on the issue of compensation: Donal O'Brien, memorandum to LSR and DR, May 21, 1987, RBF document of record no. 14,107, 12–26, RBFA.

265   CC's letter and the proposal to the National Trust: CC to Robert Bass, November 3, 1989, RBF document of record no. 14,400, RBFA.

266   "at no time": Ibid., Historic Hudson Valley, "Pocantico Historic Area Operating Program," 2, ibid.

266   RBF's plans for the proposed center: Ibid., appendix C.

266   The offer of compensation to the National Trust: Robert Bass to CC, May 18, 1990, RBFA.

266   "the level hoped for": Minutes, RBF Board of Trustees meeting, February 14, 1989, RBFA.

266   "the spring of 1992": CC to Robert Bass, November 3, 1989, RBF document of record no. 14,400, RBFA.

267   Robert Bass did not respond to the authors' request for an interview.

267   "a financing opportunity": DR Jr., interview.

267   "getting a chunk of money": Ibid.

267   "You can't blame him": Ibid.

267   "We have agreed": CC, interview.

267   "This is unconscionable": Ibid.

267   Bass's letter: Robert Bass to CC, May 18, 1990, RBFA.

268   "co-stewardship agreement": Ibid.

268   "the unrelated grant": Ibid.

268   Various amounts of money Bass was rumored to want the Rockefellers to pay for Kykuit: DR Jr., interview.

269   CC's description of the negotiations with the National Trust: CC, interview. See also minutes, RBF Executive Committee meeting, April 24, 1990; CC to RBF trustees, May 30, 1990, RBF document of record no. 14,492; minutes, RBF Board of Trustees meeting, June 14, 1990; J. Jackson Walter to CC, September 11, 1990, RBF document of record no. 14,514; minutes, RBF Executive Committee meeting, October 2, 1990; minutes, RBF Board of Trustees meeting, November 20, 1990; minutes, RBF Board of Trustees meeting, February 12, 1991; minutes, RBF Executive Committee meeting, April 9, 1991; CC to the trustees of RBF, May 29, 1991, RBF document of record no. 14,607, all RBFA.

269   "not a terribly disappointing response": Minutes, RBF Board of Trustees meeting, June 20, 1990, RBFA. Steven Rockefeller's response to the National Trust's position: Ibid.

269   CC's conviction that the National Trust would not budge on the issue of Kykuit's ownership: Ibid.

270   "he felt that if visitation was fully": CC, interview.

270   "wanted to do it right": Ibid.

270   The inclusion of the 25,000-visitor minimum in the agreement: RBF document of record no. 14,607, May 29, 1991, RBFA.

270   "found the ideal way": Robert Bass, quoted in "Historic Rockefeller Home to Be Opened to the Public," press release, RBF document of record no. 14,638, September 18, 1991, RBFA.

270   "the enhancement": DR Jr., quoted in ibid.

270   "Laurance and I share": DR, quoted in ibid.

271   DR's visible anger while speaking of Nelson's will: DR, interview.

271   "many millions of dollars": DR, Memoirs, 353.

271   "He saw this as a place": CC, interview.

271   "right down to every rose": Ibid.

271   "He was the one": Ibid.

271   DR's account of redecorating the Eyrie: DR, Memoirs, 188.

272 DR's plans to develop his property in Pocantico Hills: *New York Times,* December 22, 2002, and April 21, 2004.

272 "it would be quite a temptation": DR, quoted in ibid., December 22, 2002.

272 News coverage of DR's ninetieth birthday and gifts to MoMA and Rockefeller University: Ibid., April 13, 2005, and *New Yorker,* May 30, 2005. The earlier *New Yorker* profile of DR, January 9 and 16, 1965.

273 Description of preparations at Kykuit for public visitation: *New York Times,* November 21, 1993.

273 "slightly at odds with itself ": Paul Goldberger, ibid., May 6, 1994.

273 Recommendation that the service areas at Kykuit be included in the public tours: Charles Longsworth (who at the time was president of Colonial Williamsburg), interview.

274 "The family and the household staff": DR, *Memoirs,* 30.

274 "too flashy and ostentatious": Ibid., 31.

275 The opening of Kykuit compared to the opening of Buckingham Palace: *New York Times,* May 6, 1994.

INDEX

ROBERT F. DALZELL Jr. is the Willmott Family Third Century Professor of American History at Williams College and the author of *Enterprising Elite: The Boston Associates and the World They Made* and *Daniel Webster and the Trial of American Nationalism.*

LEE BALDWIN DALZELL was for many years the head of the Research and Reference Services Department at the Williams College Sawyer Library. The two collaborated on *George Washington's Mount Vernon: At Home in Revolutionary America.*